QUITE CLOSE TO EUROPE

QUITE CLOSE
TO EUROPE

A Memoir

Richard Carden

For David

with happy memories of a
working time together.

Richard

HILBOROUGH PRESS
2019

.978-1-5272-3605-9

Hilborough Press, Hilborough, Thetford, Norfolk IP26 5BW

I am grateful to Professor Robert Tombs for permission to include in chapter 3 the quotation from his book *The English and their History* (Penguin/Viking), and to Lawrence Sail for permission to quote in chapter 4 from his poem 'Not admitting it' (Bloodaxe Books).

Printed in Great Britain by Print2Demand Ltd
Westoning, Bedfordshire MK45 5LD
print2demand.co.uk

For Violet

who inspired me to pull these memories together

Acknowledgments

I thank those who read all or parts of this book while I was putting it together; in particular George Warren, Lawrence Sail, Friederike Jeans, Gareth Steel, Julian Tunnicliffe, Gary McKeone and David Tomlinson. They saved me from many mistakes, large and small. Thanks also to Kirsty Anderson for typesetting and expert guidance on book design and production.

Most of all thanks to Poppy who lived through the major part of this, who had to put up with my all-too-frequent absences on official travel, held the family together through thick and thin, and stood by me at those times when difficulties were greatest.

CONTENTS

Note: the family

Members of the family who come into this story,
mostly without any introduction, are:

Poppy. We married in 1971

Rosie. Our daughter, born 1981

William. Our son, born 1985

Heather. My sister, born 1947

Janice. My just-older cousin, born 1942

Nigel. Poppy's brother

Then came **Violet**, Rosie's daughter, in 2015

1

FIRST YEARS

For the first ten years of their married life my parents lived in a house in Northwood Hills. Not all place names fit the places they are given to, but Northwood Hills does have hills. Their house was near the top of Haste Hill, with sweeping views to the front, down over streets of similar houses, across school fields and the town centre, and away in the distance Harrow Hill, with its landmark church spire on top. Behind the house was open ground: Haste Hill golf course. The golf course is still there and so is the house: 59 Cranbourne Road. In 2014 when Rosie was working in Pinner, the next station up the Metropolitan Line, I went in search of this, my first home, and found the street (as described) but I would not have recognised which house we lived in. House names have been changed, house fronts have been adapted, garages and gables added.

In 1937, the year my parents were married, this whole area was newly built over. We have a book that was published in 1934 which describes how rapidly the whole of Middlesex was being built up, and transformed from green fields and farmland to dense suburbia. Since Middlesex had already been built over almost completely by the time I was a teenager (it has now effectively been written out of existence by the Post Office, which has replaced it by a set of London postcodes), it is worth quoting from the preface to our 1934 book: 'Fifty years ago [so in the 1880s] Middlesex was predominantly rural and contained less than a quarter of its present population. Now it is largely suburbanised and partly industrial, with a population which is growing at a sensational rate.' Our part of Middlesex grew along the Metropolitan Line, and families tended to move, if they moved, along this line. Ours did. One set of grandparents lived at Cricklewood, the other at Harrow; their children moved down the line first to Northwood Hills, and then one more stop down the line to Northwood.

The house my parents lived in was given to them by my father's father. So they got off to a lucky start, a debt-free first step on the housing ladder. They made good use of that advantage as time went on.

But first came the war. For five years of the ten before they moved on from Northwood Hills, my father was away on war service, in the Navy. Mother was not exactly left to enjoy a peaceful life in a sleepy London suburb. Northwood Hills was then, and still is more or less, on the extreme north-west edge of the vast built-up spread of Greater London. For German bombers coming to London from the south-east, as they mostly did, and droning across London looking for a tempting target, from south-east to north-west, if they got as far as Northwood Hills it was clear that that particular sortie had not been useful; time to offload the bombs and to head back home. If the crews were being careful not to hit civilian targets, they would aim for the dark space of the golf course rather than a street, to drop their bombs off. Quite a few live bombs thus fell on Haste Hill golf course (creating new bunkers). Luckily none struck our house. But we had an Anderson shelter in the garden and it was used. I can just remember my father trying to demolish it when the war was over. Absolutely no chance, with pick and shovel. It was made to withstand more than that.

But I am running ahead. I was nowhere when the war began. I came on the scene in the middle of 1943. This is how my mother recorded my beginnings, in *Baby's Log Book*.

Richard John Derek was born on Saturday, 12th June, 1943 at 7.50pm at St Anne's Nursing Home, West End Avenue, Pinner.

Height [sic] at Birth: 19 inches.

Weight at Birth: 5 and a quarter lbs.

My weight was then recorded month by month, rising in steady steps, to 17lbs 8oz at the end of the 7th month, after which the record goes silent.

How Baby is Fed: 'Fed on Trufood which seems to suit him very well except that after every feed he brings back quite a lot. The doctor said this was nothing to worry about. Although Richard is so small he has always been fed 4-hourly. He seems unable to take his orange juice, which I've tried very hard to make him take.'

Baby and Vaccination: 'Richard was vaccinated whilst his Daddy was home on leave on the 24th Sept when he was 3 and a half months old. It did not seem to affect him at all.'

How Baby Sleeps: Sept 1943: 'Richard sleeps wonderfully well in the daytime, but his restless time is in the evenings between the 6 and 10 o'clock feeds. He sleeps well after his 10 o'clock feed and does not wake until between 6 and 7 for his early morning feed.' Oct 1943: 'Richard has improved and sleeps better in the evenings, although he still wakes at this time occasionally.'

How Baby is dressed in his first year: 'Richard was christened six days after his daddy returned from America, on the 12th Sept, when he was exactly 3 months old, and the following week he was shortened [!] into Viyella frocks [!], which he will wear all this winter plus leginettes and woolly coats. He has never worn woolly frocks, for during the first three months he wore silk robes, as it was summer.' [Wow.]

Mother's notes on Baby's routine: June/July: 'Richard has his bath and 10 o'clock feed, then he goes into the garden in his pram and sleeps until his 2 o'clock feed. He comes in for his food and then sleeps in the garden, sometimes until his 6 o'clock feed.' Aug/Sept: 'Richard wakes now in the afternoons about 4.30 and lies kicking until 5.30 when he gets fidgety and I prepare him for bed.' Oct/Nov/Dec: 'Richard is getting very active now and when he is nursed he's perpetually jigging up and down. His most fretful time is still between 6 and 10 in the evening, but he's improving.' January: 'The day Richard was seven months old he cut his first tooth without any trouble, and its neighbour followed ten days after. He now has rusks before his 6 o'clock feed and also I'm introducing Farex and vegetable broth at his 2 o'clock feed.'

The Log Book goes on with page headings for Things Baby First Notices, Age at which Baby First Crawls, Baby's First Words, Baby's First Birthday, Baby's second year... but all these pages are blank. I suppose I had become less of a novelty.

Naturally I don't remember any of that. What are the first things I remember? It is difficult to be sure. There are things we feel we know about our very early years because we have seen photographs, or older members of the family can remember things about us and tell us about them, over and over again, so that they become firmly embedded in our minds. There are four or five impressions I have in my mind which I think pass the test of being genuine early memories. This is because they are not recorded anywhere in photographs, and they are not things that my mother (who was certainly present on each occasion) ever talked about.

First, I have a very blurred impression of being in a room, I think an upstairs room; it is after dark, and I see out through a window to a house fire somewhere in the distance. In this 'memory' there are several people, women, in the room talking about the fire. I have always supposed – because this memory has always been with me – that I was somewhere not at home but perhaps at Harrow where other members of our family lived; that the women in the room were maybe my mother, my father's mother and her two daughters, my aunts. The women are talking but I am too young to understand and perhaps only half awake. The fire could have been a house that had been bombed, or maybe it just caught fire. I look back on this as possibly my earliest memory.

The next is very much more distinct and feels altogether like a real memory. It starts with a journey by train. I see flashes of light as the train passes through stations. Most likely I think these were my first experiences of an underground train in London. Then comes a very clear memory of being taken up the side of an immense grey ship, and of being handed over once we were on board ship to a group of sailors in their kitchen area – the ship's galley – and being allowed to play with their dog. I think this little scene can be dated with near certainty to March 1946 when my father returned from a long spell of duty in the Far East and my mother and I went down to visit him on his ship, which had just docked at Devonport. We would have travelled firstly into Baker Street, then by tube from Baker Street to Paddington, and then from Paddington to Devon on an overnight train. The 'immense grey ship' was HMS Nigella. My father, a sub-lieutenant in the Navy and a qualified navigator by the end of the war, had navigated this ship from Trincomalee (in Ceylon) all the way to Devonport, an achievement of which he was quite proud and for which he received a note of commendation from the ship's captain. My father and mother were being reunited after being separated for most of my tiny life, so not surprisingly I was parked with some of the ship's ratings in the galley. Whether or not I am mistaken with my precise dating, one feature of this little scene confirms that it was a genuine experience: the dog. I told this story some 45 years later to the captain and officers of a naval minesweeper on which I was being entertained; they were deeply sceptical until I brought in mention of the dog. At this, they were suddenly convinced, explaining to me that there was a longstanding and total ban on dogs being carried on navy ships before and after the war, because of the risk that they would bring rabies into Britain, but the rule had been relaxed during wartime to make life a little less stressful for the sailors.

So I count that as my first definite memory. I was at that time not quite four years old.

Then comes another pretty vague recollection of waiting with my mother somewhere on a hill just outside the station at Northwood Hills for my father to come off a train. There is nothing more in my mind than that. If it counts as a memory at all, I think we were waiting for my father to make his first return home after being released (demobbed) from the Navy; and it will have been just a few weeks after the reunion at Devonport.

Then I have another very sketchy memory of being in my push chair (no-one called them 'buggies' in those days) half way up the hill from Northwood Hills high street to Cranbourne Road, with my mother standing talking to a friend. What sticks in my mind is her saying 'Poor Merrick Hunt has TB.' It was somehow the solemnity with which that was said that fixed it in my mind. Merrick Hunt was the name of someone who lived a few roads away from us, and I don't remember that I ever heard of any close acquaintance after that being afflicted with TB. But I guess in wartime it was a less rare disease than it has, happily, become. The location, 'half way up the hill', may seem vague. But when in 2014 I went in search of the house, not having been back at any time in nearly 70 years, the slope of the hill and the view from the hill suddenly felt quite familiar. Something told me I had been there before.

My only other memory from this time when we lived in the house in Cranbourne Road is of our air raid shelter. What I remember comes from the time when my father was back with us and living at home. The war was now firmly over. Father wanted to remove the air-raid shelter and had been out in the garden trying to attack it with a pick or a mallet. He came indoors hot and frustrated and said something to the effect that it was indestructible. This shelter was of the 'Anderson' type, solid concrete embedded in the ground. It had featured in my life during the war, in that my mother and her parents, with me, had responded to air raid warnings and slept in the shelter on occasions; I have no idea how often, but my mother left notes of sometimes doing this. I can't remember it at all. It left no impression – presumably it seemed part of normal life to a baby. I wonder how those shelters ever were removed? We didn't stay to find out. We moved house from Cranbourne Road in April 1947 to Moor Park Road in Northwood. From there my schooldays began.

2

NORTHWOOD YEARS – SCHOOLS

1947-1962

I went to three schools in Northwood.

The first was Miss Sage's nursery school, where I started after Easter 1947, three months short of my fourth birthday, and stayed until I was five. Miss Sage I remember as rather tall and thin (but then any adult would seem tall to a four-year-old, and most people were thin in 1947). She held her little classes in the hall attached to our Methodist church. It was rightly described as a nursery school rather than just a nursery. I think the emphasis was on teaching us to read and write. I don't remember that we did a lot with paints and playthings, and anyway in those bleak years immediately after the war play materials will have been in short supply, and the variety of toys and instructive playthings that are all so easily obtainable today had not even been thought of. Miss Sage in my memory is a firm and fair teacher, not warm and cuddly, not fun, but a teacher. The one lighter aspect that I dimly remember is that my cousin Janice, she being a few months older than me, came to stay with us and attended Miss Sage's with me for a short time while her younger sister was being born (this was September 1947). Family chatter was that Janice and I made a disruptive pair, and tested Miss Sage's patience. Whether or not there was any truth in that, by the time I left at the age of five I could do reading and writing.

The next step was to Miss Brown's, a little formal school nestling on the edge of the grounds of St Martin's preparatory school. These days Miss Brown's would be labelled a pre-preparatory school. It was for boys only, and wholly geared to tuning us up for entry to St Martin's in the two years – five to seven – that we spent there. I can remember nothing about Miss Vera Brown; I can't picture her at all. One memory I have, which may well be mistaken, is that we had at some stage to be fitted out with boxing gloves. At the age of 5 or 6? I can't now think it really happened. The only firm fact is that one of the boys attending Miss Brown's with me was called John Cottingham. He and I trod the same path through prep school (St Martin's), then Merchant Taylors' and then St John's College, Oxford together – nearly twenty years of education in common. He and I on reaching the age of 7 made the transition from Miss Brown's to St Martin's.

Before we leave Miss Brown behind, it is worth quoting one or two remarks she made in her final report on me, dated 'Summer 1950', remarks which seem quite perceptive pointers to the future:

- French: has done well, and shows interest and ability;
- Conduct, marks lost: rather inclined to talk too much and to be disobedient – otherwise [otherwise?] good;
- Carden has done an excellent term's work. He is capable and able to concentrate. If encouraged, should do very well as learning comes easily to him.

St Martin's   1950-56

St Martin's was a larger world. This was a proper school. I am pleased to find that it still exists today (2018) and from time to time makes the news for winning top place in a national spelling competition or some other educational achievement. In the 1950s it consisted of a large old suburban villa and a long two-storey modern wing of classrooms: half and half. It has expanded since then. There was a field in front of the school buildings, on which we rampaged at play times; a larger field beyond, through a hedge; and another substantial field beyond that, across a public footpath. Here we had organised games or athletics, according to the time of year. Outdoor games were part of the timetable on several if not most days of the week. We were not short of exercise. Most boys walked to school or came by bike; almost no-one in those days was brought to the school gates by car. The 'school run' was a thing of the distant future.

I can still picture nearly all the key members of staff, and remember them quite warmly as individuals. The headmaster was Lionel Woodroffe and he, I think, had founded the school. He seemed to us an older man, so I suppose he was then in his 40s, maybe nearer 50. He kept a dignified distance from us boys. He was not at all harsh or austere (words I could use of my next headmaster) but there was no doubt he was in charge, of us, and his staff, and the school. He dealt with the parents, who seemed to be impressed by him. He dealt with us as and when we needed a touch of headmasterly discipline, and otherwise taught us what would now be called religious studies but was then called Divinity. This consisted of a lot of reading of the bible with little or no discussion of its meaning but frequent tests to make sure we knew the bible stories thoroughly.

Mr Woodroffe's nephew Mr Allen also worked at the school. I guess he had not achieved much academically. He majored on 'games' and school administration. The most junior member of staff and the only female was Miss Folkes, who taught the most junior class and also shepherded other classes when we went for walks in crocodile outside the school grounds. For some reason we always and only addressed her as 'Please'. To the masters we said 'Sir' and I suppose to Miss Folkes we could have said 'Miss'. But it was always 'Please' and this was the only form of address we used, even though it sometimes meant our saying what we wanted to say in a rather convoluted way.

Mr Wigham taught us maths. He was hyper-thin, and his face was gaunt – probably because he was a heavy smoker. He had a cigarette in his mouth most of the time, and left the ash to build up at the burning end until it dropped off. We were amply exposed to the dangers of passive smoking but no-one thought anything of that in the 1950s. Mr Wigham had a sharp tongue and could lash out with fierce irony. In between times he could be quite warm and friendly. My mother was fond of gossiping with him as he walked past our house. He gave us a good grounding in mathematics.

Mr Wright taught us English and perhaps also history, but it is his teaching of English that I remember. By the time he had finished with us he had taken us through an impressive range of English literature. We were encouraged (made) to learn long stretches of poetry by heart and then to recite it in class. I enjoyed that, though sadly my long-term memory was not up to retaining it and I could recite almost none of it now. We had read two if not three plays of Shakespeare by the time we were 13, something which my fellow students in Germany later regarded as impressive, and enviable. We certainly read in whole or in part *Midsummer Night's Dream* and *Henry IV Part I* because I remember our acting scenes from those plays in the fields in the summer. We had made our first acquaintance with Falstaff and with Bottom the Weaver. Alongside that we were taught a lot about English grammar, and figures of speech, stuff which has fallen out of most curriculums long ago.

Mr Anderson taught us Latin from the age of about 8, and added Greek for some of us from about 10 or 11. I can remember reciting (in my head) my first steps in Greek verbs while sitting in the dentist's chair, to take my mind off the drilling. A dentist's drill circa 1954 was loud and slow. Pain was not far away. Mr Anderson would not have minded this. Pain was an integral part of his teaching method. He was another smoker, and he too could lash us with his tongue. But unlike Mr Wigham he thought nothing of lashing us physically too. He administered beatings quite routinely. We would be beaten for misbehaviour and, I think, for slovenly school work as well. The beatings were inflicted with a gym shoe that had a highly polished sole, worn smooth by years of beating, and it was of a shoe size that gave it flexibility to come down on the victim with a bit of a whiplash. Mr Anderson would accumulate a number of boys to be beaten, appoint a time, and then solemnly work his way through the queue. He beat with a firm touch and an air of enjoyment. I was part of the line-up quite often, generally for speaking out of turn (forgetting Miss Brown's warning). Some would say I was never cured of that, so perhaps I was not beaten enough. This systematic physical punishment is probably outlawed if not illegal now, but neither we nor our parents were particularly horrified about it then. I retained high regard for Mr Anderson and responded well to his teaching. He got my Greek off to a very effective start.

There may have been one or two other teachers who have faded from memory but that was the main gallery of them and their teaching methods. I look back on it as a happy school, where I enjoyed my first encounter with the range of core subjects and learned fast, in a group of similarly keen learners, competing with one another. I enjoyed the range of outdoor activities, and the straggly hedges around the borders of our playing fields were where I took my first steps in the systematic observation and recording of birds: tracking down nests, not to take and collect the eggs but to note the number of eggs or fledglings and record that on simple nest recording cards. I still have a few of those somewhere, dating back 60 years now. I like also to remember the things that our schools taught us on the side, and one thing St Martin's drilled us in was basic house cleaning. We took it in turn in small working parties to sweep the main common areas of the school building at lunchtimes. This was not punishment. I suppose it saved the school a little money on cleaners. We boys got early training in the use of brooms, dustpans and brushes, and learned how slow deliberate movements catch the dust better than over-energetic jerky action which just sends it up in the air again.

There was a downside to the quality of teaching at St Martin's. The school did its best to take the pupils who were keen to learn to as high a level as possible, to maximise their chances of securing places and if possible scholarships at the schools which they were going on to. I with John Cottingham and three or four others were aiming at Merchant Taylors'. With all the help St Martin's gave us I think we sailed over the entry requirements, and we won scholarships too. This helped our parents' pockets. But for me it meant that the first year at MT if not two years felt like treading water; recapping subject matter that had been fresh and interesting the first time. It took the edge off that year or two; I felt disappointed not to be stretched as before, and got rather bored.

However, I would not lay that at St Martin's door as a criticism. I look back on my years there as the the best of my time at school.

Merchant Taylors'   1956-62

The school that I attended from the age of 13 to 18 was Merchant Taylors', at Sandy Lodge (near Northwood), in Hertfordshire. I left at the beginning of April 1962, with six months of free time before I started university, and did not keep in contact with the school or its staff after that. So I was quite surprised when in the spring of 2016 I received an invitation to attend a 'Celebration of Classics' at the school – on 21 June. This came as an attractive idea. It was an event with a specific purpose: to shine a spotlight on the teaching of Latin and Greek and the civilisations of ancient Greece and Rome, a cause which I am always happy to support. I have not felt any impulse to attend school reunions of a general kind because I have long since lost contact with nearly everyone who was at the school with me, and as for those few who have remained friends we keep up in other ways. But this event was something different. Specific to classics, it was the first event of that kind ever, so far as I knew. There might never again be such a suitable occasion for dipping back into my school days. So I accepted.

When the date came, it could not have been at a more difficult time. I had injured my spine about two weeks before, I could barely walk, and because I was on such strong painkillers I was not permitted to drive. Poppy nobly stepped forward and agreed to be my chauffeur. The last part of the drive was quite difficult for her, threading through the outer London suburbs in dense traffic.

It was a fairly small gathering and I was, by a small margin, the oldest former pupil there. But one of the two appointed speakers was an only slightly younger person, who had been the star classics pupil two or three years behind me and had gone on to a university career, finishing up as Professor of Greek at Nottingham University. I knew of his reputation and have used some of his books, so I was interested to meet him face to face. That was a supplementary reason for going – but not the main one. It was good to meet and talk with the sprinkling of current pupils who had turned out for this 'Celebration'; six to eight of them studying Latin, only four studying Greek as well. That was about a third of the number we would have been in the 1950s. We sat with the headmaster at lunch, and met the young head of classics, Philip Harrison.

It was quite a fine day, in a summer which had been unusually short of fine days. The sun shone over the playing fields and as we looked out from our lunch table in the luxurious newly-built clubhouse for Old Merchant Taylors (OMTs) we could see tennis being played in the foreground (the school had no tennis courts in my time) and cricket being played on pitches in several directions beyond. The playing fields at Merchant Taylors' are extensive; one of the benefits of the move the school had made to Sandy Lodge from the middle of London in the 1930s.

This is the place to explain a little of the school's history. It was founded in 1561, in the reign of Elizabeth I. That was a period of high tension in England over forms of religion, tension centred on whether or not to restore the tie with Rome and the Pope which Henry VIII, Elizabeth's father, had decisively broken. Several schools founded around that time were creations of the church, with shades of allegiance that came under close scrutiny, while some were secular creations, funded by trade. Merchant Taylors' was of the latter kind. The idea of founding it came from a leading member of the Guild of Merchant Taylors, Richard Hilles. His idea did not meet with immediate support from all of his colleagues because his proposition, his prospectus, for the school was that it should teach Greek as well as Latin (and theology), and prepare pupils for careers in the service of the state as well as in the church and universities. Greek, at that tense time, was regarded with some suspicion by those with leanings towards the catholic religion and restoring links with Rome. Greek was suspect; subversive. Had it not sparked off free-thinking in Italy? What was all their renaissance about, and where was it leading? St Paul's School founded 50 years earlier was under this same suspicion, of teaching 'heretical' Greek. Not many years after the decision by the Merchant Taylors' Company to found a school on the lines proposed by Richard Hilles, credit for it was being taken by another prominent member of this livery company, Sir Thomas White. Now, Sir Thomas White had just recently (1555) founded St John's College in Oxford – of which more later – but he was a "Romanist", one of those people distinctly uneasy about where the teaching of Greek would lead, and he was *not* immediately supportive of the Hilles project. It took six years before White created the links between the Merchant Taylors' school and his college in Oxford: 1567. Links from which I benefited 400 years afterwards. More of that in its place.

Moving on, the school building was at first in Threadneedle Street, which everyone knows is the address of the Bank of England but not so many know is also where the Merchant Taylors' Company has its livery company hall; had in the 1560s and still has today; and that it was the concentration of tailors here in the middle ages which gave the street its 'threadneedle' name. The school outgrew its first building, moved next to Suffolk Lane, still in the City, and remained there through to the 1870s. The next move was to Charterhouse Square, still very central, but only for a relatively short time. By the beginning of the twentieth century it had become more and more clear that central London was not the right place for this school to be. With the rapid spread of London and the growth of the suburbs, accelerated by the opening of suburban train lines, the fathers sending boys to the school were living further and further out in the leafy suburbs, whilst the boys were spending so long commuting back into London that the school day was having to be compressed; and as for exercise, there was no space for any sort of outdoor games.

The decision was taken to move the school out, 25 miles out to Sandy Lodge, a greenfield site. Here was space for wholly new buildings to be surrounded by ample playing fields. The main school buildings that were designed and put up in the 1930s are austere verging on unsightly; sheer expanses of brick, not such as to inspire affection. But then the earlier school buildings in Suffolk Lane had been described as gloomy in their day, dark and dreary, looking exactly like a warehouse. Ugliness seems to be the Merchant Taylors' house style. The move took place in 1933, to the school as I knew it, but the centuries-old link with the City was kept up. The Merchant Taylors' Company continued to have a role in the governance of the school, and to contribute funds towards the running of it.

Coming back now to my visit in June 2016, I was expecting that this visit, the first time I had stepped inside the school buildings and spoken to staff or pupils since 1962, 54 years previously, would perhaps unlock a flood of memories. It didn't. As I looked out across the playing fields, cricket being played, it simply felt... familiar. It was a scene I knew well. It didn't trigger any interesting memories.

Why not? Possibly because I did not find my time at this school particularly stimulating or particularly enjoyable. I need to think harder to explain that. But first we need to build up a fuller picture of the school.

What sort of people were the pupils? The catchment will have changed to some extent with the move out of the City. The parents – in the 1950s mothers mainly didn't go out to work, so this means the fathers – typically had jobs of one kind or another in the City of London, in private companies, or in city-related professions such as accountancy, or in government departments or in the media – which meant, in those days the BBC because ITV hadn't started. It was not a school to which 'old money' sent their sons. This was a school for 'new money'. And in the 1950s the parents with money enough for the school's fees were, not all but many of them, spending to give their sons a better education than they themselves had had.

My father was a good fit with this picture. He was a merchant dealing in textiles and clothing, in effect almost a 'merchant taylor'. He was managing director of a fairly small company whose core business was to supply textiles for clothes-making, and finished clothes, to a selection of department stores on half a dozen Caribbean islands, with Jamaica and Trinidad/Tobago the main ones. The company, James Miller & Co, had been born around the beginning of the twentieth century and by the end of the twentieth century it was defunct. It was the final flourish of the Imperial Preference trading system. During the

1960s and 1970s British colonies in the Caribbean achieved independence one by one, and fairly soon wound down their trade dependency on Britain, building up economic links with the United States instead. My father's successors running James Miller (he died in 1970) scratched around for new business of one kind and another for the following twenty years but never seemed to make much of a success of their new ventures. A period of economic history was coming to an end. However, through the 1950s and 1960s the business did very well.

As for the general picture I am painting of parents and pupils, this is not something that I could have articulated at the time but, when I went on to Oxford and could begin to make comparisons between my contemporaries there who had been to one school or another, I think some features of the Merchant Taylors' imprint could be identified. Because we were not following in our fathers' footsteps, not going through a schooling that our fathers and grandfathers had had before us, we tended to exercise a freedom to form our own ideas and attitudes. We were more tuned to the latest cutting-edge novels and plays – and new things were happening on the literary scene in the 1950s. One of the assets of being only half an hour's train ride from the West End was that we could go into London for an evening, to see a play or hear a concert. A group of us, by the time we were 16 or 17, took full advantage of that. We went to see plays by John Osbourne, Arnold Wesker, Samuel Beckett when they were new and meeting with cries of horror from the critics. This was the period when 'kitchen sink' plays arrived on the scene, and the theatre of the absurd. We went to see some plays twice; *Waiting for Godot* for instance, and *The Caretaker*. We lapped up novelty. As for music, my closest bird-watching friend Martin happened to share my interest in classical music. So, over the summer holidays, on days when we were not bird-watching, he and I frequently went to promenade concerts in the Albert Hall. We did it cheaply. We *always* promenaded, queuing for an hour or more for tickets, then standing throughout the concert (sometimes there would be room to sit down on the floor, but often not). This way we got to hear some of the top conductors and solo performers of the 1950s, and a wide range of music, both mainstream and new. In those days the proms programme could be guaranteed to stick firmly to classical music. There were other London schools which could of course offer the same opportunities, but there were major public and state schools around the country which could not. We had a cultural benefit from being so near to London.

That was, of course, London's contribution, not the school's. In my memory I tend to run down the quality of the Merchant Taylors' education. My low rating may not be wholly justified. The quality of teaching of Greek and Latin, in which I specialised more and more, clearly gave me a good foundation for university; me and a number of my contemporaries who followed the same path. But it took my teachers at Merchant Taylors' some time to catch up with and improve on the grounding St Martin's had given, and their teaching of classics was (with one exception) sound rather than sparkling.

I have very often wondered whether it would have been better for me with my taste for languages to have specialised in modern instead of ancient languages at school, so as to have got a thorough knowledge of the history and culture of two or three modern European countries along with acquiring the skill to speak their languages with fluency. French and German for instance, or Italian, or Russian. Could that have happened? If only. It would have been a great asset for me in the career which came later.

But there is a specific and a general reason why it would not have worked. The specific reason is that I don't think the quality of modern language teaching at Merchant Taylors' was all that good – though the same may well have been true then at many other major schools. Teaching of modern languages has never been a strength of school education in England. French, for us, was taught in a bookish way. It was all about reading bits of literature (but not a representative range – I learned more about that from a couple of letters with reading lists sent to me many years later by a friend of a friend who had gone to live in France, than I ever picked up at school). A light sprinkling of history was added in as necessary to interpret the literature. If we were taught to speak – and we must have been – it was very basic and the content was far removed from everyday situations. So that although I studied French to A level I only really learned to speak it when I was catapulted into living and working in Paris for two months between school and university.

As for German, I don't recall that it was taught at all, though it must have been. Italian came as a spin-off from Latin. One of our sixth-form classics masters gave classes in Italian grammar to a few of us for a term, and I have been permanently grateful. It got me off to a confident start in teaching myself, boosted by some hitch-hiking around Italy in summer holidays.

The general reason why I do not believe that I would have gained from opting for modern languages rather than the 'classics' is that there was nothing at any school or university, to my knowledge, by way of a course based on modern languages which matched up to the courses that we followed in the classical languages, Greek and Latin, for either range or rigour. For range, classics as taught in the 1950s and 1960s (the focus has shifted substantially since then) took in poetry, drama, but also history, philosophy and politics; and that included some pretty exacting works of history and philosophy. By contrast, French and German as taught at Oxford took in a narrower range of reading: poetry, drama, works of fiction – literature in the modern sense, belles-lettres – for the most part.

As for rigour, French and German *can* be taught rigorously but weren't (or so it appeared to me). The point was to cover a large spread of writings (good) but with the priority on reading a lot, then discussing how one author's work drew on, or was related to another. The classics approach many people would now consider went too far in the other direction: minute attention paid to the meanings of words, to the forms of poetry (metre) and the techniques of rhetoric at the expense of overall meaning and significance. Not seeing the wood for the trees? There is force in that line of criticism but, in defence of the classics approach, we were made to understand the exact meaning of what an author was saying and, because the forms of expression in both Latin and Greek are more distant from the way thoughts are expressed in modern English, we came to understand that there is not always an exact equivalence between words and phrases in one language and another; that it is important to think below the surface, to the idea underlying the words used. Some of the same skill is useful in moving between any one modern language and another but, because the distance between forms of expression is not *as* great, because treating words as if they were equivalent one-for-one works more often between modern languages, the point often gets lost. The way we were taught classics in the 1950s was a method that had been honed and refined over some two hundred years of school teaching in England. Just as some scientific subjects, chemistry in particular, are rated highly as training for the mind because of their intrinsic difficulty and the rigour with which they are taught, so classics in my opinion stands out among the 'humanities' for both rigour and range. That was what it was about this subject that drew me, from the St Martin's days, and gripped me more firmly as time went on.

There is another might-have-been, another choice that I might have made: biology. By the age of 14 or 15 I already had a strong interest in natural history *and* I had taken it in several ways in a scientific direction. I had read up about basic genetics when I took to breeding budgerigars. Those birds breed rapidly and the relationship between the colours of parents and offspring can give some good illustrations of dominant and recessive genes at work. I was linked in through early membership of the BTO to its nest recording scheme; I read the scientific papers in the BTO Journal *Bird Study* (the first copies I have date from 1959); and in the school periods when we were allowed to read what we liked, I mostly at that time chose to read heavyweight volumes from the *New Naturalist* series, to the puzzlement of my classics contemporaries who were reading this and that work of literature.

Why did I not become a biologist? I took O level biology. Our teacher Mr Stokes had that opportunity to fire me up – but he stuck to the basics of the syllabus and failed to communicate anything of the excitement of life sciences. He was no David Lack. (Taught with David Lack at Greshams or taught by him at Dartington Hall, I would quite possibly have become dedicated to biology.) We had a school natural history society, and it had a little library with a few stuffed birds and a distinct smell of formaldehyde, but the society had very few members. I can remember only one. He and I didn't bond. So Mr Stokes let a potential future biologist continue to cleave to the classics. Another moment came when the scientists could have got a grip on me. I might have been a fairly easy convert. But more of that when the moment comes.

Aside from the extra-curricular culture, which we drank in for ourselves, and the mainstream teaching of classics, I credit Merchant Taylors' with giving me two experiences of practical usefulness and lasting value. One was the teaching of woodwork. For the two years up to O level (GCSE equivalent) we had a double period on a Friday afternoon for which we were offered two options: musical appreciation, or woodwork. Most of those with higher IQ were expected to opt for musical appreciation and most of my friends did so.

I opted for woodwork. The woodwork master, Mr Beech (inevitably his nickname was 'Woody'), I remember as a tolerant and patient teacher. He set no limit on the amount of wood you could use. Over the two years' tuition with him, I learned what to do with the basic range of woodworking tools, how to cut joints, turn bowls, and do some marquetry. It is amazing the number and variety of pieces of woodwork that I produced over those two years, some of which we still have. I made a full-sized work bench which has moved from house to house with us for about sixty years and which has been endlessly useful for making other things, including a succession of bird nest boxes. At the other end of the skills scale I made a marquetry picture which still hangs on our dining room wall. I didn't create the picture, I had a picture to copy. But the quality of my workmanship was good enough to be worth hanging on the wall, and still attracts admirers. Along with those things I made several huge plywood cages that served for the rest of my teenage years to house my breeding stock of budgerigars. I don't know what Mr Beech thought I was learning when I made these, and they must have used up a lot of plywood. But they were definitely useful, though they have long since gone. My O Level woodwork has served the family well, applied to DIY operations in at least four homes where we have carried out major reconstruction.

The second of what I count as useful experiences was the light touch of military service that we got through the school's Cadet Force. Many of my contemporaries scorned this. Attitudes were changing. We were on the threshold of the 1960s. The spirit of public service, all pulling together, the team playing on which public schools famously put emphasis, was under attack from the spirit of self-expression and emphasis on the development of the individual. The tension between these two attitudes broke out strongly in my school days, and the cadet force was one target for scorn from the individualists. However, until the late 1950s National Service was still in operation and, although that came to an end three years before I would have been called up for two years of real military service, we still had compulsory Combined Cadet Force ('Combined' because we had army, navy and air force options). We all had to come into school in military uniform on a Friday, and part of Friday afternoon was given over to drilling, rifle handling, map reading and so on. We all had to start for the first year in the army section. After that we could if we wished move over to the navy or air force. I chose the navy because my father had served proudly in the navy in WWII. I think the whole system of cadet force became optional soon after my time at the school, with social service becoming an alternative. However, I am not sorry to have had my small taste of what it is like to serve in the armed forces. We only played at being soldiers or sailors, but we went through the experience of being shouted at on the parade ground by an RSM (our Arthur Bell was the genuine article). We went to Bisley for rifle shooting in freezing cold weather one March, staying in barracks alongside real young teenage soldiers – a rude shock – and fired real ammunition at targets that were too far away to see. We went a number of times to Portsmouth and once to Rosyth. The train journey north to Edinburgh was a revelation – probably the first time I had been north of Watford. As for skills for life: Thursday evenings at home were spent getting the kit ready for inspection next day; producing a mirror-quality shine on the toecaps of my boots (there were various cunning recipes for doing that) and producing the concertina creases on my bell-bottomed sailor's trousers for which I think I still know the secret.

With all this, why do I not look back on my time at that school more warmly? The headmaster was bleak, austere, and cast a shadow. Much of the teaching was competent and even of high quality, but not very lively; 'competent but dull' would be my overall marking. The liveliest teacher at the school at that time was John Steane, teacher of English, enthusiast for song and a scholar of the human voice, author (some years later) of *The Grand Tradition – Seventy Years of Singing on Record – 1900-1970*, a book about recordings of opera singers which became quite famous. He was a stimulating teacher and also occasionally accompanied us on evening trips to the West End. The uniquely valuable lesson he taught us was how to pee safely out of the windows of the old slam-door trains (no toilets) that were still running on the Metropolitan Line. Always use a window on the near side of the train; if you use the offside there would be a risk of the jet hitting the conductor rail on the opposite track, with unforeseeable consequences. He then was one intellectually distinguished member of staff. Why were there not more?

All in all, my take-away memories of Merchant Taylors' contrast with my take-away memories of St Martin's. Partly my downbeat memories of the later school will reflect that I was not very good at being a teenager – and that could be laid at the door of a strict methodist upbringing in a strict methodist household. So that the extracurricular activities where teenagers practise being teenagers, such as Saturday evening parties, and any form of consumption of alcohol, were firmly frowned on. While my more sociable contemporaries were going to parties, playing in bands, or – horror of horrors – gathering in the pub, I suppose I was, depending on the time of year, either out bird-watching or having hours of bookish discussion with the one or two friends who were on the approved list and regarded as safe. That sounds like a very limiting schedule for free time. I think it was.

The process of transition from Merchant Taylors' to university was smoothed for us by history. Remember that Merchant Taylors' School, founded in 1561, was taken up within a few years of its foundation by Sir Thomas White of the Merchant Taylors' Company who had only recently (1555) founded St John's College in Oxford. The two institutions were firmly linked and had remained so. St John's College offered a number of 'closed' scholarships to boys coming from Merchant Taylors' School; 'closed' meaning that they were awarded only to people from that school or not at all. The government Department of Education had imposed a condition (since 1948) that candidates had to come up to the same standard as the college would apply to 'open' scholarships. This arrangement meant that Merchant Taylors' tended to put its best pupils forward for the St John's scholarships; our choice of university and college was therefore simplified. We had to sit special St John's entry exams in the autumn after A level and, provided we passed those, as did I and John Cottingham (both from Miss Brown's!) and half a dozen others, there was then an oral exam to be faced. These oral exams were conducted, following centuries of tradition, in the Merchant Taylors' Hall, 30 Threadneedle Street. The President and three or four Fellows from St John's came down to grill us. It was intimidating enough, and the historic setting made it more so. I remember being quizzed by the President, William Costin, who spoke in a squeaky voice, about some hair-splitting difference between the meaning of two words and, whatever I may have said in reply, he chuckled (squeakily) and said that was a foretaste of Oxford philosophy. Those of us who passed this ordeal were invited back a few weeks later as junior guests at a full-blown adult feast in the Merchant Taylors' Hall, black tie and many courses of food and wine. That was autumn 1961. I relived the memory of the interview vividly when, quite by chance, I visited the Merchant Taylors' Hall very nearly 50 years later, in autumn 2010, for a discussion about a theme for a Consultation at Windsor with a farmer landowner who happened to be a member of this livery company. Arriving a bit early for my appointment I wandered through the rooms and realised, with a flash of déjà-vu, that I was in the room where Costin & Co had put me through their inquisition all those years before.

I have been in the Hall once more since then, for a concert to celebrate the school's 450th anniversary, in spring 2011. It was a concert performance of Handel's Messiah with original 18th century instruments. In talking to parents in the interval I realised how greatly the school has changed. Around a third of pupils now have parents of South Asian (mainly Indian) or Chinese origin. A sign of the times, and of continued outward migration of upwardly mobile families along the Metropolitan Line, and a fresh source of intellectual energy for the school.

In between school and university   Summer 1962

No gap year for most of us in those days. Having sorted out university entry by Christmas 1961, I stayed on at school until Easter 1962. I then had six months to play with. I did two things of significance. I spent a month on Lundy, slotting into the post of assistant warden at the island's bird observatory, which I had held before. Then I spent two months or not much more in Paris, working full-time as a bank clerk at the First National City Bank on the Champs-Elysées.

The month on Lundy could have been just some more bird-watching, albeit purposeful bird-watching. But the arrival of a strange bird put us into the ornithological record books. The weather was bad, as it often is on Lundy. Cloud down to ground level, wind and rain. The warden, Michael Jones discovered a bird that he could not identify, feeding on the ground with some linnets. It looked like some type of lark, but not one that he knew. He came to me in great excitement and we went back to look at the bird together. We watched it over several days (7-11 May) and took detailed notes. In those days there was no such thing as digital photography – which, combined with email, settles the identification of any bird within minutes these days. Nor could we call in

31

any help from other bird-watchers. Lundy was cut off as it often was in the 1960s, when outside the summer holiday season the only supply line was a 30 foot fishing boat sailing out of Bideford, unable to make the crossing in rough weather. So Michael and I compiled a meticulous description of our strange bird's plumage, behaviour and song, and wrote it up for greater experts to pass judgement on. We were still unsure what species of bird we had been looking at. We concluded that it must be a Calandra Lark, though not all points in our description fitted that.

The process of scrutinising records of rare birds has always been rigorous. The evidence, written description and any photographs, has to be assembled and submitted to a committee of super-experts, who have to pick through many doubtful records and stories of wishful thinking. They start sceptical. To strengthen our case, I went with our written description to the Natural History Museum in London which holds a vast collection of 'skins' – the dried corpses of birds, with their feathers on – from all around the world. This is one of the great reference collections to which researchers are allowed access, but only sparingly. I still have the letter of 24 May 1962 from a Mr Galbraith at the Department of Zoology, Cromwell Road (the skins collection moved soon after that to Tring):

'You are welcome to study skins of the Calandra Lark and its relatives ...

We are usually chary about giving facilities for the confirmation of sight records, because the best watchers can be misled if they do not know the recognition characters of the species concerned; but that is clearly not the case here.'

In due course our record was submitted to the Rarities Committee, whose verdict was that what we had seen was a Bimaculated Lark (melanocorypha bimaculata), a relative of the Calandra Lark whose home range was the extreme south-east of Europe and western/central Asia – Azerbaijan and beyond. Whereas the Calandra Lark had been recorded in Britain a few times, the Bimaculated Lark had never been seen in this country before. We had a 'first for Britain' - something that keen birdwatchers dream of finding. I was within reach of the bottom rung of a career in ornithology.

Then came Paris. My father had fished for a job for me in the International Labour Organization in Geneva, where he had a contact, but they did not want to take anyone for such a short time. I had, by now, only two or three months to

32

offer. But Paris worked out better than Geneva ever could have done. The office of the bank where I was to work was half-way down the Champs-Elysées, on the left as you walk from the Arc de Triomphe towards the Place de la République. (It has disappeared now. Rosie and William and I could not find it in 2013.) I went to live with a family, a posh Parisian family who took in two or three paying guests from abroad under a scheme for immersing visiting students in the French way of life. I still remember the address: 44 rue Laugier. The family was called Jung. The mother of the house ruled the roost, with son Claude and daughter Marie-France, both in their late teens or early twenties. The main event of the day was the evening meal which we all took together, family and the 2-3 house guests. The family talked incessantly – it was my introduction to quick-fire, sharp-shooting French conversation style. I was never clear whether it was put on for show, or to get us foreigners up to speed, but it certainly came as a baptism of fire for me with my A level book-bound French. It was fun and torment simultaneously. As for office work, I had a walk of about twenty minutes through the VIIIe (posh) arrondissement, past the Arc de Triomphe to the portals of the First National City Bank. It was American-owned so there were one or two American managers around, but nearly all the employees were locals and the working language was French. I became quickly conversant with some technical terms of accounting and everyday words for filing, clipping and punching holes in bits of paper. I was given a variety of things to do, including sometimes sitting at the counter dealing with clients. It felt like a long day: 8.30 – 6.30, I think. I was impressed by how hard the American staff worked, and expected us to work. Ten hour days were nothing to them, and they didn't expect four week summer holidays. My time in Paris ran from mid-June to mid-August, so the city soon began to empty out for the holidays and shops began to shut down. No sooner had I become comfortable with one little cafe than I had to move on and find another. I walked an immense amount, but used the metro system a lot too. Paris in the early 1960s contrasted in some ways with London. There was more poverty evident on the streets: beggars sleeping over the grills covering ventilation shafts from the metro, through which warm air came up. In applying, as I had to, for a residence permit, or work permit, or both, I had to queue for hours at government offices, with immigrants from Algeria, a first encounter with French bureaucracy and sharp-tongued officialdom. France's war with Algeria had just ended, Algeria was within days of independence, and French settlers were flooding back to their mother country. I have a memory of standing near the Arc de Triomphe watching as General de Gaulle and the German Chancellor Adenauer stood side by side at the Tomb of the Unknown Soldier in a famous act of reconciliation between France and Germany. But that was possibly a year or two later, because I made one or two return visits.

If my parents had been more thought-out they would have pressed me to stay on in Paris for a month or two longer. I could have done, and would have gained by it. But by the end of August I was back home. Nevertheless Paris had made its mark, my French had taken a great leap forward, and I have felt quite at home in Paris ever since. Paris, the central area, has changed far less in my lifetime than has London, let alone Berlin – but that comes later.

3

NORTHWOOD YEARS – THE HOME SCENE
1947-1962

My years at school spanned the 1950s; we might call it the 'long 1950s', as some historians would do. Life in Britain changed very much in those years, and life for us at home changed along with it. The most important change was the arrival in 1947 of my sister Heather. She had a difficult start because she needed an intricate eye operation when she was very young. The skills of a surgeon who had performed wonders on injured RAF pilots put her right, and she was soon fit enough to be on the receiving end of trials and tests that I put her through.

Our parents changed houses like a snake changes its skin. When a house began to feel tight and itchy, they cast it off and moved to another. During our schooldays we lived in four houses in Northwood (and two more afterwards); three of these were in the same road, one just round the corner. Because these houses were so close to one another, it had no disruptive effect on us children. None of us had anything like the quantity of clothes and other possessions that have become normal now. Packing up and moving house was not a complicated operation. The largest of our houses, where we had the most room and the most fun as teenagers, was sold to developers and turned into several blocks of flats. I don't think my parents ever lost money on their house transactions.

For a few years after the war there was real austerity; considerably more bleak than what is being called austerity these days. There was one long severe winter when snow and ice lasted for months. Houses whether large or small were simple and sparsely furnished compared with today. Indoors there was no central heating. Our Northwood houses in the 1950s certainly did not have central heating. One or two rooms were heated by open coal fires, the rest hovered somewhere – but not always very much – above outside temperatures. When it was cold outside, it was cold inside. In freezing weather we had beautiful patterns of ice on the inside of our window panes. That indoor ice was something I was used to seeing well into the 1960s, in lodging houses in Oxford.

People also did not generally have a fraction of the domestic equipment that everyone has today. Kitchens were simpler. Fridges were coming in – though my mother's parents in Northwood Hills never had one. Various labour-saving machines were creeping in from America, but they were rarities. Microwaves had not been invented. Clothes were plain and utilitarian. My mother in winter went into thick coats and thigh boots with woolly lining, and wore the same every day when she went outside.

This austerity lifted quite fast as we moved through the 1950s. But life in central London at that time still had aspects that would today make us think we were in a third-world country. In the early 1950s my father sometimes took me with him to his office on a Saturday morning. Saturday half-day working was routine in the City and civil service until the mid-1950s. We went by car to Finsbury Square near Moorgate. An area behind Moorgate station had been badly bombed and was still a bomb-site. Where office blocks had stood, there were only stumps of walls and holes in the ground. These particular bomb sites were for some reason favoured by Black Redstarts, robin-like birds that otherwise nest in very few places in England. So, once my interest in birds had come alive, I went to Moorgate a few times to watch Black Redstarts. Then in the 1960s the sites were cleared, new office blocks sprang up, and the birds were driven out. But, going back to the 1950s, office work on a Saturday finished at lunch-time. My father would then drive me back home along the main roads where, at every intersection or traffic light where queues of cars built up, there would be men ready to spring forward to sell us the lunch-time papers (London evening papers in those days went through three to four editions during the afternoon) or to give the car windscreen a rapid wash. People were scratching a living on the street among moving traffic in a way that today's young people would see only in India or some even less developed country. London in the 1950s had some comparable features – though visible street poverty was in general worse in Paris.

In these years my father's business did well. Our houses and cars became bigger; our neighbours began to splash out on cocktail parties and tennis parties and the very latest model of Jaguar. My mother responded more enthusiastically to this than my father did. He preferred to spend his spare time, such as it was, on gardening or football refereeing, but had to give the latter up in his forties. He carried mixed memories of his war service in the Navy. He had had rough times, about which he never spoke to us, the children. But he took pride in what he had learned about navigation and the stars, and on walks with the dogs after dark on winter evenings he would teach me to recognise the constellations, and the phases of the moon. He kept, and we still have, his Ditty Box, the tiny treasure chest that was standard issue to officers in the Navy. Dogs became his keenest pleasure, golden retrievers his breed of choice. The first one or two of these that he bought were very carefully selected from top breeders. Jess, our star retriever of all time, was a beautiful looking dog, and father trained her with great thoroughness. She won prizes for her looks at Crufts, and carried off prizes in obedience trials at country shows. From her father bred litters of puppies several times and although most were sold we seemed always to finish up keeping one. As time went on we had three or four mature retrievers in the house, and periodically six or eight puppies as well. Dogs all round the house, walking dogs morning and evening, riding in cars with the smell of wet dogs after walks in wet weather, these were constant features of home life all through the long 1950s.

A very important aspect, if not dominant then a constant and significant part of our background while we were children, my sister and I, was the Methodist church. Both of our parents were methodists, and both came from families who had been methodists for generations. All our direct relations were, and all the earlier generations whom they could remember had been, methodists. Being methodists and belonging to methodist churches was a fundamental part of who they were. The talk between our parents when we were little was often about churchgoing, church affairs, organization of church events. Father was treasurer of the church we attended. When you look at photographs of him in younger days, and his parents, many of the pictures were of them at church gatherings, of his father presiding at formal church occasions.

Mother's parents were different. They were quieter, more modest people, who had not been at the centre of any church organizations. But churchgoing and following the strict code laid down for methodists, was if anything even more important for them than for my father's side. They regarded themselves as 'Primitive' methodists, the line of methodism which traced back to revivalist open-air meetings of factory workers in the Staffordshire potteries at the very beginning of the nineteenth century. One of the foundation stories of the Prims was the mass meeting on Mow Cop in Staffordshire in 1807. On mother's side our family carried a firm folk memory of that formative event. Methodists, for a hundred years, were divided between Wesleyan (Charles and John Wesley their founders) and Primitive methodists. The two lines had joined some time in the 1920s. But that was too recent for my mother's parents to have forgotten that they came from the Primitive line.

These two strands, Wesleyan and Primitive, were not in conflict but came from different starting points and laid emphasis on different things. Robert Tombs in his book 'The English and their History' expresses the difference in a way that matches the two sides of our family, so I quote:

> 'The Primitive methodists (the 'Prims') who doubled their members during the conflictual 1830s [the time of the Reform Bill] remained a sect of the poor, preaching a lively message of 'the three rs' – ruin, repentance and redemption, and their preachers provided a constant stream of trade union leaders. Mainstream [Wesleyan] methodism attracted the hard-working, respectable and newly prosperous businessmen, who now [as a result of the Reform Bill] had the vote, and became the most dynamic force in English politics.'

Mother's parents came from the 'three r's' tradition; folk memories of households ruined by gin were not far away. Grandpa used to sing loudly while he was shaving, songs from the music halls of the 1890s. Grandma would tut-tut and feel ashamed that these merry songs were ringing out in her house in front of a small child. Grandpa was also rumoured to have played billiards in his youth – very risqué. On my father's side they were in business, doing modestly well from it, and they got on with it.

We were definitely nonconformists. We felt ourselves quite markedly different from Church of England people. It is quite hard for today's children really to appreciate what a strong hold christianity of one variety and another had on us in the 1950s. Very few people openly proclaimed then that they did not believe in what the churches preached and saw no need for it. Most people if pressed would say that they were 'Church of England' and all the schools that we went to assumed that 'Church of England' was the default position, and wove Anglican routines and practices into the school day.

We, however, were methodists and went to churches that did things differently: next to no dressing up for the clergy, no hierarchy of bishops and archbishops demanding respect, no repetitive prayers and ritualistic intoning of psalms; instead hymns, sung with energy, written by people who had inspired our distinctive form of christianity in an attempt to shake the Anglican church of the eighteenth century out of its lethargy and neglect of the poor. We had families who kept to strict rules of behaviour: no alcohol being the rule that impinged most clearly on adolescents mixing with contemporaries to whom no such prohibition applied. I was conscious from my early days at school of being from this different tradition. It became a habit to maintain the distinct pattern of behaviour and to find positive satisfaction in being that bit different.

Mrs Thatcher came from a methodist household. She defined what it had taught her as self-reliance and working for your own well-being and that of your family, not relying on society to carry you: conservatism, Thatcher-style. That does not at all fit the methodism that I grew up with. The Primitive Methodists had sprung from the harsh conditions of factory workers in the industrial towns and the total neglect of them by the established church. Methodism offered a collective security to its congregations along with a form of teaching that they could understand, shorn of the ritual and rigmarole and class-bound clergy common at the time. The Wesleyan tradition, rather less radical, traced back to John and Charles Wesley, the originators, who had not intended to found a separate church (that came about only after they died) but to shake up the Anglicans. From the Wesleys came a vigorous style of preaching direct to a congregation, without costumes or rituals, direct messages of salvation backed by vigorous singing of hymns, written, many of them, by the Wesleys themselves. To their methodist followers these were *their* hymns, and the methodist hymn book was a much-loved part of our homes. My mother and her sister enjoyed playing the hymn tunes on the family pianos. The Church of England, let it be recorded, had no hymn book before the Wesleys came along.

All through the nineteenth century and well into the twentieth the methodist church was strongly linked to the Labour movement. They sprang from the same section of society. Many prominent Labour politicians up to and including Harold Wilson and Roy Hattersley in the 1960s and 1970s were devout methodists – as was Arthur Scargill of miners' strike fame (a Prim).

My father's mother and sisters professed to be Labour supporters. The family members who were engaged in business, my grandfather on that side and father himself, were clear that conservative economic policies served their business interests better, but would never have accepted that they were 'Tories'. As for my mother's parents, they were quieter about politics as about other things, but grandfather on that side was a Liberal with Labour leanings, one of his heroes being George Lansbury, the pre-WWII radical pacifist Labour leader. None of our family were actually pacifists but those who stood up for pacifism were ipso facto admired. One of the family's heroes was an uncle who had been arrested and put in prison for preaching pacifism in Aylesbury marketplace in the first world war. There was certainly no link between methodism and conservatism in those households. The long-running and clearly-documented links between methodism and the Labour movement make Mrs Thatcher's definition look quite eccentric.

I still in retrospect find the plainness and directness of the methodist approach has much that is appealing. Their energetic singing of hymns is still capable of bringing a church alive, in contrast with the muted, limp mouthing of hymns that is as much as many Anglican congregations can manage. To this day when I feel like humming or whistling a tune, it is not pop songs or opera that come into my head but the tunes from the methodist hymn book. The methodists gave birth to the Salvation Army which is still going strong, and providing a safety net for those who fall by the wayside. That is in the best tradition of methodism: by their fruits shall ye know them. There was very little by way of theology in methodist services. The sermon was the major part; sermons typically expressed in plain terms with some practical message about doing good in the world. Methodist ministers, and lay preachers, tended to have something worthwhile to say for themselves. They had after all gone into the methodist church for that reason. It was not a calling to take up for the sake of a comfortable vicarage and a certain social status and prospects of promotion to a post as prince of the church, presiding in some fine historic building. The most eminent methodist that I can remember was Donald (Lord) Soper, whose reputation rested largely on his preaching from a soap box at Speakers Corner in Hyde Park.

This was the positive side of methodism that came through to us: energetic social conscience, no respecter of class, status or authority. From that point of view it was inclusive. As against that, there was an exclusiveness, a narrowness, about the rigour with which the key codes of behaviour were applied. My mother was among the strict interpreters, drawing black and white distinctions between good and bad, permissible and impermissible. Almost her only remark when I told her I was joining the civil service was: 'so you have decided to join the Establishment?' – with a note of disapproval in her voice.

Going to church on Sunday morning and going to a bible study group on Sunday afternoon were routine for all the time that I lived at home. The methodist family tradition had a firm hold on me in those Northwood years, and probably left its mark on me for ever after.

Moving on to lighter matters, our summer holidays were not what people expect now. When we first had summer holidays, we went by car to Broadstairs in Kent. Going by car to Kent sounds simple, but in those days there were no motorways, roads were all much narrower and the main roads could be quite congested. The car in which we travelled was a little Austin 7, unbelievably small compared with today's smallest family saloons. In this capsule our two parents rode in the front, and on the back seat sat I and Heather, our suitcases jammed in between us and Jess the golden retriever perched on top of those. The journey from outer north-west London involved struggling right across the centre of London to the diametrically opposite corner. When we finally limped up the hill from Greenwich to Blackheath (all cars were underpowered in those days, and struggled on hills if they were fully loaded), we felt that the worst of the journey was over. But a couple of hours or more of slightly faster progress to the far corner of Kent lay ahead. Once we were on the open road, there would be a constant hiss of cars passing us in the opposite direction. We always made this journey in the middle of August, which was hop-picking season, and hops at that time were still picked by gangs, family groups, bussed out from the east end of London. We used to see them at work in the hopyards of the Weald.

Once arrived in Broadstairs we and our cousins (the two families always travelled together) were shoe-horned into the cramped rooms of a boarding house some way back from the sea front. The holiday then consisted of walking up and down between the boarding house and the beach twice a day, sitting on the beach, making sand castles, and trying to enjoy swimming in the cold and unpleasantly salty sea. It was a struggle to find entertainment in the evenings. This was our summer holiday for four years: 1949-53. After that, the parental decision was to make a break, and we headed west, to Somerset for a year or so, and then later North Devon, in caravans at first and then (luxury, we were becoming better off) in small private hotels. Other families by the mid-1950s were beginning to venture abroad, mainly on to the continent. Poppy's family did. At no point was there ever any question, so far as I can remember, of our travelling outside England; England, not Britain. I think probably the dogs were the determining factor. The retrievers were my father's pride and joy. Mother loved them too. They wanted the dogs with them when they were on holiday, and taking the dogs on the continent would have been a flat impossibility in those days. I make it sound as though our summer holidays were dismally limited. We did not feel like that, not at all. We all enjoyed exploring the hills and coast of first Somerset and then Devon. The dogs saw to it that we had many energetic walks in fine scenery. Quite often it rained, but we took that in our stride. Only when I was nearing the end of my schooldays and then starting university did we venture further afield on holidays, to Wales and then (feeling very adventurous) to Ireland.

In the summer of 1953 our parents went away for a month or more on business to the West Indies, and I was sent to board with Heather at her nursery school, Miss Maycock's. The two Misses Maycock very bravely took a group of their older pupils, and me, to London on the day of the Queen's Coronation, 2 June. I have memories, with snaps from my Kodak camera as evidence, of our walking through St James's Park in the afternoon among soldiers from Commonwealth countries relaxing under the trees after the morning's ceremonial parade, and of our being in the crowd at the Victoria Memorial in front of Buckingham Palace when the Queen and Prince Philip made an appearance on the balcony.

Times were very different for children in other ways too. Sweets were rationed, meaning effectively not available, until 1953 (home production of sugar was smaller in those days than it is now, any extra had to be imported from the West Indies, but Britain needed every last bit of foreign currency for more essential things than sugar). So I grew up with no sweets until the age of ten, and we had our first television not long before that. Good for health, and not bad for the mind. Books had a correspondingly more important place. There was a public library in Northwood – it was run by Boots the chemists, in a side room off their chemists shop. Why Boots had diversified into operating a library service, and whether they did the same in other parts of the country, I have no idea. It seems a very curious arrangement, looking back. But Boots *was* our library, and I used it and appreciated it in those early years.

Travels on the continent for me began with two trips organized from school. I first saw continental Europe with a group from Merchant Taylors', at Easter 1957. A busload of schoolboys travelled with Beano-level prejudices. We stayed at Valkenburgh near Maastricht in the toe of the Netherlands and radiated out from there into the near parts of Germany and Belgium, and up to Rotterdam. These areas still looked rather knocked about by war.

I did not go abroad again until August 1961 when I travelled with three other sixth-form classicists by train across France, through Switzerland and down the length of Italy (on their August holiday, Ferragosto, not a comfortable day for travel) to Brindisi. From there to Piraeus by boat (deck passengers) and then we spent three weeks touring the main classical sites on the mainland and Crete, hitch-hiking, sleeping in the open, often on the archaeological sites themselves. This was just before the upsurge of mass tourism. Sites were open and unprotected. Bird life was also a good deal richer than now, vultures and eagles a common sight. We touched base with our classics master at the British School at Athens, for a rather welcome health check.

This was very definitely an upbringing in the suburbs. People deride suburban life for being... monotonous, too quiet, lacking in excitement and adventure? Certainly most of the fathers of families caught their commuter trains in the morning and disappeared into London to do whatever they did. Northwood was a 'dormitory town'. The people who lived here were not a rich social mix, they were mostly middle-class, and in that sense our upbringing was more sheltered than if we had lived in inner London or some other large town. The roads around where we lived were pretty quiet and night-life (if we had been looking for it) was pretty non-existent. Against that, we had easy travel to school and got on with our schooling. We had fresh air in our gardens and a variety of countryside in easy reach, whether for walking the dogs from the front gate, or cycling, or being taken out and about by car. Most of all, the fathers who commuted into London had a bright lot of children and our schools were competitive places. Stimulus at home and a tougher form of stimulus at school came with the territory. The suburb of Northwood, what it lacked in Grade I architectural interest it made up for in providing an excellent growth medium for young people making their way up the educational ladder. The critics of suburbs make some strong points, but there are plus points that need to be weighed on the other side of the scales.

4

UNIVERSITY - OXFORD

1962-70

St John's College, Oxford

To

Mr. President,

the

Fellowes, and Schollers

of

St John's College in Oxon.

Mr President, with the Fellowes and Schollers,

I have mee recommended unto you even from the bottome of my hearte, desyringe
the holy Ghoste may bee amonge you until the ende of the Worlde, and desyringe
Almightie God that everye one of you maye love one another as brethren; and I shall
desyre you all to applye your learninge, and soe doing God shall give you his blessinge
both in this Worlde and in the Worlde to come. And furthermore if any variaunce
or strife doe arise amonge you, I shall desyre you for Gods love to pacifye it as much
as you maye; and that doinge I put no doubt but God shall blesse everye one of you.
And this shall be the last letter that ever I shall sende unto you, and therefore I shall
desyre everye one of you to take a copy of it for my sake. Noe more to you at this time,
but the Lorde have you in his keeping until theende of the Worlde. Written the 27. of
Januarye, 1566. I desyre you all to praye to God for mee that I maye ende my life with
patience, and that he may take mee to his mercye.

By mee, Sir Thomas White, Knighte,
Alderman of London, and
Founder of St John's Colledge in
Oxforde

[Obiit Anno Salutis, 1566, Regni Elizabethe, 8vo
et die undecimo Februarii.]

Those of us coming from Merchant Taylors' already knew of Sir Thomas White as one of the founding fathers of our school. But for all who arrived at St John's as scholars the relationship with this man from the past became quite personal. We were each solemnly given a copy of the above letter which he had written to the scholars ('schollers' - spelling was not subject to strict rules in his day) just before he died. His message was passed on to us as if it applied equally to us, four hundred years down the line. My copy of the letter is hanging on the wall beside me as I type this.

In this and other ways we were made aware all the time that the institution we were joining had a very long history. Our college dated back to 1555; quite a few other colleges were several hundred years older. The buildings in which we now lived and worked reflected it. That is, most of them did. By 1960, some colleges were beginning tentatively to insert ultra-modern buildings in with the old. St John's was the very first to do that. Their 'Beehive' building had only been open for two years when we arrived. So-called because it consisted of sets of hexagonal rooms, like the cells of a beehive: three sets of rooms arranged around three staircases, about three floors high, ten rooms to each staircase. The three staircases were linked on each floor via the bathrooms, so that it constituted in all a cluster of about thirty rooms, for undergraduates mainly, though a couple of rooms on the ground floor which looked out on the President's garden were reserved for tutors.

On arrival at the college we were given a choice of rooms, a choice of where we wanted to be housed, and I opted for a room in the Beehive. Most of my contemporaries went for older-style rooms, of which there was a wide variety ranging from those in the very oldest parts of the college to some from the Victorian period or the 1930s. Many of these 'rooms' consisted of a sitting room and a separate bedroom, some even came with the strong outer door or 'oak' which you traditionally closed ('sported') only when you really did not want to be disturbed. In the Beehive by contrast you got just the one hexagonal room, a bed-sitting room with wash-basin, some shiny new 1960s panelling and a wide picture window.

I don't know whether those of us who had made the bold choice to go into this revolutionary modern building had any streak of modernity in common, or of contrariness. The building itself won prizes from architectural experts but was regarded as shockingly out of place by the public at large. We made up, at any rate, a lively little sub-community in our non-traditional habitat.

Tradition weighed even more heavily in 1962 than it does now. Oxford then still had many features which have since been overthrown. All colleges were single-sex and the large majority were for men only. Gates were locked at 11pm and the high walls around each college were topped either with sharp metal spikes which revolved, or with broken bottle glass set in cement – most commonly the latter. This was a highly effective form of defence which very few people succeeded in getting over. I don't remember any serious campaigning to change that system of apartheid, back in the early 1960s. It was how it had always been. Yet within ten years it had all changed; one college after another began to admit women or, in the case of the ladies' colleges, men. Like the Soviet Union, the old system collapsed fast once a touch of perestroika was let in.

I had a girl friend when I went up to Oxford but she lived in London, and my occasional absences from college on a Saturday night seemed to go unnoticed. She was from Trinidad and went back to Trinidad during my first year, so the spikes and broken glass never came between us.

St John's had a slight feel of being on the edge of things geographically. That may seem an odd thing to say because it actually sits very close to the centre of the city. But it is on the edge of the main concentration of colleges. The cluster from Balliol to New College, Corpus Christi and Christ Church had a more central feel. Their undergraduates seemed to be in and out of each other's colleges more. We at St John's seemed to be largely self-sufficient in our own company. I at least never made friends from any of the other colleges, whereas lasting friendships were made at St John's. That was our focus.

St John's is today recognised to be the richest of the rich Oxford colleges (valued at £442 million in 2015), and must also be one of the largest. It seems to have built a large new quad every ten or fifteen years since my time. It has expanded exponentially. In 1962 it was not nearly so large, and not quite so high in the league table of wealth as it is now, but it was recognisably rich. We were conscious that our college owned a vast tract of housing, all the way from the college walls to the northern by-pass. It had profited immensely out of the expanding need for family houses during the Victorian period, when it became allowable for Fellows to get married and live outside their colleges.

The land which St John's conveniently already owned then became covered in large suburban houses (a housing stock which puzzlingly has no equivalent in Cambridge) and profits came tumbling into St John's coffers. For us as undergraduates this had advantages: when we reached our third or fourth years and needed to find lodgings outside college, there was never any difficulty. We had a plentiful choice of houses owned in one way or another by the college, or houses owned by college staff. Several of our college scouts or servants had scratched together enough to buy houses which they then let out to undergraduates. Was this a recent social step up for them in the 1960s?

So we were well aware that St John's was a rich institution. It owned not only the large spread of built-up North Oxford but also large expanses of farmland in Oxfordshire and beyond. Some of our tutors lived in college villages. We made excursions to village pubs owned by the college. Most memorable of those was the Lamb and Flag (Lamb and Flag – the ecclesiastical emblem of St John) at Kingston Bagpuize where Dudley the landlord, a large man, kept order in the bar which was crammed to overflowing at weekends, and served all manner of dubious rustic food including sometimes rook pie. This was a favourite haunt.

Once a year the Fellows of the college held a tenants' dinner. All the college's tenants from town and country properties came and were given dinner in Hall. We undergraduates never got to take part in that event, but it symbolised for us that the college was in the league of wealthy landowners, with a spread of town and country income. There was – and presumably still is – an Estates Bursar and a Domestic Bursar. The latter looked after the fabric of the college, while the Estates Bursar looked after the portfolio of property beyond the walls. I sat with him at dinner at a college feast in 1963; Arthur Garrod, a country gentleman of the land agent subspecies, who reminded me a little of the agent I had known on Lundy (Arthur Gade). Arthur Garrod, who was approaching 60 years old in 1963, therefore not quite an Edwardian himself, spoke to me about his father who most certainly will have been; of how his father had been a shooting man, and how his favourite breakfast (no doubt after an hour or two in the field) had been half a cold grouse and a pint of moselle. A pint! I have always aspired to that breakfast. The college feasts to which we *were* occasionally admitted – in my case to give a Latin address – seemed lavish at the time. They were indeed lavish for their time. But through skilful management of its property and some judicious movement in and out of agricultural land St John's has grown immeasurably richer over the past 50 years. This is reflected in the even higher quality of feasts and garden parties today.

St John's in 1962 was not as intellectually strong as it became 40-50 years later. That rise up the league tables seemed to come gradually. Indeed, one of my first surprises on arriving in the autumn of 1962 was that it was not more of an intellectual power-house than it was. Our intake of undergraduates was very mixed in talent – and in social background. There were some colleges which had the aura of being much more exclusive; Christ Church in particular. St John's was not the first choice for those from the ancient public schools or old landed families. Its mixed quality of talent and of social background was its characteristic. Neither top flight nor top drawer, it felt like a comfortably open society.

Turning now from the general to the personal, from the college to the people I knew. Because of the historic link between Merchant Taylors' and St John's several of us moved on from school to this college at the same time, and we had friends who had gone there a year or two earlier. That helped us. We found our feet more easily than those who had come up alone from their schools and were pitched into a large community of strangers. The little band of brothers in the Beehive building turned out, as I have said, to be lively, and the fact that most people inside and outside the college tended to regard our building as outré and our choice to live there similarly tended to bond us more strongly. There was one among us in this Beehive community who stood out for force of character, and who did much to bind us together: Lawrence. I quickly got to know him. He was not one to be ignored. I had not met anyone like him before. He was outgoing and exuberant but he was not trying to impose his own personality. His manner was to fire up everyone around him until they matched his level of exuberance, and to attentively draw out the different characters of a group to express themselves and contribute to the atmosphere each in their own way. There was thoughtfulness and consideration for others not far below the surface of wild animation. There would often be a quite disparate group of us from the surrounding cells of the Beehive who would find ourselves in his room in the evening. He made the mood, and made it hard for others not to join in. This was one facet of a complex character. He had quieter more reflective moods, a deep sensibility to painting and music (his father was an artist and collector of art) and literature. His use of words was a stock-in-trade. It could be like a firework display. It was the instrument with which he made the mood of the gathering, quick-fire scatter of comment, amusement, mockery – always friendly and constructive mockery, designed to draw the victim in, not to put down. His ability with words became his lifelong career. In tandem with teaching he has made his way as a poet. Lawrence, then, of all the people I lived alongside in college over those first two years had the most positive impact on me.

He struck up a close friendship with the scout, George, who looked after us on Lawrence's staircase in the Beehive and mine. Friendship based to start with on a shared love of mockery, teasing and practical jokes. George was the master at this, Lawrence had only to encourage him, and learn from him. George and he were well-matched. I don't think George could have had such fun with any of his undergraduates before then, or after. The two of them became firm family friends. George was in a small way quite an entrepreneur. He lived in a college house where he rented out a couple of rooms; and in addition he had saved and bought a house (later two) which he rented out to half-a-dozen students or more; he had a productive allotment; and he had bought a car. (People on low incomes were only just beginning to find cars affordable in the 1960s.) He drove his car at terrifying speed. We would often go out with him on trips into the Oxfordshire countryside, and after some eating and drinking he would tear back to Oxford taking delight in pushing to the limit his ability to control the vehicle. Lawrence and he remained firm friends to his dying day. Lawrence captured the spirit of George to perfection in this poem.

Not Admitting It

> Your world worked almost perfectly: in your cellar
> the beer ticked and fizzed. On your allotment,
> year after year the scarlet beans raced up
> the crossed poles, onions swelled their copper domes,
> raspberries delivered their soft drupels by the score.

You had the world's number, knew to avoid
redcaps, rozzers, all agents of the state.
During the war, you heated your steak and kidney
on a tank's engine cover. In peacetime, drove too fast
(your wife knitting like fury) but spotted all speed traps.

Perfectly at ease, you went about trailing
a tea-cloth and duster, one from each trouser pocket.
Your moustache came and went – the pipe as well,
which took its turn with hand-rolled Rizlas so thin
they almost went up in the lighter's flame completely.

Confident, too – God knows what you smuggled out,
wrapped in brown paper, from the college buttery, certain
that somebody's blind eye was turned. And proud of your fitness,
bracing your stomach muscles, then inviting
a punch: *Go on, have another go! Harder!*

Your stories, like your laughter, described a place
in which, if you kept your wits, and one step ahead,
anything was possible. Scouting the world as it was,
you tutored us to share your love of jokes,
to see that defeat was the biggest joke of all.

[...]

From: *Waking Dreams, New and Selected Poems,* by Lawrence Sail. Bloodaxe
Books, 2010.

There were other friends; friendships grew fast, and some blew over; but Lawrence's was more uplifting than any. I have known only one or two people who could 'make the weather' in a group of friends as he could.

We in the Beehives were disruptive in our way. I think the Fellows must have found the behaviour of undergraduates in the early 1960s unsettling on a

broader front. We were all pretty immature. National service had only just ended (I escaped by three years). Hence our predecessors until recently had done
two years' military service and arrived at university a couple of years older and
matured by their experiences in the forces. We came straight from school. We
could make a deafening noise, because the general rise in prosperity coupled
with new technology meant that many of us owned individual means of playing loud music: record players (individual TVs came later). On a Friday and
Saturday night rooms rang out with loud music from parties large and small.
Noisy parties were nothing new to Oxford colleges but I think the technology
at our disposal in the early 1960s brought a step-change in ability to blanket
the quads with noise. Tutors in residence must have found that a rude shock.

We had a sprinkling of hooray henries in St John's but they were not a major
source of disturbance. St John's had its home-grown version of the Bullingdon
Club, called the King Charles Club. This harked back to the early history of the
college. Sir Thomas White, always more a supporter of catholic Mary Tudor
than of protestant Elizabeth, had founded his college to be a training ground
for good catholic clergy. St John's had widened its sights by Jacobean times, but
not very much. When the civil war broke out, St John's – along with most other
Oxford colleges – was in no doubt which side it was on: the King's. St John's
gave all that it had to help finance the King's war effort, and found itself on the
losing side. The King Charles Club, remote as it was from those events of the
1640s, reflected the royalist allegiance. The Club held a dinner once a term to
which famous outsiders could be invited. Prince Friedrich von Preussen dined
with us on one occasion – not long before he drowned himself in the Rhine.
The Club's main event of the year was commemoration of the execution of
King Charles I – Charles the Martyr – on 30 January. After a good dinner the
members of the Club would process around the college carrying candles and
torches, wailing and moaning in maudlin fashion. Some glasses got broken,
maybe the occasional window. But all in all this was but a pale shadow of the
Mallard Dinner which takes place at All Souls once every ten years, vividly
documented in one of the obituaries of Martin West.

Very few of my contemporaries went on to achieve national fame. I can
think only of Simon Jenkins, journalist, for some years editor of the London
Evening Standard and then *The Times*, and author of numerous books about

buildings and architecture. One of his early books, on *Outer London*, has guided us to places around London that we would not otherwise have found. There is a hard-working and productive man.

'Greats' ... ?

The course which I chose would have been Classics at any other university: classical Greek and Latin. That was the field of study I wanted, but at Oxford that was not a straight option. The course we took was called 'Greats', sometimes referred to as Mods and Greats, because the exam we sat in our second year was called Honour Moderations. In the university's formal terminology the course was called Literae Humaniores, abbreviated to Lit. Hum. – *the* humanities.[1]

Our course consisted of five terms focussed on study of Greek and Latin texts and the languages, leading up to the 'Mods' exam. After that the course changed gear and over the next seven terms, leading up to finals, we had to study a chosen period of ancient history, plus a course of philosophy which started with the ancient Greek thinkers Plato and Aristotle and their predecessors, and then jumped to Western Europe of the 17th and 18th centuries. We read Descartes, the 'English' rationalists Locke [English], Berkeley [Irish] and Hume [Scots]; Kant, Bertrand Russell, G E Moore, Wittgenstein; the logical positivists of the Vienna School – of whom Oxford's own A. J. Ayer was counted a fully-fledged member; and this being the early '60s we came to rest with a clutch of philosophers with a strong local Oxford flavour, whose special contribution appeared to be to split hairs. These were the people whom Dr Costin at my interview in the Merchant Taylors' Hall had squeakily teased me to look forward to. We could pick up other philosophical writers on the way, but these were the majors.

All told, the course took four years, as did chemistry, whereas most other Oxford degrees took three.

---

[1] This label has had a long history. It goes back to the middle ages, when there were just two strands of studies at Oxford: divinity, or res divinae, and literae humaniores, the studies more related to man: classical Latin and (after the renaissance) Greek, including philosophy, and such science as there then was.

So this was a sort of classics-plus; classical studies with modern western European philosophy added on. It was peculiar to Oxford. It dated back at least a hundred years and had been refined over that period. It had acquired considerable prestige, in part because it was the course which a large number of British Empire administrators and a succession of top British politicians and civil servants had taken; in part because it was claimed (by those who taught and those who took the course) to be exceptionally exacting – a unique test of intellectual power. Those who had achieved double firsts in Mods and Greats were regarded as very high-powered. They had succeeded in a sort of intellectual triathlon: in difficult languages, in the study of history, and in philosophy – philosophy with politics.

The hundred years' run of high prestige which Greats had enjoyed was coming to an end by the 1960s. Change came from two directions. Many people with an interest in politics and an eye to a career in the modern world wanted to study the philosophy element of Greats without the heavy overlay of ancient Greek and Latin, and wanted to study politics in modern societies, not the societies of ancient Greece and Rome. To meet this demand a new course had been shaped: PPE – politics, philosophy and economics. This was, in its early days, sometimes called 'modern Greats', though I think that label was already dying out in our time. Pressure came from another direction for change of a different kind; from those whose main interest was in the classics, and the civilisations of Greece and Rome, who wanted to be allowed to pursue that interest through to finals and to dispense with the modern philosophy. In response to this different demand the Greats course has since 1972-73 been made more flexible. It is still possible to pursue the original triathlon, but alternatively you can opt now to take additional papers on aspects of ancient Greek or Roman civilisations. In that newer form, the Greats course of today comes closer to the Cambridge tripos or to classics at any other university. I have no doubt that if those options had existed in my day, I would have preferred them.

Was the prestige of Greats in its original form ever justified? How do the newer alternatives match up to the tests that Greats imposed?

PPE has three strands, designed to match the second part of Greats based on more modern material. The study of Latin and Greek language and literature is missing, most obviously, and with that the study of highly developed societies radically different from ours. Does that matter? Leaving aside the language learning, in-depth study of the societies of ancient Greece and Rome (their outlook on life and their values as well as their politics and systems of government) imprinted the Greats students with an objectivity and perspective about the state of things now, and a sense that (in the terms of the French altermondialistes) 'another world is possible'. This objectivity sometimes deteriorated into a detachment and indifference, but an ability to stand back and view contemporary problems from the outside is a quality to be desired in politicians and government administrators. As for economics, I am unsure whether it should be ranked alongside politics and history. Economic theories seem to come and go. It is a discipline built on shifting sands. One other thing definitely missing from the PPE mix is the study of history. Claims are made for history as the very best preparation for running the country. We certainly have some examples among present and recent political leaders of Britain who have been sadly if not damagingly lacking in knowledge of history. Greats, for all that its focus was on the ancient world, included a good element of the historian's discipline. We were expressly taught how to weigh and evaluate the available evidence; to make allowance for evidence missing; to think hard about the point of view from which the historian was writing, and what his (all ancient writers of history were male) economic or personal interests were and what slanted image he might have wished to project. We learned to apply logic, judgment and perspective to the evidence put in front of us. Does PPE do all that? A trendy criticism of PPE is that it offers breadth over depth, and a platform for the quick-witted to put together opinions on the basis of very little knowledge. This is all good fun as banter but can't be sustained as a serious critique. PPE contains serious intellectual stretch, though put side by side with Greats it falls short in two identifiable elements: hard languages, and history. Less definitely, but in my opinion, what it gains in modernity of subject matter it loses in the detachment and objectivity towards our own politics which can come from studying the politics of times when the world was very different.

The modern philosophy which is a common element in PPE and Greats (or Greats as it was) always included political and moral philosophy as well as logic and the more abstract philosophy of knowledge. This is not only a stretching intellectual training; it also gives a basis for thinking about the problems of society and the individual and the interaction between them that is clearly relevant for anyone aiming at a career in politics, public service, or political journalism or broadcasting; and to a range of other occupations too. Those who take the newer options now available in Greats in its modified 21st century form, classics and only classics, miss out on that.

Study of the languages, Greek and Latin, was quite definitely part of the fascination for me, a key reason why I pursued that path of study. It has often been argued that training in Greek and Latin, although they are dead, is an excellent basis for learning modern, spoken languages. The obvious riposte to this is that the even better preparation for modern languages ought to be to learn modern languages from the outset. But we are testing the claims of a training in the classics, through Greats specifically, to be superior to other courses in the humanities. The teaching of classical Latin and Greek was generally more rigorous than the teaching of French, Spanish or German. We were made to think precisely about the meaning of texts word by word, sentence by sentence. To make this harder, ancient Greek and Latin, in the surviving works of their literature (the same may well not have been true of everyday conversational language but we have very little of that to go on) used forms of expression that are more distant from English than are modern French or German; and, some writers more than others, used highly condensed styles where every word, and its place in the sentence, carried significance. Think of Thucydides, Tacitus, Martial or Juvenal. Faced with the demand to translate those writers into English, drawing out the full meaning, we had to think hard, unpack the sense, and then find English words to express that.

Achieving accuracy of translation, against these challenges, was one of the most highly prized skills. Just writing about that approach now sounds old-fashioned. Our contemporaries studying French and German thought it was antiquated then. Today's students of Latin and Greek are, I think, let off more lightly than we were. Certainly the strenuous effort of translation that I am describing has taken its place alongside reading of text for appreciation of the works of literature that they are (if we achieved that in our day it was an incidental pleasure but not something that we were examined on), and alongside 'reception studies' – the study of how works of literature have been understood and appreciated differently at different times and in different countries.

Hardly anything had been written about 'reception' in this sense sixty years ago. It is a major strand of classical studies now.

To resume my line of argument, our learning of Latin and Greek *as then taught* did set us up rather well for learning other languages; learning to be alert to ways in which forms of expression and the ideas behind words can differ; to be on our guard against faux amis. But it was a very time-consuming and roundabout route to have taken if the objective was to make us good linguists. From my observation and experience, learning any one or two foreign languages is good preparation for learning others. Additional languages come more easily after the first one or two.

Modern languages are simply not well enough taught in English schools – so far as they are any longer taught at all. I would happily have taken a degree in modern languages, and I would have found it very valuable for the career which I eventually followed. But I am in no doubt that I would have missed out on the more satisfying exercise of unravelling Greek and Latin and on the wider range of material that we read. The degrees in modern languages at Oxford in the 1960s (has this changed?) had a much narrower focus – on poetry, theatre plays, works of imaginative literature in those modern languages, whilst skimming lightly over works of history, politics and philosophy that were mainstream for us classicists.

To conclude this analysis of Greats: in combining the rigour of Latin and Greek languages as taught in the mid-twentieth century with the range of imaginative literature as well as history, political thought and philosophy, the last of these streaming from the fifth century BCE to the mid-twentieth century CE, Greats was a peculiar combination of subjects and disciplines, always unique to Oxford. The pressures to modernise have resulted in changes. The need to modernise was clear. Unclear to me is whether any of the variants match up to the triathlon that Greats once was. I think 'modern Greats' has still to be invented.

Teaching and our teachers

The Oxford tutorial system was flourishing, and was perhaps at a high point in the 1960s. By comparison with Oxford of the 1840s, or even the 1920s, tutors were taking their work seriously. Yet by comparison with now, we had ample time to play. Gone were the days when dons pleased themselves as to whether they paid any attention to their teaching duties. Tutors in the 1960s seemed attentive to their obligations towards their pupils. For our first five terms studying for Mods we had a single college tutor, Donald Russell. He made a lasting impression on all his pupils. He certainly did on me. He was wholly devoted to his classical learning. Then in his forties, he seemed to us to have accumulated a vast amount of knowledge. Now (2018) aged 97, he is still practising his craft although he retired from teaching at the age of 96.

He did not exactly wear his learning lightly. You were well aware of how much there was, but he was mild-mannered, unpretentious, and he did not push his accomplishments at you. You soon enough discovered them by engaging with him. He had a kindly character but you could not relax in conversation with him or treat him lightly. His mind was razor-sharp and any light-hearted remarks or sloppy conversation met with a precise response; not a hostile response but one which left you in no doubt about the inadequacy or inaccuracy of what you had just said. No banter here. (In his late nineties he is still an exacting conversationalist.) Donald had, by the time he took us on, been teaching at St John's for about 15 years. He had taught one of the young men who had taught us for our last year or two at Merchant Taylors'. He seemed to have given most of those early years of his career to attentive and devoted tutoring. Unlike the next generation of scholars he had not pushed himself to do a doctorate (those were still quite a rarity for his generation). He had not been put under pressure to publish any immature work (as I did) nor to churn out endless articles on the minutiae of his field of scholarship, as young academics are now. He produced his first (and maybe best) book only in the 1960s, while we were his pupils.

His chosen area of specialism was prose writing, Latin and Greek, the craft of prose style and rhetoric. This was typical of the man. It was an aspect of writing not particularly in favour with twentieth century readers, but was an aspect of writing which the ancients themselves paid close attention to. Using words in prose writing and speeches to best effect, for maximum impact, artful persuasion and attractive style. This was Donald the scholar and Donald the tutor.

He lived, in those years, in college, in a set of darkly-panelled rooms with an imposing carved fireplace, all very Jacobean, in a corner of the Canterbury Quad which had been built for the college by Archbishop Laud in the 1630s, at the two ends of which were mounted in niches statues of King Charles the First and his Queen Henrietta Maria. This part of the college expressed the college's allegiance to the royalist side in the civil war of the 1640s – allegiance for which it paid heavily, losing most of its worldly wealth to finance the King's army. Donald's rooms overlooked the Canterbury Quad on one side, and the great lawn on another.

Donald then was our main teacher for five terms. He made use of junior research fellows from time to time and thereby exposed us to different styles and personalities, though I think his main motive was probably to give those young men working towards their academic careers a little early practice in teaching, with us as guinea pigs. The two I can remember both went on to make university careers. One was Ewen Bowie, another was Martin West. Martin was the more notable of the two. His performance as teacher left very little mark on us. We found it extremely hard to get anything out of him. He would stare at us as if we were from another world, and there were long silences. We were merely the first to come across those silences. He went on to achieve very great eminence as a classical scholar, and his power and originality were finally recognised by his being awarded the Order of Merit. This is a crowning achievement in any field. There are only 24 members of the Order at any one time, from all fields of endeavour. It may have been the first and only time a classical scholar was given this distinction. Sadly Martin was not able to bask in it for long, He died within two years. But throughout his glittering career his silences were legendary. He was said to have been able to keep silent in seven languages. I believe that 'seven' is an underestimate, but he did indeed speak only when he had something significant – or witty – to say. We in our youth had had our first brush with a top scholar.

This was (was) the strength of the Oxford tutorial system. We at St John's were close to Donald Russell. Our contemporaries at other colleges were being tutored by other and more famous scholars. Of course face-to-face teaching was in itself of high value but the special quality came from confronting and working with someone who was firmly established in his field, with top scholars. In more recent years that has been diluted, as more and more of the tutoring of undergraduates has been turned over to teaching assistants, young scholars and research students who, brilliant or not, do not yet have achievements to their name. There has been some falling off in the tutorial system. Not that it has fed through to less good exam results, but the experience is not the same as it was.

Lecturing, on the other hand, can only have got better. Attending lectures was part of what we were meant to do, in those five terms of Mods and for Greats. The weekly tutorials were more demanding but we were advised to attend some lectures too. We classicists had almost complete freedom to do so or not. The position was very different for those studying science subjects who seemed to have to keep regular hours in their laboratories. We felt our position was greatly superior. We had to produce work for our tutor, and we had a very exacting schedule of reading to keep up with – if you did keep up with it. But as for lectures, they were largely optional and on the whole of very poor quality. Many consisted of the lecturer reading through notes, in a monotone or mumble. I can only think that standards must have been pulled up vigorously by now, as today's undergraduates have become more demanding, pushed by TV and pulled by tuition fees.

Even our star performers would probably be judged sub-standard today. Hugh Lloyd-Jones was one we were told to attend. He had been appointed Regius Professor of Greek a year or two before, and lectured on Aeschylus' *Agamemnon*. He gave his lectures in Christ Church, so they were an opportunity to enjoy the grandeur of that great establishment. But Lloyd-Jones, a fiery and rapid speaker, fired his commentary on the *Agamemnon* at us at unintelligible speed. He was later my supervisor for my D. Phil and my respect for him and his literary knowledge grew. But that first encounter for us undergraduates was breath-taking but not very educational.

There were tutorials and lectures, and then there were seminars. For us classicists in our first five terms there was only one seminar of any kind. It was run by Professor Eduard Fraenkel – a greater expert on Aeschylus' *Agamemnon* even than Hugh Lloyd-Jones. Fraenkel was one of the Jewish academics driven out of Germany by the Nazis, who by the 1960s had risen to dominate British intellectual life in one field after another. There was Ernst Gombrich in art history, Nikolaus Pevsner for architecture, Krebs and Cahn in the sciences,

Claus Moser at the London School of Economics (when he was not at the Royal Opera House). German scholars were highly influential wherever you looked. For classics we had Eduard Fraenkel. He ran seminars, along German lines, on Greek and Latin metre. A large number of people attended – for we were drilled by our tutors to go and sit of the feet of this ambassador for German high scholarship. Unfortunately for us there was no such option as sitting at Fraenkel's feet. He ran his seminars in the style of a master class. Some poor victim would be chosen to stammer through a prepared piece, then to be torn apart by Fraenkel in the strong German accent which he never lost, and in terms as unsparing as they were exacting. No concession was made to youth and inexperience. We were held up and measured against the standards of Wilamowitz and Paul Maas, and we fell lamentably short. Fraenkel's habit was, once he had mauled his victim's poor performance, to turn to one of his two or three favoured pupils and ask them to supply better answers. Michael Reeve was one of these; he went on to become Kennedy Professor of Latin at Cambridge. Colin MacLeod was another; he became a Fellow of Christ Church and produced several highly regarded books but lay down in front of a train at the age of 39. Both had benefited at different stages from the St John's Woodhouse Fund, as later I did; so we were members of the same select club of scholars-in-the-making.

Fraenkel was a formative experience. A few years later I rented a St John's flat in Museum Road which happened to be opposite the house in which Fraenkel and his wife lived. I used to see him returning home for lunch as punctual as clockwork just before one o'clock. I used to see his wife appear at the front window just before the due time, watching for her beloved Eduard to return. This was the domestic side of the emigré professor who could be so ferocious with his pupils. The couple must by then have both been in their eighties. One day Mrs Fraenkel died. Eduard took his own life the same day.

For the second part of our course we were meant to turn our attention from the literature of Greece and Rome to ancient history and philosophy. I did not take to that new agenda with much enthusiasm. Even though we had a tutor for ancient history who was what an Oxford college tutor ought to be – a real expert in his area (Roman citizenship) and a high authority on the whole field of ancient history – able to dissect our youthful views and show us what did and didn't fit the evidence. Forensic training of a high order. And for philosophy, after a term with a young Australian on probation we were taken up by Paul Grice, a deep thinker of an intensely Oxonian sub-species, who would sit for long periods of the hour we were meant to spend with him in utter silence, not asleep but thinking. After his silence, a thought or a question would come out, with intense emphasis. Both Paul Grice and Sherwin-White had Oxonian hobbies to which they gave much time. For Grice it was cricket, and when just after our time as undergraduates he was picked up and poached by Berkeley (Calif.) his price for going was that they make him a cricket pitch on the campus. Sherwin was keen on horse-racing and was, in the college, designated Keeper of the Groves i.e. he was the Fellow who saw to St John's magnificent garden, and being himself an expert on rock plants he made a major contribution to the planting of the extensive rockeries.

I was resistant to the new agenda, Greats part II. My enthusiasm for the language and literature of Greek and Latin, Greek more than Latin, still ran strong. There were university prizes on offer for those who reached a very advanced level, beyond the requirements of the undergraduate syllabus. Many future scholars had notched up one or more of these prizes. I won two: the 'Derby' and the 'Craven'. I don't know that I devoted a major part of my time to these, but it was evident to Sherwin at least that I was not giving my work for him the keenest attention, and he said as much after a term or two. Grice was too abstracted. To him, the thoughts of most of us undergraduates were so very far removed from what was interesting to his mind, working on the further frontiers of thought, that as between my level of attention and the considerably greater devotion shown by two of my peer group, he may simply not have noticed.

It did though impact on my results at the end of the Greats course. As the finals came closer I became aware that I had fallen behind. Rather than putting in redoubled effort to close the gap, I settled for what I had done, and set my sights on more classical scholarship beyond; a doctorate. My Greats results came in, a shade below the first that I would have liked. I took my place in the line of people who had preferred the language/literature line of study: A E Housman, Martin West, Colin MacLeod. These had all become serious classical scholars. My level of fame would never have reached theirs, but my preferences were theirs. At Cambridge in those days, and at Oxford now, I would not have had to make the choice. The options I wanted were always on offer at Cambridge, and were built into the Oxford Greats course soon after my time. My dose of Oxford-style English philosophy was quite enough for me. My love for and intensive training in the languages and literatures of ancient Greece and Rome has served me well, and helped me to travel the long distance I have travelled down the paths of French, Italian, then German, and latterly modern Greek.

A second degree

I went on to a D. Phil with Lloyd-Jones as my supervisor and a year and a half in Berlin helped by finance from the University's Craven Fund and the St John's Woodhouse Fund. The Berlin experience is the subject of the next chapter. The subject for my research was 'The papyrus fragments of Sophocles'. Sophocles was one of the three great writers of tragic plays of classical Athens. He, with Aeschylus and Euripides, wrote hundreds of plays of which only a very few 'survived'. Just a small number continued to be copied and read for many hundreds of years, with the result that copies were preserved in a few libraries in Byzantium and then Italy through to the era when printing was invented and books could be reproduced in quantity. The position was the same for the whole of ancient Greek – and Latin – literature. Portions of the work of the authors who were still being read in late antiquity 'survived'; huge amounts were lost, and were known to have been lost. Up until the nineteenth century it was thought that that was it; we had what we had of the work of the ancient Greek and Roman authors, a finite quantity, and the rest was forever lost.

This picture changed during the nineteenth century, through the finds of papyri in Egypt. What are papyri? Why Egypt? What has that to do with ancient Greek and Latin? Papyrus (from which our word paper comes) is the form of writing material that was most commonly used in the ancient world. Papyrus is firstly the name of a plant, a type of reed which grows in the valley of the Nile. Papyrus the writing material is made from the pith and fibres taken from the hollow stems of the papyrus plant. Strips were laid side by side one way, then covered with strips laid at right angles to them, and the two layers pressed hard together and dried. This made a flexible and very durable form of 'paper'. It was produced only in Egypt, exported to Greece, Italy and elsewhere around the Mediterranean, and used by scribes everywhere for more than a thousand years. Papyrus the writing material decays if it is exposed to damp, and over time the vast amount of written material that must once have existed in Greece and Italy just melted away. Egypt, however, has an extremely dry climate. In the valley of the Nile the river flooded every year – until the Aswan Dam came into operation in the 1950s – and the water table rose across much of the area where people lived. But around the edges of the area that had been inhabited 2000 years ago, on the higher land away from the valley floor, the ground could be almost completely dry, permanently. It almost never rained.

The idea of exploring Egypt and excavating for antiquities was launched by Napoleon. He – showing his wide range of interests – took a group of learned academics ('savants') with him when he invaded Egypt in 1798. Nelson cunningly burned his fleet and Napoleon himself soon fled back to France but the savants stayed longer and published a lavish description of all that they had seen. (A copy of this Description de l'Egypte is one of the treasures of the Travellers Club library.) The idea of exploring Egypt took hold. Gradually through the nineteenth century German and British and Italian archaeologists followed in the footsteps of the French. Not until the 1880s did scholars' interest really shift from stones, tombs and temples to the papyri which they were finding everywhere.

Once attention was focussed on those, it was found that the writings on the papyri were extremely interesting. There were writings of all kinds: lists and bills, letters of an official nature, personal letters between parents and children, and works of literature. Quite a lot of this material was in the local language of Egypt, Coptic, or in medieval Arabic or Byzantine Greek, but a large amount was identified as classical Greek. Why Greek, in Egypt? That was the legacy of Alexander the Great. Alexander conquered Egypt and his successors colonised and ruled Egypt from 323 BCE until the Romans conquered them: Octavian, the future emperor Augustus, beating Cleopatra and Antony in the sea battle of Actium in 31 BCE. First under Alexander's successors and then under the Romans, the country was administered by Greek-speaking civil servants. The Romans seem to have been content to leave these Greek-speaking administrators in place, and there they stayed. For most of a thousand years, until Mohammed's armies swept them away in the 630s CE, there was a comfortable educated middle class in Egypt, speaking, writing and reading Greek.

What they read was a lot of Homer, some of the works by tragedians like Sophocles, and a wide variety of other poetry and prose. When they had no further use for a 'book', they often used the other side of the papyrus for everyday purposes: documents, letters, shopping lists. And when they had finished with that, they threw it away, usually tearing it up first, as we do with our waste paper.

In the 1880s and 1890s European archaeologists swarmed into Egypt, many now in search of papyri. News had reached the major museums and universities that unbelievable treasures were being found: chunks of ancient Greek literature, some of it hitherto unknown. As the papyri-hunters gained in skill they learned to recognise the best places for their hunting: town rubbish dumps on the fringes of the inhabited area, close to the western desert. Huge finds were made; vast quantities of papyrus were carted off – to the despair of the Egyptian Archaeological Service – to the major museums in Paris, Berlin, Vienna, London and Oxford. In the 1920s the Italians and Americans muscled in too. Because there was such hot competition, a single hoard was sometimes split between several of these cities. Even pieces of a single document sometimes finished up in several different places. That explains why my research took me from Oxford to London and Berlin, and even then I needed a helper to look at pieces in the US.

The quantity scooped up from Egypt between the 1890s and 1914 was so vast that even now a hundred years later scholars are still working through some of it for the first time. Much of it was examined and published more quickly, but the process of working out which piece might go with which still continues. This explosion of new material resulted in a large expansion of what we know about ancient Greek literature. The classics, which had seemed for the previous 300-400 years to be a fixed amount that had come down through the monasteries of the middle ages, had suddenly come alive. The limits were having to be discovered all over again.

My research subject, the Papyrus Fragments of Sophocles, was taking me into this new field of study. My task was to examine closely all the pieces that might be by Sophocles, to look at the original papyri – all mine had been previously published and were held in museums – to see whether I agreed with the way they had been deciphered, perhaps in haste, by the first editors; then to draw on my knowledge of the known plays by Sophocles and of Greek literature more widely; to form a judgment on the strength of evidence for this and that piece being by S. and not some other author; and to put together a commentary. The work called for great precision in checking the visible evidence and determination not to rush to conclusions (some similarity here with identifying difficult birds in the field). This sounds and indeed could be pretty tedious. But there was a thrill in handling 'paper' written 1800-2200 years previously, and reading the handwriting of unknown scribes. Also I was getting the opportunity to read around in Greek literature more widely than before.

In the first term or two I had to be tutored in reading the ancient scribes' handwriting. To learn this craft I sat at the feet of Peter Parsons. Peter was at that time a young scholar, not many years older than I was, who had been singled out early to be groomed as a papyrologist. He had spent a research year in Michigan learning from Prof Youtie, a legendary American, world leader in this specialism. Peter had an elegant high-ceilinged room in the elegant Peckwater Quad at Christ Church. It was the inner sanctum of an ivory tower. Peter was a striking figure to look at, tall and well-padded (cookery books were never far from his working area), and had what I would without the least sense of unkindness describe as an egg-head. His head was large, domed, with no very prominent covering of hair. He was immensely kind and gentle in manner, and took great pleasure in passing on to new entrants his already great knowledge of papyri and the problems of deciphering them. These were pleasant sessions, from which I learned adequately fast.

I must soon have made my first trips to the British Museum and started to hold in my hands relevant pieces of papyrus, clamped between plates of glass. Later I was let loose on some raw scraps that had not yet been deciphered by anyone. What I remember more clearly from that first D.Phil year were the sessions with Hugh Lloyd-Jones, my supervisor. Lloyd-Jones was always overpoweringly learned but again patient with a new apprentice, and extremely patient with my first efforts that were untidy and make me ashamed to think back on. His rooms too were in Christ Church but less elegant than Peter's. It took some courage to knock on his door and enter, as I often had to, without any sound of a response, to find Lloyd Jones having his after-lunch sleep – a habit of which I firmly approve. He would spring from his bed and go from 0 to top speed in

60 seconds. A formula one performer.

I remember clearly from this year too the master class which Lloyd-Jones conducted, where six or eight of us assembled to analyse and discuss a piece of literature recovered from a papyrus. Our text was by Callimachus, a scholar-poet who had lived in Alexandria, attached to Ptolemy's famous library. He wrote poetry to dazzle his contemporaries with his great learning, full of riddles and puzzles and glancing allusions to history, myths and legends. Now in the 1960s dazzling a new generation of readers, it was giving the opportunity to the cream of Oxford classicists to out-dazzle one another in their ability to unravel what Callimachus had wrapped up. Lloyd-Jones was far ahead of the rest of us. Peter Parsons kept up, as did one or two other young scholars a year or two ahead of me on the academic ladder. But the members of this group that I remember more clearly are two who did not make Greek literature their career. One was Peter Levi, who had started out as Jesuit priest, and attended these master classes in his dog collar (he resigned from the priesthood later). He was widely read, and a deep lover of Greece ancient and modern, and himself a poet. He brought a fresh non-academic tone to the table. The other was Leonard Ingrams who like me was being groomed for a career in classical scholarship but who went off the next year to become a high-earning international banker, and who will make an appearance again in later chapters of this story.

Those were some high points and the start of a new phase in my study of the classics. All through that first D. Phil year I methodically started each day with an hour or two of learning German – to ready myself for continuing to study at the same high level in Berlin in the year ahead. I would be joining master classes where all the discussion would be in German.

Berlin next, and then a year back in Oxford writing up and doing a little teaching for Donald Russell. By the end of eight years Oxford had given me an excellent education, and a first-class preparation for a career as a classical scholar. But I still had a good deal of growing up to do. I had spent much of my time in libraries and museum reading rooms. The final selection board that decided on my entry into the civil service in 1970 did raise questions as to the relevance of Greats and all that ancient literature to a career in the twentieth century public service, but they chose to let me pass. There was work left for the ministry of hard knocks to do.

5

UNIVERSITY – BERLIN

1967-69

O ne day in early October 1967 I packed my VW Beetle with clothes and
books and set off for Berlin. I had a travelling companion, Jonathan, a
friend from Oxford who remained a good friend to us and to Rosie and William when we lived on the edge of Bedford twenty years later, until he tragically
died young in an epileptic fit.

I was glad to have company on this two-day drive. In those days – people
find it hard to imagine the reality of it now – the Iron Curtain was a physical
fence of steel running unbroken from the Baltic coast through the middle of
Germany, and on round the edge of Austria and Hungary. To get by road from
the western part of Germany (the Federal Republic) to the western part of Berlin you had to go through a crossing point, one of three, and drive something
like 100 miles through East Germany (the German Democratic Republic or
DDR) to another crossing point, in the barricade which had since August 1961
totally encircled West Berlin.

The permits for cars making this transit had a time limit. The purpose was
to put western travellers under pressure to drive straight from one end to the
other and not roam about off their route, poking their noses into life in the
communist east. So you had to hope you did not break down, or you would
face awkward questions before you were let through into West Berlin. It was
a comfort on this outward journey to have Jonathan with me. Subsequently I
made the same journey several times on my own, always feeling rather tense.

On our way through West Germany we made an overnight stop in or near
Hamelin, and gazed at the huge half-timbered houses of the old town, impressed by the size of them. Houses in Germany whether old or modern are
so much bigger than in England. We passed through the Teutoburger Wald,
the forest where German fighters inflicted a major defeat on a Roman army in
9 CE, a rare experience of defeat for the Romans and the first appearance in
history of German effectiveness in battle. Then we made for our crossing point

near Braunschweig – at one time called Brunswick in English but is that name ever used now? Next stop, Berlin.

I knew where I was making for because my Oxford supervisor, Professor Hugh Lloyd-Jones, had recommended to me that I should lodge with a lady called Ursula von Krosigk who kept a bookshop near the Kurfürstendamm, in the centre of the city, and lived near there. His very short note to me about her mentioned that she was the niece of a man who had served as finance minister in Hitler's government and had briefly been chief minister in the 5-day government which bridged between Hitler's suicide and the final surrender of Germany that brought WWII to an end in Europe. I took that information in my stride, glad not to have to search out my own accommodation for the year, and I had made an introductory call on Ursula over the summer.

Her apartment was on the fourth and top floor of a massive block of flats on the corner of a square in which stood a massive red-brick church from Kaiser Wilhelm's period with a bell that tolled mournfully from time to time. These Berlin churches seemed to have no equivalent of the cheerful peals that English churches can put out. My room was long and narrow with a high ceiling and something of a view out at rooftop level. Slightly monastic. This was to be home for the next nine months or more.

Jonathan stayed for a day or two while I settled in here. He stayed long enough to be with me when I drove my VW Beetle into the front of a bus. The layout of the crossing had confused me, the bus driver was unforgiving and took one wing off my car, at little cost to the bus. There was no doubt I was at fault. It didn't happen again. Jonathan delighted for years afterwards in repeating back to me the indignant phrase in broken German with which I had tried to shift the blame on to the bus driver.

After a few days it was time to enrol at the Free University (FU). My supervisor here, Professor Rudolf Kassel, had prudently arranged for one of his postgraduate students, Otto Zwierlein, to come with me and shepherd me through the enrolment procedure. Just as well, because searching questions were asked about my competence in the German language and ability to follow a postgraduate course. I had worked through the school course *Deutsches Leben* and then Linguaphone, I had a lot of German in my head by now, but not much on the tip of my tongue – and absolutely no formal qualification to show. I could have fallen at this first hurdle, if Otto had not brushed the questioning aside and spoken up for me.

The university could not have been more different from Oxford: no colleges, no dreaming spires, no airs and graces or traditions. The Free University was not quite twenty years old. It had come into being in 1948 when a group of students at Berlin's original nineteenth-century Humboldt University, by then in the soviet sector of the city, rebelled against the steadily tightening pressure from the communist government on academic staff and students alike to fall in with communist thinking. To the students who rebelled, this was political pressure of just the same kind as the national socialists, the Nazis, had exerted only very recently. It was the principle of political pressure, not the fact that it was communist politics, that triggered the rebellion. The rebels moved to the western side of the city and petitioned the allied powers to set up a 'free' university. Thus the Free University was born. By the mid-1960s you could be forgiven for thinking it was dominated by communist doctrine, and with pretty strong pressure on students to conform. But more of that later.

So the Free University that I joined in 1967 was still quite new. There was a small campus of central facilities: a library, the 'mensa' (student canteen), one or two scientific and medical buildings, all in modern concrete. For the rest, much of the activity was housed in big nineteenth century villas with which the suburb of Dahlem was well provided; villas on the expansive scale common in many German towns. The classics faculty was housed in a pair of these villas, converted to provide library and seminar rooms. That was where I spent my study time.

I shuttled daily between Ursula's apartment in the Pariserstrasse round the corner from the Kurfürstendamm, and Dahlem in the south-west of the city. It may help to describe a little more of the geography. The Berlin that I knew has changed utterly. The centre was massively rebuilt following the reunification of Germany in 1990. In 1967, the Wall, still only six years old, was a stark reality. The city was firmly, unmistakeably, divided, with the Wall cutting north-south down the middle. West Berlin where I spent most of my time and which I came to know very well indeed, was half a city. Imagine it as half an apple, core at one side. When, for instance, I refer to Ursula's apartment as 'central', it was certainly not in the centre of West Berlin but of Berlin as a whole; it was midway between north and south but firmly to one side, towards the eastern edge, of the West.

Dahlem, the university quarter, was a leafy suburb with villas, open green spaces, and quiet streets. A little west of Dahlem is the Grunewald, extensive woodland where the villas grow even larger, and where the more successful academics had their homes; Professor Kassel among them. To the south of Dahlem was a busier suburb, Zehlendorf, which had a flourishing shopping centre (there were few shops in Dahlem). In between these and the leafy Grunewald was an area of very attractive lakes fringed with pines. Good for walks and quiet contemplation; the nearest equivalent of Oxford or Cambridge college gardens.

This begins to make cold war West Berlin sound rather attractive. It was. Down the western edge ran the Havel, a river that widens out in several places into beautiful calm lakes with wooded banks, real countryside except that, at the southern end where the Havel left West Berlin and flowed on into East Germany the border was defined as running down the centre of the river, and the apparatus of the border, and border guards, became visible on the far bank. There was even some farmland.

In the early weeks of my first term, through October as the leaves slowly changed colour under clear skies with cooler nights but warmth in the afternoon sunshine, I took myself off several times after lunch to explore this Havel countryside, particularly around the Wannsee. Kleist's grave was a favourite place to sit. I did not feel I was doing anything reprehensible in taking an hour or two out, in the delicious autumn weather, for some fresh air and exercise. But I was not allowing for the pressure which Germans exert on each other to conform. One of my fellow classics students – he was perhaps more serious-minded than most – told me, when we had got to know one another a little better, that I was in his eyes a 'chaotischer Typ' – apparently because I did not spend my afternoons uninterruptedly at my desk in the library.

That was just a first brush with what I found to be a very censorious society. There were others. On the streets it became a familiar experience for me to be shouted at, geschimpft, on the streets because, by Berliners' standards, I wore my hair long. That was something we allowed ourselves in the chaotische society of Oxford but here it was taken as a political, and politically dissident, statement. Stepping out of line. I was regularly the subject of fierce catcalls from the older generation, the Rentner, on the pavements of the Kurfürstendamm.

It was quite possible to go for days without coming face-to-face with the Wall, indeed for many people living in West Berlin there was no need ever to do so. Unless, like me, you needed sometimes to visit the national collection of Greek papyri which was held in the Pergamon Museum, on Museum Island, in the East. For most of the time my academic work centred on the two villas in Dahlem: working in the library, attending lectures given by Professor Kassel, participating in his seminars with his little band of graduate students, six or eight of us; and participating also in seminars given by Professor Keydell for an even smaller and more select group. Kassel was then in his forties, at the height of his career as a Greek scholar. He had done war service, had spent a term or two in Oxford in 1962 as a guest lecturer, and his alliance with Lloyd-Jones must have dated from then. He could be severe with his students but valued his link with Oxford to the extent that I was treated with respect (only once that I can remember was I told off a little sharply, for gazing out of the window during one of his lectures). He was an authoritative guide to Greek literature, poetry in particular, and an exacting and stringent if not memorably stimulating superviser. Lloyd-Jones was more exciting. Keydell was from an earlier generation. He had been an undergraduate in Berlin in the early 1900s, studying under the hugely eminent Eduard Norden, his doctorate supervised by Wilamowitz. The latter was a giant of classical scholarship, a famous name to all classical scholars, Ulrich von Wilamowitz-Moellendorf to give the name in full. Here was a living link with that great man! Keydell was around 80 at the time when he taught me, and went on to retire at 85. With him I was drinking at source the very finest of German scholarship.

This was *most* of the time. But I also had to do some personal research on papyri. For that I had to make my way to the Pergamon Museum in East Berlin. I had to go in my car (bus damage now repaired) through the famous Checkpoint Charlie – a checkpoint specifically for non-Germans. The Prussian border police who manned all the checkpoints were not trained in good humour or customer relations. They did not like to be trifled with. My VW Beetle rubbed them up the wrong way. It looked to them at first sight like a vehicle they were familiar with but it was right-hand drive and I sat (naturally) in the driving seat. Time and again the guards would come to the passenger window to look at my papers, only to find me lurking on the other side of the car. So they had to walk round, and they had lost face. This got us off to an unsatisfactory start. There was a sense in the air that I had done something deliberately to confuse. When I then explained that I was going to visit a museum to look at ancient Greek manuscripts, the guards' suspicions deepened. This was clearly some devilishly original new cover for illicit activity. I was never subjected to any active obstruction but crossing through Checkpoint Charlie never felt simply routine.

At the Pergamon Museum the Greek papyri were housed in the most remote and shabby back room. I only ever met two members of the museum staff there: Herr Poethke, a gaunt man of maybe 30-40, and an older assistant whose name I can't remember and who seemed to have no duties. Perhaps he was the Stasi's watcher. Poethke knew some Greek and appeared to enjoy his subject. But he cut a pathetic figure. Studying ancient Greek was for certain low on the scale of priorities in the communist system, and he seemed to work in complete isolation. It created interest that I had come all the way from England to study some pieces of papyri from their collection. Poethke was helpful. I scrutinised two or three fragments of Greek tragedy. I did not really need to go there more than a few times, to make my transcripts. I published a couple of academic articles about this work which were well received by the elite band of scholars working on Greek papyri.

On one occasion I was in East Berlin towards Christmas and I found my way to a Christmas market, where the main customers were young Russian soldiers in uniform, complete with fur hats (winters in Berlin could be seriously cold) with the Red Army insignia on the front. They were taking great interest in buying toys which, since many of these soldiers looked to be only around 15 years old themselves, I reckoned were more likely presents for their younger brothers and sisters back home than for their offspring. It was a strange feeling to move from the Wall, where the guards had their guns trained at all times, and to be wandering on this market rubbing shoulders with the enemy's troops off duty.

Meanwhile Ursula and I were slowly getting to know one another. In the first few weeks I came and went without wanting to bother her. We did not talk much. But she became concerned when she questioned me about what I was doing for an evening meal and discovered that I had been slipping out to Aschinger, a soup kitchen under the Zoo Station, the central station for West Berlin at that time. I had been quite happy with a bowl of Erbsensuppe for my evening meal, as I was getting a proper lunch at the university mensa. But Ursula called a halt to this and began to insist on making a meal for the two of us. That became the normal routine, and an opportunity to talk more.

It would be wrong to describe Ursula as guarded, but she only opened up to strangers with caution. It took me a long time to build up the picture I give here.

She supported herself by running a little bookshop in the Knesebeckstrasse, minutes from the Kurfürstendamm. Hers was one of three bookshops close together here. The greatest of the three was Schoellers. Marga Schoeller was part of the literary scene. Ursula always spoke of her shop with reverence. It was regularly visited by famous authors, and it carried a fantastic range of literature in German, English and other languages. Then there was Camilla Speth. Ursula's little shop was a clear third to those other two, smaller, less inspirational. Ursula struggled to give her shop the same sort of allure as the other two, because she didn't really have their talent. It was hard to see how she kept going. I concluded that she had a loyal following of friends and customers from the past just sufficient to keep the business afloat. Over the next year or so I did my bit for the business too. Her shop was my prime source of books to widen my range of reading in German. With advice and suggestions from Ursula – and a certain number of free books, though I paid for most – my knowledge of German writers expanded steadily.

Ursula had a family history and a personal past. Her family were Prussian aristocrats who had owned land in Mecklenburg, a region north of Berlin towards the Baltic. She was born and brought up in a country house there, with an English governess from whom she had acquired polished English and an upper-crust accent. Ursula Adelheid Anna Hedwig Adolphine von Krosigk, born 1904. Into her old age she had a striking head of Prussian-blonde hair, and features that were unmistakeably from a good stable. Once, but only once, I heard her greeted by a friend at the theatre as 'gnädige Frau' (Your Grace), an honorific form of address pretty much scorned in 1960s Berlin.

74

She had an uncle, Graf (Count) Luft Schwerin von Krosigk who, as Lloyd-Jones had told me when he recommended Ursula to me, served in Hitler's government from beginning to end (1932-45) as finance minister, and then as chief minister to Grand Admiral von Doenitz in the short-lived government that bridged between Hitler's suicide and Germany's final surrender. I did not know until researching just recently (2016) that the said uncle had been put on trial at Nuremberg and condemned for war crimes but reprieved (for what reason?), and that he lived on in West Germany until 1977. So he was alive at the time when I was in Berlin. As far as I know, Ursula was not in contact with him, though she might have been. It was something we never talked about. I was in Germany to experience the present, and I never questioned Ursula about the past, hers or her family's. [2]

Her own past, so far as she gradually told me about it, included a spell working as a secretary at the Lausanne peace conference in the 1930s. During that period she had clearly known a number of fairly prominent English people in Berlin. One was Sefton Delmer, correspondent for the Daily Telegraph. She went to look him up during one of her visits to England in the late 1960s, and came back disappointed, commenting that he drank too heavily. That attempt to reconnect with her past had misfired. She had also known Leonard Ingrams, banker... and spy? I reckon she had been particularly fond of him. Leonard Ingrams was the father of Richard Ingrams, founder of Private Eye, and of Leonard the younger, who by coincidence attended Lloyd-Jones's master classes with me in 1966-67, then went into banking with Barings, and founded the Garsington opera. With Ursula I went to visit Leonard the younger and his wife Rosalind in London one day. With Ursula I went looking for the grave of Leonard the father, in a churchyard on the shores of the Starnberger See south of Munich, at a village called Tutzing. We had to hunt for a very long time but Ursula was clearly intent on finding his grave, and we did. She was lost in contemplation of times past.

---

2 The family is once again prominent in politics. One of Luft Schwerin von Krosigk's grand-daughters, Beatrix von Storch (née Beatrix Amélie Ehrengard Eilika, Duchess of Oldenburg) took up a seat in the Bundestag after the September 2017 election, sitting for the Alternative für Deutschland, the first far right party to obtain any seats in the German Parliament since World War II.

This was just one of many threads that had connected the British and German upper classes in the 1920s and 1930s. The infamous uncle, I find, had spent a year at Oriel as part of his education. He will have been one of the Germans who paid misguided attention to the famous vote on King and Country in the Oxford Union in February 1933. Perhaps, being as close to Hitler as he was, he was a key adviser on the weight to be given to that vote as an indication of British government policy. Ursula's true best friend was Gisela von der Goltz, Freifrau (Baroness) von der Goltz, member of a very ancient Prussian family which had supplied senior officers to the German army and navy in the Franco-Prussian war of 1870 and in First and Second World Wars. When Gisela spoke to me, whether she spoke in German or English, she did so in the manner of a general addressing a junior staff officer who could not be expected to know very much.

By the 1960s Ursula had reinvented herself as a bookseller, but picking up these threads of connexions with England from before the war was significant for her. I was, I think, the first student from Oxford that she took in, but the flow continued for quite a few years after me. She had a particular weakness for lodgers from Oxford. Some of my successors through the 1970s were classics students from the Lloyd-Jones stable, but there was also James Fenton, poet, and Timothy Garton Ash, who made his name as a scholar of international relations by studying at first hand the overthrow of communism in Poland by the Solidarity movement, and wrote a book, both vivid and grim, about his experiences in Berlin with the Stasi, the secret police. In that book, *The File*, he gives a short pen picture of Ursula. He maybe tried a little more than I did to draw her out about the past. In my time living with her she was visited by James Cameron, an English investigative journalist who set up an interview for the BBC in her flat and tried to draw her out about her experiences in wartime Berlin. I remember him saying to me afterwards that it had been hard going. I don't think he got anything interesting out of her, and I don't think the interview was ever used.

Ursula was, and perhaps had always been, fairly bookish. Life revolved around the bookshop, and taking home books from the shop to read in the evenings, with distinct fondness for books in English. Over the years the books she recommended to me included a good many new works in English that she came to know about before we did.

Ursula was a major support to me in finding my feet in Berlin. The year might have gone quite differently without her. We kept in contact for more than twenty years afterwards, until she died in the early 1990s. On one occasion she came to stay with Poppy's parents, Lancastrians both, at their home in Lancashire. As a lover of mountains who spent a week or two every year if she could in the Engadine, she was curious to see the English so-called mountains in the Lake District. On the day we went up there the sun shone strongly from a cloudless sky, so she didn't really see the scene as others see it. The most memorable event of the day was Ursula reciting *Albert and the lion* in the kitchen in Ormskirk from memory in a very credible Stanley Holloway/Blackpool accent.

What about my fellow students? The little group around Professor Kassel specialising in ancient Greek were marginal to the Berlin mainstream. One or two of them were from homes in West Germany and had opted to study in Berlin as a way of escaping military service. Only one that I can remember was a native Berliner. One was exceptionally talented, fiercely critical, fiercely self-critical, and fed her zest for literature into my thesis while doing her own work on Hesiod and Callimachus: Ljuba. Our intense conversations ranged widely. Her partner Roderich and one or two others were there, drawn to a Belgian professor who was building up a centre of expertise in the manuscripts of Aristotle. Why *he* was in Berlin I never made out. And there was Otto Zwierlein, the man who had helped me through the university entry procedures on my first day. He was more of a Latinist, and went on to write about Roman playwrights.

Whether on the instructions of Professor Kassel or not, Otto continued to take me under his wing and when it came to the winter vacation took me travelling with him. We did not have three terms like English universities but two semesters: a winter semester that ran from October to mid-February with a minimal break for Christmas and New Year, and a summer semester that ran from late March to the end of June. In between was a vacation of four or five weeks. Otto suggested that I travel with him (in my car) to Austria for a bit of skiing. This didn't work out terribly well – for him – in that he and his group of friends were adept skiers while I floundered on the nursery slopes, made no progress and soon got fed up. I was contented enough reading Goethe's *Dich-*

tung und Wahrheit at the mountain-top restaurant while the others skied but Otto decided, after a day or two of that, that I must be entertained more, and we set off on a tour of the baroque monasteries that nestle in the foothills of the Bavarian Alps. On these he was an excellently informative guide and I enjoyed being introduced to a landscape and forms of architecture that were wholly new to me. Riemenschneider's woodcarvings and the Wieskirche were highlights. On the way back to Berlin we stopped for a night in Otto's home village of Heustreu ('Hay-Strew') and stayed with Otto's parents. With much unnecessary apology he explained that his parents were simple peasant farmers and that he was the first in his family to go to a university and to aim for a career as an academic. The Zwierlein parents did indeed live simply, in a farmhouse which in the German style was grouped with others in the centre of a village, working land outside the village. There was not much I could do to communicate with them because they spoke only the local dialect. My Hochdeutsch was by now pretty competent but the dialect was beyond me.

Some time in this winter vacation I made a brief return trip to England for an oral interview at an Oxbridge college, either Balliol in Oxford or Christ's in Cambridge (where William worked many years later). I had applied for research fellowships at both, but those applications came to nothing.

Late in the winter semester I had delivered my first paper to one of Kassel's seminar groups, describing one of the pieces of research I had been doing in East Berlin. I have no doubt that my paper was a pretty ragged effort in terms of written German, but it represented for me a rite of passage. I had managed to become a fully-fledged postgraduate student, despite having no formal education in the German language. My fellow students in the seminar group were all very friendly and supportive.

Summer came. Study continued. One of my contemporaries from Oxford came to join us, Peter Brown, like Otto an enthusiast for the Roman playwrights. This was not a form of literature that I could find any interest in, but I linked up with Peter for excursions from time to time. On one memorable occasion we went through Checkpoint Charlie to East Berlin on the May Day holiday, parked the car somewhere near the centre, and proceeded to attach ourselves to the May Day procession as it shuffled towards the central square. So it was that Peter and I paid our respects to Walter Ulbricht, General Secretary of the Communist Party of the German Democratic Republic, infiltrated into the contingent of radio operators from Köpenick.

1968 was the year of student protests all across the western world, fiercest in Paris where protests started by students and picked up by the working population, after months of unruliness on the streets, forced the august President Charles de Gaulle to resign. In England the only serious protests were at the London School of Economics; in America, fashion meant that various university campuses erupted. There were differing local causes of discontent but a unifying thread was opposition to America's war in Vietnam (from which the British government stood firmly aside).

In Berlin, student protest was already running strongly in the summer of 1967. The last thing my conversation tutor said to me before I left Oxford was: the German students will find you very unpolitical. She was right. From the day I arrived at the Free University (FU), political activity – not protest but animated noisy discussion of politics – was in your face on the campus. Politics in Oxford was no preparation for this. To label it all as 'protest' would miss the point, very badly.

Because I was there in this hotbed of political activity, and because I think there were big differences between what was going on then in Berlin and what came later in other countries in 1968, differences which I could perhaps see more clearly from close at hand than external commentators saw, I shall explain what I think it was all about, and what it said about German character and the state of German society – at that date.

There are several strands to disentangle. First is the origin of the FU. As already noted, it was born out of resistance to political pressure (from the soviets) on academic freedom and student debate. However, once the FU had been set up, this matter of principle was quickly lost on the general population of West Berlin. They regarded the FU as an anti-communist institution. As the soviets tightened their grip around West Berlin, there was growing sensitivity in the city government that any activity – student activity – critical of the allies – usually meaning the Americans – was at least undesirable, and possibly life-threatening to West Berliners. The population on the streets of West Berlin readily fell in with that view.

As for the students at the FU, they consistently stood up for their rights to free expression, but the issues on which they took their stand tended, as the 1960s went on, to be issues which brought them into conflict with the city and university authorities, both. By the mid-1960s the hottest issue was opposition to the US over the war in Vietnam and the Americans' increasingly destructive military actions there. Berlin students were not alone in feeling strongly about this. Opposition was growing in Britain too, where the Wilson government from 1964 firmly resisted being drawn in by the Americans. However, in Berlin, opposition to the Vietnam war fell into the class of activity that the authorities were inclined to crack down on.

The already heated situation was made sharply worse in June 1967. The Shah of Persia made an official visit to Berlin. Students protested. During street scuffles the Berlin police managed to shoot one student dead. As it happened he was Norwegian. A cursory enquiry exonerated the police officer, though without producing any real evidence that the shooting had been necessary.

So, by October 1967 when I arrived on the scene, the mood was grim. Fiercer clashes were in prospect.

Alongside this conflict around specific issues, there was a more deep-seated clash of mind-set between a large body of students who held left-wing views and a large proportion of the academic staff who, regardless of politics, took the view traditional in German universities that a professor, the 'Ordinarius', should be treated with academic respect *and* personal reverence by the students. That view among academics ran strongly in Berlin and was in sharp contrast to Oxford, where thanks to the tutorial system even beginner students are encouraged to challenge professors face-to-face, however eminent they may be. To say that all the Berlin students were Marxists would be a simplification – but not a gross simplification. A significant number had studied Marxist philosophy deeply. When you say that German students have studied something deeply, that means deeply. These were world-class exponents of the mid-twentieth century version of Marxism, its application to politics, international affairs and personal relationships. These experts were a significant proportion of the student body and exercised influence beyond their numbers. They were looked up to. They found a willing audience among their less specialised colleagues. The default position of very many Berlin students at this time was sympathy with the Marxist world view. It chimed in with what students in Germany and elsewhere in the world considered to be wrong with America's leadership. It chimed in with what very many disliked about the authoritarian attitudes of their senior academic staff. Along with this, owing more to Freud than to Marx, was a highly-developed set of views on individual behaviour: the qualities prized were respect between individuals, equality of the sexes, independence of mind and absence of authoritarian attitudes. This concern with personal behaviour expressed itself in a running commentary on the behaviour of friends and associates. To be unpolitical was not permissible. It was the duty of the citizen to be politically engaged.

What was I to make of all this, utterly foreign as it was to anything I had come across before? Looking back now, I think I saw the respect paid to Mao and Che Guevara as no more than wall-paper. I could not see what those heroes really had to offer to the Berlin situation, nor could I see that many of the students I came into contact with really had worked-out ideas about that – though it was never hard to find a student of Marxism who would argue the case. The views on individual behaviour were refreshing, a probing and penetrating analysis that kept one up to the mark. The attitudes that made most sense to me were the condemnation of authoritarian behaviour and the readiness to stand up to it. The high-handed attitudes of the professoriat were alien to the Oxford spirit of challenge; they were also – quite rightly – perceived as too close for comfort to the top-down authoritarian views on which the Nazi system had rested. A fair number of the academics did in fact have their Nazi past. This was an epoque when a younger generation in West Germany was trying with great energy and thoroughness to create a new, free and democratic society. The heroes of that effort were such people as the Hamburg journalists of *Die Zeit* and *Der Spiegel*: Marion von Dönhoff, Rudolf Augstein, Theo Sommer. Academics, or judges, or politicians, or police officers, clinging to dictatorial attitudes, needed to be shaken up and dragged into the new world. I had much sympathy for the students homing in on that.

The opposing views that I am describing did not simply play themselves out in dialogue and debate – though my tutors back in Oxford quizzed me as to why it could not have been done like that. No, the clashes took the form of mass meetings and sit-ins in the university buildings, and periodic demonstrations on the streets which might begin with thousands walking a route, and stopping for speeches from one or other leader over a loudspeaker, but always finished up with a confrontation with the police, and a certain amount of smashing of windows in the more expensive shopping streets. There was an element of carnival about that, but also (I felt then) a ratcheting up of the mood of conflict by the police, through their dressing up in paramilitary gear and deployment of high-powered water cannon, with helicopters clattering overhead. This played to the demonstrators' narrative of an oppressive state. Could the differences not have been sorted out in a more controlled fashion? In pure theory, but... this was a battle for a new form a society between two sides whose views were far apart, tenaciously held, with little or no inclination for compromise.

The battle for the new form of Germany was fought out on many fronts through the 1950s and 1960s. Taken on one level, the student unrest in Berlin 1967-68 was part of that. Some of the protestors went on to make careers as respected politicians; Joschka Fischer for example, or Daniel Cohn-Bendit. Some of the key student leaders died, or almost died, for their cause. Rudi Dutschke stood out as a charismatic leader of the protests of 1967 against the shooting of the Norwegian student, and was then himself shot in the head and almost killed. He was capable of writing the most dense and scholarly Marxism, but as a speaker at student meetings he had force, charm and leadership. Some few persisted to ever more extreme protests against the form that West German society was taking; the high value given to successes in business and industry which they construed – again not wholly wrongly – as a mask for Nazis and Nazi attitudes unreconstructed. I don't recall ever meeting Baader, or Meinhof, but I certainly sat in a bar at the next table to a law student who later made a name for himself as defence lawyer for Baader-Meinhof. I was an exotic visitor from an alien culture, so I was occasionally filtered into the inner circle of the highly-intelligent highly-motivated student leaders.

It was a time of fierce conflict – in which a new and gentler West Germany was being born. I say West Germany deliberately, aware that that state no longer exists. With the reunification of Germany new stresses came into being, and are still (2018) being played out.

Come May 1968 the Berlin scene went strangely quiet. This was because Paris had come to life. The protests there spread from the universities to a wider swathe of society and there was a prospect that they would lead to changes in real life – as they did. So the seriously engaged among Berlin students all decamped to Paris for several weeks.

Over the summer term I continued to make the most of the scholarship offered by Kassel and Keydell. All the time I was reading my way through German literature, and enjoying it more and more. It appealed to me as French literature had never done, and it was all new. I read unsystematically but widely, picking up recommendations from friends, and mixing in my own choices. I soon came to Goethe: such an amazing range, and a writer who told us so much about himself. I began with *Dichtung und Wahrheit*, then *Werther*, and that led to the Bildungsromane of Goethe and other authors. Stories built around the personal development of a central individual: this was something new, and interesting. I read Goethe's poetry in small doses (Schiller appealed less) and Heine with relish, discovering that the use of rhyme by these poets which would sound like jingles in English had a different and more serious effect in German. Goethe's mock epic *Reineke Fuchs* was a delight. After a brush with Lessing (*Laocoon*) I was moving (but never systematically) into the nineteenth century. I enjoyed unravelling and savouring the long rolling sentences of Kleist's short stories. Fontane had been recommended for the atmosphere of Wilhelmine (late Victorian) Berlin, so I read *Effi Briest* and *Irrungen Wirrungen*. But Jean Paul and E T A Hoffmann (*Kater Murr*) were more fun. For long rolling sentences, Thomas Mann was more exacting than any of his predecessors; his sentences as long as other people's paragraphs. The key, I found, was to listen to recordings of Thomas Mann reading his own works. I listened over and over again to those that Ursula lent me, and could then settle into the right pace for reading and savouring his enormous winding sentences, parenthesis piled on parenthesis. *Buddenbrooks, Felix Krull*, the short stories.

Moving on into the twentieth century I dipped around in the Viennese von Hoffmannsthal (needs to be taken with a dose of Stefan Zweig as health warning), and Musil. Rilke was made accessible by the dual language Hogarth editions with English translations by the St John's College English tutor, John Leishman, who died tragically in a climbing accident in the Alps in my first year at Oxford, so that I never met him. Here was someone else who had been diverted from his mainstream subject by the fascination of writings in German. His translations of the deeply difficult Rilke were superb. I read some Brecht plays – but why read those when we were able to slip across to East Berlin and watch them performed in sparkling style at the Brechttheater on Unter den Linden? Forward then to modern times, I read everything from Böll and his stories of the post-war years to the stories and plays that were beginning to emerge from writers in the DDR, depicting the stresses and subterfuges of everyday life 'over there', carefully not painting such a black picture as to fall foul of the censors.

All this, evidently, I lapped up with real appetite. I had not been sent to Berlin to immerse myself in German culture – but I did. It opened up a whole new world. I read so much that it was inevitably eating into time that I should have been giving to my thesis and to widening my knowledge of Greek rather than German literature. But my keenness to progress as a Greek scholar and prepare myself for life as a university lecturer in classics was imperceptibly ebbing. It ebbed further in the two years that I spent back in Oxford completing my doctorate.

Epilogue

Once I had finished my study time in Berlin and joined the British civil service, I did not see much more of how events in the university went on. Professor Kassel moved to Cologne. But curiously I made three or four short visits in the 1970s and early 1980s, on Ministry of Agriculture duties.

There was an annual food and farming exhibition held in Berlin at the end of January: Green Week. Throughout the 1970s and 1980s the committee of officials which met normally in Brussels once a week to deliberate on Common Agricultural Policy business, the 'Special Committee for Agriculture' (Coreper equivalent), took itself off to Berlin in the Green Week and held its weekly meeting there, as a symbol of European Community support for West Berlin. These meetings were held in the Reichstag building. At that time the building was a shell, very little used. The outside stonework still showed the pockmarks of the frenzied gun fighting in the very last days of the war. No-one in the 1970s could foresee that the soviet empire would ever end, so we all assumed that the Reichstag building was doomed to remain as a relic of that conflict of 1945. The building stood immediately up against the Wall, well within range, we reckoned, of Russian listening devices. We mused on what sense the Russians could possibly make of our arcane technical discussions about the finer points of EC management of agricultural markets. The coefficients for different cuts of the sheep carcase? The rate of subsidy for extracting starch from grain? Were these some fiendishly obscure codes for plans to subvert the Russian market?

After a break of some years I once more needed to travel to one of these Green Week events in January 1990 – just weeks after the collapse of the communist controls over travel between east and west in November 1989; the Fall of the Wall. People were suddenly free to move backwards and forwards between West and East Berlin, and from other eastern countries that had for decades been locked up behind the Iron Curtain. Our minister of agriculture, John Gummer, was invited to speak at a special ceremony to open the Green Week, and I was to travel with him. He was absolutely intent on going. He could see this being a big day, himself as one of 4-5 ministers nominated to speak at what was bound to be a high-profile occasion if not a moment of history.

Two hurricanes have struck London in my memory. One was in October 1967. The other was on 30 January 1990 – the day we were to fly to Berlin. Arrangements had been made for the four of us (a private secretary and press officer were to come with us) to fly on an RAF plane from Northolt. Around 11 am the RAF phoned to tell us they were closing Northolt because the wind was too strong. Gummer was adamant, he must fly; we must find a private company, anyone, who would take us. All things are possible, so we did find a private company willing to take a four-seater plane out from Heathrow that afternoon.

Setting off from Whitehall by car around 2 pm, we had to go via Ealing to check that Gummer's house was still standing. He eyed the roof rather apprehensively before we went on our way to Heathrow. In the VIP lounge, rain lashing down, we were told that one of the two runways had had to be closed because a jumbo jet had skewed across it. Landing and taking off was now all on the one runway remaining open – but flights were continuing. We were taken to our plane, which looked extremely small as it taxied out among the large and very large passenger planes all around. The wind was intense, and rain obscured the runway. Take-off was frankly scary, out titchy plane felt very close to being blown away, the pilot gave it full power and kept accelerating with full power until we began to rise above the worst of the cloud. We the four passengers had dealt with one bottle of champagne before the plane levelled off. Helped by the following wind we got from London to Berlin in record time, not much more than an hour, and the descent was calmer. Once on the ground at Tegel we were transferred to a British Military Government bus with a blue flashing light on top. Here began the next scare. It was by now only half an hour to the start of the Green Week ceremony. Gummer was in a hurry. The blue flashing light went on and we were driven through the evening rush hour traffic, across red lights, narrowly missing the indignant Berlin commuters who were ready to see the back of the occupying military powers and not inclined to make way for us. (BMG in fact closed down later that year.) In the nick of time, after this doubly nerve-racking journey, Gummer stepped up on to the podium and delivered a brilliant spontaneous speech full of emotional praise for freedom, with an admixture of (to me) fictitious-sounding anecdotes. It was just what the audience wanted. It brought the house down. The speeches from the other ministers who spoke before and after contrasted miserably; all wooden, prepared and read from scripts in lacklustre tones – and that included the speech by the German host minister. Something about the Westminster Parliament equips our ministers to rise to an occasion and speak as if from the heart, something that wholly eludes their counterparts from less adversarial systems and tamer parliamentary assemblies.

So British involvement in the governance of Berlin went out on a high, and later that year West Berlin came to an end.

6

FAST FORWARD IN WHITEHALL
AND BRUSSELS

1970-83

During the autumn of 1969 I decided to take the civil service entrance exams. This was not something to be undertaken lightly. The exams came in three stages: first, one day of written papers, then two days of group work and interviews, lastly a face-to-face interview with a final selection board if the two earlier stages had gone well. From beginning to end the process generally took around six months. I was still half-inclined to pursue an academic career as a university lecturer in classics. But I had not yet secured an academic post.

There was no tradition in my family of going into the civil service, rather the opposite. Were we not non-conformists, anti-establishment? I can be quite precise about what drew me towards the civil service at that stage. Sir William Nield, the father of a school friend, was my inspiration. I had known him by then for more than ten years and had followed his rise from the middle ranks of the Ministry of Agriculture, Fisheries and Food (MAFF) to become a permanent secretary in the Cabinet Office. Apart from being a magnetic personality he was highly articulate about the ups and downs of his life inside the government machine, and gave an unvarnished account of it to those of us close to him. He had taken a steady and friendly interest in my progress. The bond with him and his family was strong. I felt comfortable about following in his footsteps.

The written exam which was the first stage of the entrance process should not have been much of a hurdle to me, but I was sensible enough not to take it for granted. To prepare myself for it, I retreated into the old round Reading Room at the British Museum which was then still the heart of the British library system. (It was closed only in the 1990s, after the new British Library at St Pancras had been built. My accidental involvement in that comes later in this chapter.) That was a far quieter place for reading than is the new British Library. The rules on admission were stricter, and silence was strictly enforced. I sat under the vast dome at one of the desks where famous English writers had sat (and some non-English, like Marx and Lenin), and there I spent concentrated hours with a selection of books on politics, social sciences, diplomacy and current affairs. This preparation paid off. It meant I was on the right wavelength (re-tuned from Greek papyri) to dash off the sort of essays called for in the question papers. I passed, I was told, with exceptionally high marks.

Then came the two-day process of group work and interviews. I knew that my performance here had been more hit-and-miss. Sitting in libraries and writing academic articles was a far-from-adequate preparation. But I passed, and then came the Final Selection Board. The assembled handful of the great and the good made some pointed remarks about study of classical Greek and Latin not being the obvious grounding for government in the late twentieth century. But they let me through. It would not have happened in many other countries, and my foreign friends have always struggled to understand how it could happen in Britain.

At the very end of the admission process we were handed scraps of paper and invited to write down the names of four or five government departments that we would not mind working in. Along with 90% of other applicants I put down the Treasury. Bearing in mind some advice of William Nield's that government departments can be divided into two broad groups, economic and social, and with a vague thought that the economic side would bring more openings for work abroad, I plumped for that. I probably put trade before agriculture, but MAFF went on my list.

MAFF it was to be. A letter came telling me I had been accepted into the civil service and had been assigned to the Ministry of Agriculture, Fisheries and Food, to whom I should report at the beginning of October.

This was of course welcome news, but I had by then received another job offer. Because the civil service process had stretched over six months, I had proceeded in parallel with an application for a lecturer post at Edinburgh University. I had been called for interview with Professor Beattie, head of the classics faculty; he had offered me the post; I had accepted and had taken lunch off him at the New Club in Edinburgh, which I remember as rather dour – both the surroundings and the atmosphere at lunch.

Now what was I to do? The lecturer post at Edinburgh, a major university with its strong reputation in classics, would have been a more than adequate start to an academic career. It would be good if I could record that I weighed up my options in a careful and analytical way, but I don't remember that I did. I chose the civil service and the choice shaped the rest of my life. I simply wrote to Beattie pulling out of the post I had accepted. He was furious. I don't know whether he could have taken legal action. He contented himself by expressing his fury to my Oxford supervisor Hugh Lloyd-Jones, who wrote me a very polite letter saying it was my life and I could choose what to do with it; and he certainly bore me no malice, making generous references to my academic work on the Greek papyri on several occasions, and in his books, subsequently.

I fear the worst impact may have been on David Bain, a contemporary at Oxford, and a Scot by birth, who had competed with me for the Edinburgh post and who might well (though I do not know for certain) have got the post if I had got out of the way sooner. He finished up instead in a post at Manchester where he taught and wrote about Greek drama for the remainder of his career, but died young, reputedly from drinking too much. It sits on my conscience that he might have had a happier life if he could have had that lecturer post in Edinburgh.

Starting work in a Whitehall office after eight years at university, where I had been subject to very light timetabling, with great freedom to work when the mood took me, was quite a difficult transition. I found it terribly hard to get out of the habit of dozing for half an hour after lunch. The days were long, with an hour or so of commuting, initially from Northwood, morning and evening. The weeks seemed long, the weekends short, and holidays unbelievably short.

The work itself was light to start with. The belief was that young graduate entrants would learn on the job, if they were attached to a 'Principal' (later known as Grade 7). The style was for us to learn by watching, as understudies to people five to ten years into their careers. We were to be moved from one post to another fairly quickly, every year or two, to be given a taste of different types of work in our department or ministry, and a touch of tuition from a variety of mentors. Because I had spent eight years notching up two Oxford degrees I was four or five years older than some of the others who joined MAFF when I did, and I was moved along through this training phase a little faster.

My first post was in Fisheries, on the research side. This meant studying the programmes of research which MAFF supported. The laboratory for freshwater fisheries research was, in 1970, in the basement of the ministry's office in Whitehall Place, where it stayed until the IRA blasted one side of that building with a big car bomb in March 1973. The fabric of the building was pretty solid and not much was damaged, but the fish tanks were shattered. Research into sea fisheries, a much larger programme, was run from an imposing laboratory right on top of the cliffs on the southern edge of Lowestoft, facing straight out east across the North Sea from the easternmost point on the coast of England. I visited that laboratory two or three times during the first few months of this, my first civil service post. Whether or not I learned much, this posting laid the foundation for my being appointed years later as head of the whole of the ministry's fisheries operations (see chapter 10). More immediately it led to my being included in the delegation for a conference in Moscow.

The UK as a major fishing nation provided the secretariat – the support staff – for the North-East Atlantic Fisheries Commission (NEAFC). Accordingly many of the meetings of the member countries were held in London, but if the meeting was important then sometimes another country would host it. There was to be a high-level meeting, attended by ministers, in the late autumn of 1971 and it was to be hosted by Russia, in Moscow. I was very keen to go. Russia in 1971 was part of the closed world of the Soviet Union. The Cold War was at its height. It was difficult at that time to visit the Soviet Union as a private tourist. The opportunity to go on official business with MAFF was exciting. I had rubbed shoulders with Red Army troops in Berlin; Poppy had recently had brushes with Russian diplomats in London, and had been schmoozed behind the aspidistras at an Embassy party, only just before Alec Douglas-Home expelled a record batch of 105 Russian diplomats for undiplomatically zealous spying, in September 1971. I was getting a rare chance to see one of the two power centres of the world.

We were a small team that set off from Heathrow, just five of us: two secretaries, two of us juniors designated to take minutes of the delegates' discussions, with the self-assured Peter Pooley in the lead. This was no holiday. We had very little free time. Tony and I as minute-takers worked long days, from morning till night in a bleak conference centre. We took notes by turns, half an hour or an hour at a time, while the formal discussions were in progress. In the gaps between taking our notes we had to dictate them as minutes to one or other of the secretaries, and then later check them through and polish them up. There was a little secretariat of Russians who worked alongside us, doing not much more than seeing that we had enough paper and staples and paper clips, and ferrying documents to some other part of town when photocopying was needed. Those Russians I remember said to us after a few days: 'You work like *wolves*, you must be very highly paid.' If only we had been.

There were lunch breaks, when we sometimes went back to our hotel, the Ukráina, but the service there was so slow that we were always kept waiting for more than an hour before any food reached the table. There was, however, no such difficulty in obtaining drink, if you wanted to fill in the time. It was not unusual to see some guest sitting on his own take a small carafe of neat vodka and drink his way through it while waiting for something to eat. Occasionally the drinker would slump head down on the table dead drunk. Then two waiters would come and cart him gently from the table to a place of rest, well-trained to handle this with no fuss or stigma, as it was clearly a routine occurrence.

Heavy drinking was not unknown among the delegates. One evening there was a gathering in one of the upstairs hotel rooms; it must have been an evening when there was no formal reception in a smarter venue. In the course of the evening I was introduced to a fishing boat captain from Murmansk, who had a memorably bone-crushing handshake. The room was set out with some half-height small tables on which we could rest our glasses. As the evening went on, the number of glasses on these tables built up. Eventually there was a tremendous crash and we all turned to look. One of the Dutch delegates, a huge man, tall and strongly built, was lying flat on the floor in a litter of glasses. He had taken one of the tables down with him and was now lying on his back, not unconscious but murmuring '1917, 1917'. My first thought was that this must be some form of curse on the Russian revolution but no, it was his hotel room number. This was not a first-timer. Past experience had taught him that if you recited your room number friends would rally round and take you there. It took a team of us, because he was a big man, and it seemed to be assumed that the British, in their secretariat role, would form the core of the party of bearers.

I think Tony and I were only given one half day of freedom from the conference treadmill. We were put in the hands of an enthusiastic young Intourist girl who took us to admire the Sputnik monument and one or two other marvels of Soviet industrial achievement. We must have given her the slip after a time because we finished up in a cinema watching a wonderfully fast and furious film about the final days of the Red Army's assault on Berlin: Битва за Берлин.

All our movements were no doubt carefully watched and recorded somewhere by the security services. We put this to the test in an idle moment in the secretariat office at our hotel, by rolling back the carpet and fiddling with what looked like a bolt set into the floor, something like a fixing for a chandelier on the floor below. Within minutes a soviet official came into the room to see what we were up to. We had presumably caused a hiccup in his conversation recorder.

Those were my brief glimpses of Soviet Russia. Ministers and heads of delegations got to see Red Square and to a reception inside the Kremlin. I was, for that occasion, a menial note-taker.

Over the first winter in London, Poppy and I decided that we were going to be more than just good friends. We had met three years earlier when Poppy called in at our Northwood home on her way back from a trip to Russia that she had made with my younger cousin, Gillian, the two of them students together at St Andrews, and sister Heather. Now Poppy and I were both working in London. Poppy was well ensconced at the Foreign Office, Marine and Transport Department, which had some official contact with the Fisheries Department of MAFF. We met more frequently than fisheries business required. Helped by weekends away at Skilman's Hill on the southern slope of Southwold, spurred on by parents, we went for a quick and simple wedding before the end of that winter, in Lancashire. There was snow on the ground. The little chapel in Lathom Park where we were married (a place of significance in the Wars of the Roses, with Margaret Beaufort connections; and in the Civil War, putting up lonely defence of the King in mainly Cromwellian Lancashire) was bone-chillingly cold. It was hard to sing hymns to the approximation of hymn tunes that the local organist pedalled out, and the cold air made singing harder. A weekend honeymoon at the comfortable Devonshire Arms hotel at Bolton Abbey, and we were back in our offices by Monday afternoon. A two-week holiday in the Lake District came later, when spring arrived. Then we settled into a small flat in Blackheath. From this point on, Poppy has a key role in this story.

My next work assignment in London was to the 'Meat Group', a section which dealt with international trade in meat, and support for the production of meat in the UK. We were by then (1971-72) just beginning to make preparations for entry into the European Community (EC) – though we more often in those days called it the European Economic Community (EEC). This posting for me lasted about a year. The under secretary who headed the Meat Group, Keith Dexter, was a professional economist who had risen at a young age to be chief economist for MAFF and had then made what was quite an unusual transition to become a policy under secretary. He was very attentive to the younger members of his staff, and interested in making links between his former staff, the professional economists, and the generalists in his new policy group. He became one of my mentors in my adjustment to civil service work, and was instrumental in moving my career forward at a brisk pace.

One part of my job, working with two other young policy colleagues at the same stage as I was, and with two economists, was to work out the details of how we were to adjust to the Common Agricultural Policy (CAP) systems for supporting production and regulating trade in different types of meat and meat products, and in what ways the systems the Six had put in place might need to be adjusted to fit UK circumstances – and preferences. This was fiddly work but not intellectually challenging. I found more interest in listening to the economists telling us how they expected the pattern of farming in the UK to change in response to the CAP and the higher prices which farmers would obtain for some of their main products. They predicted, for instance, that production of grain would become so much more profitable that where conditions were best for growing cereal crops our farmers would concentrate on those and cut back on milk and cattle. Production of milk, beef and sheep, they predicted, would concentrate over to the west and north of the UK, areas with wetter and milder climate where grass grows best. These predictions all seemed very theoretical to me in my innocence. Yet exactly these shifts of production took place within ten years or so of our joining the EC. Mixed farming was replaced by specialisation which, together with intensification that was driven by greater use of chemicals and advances in machinery, brought about major changes in the environment and adverse effects on wildlife (birds in particular) that then met with widespread public concern.

That part of the job was looking forward. But we were not yet in the EC. Britain was still running its own agricultural policy, supporting farmers at home with deficiency payments, whilst taking in lower-cost produce from the distant Commonwealth (Canada, Australia, NZ) but also from our near neighbours Ireland and Denmark. For those two countries the British market was crucial. We had bargains with each of them to limit the quantities of meat and butter that they sold us, so as to ensure that a share of the home market was kept for British farmers. These cosy arrangements ended when we joined the EC, but they were still alive and important in 1971-72. Both the Irish and the Danes put their most able and sharp-witted officials on to trying to extract the best deals they could from the British. I remember a tense bargaining session with a large team of Danes in a Whitehall conference room one winter afternoon, which had to be held by candlelight because the electricity supply had shut down ('power cuts' were nothing unusual in the 1970s). The light faded but the keenness of bargaining did not.

Blending European law and British tradition

The next post projected me into work where I had much more freedom of movement, and more responsibility. Here again we were looking forwards, to our future in the EC. In the late summer of 1972 I was posted to work on wine standards!

One unexpected requirement of our joining the EC, as we were now about to do, was that we needed to bring in a system of documents to accompany consignments of wine, whether in bulk or in bottle, moving along the supply chain between vineyard and retail outlet. This was a system that had clearly been dreamt up by the French, as a mechanism for preventing the names of wines being fraudulently altered. The system was obviously not designed for the British market, with wines coming in from all around the world, mainly in bottle. We were very doubtful from the start whether it would have any use-

94

ful impact in Britain, but there it was, a legal requirement that came with our membership, and someone had to get down to thinking how we would do it, and then make it happen. That was to be my job. No-one had done it before; give it to the young apprentice.

We were going to need an inspectorate to monitor the movement of these 'accompanying documents' and to take disciplinary action if they found signs of fraud – wines changing their names as they passed from one stage to another. We were inclined to keep this inspectorate small, but it would cost a certain amount of money. Just then the Vintners Company, one of the really ancient livery companies in the City of London (its first charter was given in 1363), made it known that they would like to do something new and useful with their considerable wealth. It was not that they had had a rush of social conscience to the head. More hard-headed than that, they along with other livery companies felt uneasy that if the Labour Party under Harold Wilson gained power again at the next election it might well make moves to confiscate the wealth of the livery companies, taking the view that they were survivals from past history, no longer had a place in twentieth century Britain, and were sitting on far too much money. No doubt the Vintners had done their homework. Wilson's Labour Party had been in power from 1964 to 1970, and the Heath government currently in power was struggling to govern the country (see below), so the likelihood was quite high that Labour would win the next election when it came. They did, in March 1974.

The Vintners with a good sense of which way the wind was blowing put out feelers through their contacts, one a Fellow at Christ's College Cambridge, and another my under secretary at MAFF who, putting two and two together, got us into talks with the Vintners about their taking ownership of the new inspectorate of wine labelling that government needed to set up. This seemed to be in their line of business. A deal was done, and I was put in contact with the Company's Clerk, a retired naval commander. We had financial backers. Now to make things happen.

The next problem I had to solve was where to find staff for our little inspectorate and here a second accident played into our hands. Customs & Excise were having to cut their number of staff and had just made redundant a dozen or so senior inspectors, known in the trade as 'Collectors', coming towards the end of their careers. These were people with long experience and proven competence. They were just the kind of people to give backbone to a new organization, and they had a few more years of working life ahead of them. We jumped in and recruited, I think, eight. This would give us a really high calibre top tier for our new inspectorate. Men with a lifetime of rooting out contraband and fraud – some of it from France. Just the job!

I meanwhile had some more pedestrian things to do like adapting the design of the EC forms for accompanying documents to British needs, and arranging for security printing. Talks went ahead with the Clerk of the Vintners Company and Customs & Excise on knitting together our new team. I made one or two trips to Brussels – the first of what was to be a very long series – to sit in on meetings of the EC's Wine Management Committee, and to keep them in the picture about the steps we were taking, yes seriously, to comply with their bureaucratic requirements. There was little interest shown at that stage from the EC colleagues-to-be.

Through these visits I made contact with the French Inspecteur des Fraudes. He was a key figure in their delegation; his was a prestigious position in a major sector of the French economy. M Tinlot was proud of his eminence among inspecteurs, inspecteurs having high standing in the French administration. So when – in an early surge of diplomacy – I asked him whether he would be willing to come to London and speak to our fledgling team of inspecteurs des fraudes in Britain, he leapt at the offer.

Our preparations matured, and I with the Clerk of the Vintners Company had put together a programme of training for our new team (we needed to go lightly on the use of the term 'training' because these were hardened and seasoned and proven recruits in their 50s). It was all to be held in the Vintners Hall. The Vintners Hall in Upper Thames Street stands overlooking the Thames a little to the west, upstream, of the Monument. The original medieval Hall was completely burned down in the fire of 1666, but replaced in the 1670s. A very splendid core of the present buildings dates from then. Our training course was held in a spacious upper room, deeply Jacobean in style and furnished with some high-backed embroidered chairs in which our eight inspectors were to sit for their tuition by the visiting Inspecteur. M Tinlot spoke English only hesitantly, so he had sent me the text of what he wanted to say, in

French, and I had translated it for him. He was happy to deliver it, reading from my English version.

All carefully prepared then, but what we had not allowed for was a power cut. This was a time when industrial disruption was at its height, the unions conspiring to bring down the Heath (Conservative) government. Power stations were at that time all, or almost all, fuelled by coal, and the coal miners were holding back stocks. Electricity supply had become so tenuous that London was subject to a timetabled rota of power cuts. Our power was cut off that afternoon. It was winter and the light faded early. M Tinlot started his talk, reading his script by the light of an anglepoise lamp which, as I remember it, we were managing to keep lit despite the power cut. It may have been running on a battery. The Vintners had provided candles for each of the eight collectors of customs, sitting in their high-backed embroidered chairs. The rest of the large room gradually disappeared in darkness, until the listeners were visible only as points of flickering light. I have no idea what impression this bizarre scene made on M Tinlot. I can only hope he went away with some satisfaction that he had carried his message to the outer edge of the European Community.

In parallel with constructing this new inspectorate I was in demand from companies in the wine trade to come and explain to their staff what the new system was all about, and help them prepare for it. I had had little experience of public speaking and suffered from stage fright on the first occasion or two, but practice soon broke that down. It was of some help that the wine traders dispensed their product generously, and would offer me samples, starting with goblets of sherry any time after about 10 in the morning. That help with my performances had to be treated with caution.

The Vintners will have felt vindicated when the Heath government fell in March 1974 and Wilson's Labour administration returned; returned in March and returned with a larger majority in October. 1974 was the year of two general elections. The Vintners continued to act as foster parents for the Wine Standards Board for more than thirty years, and I think operated a system which was moderately effective in keeping the lid on the endemic fraudulence in the wine trade. But eventually times had moved on and the Wine Standards Board's work was absorbed into a new creation, the Food Standards Agency, in 2006. The Vintners Company meanwhile has expanded into other charitable and educational activities, and lives on securely in Upper Thames Street.

During this time I nearly died twice. My first brush with death was on 8 March 1973. On that day, without any forewarning, the IRA planted four substantial car bombs at different locations across central London. I was working in my office in Whitehall Place, just off Whitehall, and for those of us there it was a pleasantly quiet day. The trains were on strike, and as this was the latest in a series of strikes many people had opted to stay at home. After an undisturbed morning at my desk I wandered out at lunch-time to buy a sandwich, and ran into a friend of the Nields, Rosh, who asked me in some agitation where she could leave a car for a short time. She had borrowed her boss's car (because of the train strike) and needed to park it somewhere safe just for an hour or so. I pointed her to Great Scotland Yard, the little street running off Whitehall parallel to Whitehall Place, behind our ministry offices.

Not long after lunch, towards three o'clock, alarm bells went off in our building and we received a loudspeaker warning to leave the office immediately, there was a bomb alert. There were very few of us. I linked up with two colleagues at the front door, and we ambled slowly out, not sure where we should go. We saw a few police on the corner of Great Scotland Yard and asked their advice. Without any great urgency they suggested we head away from our building, to the other side of Whitehall. The three of us had just crossed the road and reached the archway that leads through to Horseguards Parade when there was a tremendous blast. In an instant we saw a column of smoke rise high into the air above the roof of the ministry, with files fluttering and dancing on top of the plume. We were immediately hustled through the arch on to Horseguards Parade and solid steel doors came down to block our way back

It was three or four hours before I could get back anywhere near my office. When I did so, it was to see a tangle of hoses and cables running all the way from Trafalgar Square along Whitehall to Whitehall Place. The police, rather surprisingly, allowed me to go back into the building, where the scene was a great deal more terrifying. A very powerful car bomb had exploded in Great Scotland Yard (what became of Rosh's boss's car?) up against the back wall of MAFF's offices. Windows on the whole of that side of the building had been blown out. Shards from the glass had been embedded in the inside walls and even into the steel cabinets. Had anyone been left in offices on that side of the building, the glass would have caused horrendous injuries. Thanks in large part to the train strike, no-one was hurt at all. All that afternoon Poppy, who was working at the London School of Economics in the Aldwych, had been frantic with worry. News had reached her of a bomb blast in Whitehall (and another at the Old Bailey). Central London went into lock-down, mobile phones did not exist, she had no means of finding out more until she, like me, hours later found her way through and we met at the scene.

From that day onwards the bomb drill became sharper. Just as well, because I came within sight and sound of IRA bombs on two later occasions. But on that day in March 1973 I reckon I escaped with no more than three or four minutes to spare.

My second near-death was in March 1974. I had been in Paris for a few days to attend some talks at ÉNA – the École nationale d'administration - where the best brains in France are polished for careers at the top of their civil service. It was the fashion in Britain at the time to regard ÉNA, and the French statist system of government, as models to learn from. The group I had gone to Paris with included Richard Cowan, a colleague from MAFF who was completely blind. With UK law as it was at the time, he had not been able to take his guide dog across to France. I was his guide dog. We hung together. At the airport in Paris we had time to transfer to an earlier return flight than the one we were booked on, so we put our names on the stand-by list for a Tristar flight. Tristar was one of the biggest passenger aircraft then flying, with hundreds of seats. The chances looked good. For the first and only time in my life when I have gone on a stand-by list, I – with Richard Cowan – was not taken. How fortunate we were. That plane with large numbers of civil servants from Ireland and the UK returning home from a conference never reached London. A cargo door fell off in mid-air and the plane crashed, with all lives lost. It is still rated as the fourth worst crash in aviation history.

Promotion into crisis

My next move, in June 1974, was a promotion to the first solid rung of the career ladder, as Principal – one of two – in Beef Division. My colleague was a much older man who had spent most of his career in the Colonial Service, and was working out his final years in a home post. Together we dealt with cattle farming, beef production, and international trade in cattle and beef. There was not a moment for complacency that I had reached the respected rank of principal in quick time. There was trouble looming on the cattle market and within a week or two I was pitched into chaos which then lasted for about two years. I was on trial from the very beginning, tested in crisis management, and immersed in non-stop negotiations in Brussels.

It was among other things a lesson in the law of supply and demand, and how harshly this can operate on the markets for farm products. Demand is not very elastic, whereas supply is very elastic indeed. The result can be wild swings in the price.

Production of cattle in Britain had been building up and in the summer of 1974 unusually large numbers of cattle were put on the market. The wholesale price of cattle normally dipped from mid-summer through to the autumn but this year it dipped and then fell... and fell. Farmers brought more and more cattle and calves to market, and the market went into a vicious spiral. Soon, calves were all but worthless. Farmers in desperation brought some to the steps of MAFF's building in Whitehall Place and left them there. That was a publicity stunt but there was widespread desperation among farmers at the losses they were making.

Britain was by now a member of the European Community, and there were mechanisms in the CAP to deal with situations like this. The CAP system for supporting the market and ensuring that farmers got a certain minimum price included what was called 'intervention' buying: governments would buy up unlimited amounts of produce if the market price threatened to fall below a predetermined guaranteed level, and this government buying steadied the market, so that prices did not dip any further.

Britain was now in the EC, but not 'well and truly' in it. We were in a five-year period of transition, we were not applying the full EC levels of support price, and we were in particular not applying the system of intervention buying, not for beef nor for any of the other major products for which it was available. There was a point of doctrine behind that.

Joining the EC required Britain to switch over from a system of 'deficiency payments' whereby imports were allowed in at prices lower than the government wanted to guarantee to our own farmers, and farmers were paid a deficiency payment to make up the difference. That part of the farmer's income was paid by taxpayers. The EC system was fundamentally different, in that imports from countries where costs of production were lower were all but excluded by levies at the frontier, and the level of price on the home market was kept at the level that government wanted to guarantee to farmers by means of the 'intervention' system – government buying up and taking produce into store. This arrangement meant that consumers paid higher prices than consumers in Britain, and consumers paid a larger part of the farmer's income than in Britain, taxpayers less. In that the tax system is progressive, meaning that people pay more as their level of income rises, the British system of farm support was, at least as seen from Britain, the more progressive, or putting it the other way round the CAP hit those on lower incomes harder.

This difference between the two systems had been a major point of contention during Britain's negotiations to enter the EC and remained a hot political issue in these years of our transition. The choking off of imports from our traditional suppliers in mainly Commonwealth countries was one focus for our objections; the ratcheting up of prices paid by consumers was another. These issues were even more hotly contested under Labour than under the Conservatives, and a Labour government had just been returned to power.

So we were, at this early stage in our transition, clinging as firmly as we could to deficiency payments, and had not started to operate intervention buying. There were limits, there must have been, to the amounts we could pay by way of deficiency payments. So with the flood of supplies in summer 1974 prices fell, and fell. No safety net stopped the fall.

For me at my desk in Whitehall the impact was a deluge of questions to our ministers, to the prime minister, debates in Parliament, correspondence, demands for new policies. My in-tray turned into a pile of papers a foot deep, half of them bristling with red labels. It was a crash course in working under intense time pressure, doing things very quickly, just in time, and giving short answers.

Not only did I not have enough hours in the day to give longer answers, or to think for very long about how to answer each demand; more importantly I learned from observation that the people to whom I was feeding my drafts and my speaking notes were themselves under time pressure, from many other directions than mine, they did not want and could not use long stuff. This was a valuable lesson. Over time I saw one or two who like me had been good at advanced and complicated academic work struggle to make that adjustment.

I was pitched into dealing with situations that would in calmer times have been dealt with by people two and three levels above me in the hierarchy. There was no time to worry about that, I simply got on with chairing meetings of leading traders that the under secretary Keith Dexter had been in the habit of chairing. He was tied up elsewhere. It was not so difficult because, in a crisis, the handful of people in the front line are pooling information constantly, so I knew what there was to know, and felt confident in explaining to the agitated traders what government could and could not do. With Keith Dexter I went to various ministers' offices to explain what the chaos was all about. Without Keith Dexter, accompanied only by a bewildered chief constable from Wales, I had to go and see the home secretary, Roy Jenkins at the time, to explain why there was civil unrest in the far west of his kingdom. Welsh farmers had repeatedly blocked the railway line out of Holyhead to the mainland. They were intent on preventing any cattle shipped from Ireland from coming on to the markets in Britain. This was behaviour that would be entirely normal in France. If the French farmers are not burning meat shipped from Britain they are burning fruit and vegetables trucked in from Spain. Routine behaviour, to which French police react with tolerance. But Roy Jenkins, seated behind an immensely long table with a coal fire glowing behind him and a gin in front of him felt he should be trying to restore public order. I provided him with the facts, but not a solution.

All this on the home front would have been enough to keep one person fully occupied but there was constant activity in Brussels too. There was a Management Committee where the member states with the Commission debated and took decisions on regulating imports and exports, intervention buying and so on. This met regularly, every two weeks or so. I had to attend these meetings, gradually becoming used to the fact that the end-product of our discussions was generally two or three EC Regulations which would be published within a day or so in the Official Journal of the European Communities and then had immediate and direct force of law in all member states. We made laws, on the hoof.

As that year went on, discussions developed at higher level, in the Council of Ministers and in the official committees that prepared business for Council. We British were fighting to hang on to our deficiency payment system. After the searing experience of farmers struggling to get any price at all for their cattle, and with political objections to the idea of taking beef off the market into intervention stores still running strongly, we wanted new EC legislation that would allow us to keep operating something by way of a deficiency payment. The Six, the founder members of the EC, were equally strongly opposed to that, to start with. They saw it as too hard to administer, altogether unfamiliar to all of them; but also they were suspicious that it would be the thin end of a wedge, the Brits trying to shuffle back to their old ways of taking in cheap food from the Commonwealth. That was a habit the Six were determined to break.

This grew into a long-running negotiation which fuelled many long meetings of ministers, and agriculture ministers' meetings were quite capable of running well into the night, sometimes all night. That was no myth. So another lesson from this period was how to stay awake and concentrated, when necessary, for 24 hours at a time. We not so infrequently needed to.

Our minister through all this turbulence was Fred Peart. Fred Peart had been a junior minister in the post-war Attlee government, assistant to an agriculture minister of high renown, Tom Williams, who had laid the foundations for the system of farm support which served Britain well, fed the nation, and raised the nation's standard of farming through the 1950s and 1960s. Ministers who knew about agriculture were a rarity in the ranks of the Labour party, so Fred Peart was highly valued, had been in charge of MAFF during the 1960s and was put in charge of MAFF again in 1974. He was an endearing character, he knew and had a feel for the farming scene (his constituency was in west Cumbria), but he did not have a mind for detail and he – in common with most of the rest of us – knew nothing about operating in the snakepit of EC negotiations. He liked drink, and would happily schmooze his EC counterparts with gin (in the mornings) or beer (later in the day and through the night). But when it came to details and specifics he leaned heavily on his officials; and on one official in particular, Freddie Kearns.

Consequently Freddie Kearns, who held the rank of second permanent secretary, had to carry an uncomfortably heavy weight of responsibility. His task was to extract agreement from unwilling Community partners so as to meet pressures at home on an issue of high sensitivity for the Labour party, and for public opinion more widely. In the background was the build-up to Wilson's In-Out referendum of 1975. Kearns saw this through, but only after months and months of intense and hard-fought negotiations – in which several other matters of importance were in play too. His position took its toll on him. After a year or so more, his behaviour became erratic, aggressive, until he crossed a foreign secretary, David Owen, who insisted he be taken off the battlefield and confined to barracks.

That was how it was at the top. For me, down the line, mostly sitting in the delegation room in the Council building while ministers with their one or two top officials were in session on the floor above, the game was to keep track as best one could of what deal we were likely to be offered, to check that it would not cross any red lines, and to be ready with short, well-focussed 'speaking notes' in case the call came suddenly from the negotiation room. Day or night, most often at night, we had to be on our toes. The art of the speaking note writer was to fit a situation that you could only guess at, with just a very small number of 'bullet points', simply worded; simple for our minister, simple for the translators. In learning this craft I was able to watch in action one master operator who had it to perfection: Brian Hayes, then deputy secretary and very soon permanent secretary at MAFF, he won especial praise from a succession of ministers for his skill at compressing essentials into short and simple form. In the hot-house of the delegation room through many long days and nights I had the luxury of watching and learning from a master craftsman. It was an exciting time.

The end of that episode was that Britain won the right to keep a stunted form of deficiency payment, which became known affectionately among the other EC countries as the 'Peart premium'. They could afford to relax and treat it with some amusement by then. Because on the long road to that agreement they had taught us the lesson that you get no concessions, in that Community, for nothing. Prices are extracted on the way, as many as can be extracted from the country seeking concessions or exceptions. The process is unrelenting; the methods used include attrition and bullying, the testing of nerves and of physical stamina. The all-night sessions were not a form of fun or inefficiency, they were part of the armoury of attrition. At least, that is how it was then. We shall see whether it is any different with Brexit.

During 1975 I made 44 trips from London to Brussels. In those days every trip meant going by air. Eurostar did not exist. Occasionally, when we travelled as a large delegation with the minister, we had a private plane. By the 1980s and 1990s private planes were comfortable and fast. With Fred Peart in 1974-75 it meant getting a Dakota from Northolt. There may have been grades of Dakota. The one the RAF gave us was really very uncomfortable; noisy, lots of vibration, and slow, very slow.

On those days when I was working at my desk in Whitehall, there was the referendum in the background. This sparked countless questions in Parliament and letters to MAFF ministers on the subject of food prices, and whether they were higher as a result of our joining the EC. We junior officials were expected to draft soothing replies and for a time we made much of a temporary surge in the price of beef on the world market and argued from this that membership of the EC sheltered British consumers from such swings in prices. But we knew that situation was unusual and temporary. The young bureaucrat's conscience felt uneasy.

Going into 1976 the worst of the beef crisis had passed, and the referendum had been won. A new issue surfaced. Botswana, the small land-locked kingdom in southern Africa, was trying to win agreement to send limited quantities of its beef to Europe. Cattle farming was a big part of the Botswana economy, so they put their top people on to their campaign. The details of what would be a worthwhile deal for them turned on quantities (easy enough to define) and a concessionary reduced levy (rather a technical matter). When the negotiation had matured, it was to be referred to a Council of Ministers for final decision and this was treated by the Council secretariat as more an issue of external trade than of agriculture, so it was put on the agenda for a Council of Foreign Ministers (since they dealt with matters of external trade as well as foreign/ diplomatic relations). However, the Foreign Office felt they had better have an expert from MAFF on hand to advise on the technicalities. That was where I came in.

The ministers' meeting was to be in June, one of the months when all Community ministers' meetings are in Luxembourg not Brussels. Communications and facilities are all less good in Luxembourg. The weather was hot. I turned up at the Council of Ministers building and found that the Botswanans were there in force. They had, of their own choice, sent a high-level team led by their formidable lady minister of agriculture, Miss Chiepe, all of them dressed, with a sense of the importance of the occasion, in splendid colourful formal robes. They were all tall people, Miss Chiepe as tall as any of her male colleagues. They made a bold splash of colour among the drab sub-fusc suits normal among EC delegations. Their behaviour was entirely quiet and courteous but their mere presence (which we had not suggested) provoked considerable muttering among the other member states about the British 'bringing their clients along to put pressure on us'.

The foreign secretary for Britain was Jim Callaghan. The Irish held the Presidency, and their wily foreign minister Garret Fitzgerald was in the chair. I was kept for some time in a back room, doing my usual run through what possible twists the deal might take. As the time came for 'our item' to be dealt with, I was called into the ministers' meeting room – and here, from the point of view of the Foreign Office, everything went downhill. The UK Permanent Representative, our ambassador to the EC, was Sir Michael Butler. Formidably intelligent, formidably precise, a stickler for detail. His place during foreign ministers' discussions was in the seat next to his foreign secretary. However, Jim Callaghan said he wanted his technical expert next to him when the Botswana item came up. He may have thought – though it was always unlikely – that his foreign minister colleagues might launch into discussion of the details. Anyway, I was put next to him and this being a rather cramped Luxembourg meeting chamber Michael Butler had to hover not far behind us, twitching nervously.

From here on, things moved fast. Jim Callaghan spoke forcefully and with some emotion in favour of the deal on the table. France's foreign minister Claude Cheysson, a crafty heavyweight operator, spoke against it. The honour of French farmers required that. No other minister spoke. After a pause, Garret Fitzgerald with a touch of tease in his voice said: 'I note, Mr Callaghan, that the proposal you want has been passed by a qualified majority of this Council'.

Those words were enough to give pangs of anguish to Michael Butler and the assembled ayatollahs of the Foreign Office. It had been a fixed principle for the Foreign Office that, although Council rules allowed for decisions to be taken by majority (qualified majority, where each member state's votes were weighted roughly in proportion to the country's size), decisions in the Council of Foreign Affairs were only ever in practice to be taken by consensus, by unanimity, thereby upholding the notion that the UK could never be overridden on a matter of foreign affairs. No foreign affairs decision had up till that day been taken by qualified majority. Lower forms of the Council, like Agriculture Ministers, might indulge in that squalid practice. But now, with this Botswana decision, I had imported the squalid agriculture practice into 'their' Council! Butler was livid. Callaghan was relaxed – as ever, Sunny Jim. Fitzgerald was amused (he knew the British points of sensitivity as well as they themselves). Cheysson went away satisfied.

The Botwanans were jubilant, delighted with our efforts on their behalf. I was invited to visit their country at the first opportunity. To my chagrin, I was transferred from Beef Division to the Treasury before I could take up their invitation, and my successor picked it up. As I learned from his sons at his memorial service forty years later, it was an unforgettable experience for him.

On loan to the Treasury

The Treasury, where I worked for two years, in the Public Expenditure Group, felt like a different world. Treasury officials took very seriously their responsibilities for keeping the national economy on track, and many of them seemed to take themselves very seriously too. The atmosphere was serious, heavy with responsibility, and rather dull. People worked behind closed doors. The corridors were endless, since the building itself was a complex structure of circles set inside squares. You could easily get lost, so it often happened that you found yourself at the wrong end of the building from where you were meant to be. The corridors were hushed, all those closed doors. There was an absence of the informality and collegiality that I had been used to in MAFF.

The permanent secretary, head of the Treasury, at that time was Sir Douglas Wass. He was, to me, most of the time a very distant figure. He barely impinged on my life but on one occasion he called me in, to look me over, and I had the impression of a serene and distant person of immense authority, seated behind his large desk in his cavernous office. Years later, reading his obituary, I realised that he was soon after that going to be unsettled by a change of government and sea-change in economic policy that he would find hard to keep up with. He was to find himself a lone Keynesian in a rising tide of monetarists. He would experience, as I came to experience at the peak of my career, that for a Whitehall official life is much more insecure at the top than it ever is in the middle and lower reaches.

My particular area of responsibility in the Public Expenditure Group was for higher education: the budgets for universities and for student grants (a major area of public expenditure then, but now largely shifted to student loans), and direct grants paid to various national museums and libraries, and to the BBC World Service. Most of this work meant dealing with officials at the Department of Education and Science (DES). The nature of the work was so different from the work I had been doing at MAFF as to be quite a shock. All of a sudden there was much less external pressure. There were deadlines to meet in the annual cycle of public expenditure control, but you could see those coming months ahead. There were demands from on high for pieces of analysis. But I had quite considerable freedom to choose what to do from day to day – and when to take my lunch break. Gone were the days of snatching ten minutes to buy a sandwich to be eaten back at the desk while dashing off the next dozen PQs and briefs for debates later that same day. Not just this, but the officials with whom I mainly dealt with at DES did not seem under much pressure either. The striking difference between their work and work I had been doing (and did subsequently) at MAFF was that they were not dealing with the people whose lives their work was affecting, not having to come face-to-face with and defend their decisions to those people. No, DES officials dealt with other layers of officials, in the local authorities and the universities and the University Grants Committee. Theirs was a calm and comfortable life compared with the rough and tumble of many MAFF officials facing day by day the farmers and traders whom their decisions affected, and – horror of horrors – the foreigners with whom we now had to hammer out our decisions on agriculture policy. In this respect I found the Treasury work lacking in excitement. To set against that, we did have the luxury of being able to take time to think new thoughts about the direction of national policy. But on the whole I'm inclined to think the quality of decisions is improved by some time pressure and external challenge.

The Treasury's image of itself took a knock when, in May 1979, the Conservatives won the election, putting Callaghan's Labour government out of its long period of misery, and Mrs Thatcher became prime minister. It was very interesting to see the Treasury struggling to absorb the shock. These consummate mandarins, headed by the immensely august Douglas Wass, he presiding over a perchful of permanent secretaries, failed for some months to get the measure of how radically Mrs Thatcher intended to change economic policy. Her Chancellor of the Exchequer at the beginning was Geoffrey Howe. He sent down instructions to us that we should cut back a lot of public expenditure, including some that fell in my area. In particular he proposed increasing fees charged to overseas students, cutting the grant to the BBC World Service, and axing or severely cutting down the size of the new British Library, whose construction at the St Pancras site was now firmly in the public expenditure plans. The Treasury gives freedom to quite junior officials to put views on paper direct to ministers. I found that refreshing, and a contrast to practice at MAFF. I was allowed to express doubts about the wisdom of discouraging overseas students and of reducing the reach of the World Service, as damaging two areas where in my view UK 'soft power' brought us long-term benefits including economic benefits. My thoughts on that cut no ice. However, with the British Library I think we were able to fend off the worst of the Chancellor's cuts, though the building as it was eventually built at St Pancras was a sorry rump of the architect's original design.

One reversal of policy which Geoffrey Howe did carry through is worth mentioning here because – peripheral though it was – it had an unexpected impact on my fortunes twenty years later. I'll call it the curious case of the European Brookings.

Under Harold Wilson and then Jim Callaghan the head of the prime minister's policy unit was Bernard Donoughue. Poppy had come across him a year or two earlier when he was a lecturer at the LSE. He had spent some time at Harvard and had been impressed by the Brookings Institution, one of America's most prestigious think tanks. He had conceived the idea of creating a European equivalent, a European Brookings. While I was in the Treasury, in 1977 or 1978, Bernard was actively lobbying some of his counterparts in European countries to work that project up with him. He wanted a London-based official to help him organize contact-making and shape up the arguments. He approached the Treasury, who were rather at a loss, not having many people in those days with any European experience at all, but then they thought of me; here was someone on their books who knew his way around in Brussels, and a think tank bore a passably close relationship with the sort of institutions that came within the scope of my Treasury job. So it came about that one day I walked up Downing Street and knocked on the door on No 10 for the first time. Bernard Donoughue and I struck up a partnership, and he and I made one if not two trips to Brussels together. Our meetings there were with a rather exotic collection of high-ranking advisers culled from prime ministers' offices, most of them political appointees (as Bernard was) rather than neutral officials as I was. These meetings and discussions went slowly and fitfully. It was the UK team of Donoughue-Carden that made the running, with the others only gradually warming to the project.

Then came the 1979 election. Donoughue was out of office and Geoffrey Howe did not hesitate for a moment before decreeing that the Brookings project was not worth a penny. I had the distinctly awkward experience of going over to Brussels and meeting the eminenti of the Brookings group and expounding to them the reasons why our new government thought the project a thoroughly bad idea. Since most of this group were political appointees as Bernard had been, I think they found it hard to understand how I could have reversed my position so completely, and since (with Bernard) I had been instrumental in whipping up their enthusiasm (such as it was) there was a distinct chill in the room as they heard me parrot my new master's instructions.

No more was heard of the project, but there was a more cheerful legacy. When Labour finally returned to power in 1997, after 18 years of Conservative government, the incoming ministers who took office were all deeply suspicious of the senior officials they inherited. They were convinced that we must all by now be died-in-the-wool conservatives. Jack Cunningham taking office as minister of agriculture, MAFF's minister in chief, shared that prejudice. Until Bernard (by now Lord) Donoughue, taking office as one of his parliamentary secretaries, spotted me in the ranks and remembered how we had worked happily together over that Brookings project. To him, that was reassurance that I was someone he could work with; so his colleagues could too. He put in a good word with Jack Cunningham. Relations immediately warmed. The politicians' prejudice against us all was largely unfounded, but I had no objection when that past history worked in my favour.

Back in MAFF

This is not a CV that I am writing, where I must describe my career year by year and leave no gaps unaccounted for. I am inclined to skip lightly over the next four years. On returning from the Treasury to MAFF I was posted to the Cereals Division. Like the Beef Division this dealt partly with home production, partly with international trade, and as with Beef there was a management committee that met in Brussels, this one every week. The work here consolidated my previous experience, with nothing like the same thrills and spills.

Just as well because at this time Poppy and I took on an Edwardian house in Shooters Hill Road on the edge of Blackheath which required deep renovation, and then within a short time baby Rosie arrived. I could not have dealt with the intensity of work that had been thrown at me in the Beef years, and coped with everything on the home front as well.

There was no turbulence on the cereals market to rival the chaos five years earlier over beef. It was an entirely different scene. We had come to a watershed in the evolution of the CAP. For the UK, the period of transition had been completed and we were operating Community support mechanisms (including the intervention buying that we so disliked) at full Community price levels. UK growers of cereal crops were powering ahead, achieving ever higher yields from ever higher acreages. Much the same was happening all over the continent. Intervention stores were full, including in Britain where we had commissioned disused aircraft hangars from the RAF – a peace dividend? This was the time of grain mountains, and beef and butter mountains, and wine lakes. The system was now costing European taxpayers a fortune. The agricultural policy created by the Six in the 1960s had met its purpose of feeding Europe and had overshot its target. However, not many member states saw it like that. Farmers were happy everywhere and many governments basked in that farmer contentment. Not so in Britain. We were net contributors to the Community budget – by a large margin, and we were counting the cost. None so fiercely as Mrs Thatcher. Her battles with Europe to get 'her money back' were just getting into their stride. So for MAFF officials in the front line of annual negotiations over CAP support prices – much the largest determinant of the total Community budget – our instructions were clear. Bayonets fixed: hunt down every possible saving, block every possible new form of expenditure. This was enjoyable enough but year after year the spending went up, here and there MAFF had an impact in holding expenditure at less than it might have been, but it was almost impossible to prove that, and to convince other Departments in Whitehall that it was so. A handful of colleagues in the Foreign Office and Treasury and around the Cabinet Office table, who were deeply into how the EC worked, could see where MAFF was being useful and supported us. But on the whole we were putting much effort in for very little reward, very little fellow-feeling from other member states, very little recognition at home.

If that sounds pretty frustrating, there were just a few brighter spots. One regular annual bright spot was provided by the Italians, through their state organization for the support of their rice (risotto rice) growers: Ente Risi. The remit of Ente Risi in Brussels was equal and opposite to ours: to hold tight to Community support for Italy's rice growers and to boost it if they could. Ente Risi fielded one, sometimes two, men with strong physique at the weekly Cereals management committee. Built like rugby full backs, their role was to repel any raids on their bit of the CAP. Their tactics were not all defensive. Once a year they went on a charm offensive. This consisted of entertaining the entire Cereals management committee, three per member state and a clutch from the Commission, to three days of high living in the rice growing areas, centred on Vercelli in the Po Valley. There was a light dose of themed visits to paddy fields (some bird-watching interest here) and rice mills, but in the main the focus was on sight-seeing (Verona and Mantua came in one year, Portofino another) and tackling elaborate meals in the most expensive restaurants (among which an eleven-course meal in the Dodici Apostoli in Mantua sticks in the mind). There was no chance that all this hospitality would deflect the British delegation from their puritanical line on CAP spending, nor did it, so we did not feel corrupted. Nor will the chums from Ente Risi have remotely expected to get any change out of us. Their charm was directed elsewhere. We were free riders on a deal struck between the Six way back at the creation of the CAP. There was only one time when the mood towards the British was less than friendly. That was in May 1983, when the Falklands War was in full swing at the time of our rice trip, and the Italians made no secret of their sympathies with the Argentinians.

By now we can perhaps see a glimmering of sense in the decision someone took way back in 1970 to pitch me into the Ministry of Agriculture, Fisheries and Food. The thought could have been that I appeared to have some suitable qualifications for CAP negotiations: a mind for detail, and for seeing through details to essentials; ability to work in French and German. In many ways that mystery person's decision was looking rather clever. My career was taking shape around working with and in the EC. On trade and agriculture my language skills and ease in assessing other countries' outlooks made it an area where I could have impact.

Yet after four years the negative aspects of this job began to blunt my enthusiasm and my thoughts turned to trying something entirely different.

7

A FAMILY IN SHROPSHIRE

1983-87

One dark afternoon at the beginning of December 1983 we drove off from Shooters Hill Road in south-east London for a new life in Shropshire. The car was heavily loaded: three of us including Rosie who was not quite two and a half; as much of our belongings as could be crammed inside the car; and several well-grown trees uprooted from the garden, tied rather precariously on the car roof.

We had sold the Edwardian house in Shooters Hill Road on which we had worked every spare hour of the past five years to make it habitable. Our work on this house had been no mere redecoration job. It was barely fit to live in when we started, but well up to twentieth century standards when we left. We had peeled off sixty years of wallpaper and burned off sixty years of paint. I had painstakingly sanded down and painted up every inch of woodwork, taking pride in bringing the original sash windows back into smooth-running operation (the next owners rapidly replaced them with modern double-glazing). We had expelled cockroaches from the kitchen and the cellar, and replaced all the light flexes which our predecessors' parrot had chewed through to bare wire. We had even, though not with so much pride, covered most of the front garden with paving so that we could get our car off the road, out of reach of the vandals whose idea of fun was to twist windscreen wipers into artistic shapes. 203 Shooters Hill Road had put us through back-breaking work, skin-stripping work, much dust and dirt – and terrific satisfaction at creating, room by room, a clean and comfortable home. We had very nearly finished the job. Just one room remained to be brought into the modern age when the need to move came up on us.

Selling that house was a financial mistake. We would have been better off if we had kept it, and put tenants in while I was working in the West Midlands. But I don't think we fully accepted at the outset that this move out of London would inevitably be followed by a move back to London, and we certainly did not foresee how the gap between house prices in London and in the West Midlands would open up in the following three to four years. We did not like the idea of letting tenants live carelessly in the house on which we had spent those five years of back-breaking effort, then to return to the house and see how it had suffered under someone else's occupation. We came to regret our decision, but that was later.

As for the trees tied precariously to the car roof? They told the story of how Poppy, who did not come from a family of gardeners, had turned herself into a real expert on trees in our five years in Shooters Hill. She read into the subject with all the skill of a well-trained student, starting with Brigadier Lucas Phillips (his brilliant military manuals, the *Small Garden* and the *New Small Garden*). With that good general grounding she progressed, on tree studies, by leaps and bounds. After a year or two we were visiting Hillier's famous arboretum in Hampshire, and then Poppy spent hours immersed in Hillier's handbook of trees. From the pages of that she carefully selected two or three that might be willing to grow in our inner-city back garden. The idea of tree-planting was in part to compensate for a mature weeping willow, a beautiful tree, that we had with sadness to chop down when it became clear that it had grown as well as it had by tapping into our drains for its water supply. Our two or three replacement trees were still young enough by the time of our move for them to be uprooted to join us for the new life in Shropshire. These it was that we put on the roof of the car.

What was the cause of this disruptive move? It was brought on by my putting myself forward for a Ministry of Agriculture job outside London. I was setting off now to take up the post of Chief Regional Officer for the Midlands and Western Region. Why on earth did I want to do this? Most of my contemporaries thought it inexplicable: to choose to go from challenging front-line international work with the European Community, where reputations were being made, to dabble around in old-fashioned work in the countryside? I trace it back to six weeks that I had spent, very near to the beginning of my civil service career, at the Ministry's offices in Harrogate and Leeds, learning about MAFF's work directly related to farms. Poppy and I had had a very enjoyable time there, being together after the quite short working days, roaming around the Yorkshire Dales in the long summer evenings, but apart from that I had formed an interest in and admiration for the work that MAFF staff were doing directly with farmers. I had spent a little time shadowing the Chief Regional Officer in Leeds who was at that time John Holroyd. He was a rising star from the Ministry's headquarters in London, on a three to four year posting in Leeds before going back to higher things in London. John was ever the enthusiast for what he was doing, and some of his enthusiasm for his Chief Regional Officer work infected me. That was back in 1971. Between then and 1983 I had been spending most of ten years coming and going to Brussels, sitting on EC agricultural committees, where the remit of the UK representative was generally to try and keep the lid on expenditure, whilst preventing the UK from being picked off for special economies. This was quite challenging work and I was fascinated by it, but after ten years I wanted a change from damage-limitation to something more positive. So when, in the course of 1983, two Chief Regional Officer (CRO) posts fell vacant, and applications were invited, it caught my interest. I had a chat with John Holroyd who as it happened was then head of the personnel department (or, in the terminology of the time, 'Director of Establishments'). He was unsurprisingly all in favour of my putting in an application. He could see the value for my career in giving me this experience (it had done him no harm) and he rather liked the idea of having at least one CRO with London and Brussels experience to spice up the team – the others in these CRO posts tended to be people who had spent most of their careers in the regional system, technical specialists with proven managerial ability, coming up to retirement. As seen by senior management in London, a bright young thing with more political sense was a welcome part of the mix – not that those more mature out-of-Londoners welcomed it so much, as I would soon find out.

Before that dark day in December when we transported our household and little daughter in the direction of Wolverhampton we had made several visits to the area, prospecting for somewhere to live. My new office was in Tettenhall, on the very far north-west edge of Wolverhampton and the furthest north-west corner of the Black Country conurbation. For house-hunting we had looked first at the villages just a mile or two out into the country from Tettenhall, without finding quite what we wanted. Not that we could complain about the range of choice. By 1983, Mrs Thatcher's economic policies had driven many manufacturing businesses to the wall. The Black Country is or was all about manufacturing businesses and many of those, large and small, had been recently driven into bankruptcy. In house after house that we visited, the story was that the household had been hit by the slump in the local economy. Husbands and wives were working from home – home computers were then in their infancy, just beginning to open up possibilities for working from home. However, the villages nearest to Tettenhall didn't quite come up with a house in which we felt we would be happy. So, that December, we moved initially into a small rented house in the main street of the village of Albrighton, as our temporary base for continuing our search. Within a month or so, after looking progressively a few miles further out, we had arrived at a short list of target houses, and top of our list was a half-timbered house near the village of Worfield, some nine miles west of the office. We sifted through various problems about the state of the house and legal questions about its site, but swallowed hard and clinched the purchase.

By February or March 1984 we had moved from our Edwardian semi-detached house in London to this half-timbered house built in 1620, recently restored and in good decorative state, in a Shropshire village. For the staff of my office our choice was puzzling: not because of the age and state of the house but because of its location. Nine miles from the office? Why would you want to live so far away? When it is perfectly possible to live within walking distance of the office or in one of the villages much nearer, why submit to a nine mile journey morning and evening – unless you deliberately want to keep your distance from your work colleagues? To me, that drive, which took 15 or 20 minutes at most, was a dream after years of commuting in and out of London with an hour the minimum commuting time, often an hour and a half or more each way. But my staff made clear that they thought we had made a strange choice. It was a sharp encounter with provincial thinking.

The house did give us some problems, though they were problems we had reckoned with and took in our stride. The size of these problems paled by comparison with the years of hard slog that we had put in at Shooters Hill Road. The previous owners had done wonders with re-engineering five old cottages into one house with spacious bedrooms – re-engineering the main tie beams had been their boldest contribution; and they had made good work of decorating. However, they had neglected damp-proofing, and had passed over the fact that the house had a patently failed drainage system; foul water dribbled out from the bottom corner of the garden on to the roadside. We moved in on these problems resolutely. In our first weeks, the outside walls at sole-plate level were injected with damp-proofing chemical (which gave us some health problems later). As for drainage, a JCB came and dug a deep hole in the garden and a herring-bone system of trenches, and a septic tank was sunk in, at the price of scarring the part of the garden that faced the road. We very soon had a well-functioning drainage system, but not before a rumour had run round my office that their CRO was having a swimming pool installed. Suspicions of the new boss from London were running strong.

By Easter that year we were settled in and enjoying our 1620s new home, and absorbing the feeling of history. It became a pretty comfortable home, though the need for care and maintenance was never far away. When the wind was in the north-west, a fine mizzle of rain came through the wall of the principal bedroom. The outer wall here, we found, was only one brick thick. We had to coat this with water-proofing substance every spring time as if it were the hull of a boat. When the wind blew strongly from the north or south it went right through the main living room and could not be stopped even with the thick velvet curtains that we hung against the outside doors to prevent it. Two enormous grates served us in winter with enormous log fires. Spiders: the ancient oak beams, deeply fissured in places, were home to a variety of spiders that I have never seen before or since, some quite meaty. But on the whole they knew their place, and those that strayed far out into the open gave fun to the two little kittens that we gave to Rosie for her third birthday.

Not so the mice. Kittens, keep away from the mice! Rosie was very tender-hearted towards the mice. I have always found that 'Little Nipper' traps work well. But we had absolutely not to use killer traps on our mice in the Old House. Instead we used little plastic boxes that the mice could walk into for a feed, and stay happily feeding when the door dropped shut behind them. Then Rosie and I would carry the trap outside and walk five or ten minutes up Sandpit Lane to the nearby haystack where we clambered up the bales of hay to a high point before releasing the mouse to scamper away. On a strict interpretation of the law this was probably an offence, releasing vermin on someone else's land, for which the farmer could have reprimanded us. But no-one ever did, and this recycling of our house mice continued for as long as we were there.

Not many weeks after we had moved in, and before I had got very far into the new work I was supposed to be doing, it was time to go to America.

America

For the previous four years in London I had been involved with the international trade in grain. Over this period the European Community had been producing steadily more grain and exporting increasing quantities on to the world market, all subsidised. This aggravated the Americans – a lot. Massive quantities of grain were traditionally exported from the United States to those countries which the Europeans were now beginning to target. Income from these grain exports was important for the farmers in the mid-west, and the exports were handled by two or three very large, very rich US companies which exercised powerful political influence. American government officials therefore took close interest in the European Community's grain market: what next year's levels of production were likely to be, what the export policy was likely to be, and so on. I was one of a handful of people in London with an insider view of these things. The US agricultural attaché, the specialist at their London embassy, was in regular conversation with us, and we were at that time very open with him and his government colleagues in Washington about European intentions. My own senior colleagues in MAFF who had grown up with the pattern of trade before Britain joined the EC, when Britain had traded freely with the US and Canada in grain and other foodstuffs, were receptive to the US argument that the EC was trading unfairly by subsidising exports in the way and to the extent that it did. As time went on I became less receptive to American claims that they were the exemplary free traders of the world. A few years after this I became more closely involved in international trade negotiations – the GATT Uruguay Round. The Australians and New Zealanders led the way in developing a mathematical method for comparing one country's system of support for its farmers with another's. This exposed the issue more clearly. The Americans, once all their complex schemes for supporting their agriculture were put under this microscope, no longer appeared as pure as they would have us all believe. But I am jumping ahead. The point for now is that as a result of my close involvement with the American Embassy in London I received an invitation to visit the United States as a guest of the US government. This was quite a rare distinction for someone at my relatively early stage in my career. Some of the guests of the US Visitor Programme were people of note in politics or business, not perhaps at the peak of their careers but far enough forward to attract notice and to stand out as likely to be in positions of real influence in a few years' time. The scheme was a way for the Americans to shape such people's attitudes on their way to the top; to win hearts and minds.

I had received my invitation and I was very keen to take it up. Not that I was desperately keen to visit America. True, I had never been there. I had travelled widely in Europe, but not beyond. However it was more the distinction of being invited that I did not want to let slip. So it was all arranged that although I had just moved on from my London post involved with the grain trade to this new work with farmers in the countryside, my deputy in Tettenhall would take control for a month, from mid-May to mid-June, and off I went.

The organizers in the US gave me a great deal of freedom to choose what to do with my time and spared no expense. The only requirement was that I should spend the first week in Washington, learning how central government worked, meeting with government officials, and learning how Congress worked too. The remaining three weeks were mine, for me to go where I wanted, meet whoever I wanted, see whatever I wanted to see. I was actively encouraged to make it an ambitious itinerary, to zigzag across to the Pacific coast and to take in some of the southern states too.

The week in Washington went fast. The opulence of Congress was an eye-opener: the vast offices and large staffs that each Senator had at his or her disposal; like mini government departments. There was ample time for tourism once the scheduled meetings each day were over. I dipped into the museums and remember marvelling, in the Science and Space Museum, at the tiny size of the capsules in which the first space men had spun round the earth. I visited the Arlington memorial (I happened to be in Washington over the memorial weekend), and took myself out on excursions to some civil war sites: Annapolis, Gettysburg and Harpers Ferry. I did not feel lonely at this time because the British agricultural attaché in Washington was a friend and took me out once or twice. I was invited to dinner with the EC's agricultural attaché – someone who made no secret of his dislike of the Americans and disdain for their lack of culture and history, and for having invented a new culture which in his eyes was nothing but rubbish. He was, I am afraid to say, one of the shallower, less talented English civil servants who had gravitated to the Commission when the UK first joined the EC. There was a problem for Britain at that time in attracting really talented people to hazard their career in Brussels; and the problem persisted for ever after. It simply got worse in later years and is now (2018) incurable.

I had a crucial meeting with the visitor programme people at which all the plans were made for my three weeks away from Washington. There were no constraints. The programmers wanted me to travel far and wide and to see as much of the States as I could manage. With a map on the wall and my recent interest in crop production and international trade in grain as one leitmotiv, we spun an itinerary that took me from Minneapolis-St Paul in the north, to Denver and Colorado in the mid-west; from there through the Rocky Mountains to Salt Lake City; thence up to Washington State (from Spokane across to Seattle); down the west coast to San Francisco, over to New Orleans (Louisiana) and finally up to Chicago.

There were only two moments of tension between me and the programme planners: when I said that I wanted to travel from Denver to Salt Lake City by train, and to take a car from Spokane to Seattle, in both cases so as to see the countryside rather than to overfly it. I had to work quite hard to make the case for travelling these stretches other than by air. 'We don't normally send our visitors by train, we always travel by air.' 'Are you sure you'll feel safe driving on American roads? Don't you British drive on the other side?' I got my way, and these overland travels gave me much more feel for people and ways of life than flying over the mountains would have done.

There would not be much interest in giving a stage-by-stage description of my travels round this circuit. The generosity of the scheme was matched everywhere by the generosity of the people who put me up in their homes and took the trouble to give me the flavour of life in their areas. Representative Uphus in Swedish upstate Minnesota pushed me into broadcasting a discussion with him on local radio, my first and so far only live broadcast. Somewhere in Colorado there was a visit to one of the vast mid-west feedlots, half a million cattle in pens spreading as far as the eye could see. There were visits to large and not-so-large cereal farms, mildly interesting. Salt Lake City – the cathedral like nothing so much as a Disney creation. Driving through the Blue Mountains of Washington state was not frightening in the least, but a chance to do a little birdwatching on the way.

I think the places I warmed to most were San Francisco, with its switchback of roads and its period architecture, and New Orleans for sheer exotic atmosphere. Perhaps this bears out what the EU attaché, whom I have disparaged, had been trying to say. Those of us used to travelling in Europe expect to see differences in architecture, history and, yes, culture, as we move from place to place, and US towns and cities provide all too little of that. I was startled to find that in most cities where I stayed the 'downtown' area was all but deserted by about six in the evening. Offices closed, everyone went home to the suburbs, there was no street and café life of the kind that we take for granted all over Europe. I was startled too by the prominence of religious practices and enthusiasms, many of them (to my mind) extremely weird. Some of my journeys by car were on Sundays, and I tuned to all-day religious channels on the car radio, where extended hell-fire sermons were a routine part of the Sunday offering. In my city-centre hotels there were sometimes massive gatherings for prayer meetings any time from five in the morning. Salt Lake City is Disney architecture founded on crazy beliefs. I have nowhere felt so cut off from home, and news of home, as on the Pacific coast of the US where neither at airports nor from city centre newsagents was it possible to pick up any form of paper or magazine other than the native American press; not even the supposedly transatlantic *Economist*. The Americans struck me then as very... insular.

Less unexpected and more settling was the grandeur of the American scenery. But the vast scale of it made it seem inaccessible compared with the finer-grained geography of England. My closest encounters with the American countryside came through bird-watching: by some lakes in the Blue Mountains of Washington, on a drive down the west coast from San Francisco to Monterey peninsula (where I spotted a rare Pacific species of gull). Best of all, my programmers had allowed me to designate a day for indulging a non-professional interest, and so I had a day in the field in the Mississippi Delta with a dedicated birder, Nancy Newfield of the Audubon Society of New Orleans.

(She has since built a high reputation among ornithologists of the world for her work on hummingbirds, and has an interesting website.) Nancy took me into the marshes of the Delta, where I would never have found my way on my own, and – with the liberal use of taped bird calls – she gave me a feast of marshland and woodland birds. Before the end of the day we drove over the 20-mile long pontoon which crosses Lake Ponchartrain (between New Orleans and Baton Rouge), in sheeting rain. Traffic came almost to a standstill. We crawled forward up the slow-moving queue, as car after car in front of us edged out to overtake some slow-moving vehicle which we could not make out. When we actually made it to the front of the queue we found it was a battered old car with pieces of bodywork trembling and flapping around it, the driver with his window wide open despite, or rather because of, the heavy rain. Because he had one arm stretched out and was struggling to wipe a small patch of the windscreen clear enough for him to see out ahead. No sign of windscreen wipers. No MOT system in America, then!

My overall impressions of America were distinctly mixed. I wrote up my trip for MAFF when I got back. The report was focussed very much on what I had seen of the farming, and learned about the systems of support for agriculture in the US: official stuff. I do remember John Holroyd commenting, with some surprise, that I had said very little about the people I had met. Maybe that was a defect in the report but it also reflected that I don't think I had been particularly impressed by any individuals, neither from the Washington scene nor on my grand tour zigzagging across from the eastern ocean to the western sea and back again. For better or for worse, I did not keep in touch afterwards with any of the people I met on these travels and although I met and worked with many US officials in later years, the people I had met through the Visitor Programme were not (as it happened) among them. I have had mixed feelings about America from then onwards. The US Government might have mixed feelings about whether they got value for their money in giving me that superlative experience.

Now down to work in the Midlands and Western Region

When I came back in late June there was work to do. Much of my work consisted of a cycle of meetings with the senior staff of four technical services at the Regional Office in Wolverhampton and in the four district offices which carried the main burden of dealing directly with individual farms. Then there were fairly frequent visits by ministers to one part of the region or another and it fell mostly to me to prepare their programme and accompany them on the day. There were events at which I represented our part of government. MAFF had specific responsibilities for civil defence and civil emergencies, which we rehearsed periodically with other departments of central government, and the police and local emergency services. Occasionally I represented the Queen, in presenting awards given to local people under the Honours system, always in company with the Lord Lieutenant. All this was new to me.

I was in direct command of the administrative staff at regional and district level, and was expected to coordinate these administrators with the four technical services as and when events called for us all to work together. This coordination function was the main justification for having someone at my level in the system at all; there was no other person whose job it was to draw efforts together when needed, and to see that all the various specialists were operating at least roughly in line with the policies of the government of the day. This was not as easy as it should have been.

There were four technical services, of which the most numerous were the vets, followed by the agricultural (farm) advisers; the teams of agricultural scientists and land surveyors were smaller. Each of these sets of professionals reported to small teams of the same profession in London. Their annual performance marks and promotion prospects depended on keeping faith with those senior officers in London. Complying with the wishes of their Chief Regional Officer came second to that – second by a long way, was my clear impression. In an absolute emergency it was not difficult to get them all to pull together. But absolute emergencies were thankfully rare. More commonly there was a need for the component parts of the Ministry in the countryside to be seen to be pulling in roughly the same direction, and at least not working against each other.

I guess there had been quite a long period, through the 1950s and 1960s, when this management structure worked harmoniously enough. In the 1970s Britain began to switch its method of farm support from the post-war system of deficiency payments introduced by the Attlee government, over to the systems of the Common Agricultural Policy of the EC. In the early years of this transition, prices which British farmers could obtain for their staple products, thanks to the EC's safety net of 'intervention' prices and free-wheeling decisions by EC ministers in their annual farm price reviews, went up by leaps and bounds. Everyone in the countryside was happy.

But after a few years of that generosity, which operated all across western Europe (the twelve member states as they then were), uncomfortable consequences began to emerge. Levels of production rose and rose. No surprise here; farmers responded to ever-higher guaranteed prices by stepping up their production, to the limit – and the limits were being lifted by new technology, chemicals, and new farming techniques. Those advances came at some cost to the farmers, but a cost which they could afford, at the levels of price they were getting.

Already in the late 1970s, the EC was producing quantities of meat, milk and grain which were giving cause for alarm. The cost to European taxpayers was shooting up, because the CAP was giving open-ended guarantees to farmers that any amount of produce that could not be sold at a good price on the domestic market would be bought up and held in government stores – at taxpayers' expense. This was the era of beef, butter and grain mountains, and wine lakes. As the mountains grew higher, steps were taken to offload some of the surplus on to markets outside the EC, where prices were nearly always lower; so these exports had to be subsidised. At further cost to the EC taxpayer.

The EC moves slowly. It was already clear by the late 1970s to policy-makers in central government that this system had somehow or other to be reined in. The 'somehow or other' was the issue at endless meetings of EC ministers and officials stretching over a good many years. But by 1983-84 a radical decision had been taken that, as regards milk at least, the time had come to get a real grip. The decision was to introduce milk quotas across the EU: strict limits on the total amount of milk which each member state was to allow its dairy farmers to produce, with the member states left to decide how exactly to carry that through into practice with limits on each of their individual dairy farmers.

The quota system took effect in April 1984. The process of translating the national quota for the UK into quotas for individual dairy farmers was a major operation which ran through the following twelve months and beyond. It was enormously tricky. In principle each dairy farmer was given a quota based on his/her recorded production over a period in the recent past. But in the UK we allowed this figure to be adjusted for a variety of reasons. If a farmer could show that he had committed significant investment on plans to increase the size of his herd or his dairy, he was allowed some extra quota. Then there were hardship cases: farmers who could show that the basic quota would cripple their business. Naturally, as many farmers as thought they could make a case for additional quota did so. Special arrangements were needed for the small number of farmers who did not deliver their milk daily to a dairy (where quantities were independently recorded) but sold it direct to retail customers (less reliable records). Tens of thousands of stories had to be crawled over and assessed. The brunt of this was done by a very small team in London who worked themselves to the bone. Two very level-headed and meticulous senior officers went the rounds of the regions, explaining what was going on. Once the officials had come up with a decision, the farmer could appeal against it, and naturally very many did. Such appeals were heard by panels of experienced local farmers, region by region.

In my view this vast operation was the thing that MAFF did best in the whole of my working time. BSE cannot be counted as such a brilliant achievement. Foot-and-mouth in 2001 overwhelmed MAFF's skills and resources and had to be shored up by Army skills and scientific advice from outside. The introduction of a new basic payment scheme a year or so later proved almost impossible to operate because of the highly complex formula on which the then minister insisted, and that system is still proving hard to deliver, year by year. The introduction of milk quotas I regard as a historic accomplishment, perhaps MAFF's finest hour.

Down at my local level it created huge tensions within the farming industry and in the ranks of our own staff. Much of 'my' region, to the west of the Pennines, enjoyed mild temperatures and high rainfall. Grass grew well, and the growing season was long. Dairy farming was the predominant type of farming. We had large concentrations of dairy farms in Staffordshire, Cheshire and Lancashire. The introduction of milk quotas sent shock waves through these counties, and sorting out individual quotas was a huge task. I turned out to speak at many meetings of farmers, often in country pubs in the evenings, and became very used to standing up in front of angry audiences, doing my best to explain the main lines on which we were working, and fielding questions. I could only explain, and explanation only went so far. The level of anger in these milk-farming areas was real, and went on for months. Only one farmer actually set his dog on me (sharp teeth drew blood). Much harder to deal with was that a number of farmers committed suicide out of despair that they would be able to make a living with a fixed ceiling on the amount they could produce and sell. It took a good few years before everyone had come to terms with that.

In retrospect this was a formative experience for me. I learned that you cannot always expect to win approval, or even acquiescence, from your audience. Up till then I think I believed that provided you prepared your arguments carefully enough, presented them with due attention to the particular interests of your audience, and showed sufficient recognition of their special interests, you should be able to come out of a speaking engagement with a fair measure of approval from your listeners. Talking to farmers about milk quotas, I had to learn that the value here was in simply appearing, and listening, and discussing. There was no way these farmers were going to be happy about the policy I was defending, nor in the least grateful to the messenger. Talking about the unwelcome policy face-to-face with those adversely affected was all that the civil servant could do, but that in itself had some value.

The stresses played out in the tensions between our specialist services, something of which I have said a little already. The State Veterinary Service dated back to the 1880s and was in no doubt about its role: keeping the multifarious diseases of farm animals at bay, and leading the battle when a killer disease erupted into a major outbreak. Combatting the last outbreak of foot-and-mouth disease in the 1960s had been a high point to which our vets in the 1980s looked back with collective pride.

The next largest of our specialist services, the agricultural advisers – known in the 1980s as ADAS, the Agricultural Development and Advisory Service – had a culture which went back to the Agriculture Act of 1947 and the post-war push to produce more food at home in Britain. The need to modernise Britain's farms, educate farmers in modern techniques, with production of food as the clear and only objective, had been economically vital through the 1950s. The process of drilling farmers to produce more had got into its stride in the 1960s and continued to run strongly. The advisers saw it as their job to hand-hold any farmers who seemed to need it (a good many still did), and to help them to produce more. Many if not most of these advisers in government service came from farming families; many were the younger sons who had not inherited the farm but had close relations who farmed. Their family interests as well as the training they had been given was of a piece with the Dig For Victory culture of 40 years before. If – as was beginning to happen in the 1980s – the message from ministers was that enough was enough, over-production was beginning to cost the country's taxpayers too much, intensive production was having some negative impacts on the environment, wildlife and the look of the landscape; if, as was now happening, these messages from politicians and the man from Whitehall were beginning, just beginning, to signal no more production, please – the advisers took these as no more than deviant political interference, a temporary inconvenience, not to be listened to. They were wholly averse to falling in with the message. They were not at all averse to briefing against the message, and in my case not at all averse to briefing against the man from Whitehall who was, for certain, only going to be around in their region for a short time. So I had to contend with this current of dissidence. The dissonance over milk quotas was quite sharp. It made all the harder my uphill attempts to win farmers over by explaining to them what the fundamental economic reasons behind the policy were, and why it mattered to carry it through. I was battling on two fronts.

This difficulty with insubordinate agricultural advisers was dealt with a year or two later by Thatcherite economic policy. The countrywide army of advisers dispensing free advice in a maternalistic style did not fit with the general direction of economic policy in the 1980s. It was the nannying state in action, and what is more it was boosting the over-production of farm produce which was costing the taxpayer. A new director-general was appointed to ADAS with the remit of introducing charging: farmers must pay at least some of the cost of the advisory service. Charging was then introduced in several stages. Not surprisingly, demand for advice fell, gradually at first. A few years later, after I had left my CRO post, the advisory side of ADAS (but not the State Veterinary Service) was privatised altogether, and within a few years more it had shrunk to a fraction of its former size. The farmers most in need of advice, those who were older and less capable of keeping up with technical progress, whose businesses were coming under pressure, were – no surprise – least able, or least willing, to pay. That type of customer dropped away, leaving only the smarter and more capable larger farmers to support the new leaner private-enterprise ADAS.

It was the end of an era that had begun in the 1950s. Ending it had some adverse effects. Thirty years on, there are signs of how this change has damaged the performance of farming in Britain. Evidence is accumulating that since the 1980s the performance of farms in Britain has fallen behind that of farms in France, Germany and the Netherlands let alone the US. In those countries there are ways in which knowledge of latest developments (and methods in agriculture are constantly changing) from scientists and business experts is passed down to individual farmers; knowledge transfer, in the jargon. Either the state finances advisers or farmer cooperatives do the job. British farmers were in the lead in the 1980s, and in my view part of the reason for them slipping down the international league has been the killing off of the state-run maternalistic advisory service, along with cuts in government's funding of science for food and farming. There was an adverse impact too on the quality of policy work at the centre. As the senior specialists dwindled, we lost the ability to involve people with practical experience in the process of developing new policies, and thereby lost the ability to assess the practical impact that policies would have on working farms. MAFF began to lose this, and its successor department, Defra (from 2001), never acquired it. That showed. Farmers sensed that the focus of attention was no longer on them.

But this is running head. One episode from my time as CRO is worth telling. It was probably in 1986. Our permanent secretary, Sir Michael Franklin, had been invited to speak to the Shropshire Chamber of Agriculture, one of the oldest county-based farmer societies in Britain. Shropshire was and still is a quiet county in terms of industry and tourism, but its farming is its strength, and there are many farmers in the county who are both good at their farming and alert to what is going on in the wider world. The Shropshire Chamber of

Agriculture is one of a number of such chambers and societies which date back to the early nineteenth century, and which stand apart from the campaigning organizations that rose to prominence later, the National Farmers Union and Country Landowners Association, in that they do not exist to champion farmers' rights and to lobby government; more like Rotary Clubs, they encourage thoughtful discussions and debates, engage in some charitable work and, over the years, have supported experimental work and career education. This Shropshire Chamber had invited Sir Michael Franklin to talk to them and had high expectations of the top man from Whitehall. Michael turned to me for advice on what he should talk about and I drafted a speech for him which was mainly about the changes in ADAS; the changing economic climate, how it fed through to government support for agriculture, and the plans to move ADAS on to a more business-like footing. Michael was, of the permanent secretaries I worked for, perhaps the most friendly towards those he saw as rising talent. He was always well-disposed towards me, and gave me help in my progress up the civil service ladder. He accepted my advice for this event, and delivered my draft speech with little alteration. It was received in polite silence. I, sitting in the audience, felt the chill. Michael must have felt it too. His speech was followed in the customary way by a question and answer session. Not one of the questions related at any point to the content of the speech. The audience wanted to hear his views on the state of the markets for the things they produced, mainly beef, sheep and milk in that part of the country, and what the government thought was going to happen in those areas. I felt I had fed Michael the wrong speech. But he never breathed a word of criticism to me. And it was not really such a misjudgment. As things unfolded, possibly some of the 'thinking' farmers who had sat in that audience may have come to think that, well, that permanent secretary fellow, perhaps he was trying to give us a heads-up on changes in the offing that we needed to know about.

Other events tested our operational capability. The explosion of the nuclear power station at Chernobyl was one. I have given a separate chapter to that. It tells of a fraught occasion when Michael Jopling was our minister. However, some ministerial visits had a lighter side. Michael Jopling made a faux pas in his very early days as minister by arriving at the Royal Show on his motorbike, in leathers. The country's leading farmers were not amused. However, Mr Jopling was an extremely keen motorcyclist so he continued to travel to official events on his bike when it suited him, but the first requirement for his Chief Regional Officer was then to identify a safe place close to the official event, where he could tuck his bike out of sight and change his outer clothing. I rose to this task once or twice.

Mr Jopling was also extremely keen on fast cars, and regularly won the House of Commons speed race. On one occasion with Michael Jopling at the wheel I travelled faster than I have ever travelled by car before or since, even on the German autobahns. He was due to speak to a farmers' audience in Preston at 6.30 in the evening. I linked up with him in Whitehall around lunch time. He was to travel in his own car, and travel on after his Preston engagement to his home in north Yorkshire. A little delayed, we set off from the Whitehall office around 2, I suppose. It was just after 3 when we got to the base of the M1. I felt, with relief, that we were now on the road: M1, M6, and Preston was within our sights. Jopling turned to me and said, 'what route do you suggest we take?' 'Well', I said, thinking this was obvious, 'M1, then M6'. 'Hm', said Jopling, 'we might hit Birmingham in the rush hour, I think I'll go M1 to Leeds, then M62, and from there to Preston'. I choked back rude comments and said something to the effect that it would mean going a much longer distance. 'Yes', said Jopling, 'but it will be quicker'. I couldn't make much sense of that. Somewhere near Leicester I think I began to. Michael Jopling was not only pretty adept on a motorbike, he was, as I was finding somewhere near Leicester, pretty good at the wheel of a car. This car was a Ford Capri, lean and mean, wheels mounted just a little wide of the body. We sped up the M1, sped past the junction with the M6 and continued north, fast. Our speed was mostly close to 115 mph. In the outside lane all the way. If there was a car in front of us, Jopling went up close, very close. For a time I was terrified. After a time I grew more confident that my driver knew what he was doing. We sped on. Mainly at 115 mph. It didn't seem long before we reached Leeds and turned left on to the M62, in fact it didn't seem long at all after that before we had arrived at Preston. We had gone from the base of the M1 to our Preston office, about 270 miles, in three hours, an average of 90 mph. Showing his mettle as a politician, Michael Jopling rose to his feet right on time after that furious drive and spoke calmly and lucidly to his local audience. Mission accomplished.

John Gummer, then a junior minister, was quite a frequent visitor. On one occasion when he had engagements in Manchester and Liverpool he asked me to set aside a bit of time in the programme for him to visit a deconsecrated Victorian church in Liverpool city centre. He had a passion for Victorian church architecture and ecclesiastical practices and was on the look-out for some fittings that might be for disposal. We found the church. It was winter time, and mid-afternoon, and the daylight was going. We had a key and let ourselves in, John Gummer, his private secretary and me. Gummer was looking around when there was a loud hammering on the door. I went to see what it was, and came face to face with an agitated special branch officer who had been detailed off to keep a protective eye on us. Now, I had been on tour with Gummer for a day or two; several red boxes had been delivered to us from London, and were stacked up in the back of my car waiting their turn. The security man told me in no uncertain terms that it was far too hazardous in the centre of Liverpool to leave them on view, and that unless we returned to my car at once he could not be responsible for the consequences. Did we not know what the locals were like?

If I didn't know it then, I had another reminder on a different ministerial occasion. It was at the time of the Liverpool Garden Festival. A German minister of housing had come over to see the Festival and what it was doing for the regeneration of a run-down part of Liverpool, and had asked then to visit a modern housing estate. The estate chosen was in St Helens, I think, on the northern fringe of Liverpool, and for some reason, perhaps because I spoke German, I had been asked to accompany him. I picked him up and we found our way to what seemed to be the right spot where local housing officials were to meet us, but I could see no sign of them. Then I noticed a curtain twitching on the window of what looked like an office. The door opened, furtively, and a hand beckoned us in. The officials talked about the housing project, the German minister listened, the officials in their narrative made frequent mention of vandalism and the problems it caused, the minister frowned and looked puzzled. When the narrative ended he asked whether he might go up in a lift to see the buildings from a higher level. With shock the officials said this was out of the question; the lift had been vandalised,, and the staircase was in an unfit state to show a visitor. At this point there was an outburst of real fury, to the effect that 'in Germany we would not allow this to happen'. I guess not. But that is normal for Liverpool – and the reason why the regeneration brought about by the Garden Festival was short-lived.

Garden festivals as a means of city regeneration were tried in other places. Poppy and I were invited to the official opening of the garden festival at Stoke on Trent. The Queen was to perform the opening ceremony. The invitation made clear that small children were not allowed to attend, but we had no friends or family with whom we could leave Rosie for that day so we decided to take her along. We dressed her smartly and gave her some tulips from our garden to carry, to keep her happy and give her a sense of occasion. The morning programme proceeded and the invited guests were paraded after an hour or so for the Queen to walk down the line. Rosie was indeed the only small child in a long line of adults so inevitably she caught the Queen's attention. There was Rosie, still clutching her bunch of tulips, their flower heads by now drooping miserably, and as the Queen came up to Rosie she reached down and took them from her with immense dignity and passed them (as she does) to her Lady in Waiting who barely hid her disgust at the sight of our dejected bouquet. Rosie was not overwhelmed, in fact did not seem terribly impressed by the encounter. We found out why. She had only recently seen the Queen on television for some important event, dressed in daffodil yellow. This was 1985 or 1986, Mrs Thatcher was at the height of her powers, and frequently dressed in power blue. The Queen for the Stoke on Trent event was also dressed in blue. So Rosie's question was: did I meet the yellow queen or the blue queen? An understandable confusion in the circumstances.

It was a constant pleasure for us as a family during this period that work and home were not, as is normal in London, two separate worlds. There were many times when we could all share in a work-related event (more legitimately than at Stoke); friends and neighbours understood and could relate to what I did in my office time. Quite a few were themselves farmers, or involved with farming. They knew something about what MAFF did and had some idea what the man from the Ministry in Tettenhall was there for. This was unique, in my career. At every other stage I would disappear off into London (or Brussels) and the people living around us in the suburbs had no idea what work I did, and not much interest in knowing about it. And in our leisure time we got to know the great quiet areas of Shropshire, its gentle hills and valleys not much changed since the time of the Shropshire lad. It is all the better for being little known; perhaps protected in a way by the M6. Travellers with destinations beyond the West Midlands are sped along with no temptation to deviate through slow Shropshire. We loved it. So we were quite unhappy when, after less than three years, the central powers in MAFF let it be known that they would want me to move back to London to resume a London-and-Brussels based career. This terminated a posting which had not been short of interest and had given us a quality of life simply not available to the worker in Whitehall.

The removal van carted us back from Shropshire in April 1987, by then a family of four, because William had arrived on the scene.

8

CHERNOBYL

On 26 April 2016 various newspaper articles and broadcasts reminded us that it was the 30th anniversary of the Chernobyl disaster. On 26 April 1986 there was a major fire at a nuclear power station at a place called Chernobyl in the Ukraine, then not a separate country but part of the Soviet Union, the Russian empire. Radioactive material showered over the surrounding area but also rose high into the atmosphere and was carried by the wind across wide areas of central and northern Europe. Sweden and Britain were among the countries over which the radioactive cloud drifted.

I became directly involved through my work as one of MAFF's Chief Regional Officers at that time.

I can well remember where I was when the news broke. Once a year the Chief Regional Officers (CROs) met in one of the five regions for a two or three day programme of visits to farms or food businesses, and some informal discussion on current issues: the latest news on policies and management from London (the senior official responsible for the 'regions' from the Ministry's headquarters in London led our discussions); and we pooled thoughts on what was going on across the range of business that regional staff had to handle. That makes it sound rather serious. It was anything but. Ted Smith, the senior official from London, managed us with a light touch. He had an acute brain but he reserved most of his brainpower for other parts of his job, and an excursion into the countryside was a welcome break from more stressful matters.

So the CROs' annual conference was altogether quite casual. We were sitting out of doors on the terrace of the hotel where we were staying, in Kent, when someone picked up the news about a nuclear accident at Chernobyl. This was well before the days of mobile phones let alone smart phones, or we would all have immediately been scanning for further details. That was not how it was in 1986. One of our group had heard something on the radio. Moreover this was not news that had flashed round the world immediately the accident happened. No. The fire had actually happened two days earlier. The Soviet Russians were so secretive that they kept the news to themselves, meaning to the inner circle of their government, keeping their own public in ignorance, while they proceeded to evacuate people from the area around the power station. The outside world only learned that there had been some kind of nuclear accident when scientists in Sweden started to pick up signs of high levels of radioactivity in the atmosphere through routine monitoring. That time-lag could not happen now. Everywhere in the world is under constant satellite monitoring. A major fire at a known nuclear site would be world news in minutes. But that is not how it was in 1986. The world learned on 28 April 1986 of the major incident at Chernobyl that had taken place on 26 April.

One of our important responsibilities as CROs was to monitor radioactive releases and their impact on foodstuffs. We had a well-rehearsed drill for swinging into action and liaising with the emergency services if there was a leak from any UK nuclear establishment. This was work that was given high priority on the very rare occasions when there was a real need; ever since the serious leak from the nuclear power station at Windscale (now Sellafield) in Cumbria in October 1957. We had also each had a course of training at the government's civil defence college somewhere underground in east Yorkshire on what we would do in the event of a nuclear attack on our country – which was always assumed to come from Russia, and the civil defence training made the optimistic assumption that the Russians would leave us in a fit state to resume life after a nuclear bomb or two had hit us. In this scenario too, MAFF regional staff would have a role, for which we occasionally drilled.

So we pricked up our ears at the news of this explosion in far-off Ukraine. I think we probably commented that it might need some attention when we got back to our home bases, but it was far from obvious that it would really affect us. We certainly did not drop everything and send urgent instructions to our monitoring teams.

It took only a day or two for it to become clear that we were indeed going to have to do something. The cloud of radioactivity from Chernobyl was dispersed by the wind in various directions: over Russia, south to Austria and Switzerland, and north over Sweden. The cloud that drifted first over Sweden then swung south and west, over Scotland and into England and Wales. Our monitoring teams went into action and for several weeks collected samples of milk and field crops – fruit and vegetables. The samples went away to a government laboratory for analysis, and a copy of the results for the samples collected in 'my' region – that was the West Midlands and Lancashire – came across my desk.

Nearly all the readings I saw were zero, but there was just one isolated reading that was really quite high; significant enough to have caused alarm if it had not been entirely isolated in a sea of zeros. This came from a fruit farm near Evesham in Worcestershire.

Meanwhile, it was becoming apparent that quite high levels of radioactivity were being detected on the ground in areas of south Scotland, and on the high fells of the Lake District, and in Snowdonia in north Wales. The explanation, we were told, was that it had rained in those areas while the cloud of radioactivity was passing over; it was rain that had brought the radioactivity down on to the ground. Where it had not rained, the cloud would have passed over harmlessly. Those areas where radioactivity was now being recorded were areas when high rainfall is normal. That was not the full story but at least there was an explanation that made sense.

So what of 'my' isolated high reading from Worcestershire? There was by now a fair degree of public alarm, and the government's response was under intense media scrutiny. The results of government monitoring were themselves closely monitored. Commentators quickly picked up what looked like a wayward result, and ridiculed it. 'How can this one be right? It just shows that the government's officials can't even monitor the situation competently. They don't understand their own results.' Comments of this kind naturally fed a level of unease that the government didn't really have a clear view of what was happening; or else was hiding something.

Several weeks went by and we had to ride out this current of public criticism. Then came new information in the form of more detailed localised weather reports, with precise data on rainfall over the days when the Chernobyl cloud had been passing over us. Evidence showed that an extremely local spot shower of heavy rain had fallen precisely over the area of Worcestershire where we had picked up a high reading. We were right after all! I remember feeling great relief, but I also remember seeing no mention anywhere in the press that the stray result which had been so much criticized had turned out to be correct.

A few more weeks passed, May turned into June. No new fall of radioactivity was detected. The damage was what it was. The level of concern among the general public subsided – but not among farmers. Those farmers with sheep on the hills in Cumbria, Snowdonia and south Scotland were being told that they might face restrictions on selling their animals, possibly for many years to come. The radiation would be taken up from the soil into the grass and plants that sheep grazed. Farmers across the whole country shared the anxiety, fearing that the taint of radioactivity compounded with the always high level of public dread of it would cause their sales to drop, and prices to fall, not just for lamb but other kinds of homegrown foodstuffs as well.

We were all by now familiar with a clutch of technical terms: becquerels per kilogram, millisieverts, the differing half-life of different types of radioactivity. Chernobyl had showered us with caesium 137, which we were told had a half-life of about 28 years (I think it is now put at nearer 30 years). This was taken to mean that, in the areas from which it was liable to get into foodstuffs, the restrictions might have to be applied for the next 28 years. That seemed hard to take in. For the sheep farmers of Cumbria and Snowdonia the prospect of restrictions on what they could sell being applied for decades into the future naturally caused huge consternation. (In fact restrictions *were* imposed, and *did* apply for nearly that long. They were only lifted, after careful debate in the Food Standards Agency, in 2010 in Scotland and in June 2012 in England and Wales; 26 and 28 years on.)

So by June 1986 there was a lot of anger among farmers.

Part of my job as CRO was to accompany ministers on their official visits to my patch. At the very end of June every year the Royal Show was held at the Royal Showground at Stoneleigh near Warwick. This was, until it went bankrupt in the year 2009, the biggest agricultural show in Britain. It drew visitors from all over the country, farmers and others; and was always well attended by leaders of the farming and associated industries from all around the world, including a sprinkling of ministers. It was a very valuable showcase for the latest British technologies and the best of British livestock. Some major deals used to be done, especially with the state buyers from centralised states like the kingdoms of the Middle East, and the soviet communist countries.

In 1986, as it happened, the guest of honour among foreign politicians was to be the Agriculture Minister from Russia. Our minister always rolled out the red carpet for the top visiting minister. This year our minister, Michael Jopling, was to give the red carpet treatment to his Russian counterpart. I was as CRO involved in the planning of this hospitality, and had to look after our minister for that part of his Show programme. On this occasion the plan was that Michael Jopling would host a small private dinner for the Russians on the evening before the Royal Show opened. I, with just three other officials, was to attend this dinner in support of Michael Jopling and his wife Gail.

The weather was unusually warm that evening. For the dinner, we had booked a room at a country house hotel not far from Stratford-on-Avon and not far from the showground for the morning. The Russian minister and his entourage were booked in to stay the night here, though we were not. An officer from Government Hospitality (an offshoot of the Foreign Office) was designated to meet the Russians at Heathrow and bring them to this hotel during the afternoon, with a tourist stop at Stratford-on-Avon on the way.

I got to the hotel in good time for the dinner, so as to be in place before Michael Jopling and his wife arrived. I was met by the officer from Government Hospitality – in a state of high agitation. He explained that we had got off to a very bad start.

What I think none of us had been told by the hotel management was that this had been a privately owned country house until not very many years previously. It had belonged to one family for many hundreds of years, and they had obtained permission to come back and hold a large family gathering in the grounds that afternoon, to commemorate their long history there. For this, a temporary theatre had been erected alongside the hotel, and the celebrations had gone on all the afternoon with a series of pageants. The Russians meanwhile had landed late at Heathrow, made their tourist stop at Stratford, and had arrived at the hotel only an hour or so ago – while the pageant was still in progress. The family event had culminated towards 6 o'clock with a deafening fusillade of thunderflashes. We had to imagine the Russians, hot and tired from a long hot drive, unwinding in their hotel rooms, showering or dozing. They had had the fright of their lives when the thunderflashes went off. The poor government hospitality man had been on the receiving end of scorching complaints from his guests. The scorch marks were still fresh when I met him.

He was visibly shaking. We warned Michael Jopling when he turned up that he would have to be at his most charming to retrieve the situation. Michael Jopling was not a natural master of charm and diplomacy, but he could be dignified and courteous. This would have to do. The room where we were to have dinner was, as I remember it, rather long and narrow, with a fairly low ceiling. On this warm evening it was a little airless, not ideally comfortable; but it would have to do.

The Russians trooped in for pre-dinner drinks. Conversation was not easy. Except with their ambassador who spoke fluent English, all the conversation had to be through interpreters. Some pleasantries were exchanged, and then we sat down to dinner, 5 or 6 a side. Once some food had been eaten, Michael Jopling rose to his feet and made a little speech. He welcomed his counterpart and then moved into some explanation of what was to be expected the following day. He referred of course to Chernobyl. Choosing his words carefully he expressed our great sympathy with the Russians for the disaster and its effects on their people. He then turned to the impact on us in Britain, and the concerns felt by British farmers. Specifically he forewarned the Russian minister not to be surprised if he had to face some anger on the showground. We are, he said in effect, a democracy and we have an active press; so you must not be surprised if farmers express anger at the problems that the Chernobyl radiation is causing them; and if journalists put microphones in front of you and ask you to comment. That's how it is in our democracy. I just want you to be prepared for some of this as you tour around the showground.

Michael Jopling had hardly finished, indeed may not have finished, when the Russian ambassador sprang to his feet. He started in a ferocious tone and his voice rose in volume as he fired himself up. The British minister's words had been insulting. Chernobyl was 'not just disaster for the Russian people, it was disaster for humanity'. The Soviet people deserved our gratitude for what they had done to contain the explosion. The pilots who had flown helicopters over the power station to drop water on the fire deserved the highest praise for bravery and self-sacrifice. We should all be expressing our gratitude to the Soviet people, not poking petty criticisms at them. And so on in this vein, with frequent reminders to us that the Soviet Union was a *big* country and didn't need to take notice of criticism from small countries such as ours. The atmosphere had become extremely tense. I remember glancing along our side of the table at Gail Jopling and seeing that she looked frozen with fear. Remember that we were still in the cold war. The Russians could be overbearing and threatening. Here we were in a small overheated room with some powerful Russians just feet away from us across the table, clearly in a state of great anger. We could not be sure just where things were going.

The evening ended uncomfortably. I have no recollection of how things turned out next day on the showground. I doubt whether any valuable deals were struck with the Soviets that year.

That was what came back to me in April 2016 about the events of 30 years before.

9

CONSTRUCTION OF EUROPE

1987-91

At the beginning of October 1987 I was put into a new job. The most important thing expected of me was to coordinate the work of MAFF that
connected with the EC, and it was for me and my team to put together the
briefing for our ministers for EC Council of Ministers meetings. This briefing
pack would come under close scrutiny not just by our ministers but the team of
top MAFF officials who went with them, and key officials in the FCO, Treasury and Cabinet Office who would read it with hawk-eyed attention.

The Council of Agriculture Ministers met once a month throughout the
year. The first such meeting on my watch was scheduled for 19 October, and
the briefing for this had to be all done and distributed on the preceding Friday,
16 October. The subject matter had all been talked through on the Thursday
morning and the specialists went away to write their contributions. Putting the
pack together should have been a straightforward operation for my team, the
top two of whom were as keen as mustard, very practised at this, and raring to
show me that they were on top of it. My role then would probably just be to
oversee, and to step in only if some briefing came forward that seemed to conflict with lines agreed the previous day.

On the domestic front we had moved house from Shropshire to Bedford a
few months before. On the Friday morning in question Poppy's brother Nigel
who also lived in Bedford phoned us up before 7 o'clock in great agitation. The
weather had turned extremely rough overnight. High winds had brought down
power lines and no trains were running from Bedford to London. Apparently
it was even worse in London, fallen trees blocking roads and crushing cars. Advice to the public was not to travel unless it was strictly necessary. Stay at home.

The weather was indeed worse in London. On the night of 15-16 October
a true hurricane struck south-east England with winds of 100-120 mph. The
BBC weather forecaster Michael Fish became famous – infamous – for ever
after, because on TV at lunchtime the previous day he had made the mistake of

142

his life: a lady had phoned the BBC, saying she had heard a hurricane was on its way. 'Well, there isn't', Fish told the viewers.

The hurricane reached its highest intensity around three to four am and London was right in its path. It brought down trees by the hundred, including famous landmark clumps on the South Downs and stands of beautiful mature trees in central London parks. Nigel had not exaggerated. Advice to the public was not to leave home unless strictly necessary. But I judged my journey to be strictly necessary. Yes, I had a reliable team but how did I know whether they would manage to get to the office, or what other difficulties there might be? My place was in the office that day.

So I got in the car and drove to London. The drive – nearly 60 miles – was remarkably easy, traffic was light, there was none of the usual congestion as I came closer in towards London. I think I was well into the West End before I met visible signs of the storm. There were fallen trees everywhere, branches on the road, the sad sight of London planes lying flat in the parks. But nowhere was I seriously held up. I left the car behind the Ministry of Defence, just off Whitehall, and settled down to the day's work. Many people were absent but my heroic team turned out and coped. The task was completed to time, and all that remained was to drive the 50-60 miles back out to Bedford, through a non-existent Friday evening rush hour.

That was a rough start. Let's take a step back. My move to this new post was part of a chain of moves at the top of MAFF, triggered by the retirement of Michael Franklin (whom we last met in Shrewsbury). The first link in the chain was David Williamson, a MAFF alumnus, being moved from the Cabinet Office to become secretary general of the European Commission, that is the top civil servant in the Brussels system. David was going to be only the second person ever to have held the post. His predecessor, Emile Noel, a Frenchman, had been appointed when the Commission was created in the 1950s and had been there for thirty years. The chain of our moves continued with Derek Andrews being promoted to become MAFF permanent secretary, succeeding Michael Franklin; David Hadley to move up to replace Derek Andrews as deputy secretary; and I to replace David Hadley as under secretary, Head of EC Group.

David Williamson's appointment in Brussels had been in the balance till the very last minute, no doubt contested behind the scenes by this or that other member state coveting the post for one of its own people. Had David Williamson *not* won that slot in Brussels he would have been front runner for the MAFF permanent secretary position. Then there would have been no promotions for the rest of us. That made clear to me after the event why I had been kept idle for the previous three or four months, doing work of little or no significance, fiddling around with the management of the regional organization that I had just recently left. I had been parked while the Williamson appointment was settled.

This was, for me, a significant step up in my career. I had reached the rank of under secretary in just under 17 years from entering the civil service. In France they promote some people much faster than this, but by MAFF standards I had made quite fast progress. It was a step up into the sphere of people who were judged to matter to the wider public. Under secretaries, at least then, were invited to have their names entered in *Who's Who*.. When I had first started out in the civil service, I had vaguely thought I should be satisfied if I reached the rank of under secretary in due course. Now I had. William and Gwyneth Nield, ever supportive, sent me a letter of congratulation.

That said, my new job, Head of EC Group, was something of an insider's civil service post. I was to coordinate MAFF's work related to the EC. Was there much need for coordination? By 1987 large swathes of MAFF were caught up in the Common Agricultural Policy, and subject areas that were not involved in that way – sections dealing with food standards, and with animal and plant health – were about to be drawn into the EC net via the Single Market campaign, which was just then cranking up into higher gear. Of course other government departments dealt with a scatter of different things and these had to be kept in line, coordinated. The people working on different subjects develop their own objectives and all tend to think they should have high priority. It is ultimately for ministers to say what they want the priorities and guiding principles to be, and for the permanent secretary and his/her top team to filter that down and do their best to keep everyone on track. With any department that was dealing with the EC, this need to get people marching to the same tune took on more urgency. A timetable was imposed from outside. The EC's Council of Ministers met with differing frequency on different subjects but none more frequently than the Agriculture Ministers. When that Council met, the agenda was a blend of what the Commission wanted it to be (e.g .proposals for new legislation); what the Presidency country whose minister chaired the meetings wanted to move forward faster – or slower; and events. With agriculture, events impinge frequently: weather, disease, shortages or surpluses on world markets. Agricultural policy was almost entirely a matter of 'Community competence'; and the budget was very large.

What this meant from the point of view of coordination was that for any meeting of the Council of Agriculture Ministers a varying mix of six to ten different divisions in MAFF would have to serve up briefs – instructions/suggestions/speaking notes – for our minister once a month; and similar material for the high-level committee of officials which met in Brussels every week in between, sifting and shaping up what needed to go to ministers for decision. Some subjects had a long history; some, however, bubbled up all of a sudden, unexpectedly, with little time to test where they stood on the minister's scale of priorities.

As coordinator I chaired a weekly meeting in the ministry where we discussed at a fairly brisk pace the menu for discussion in Brussels in the week ahead: what the topic was, what the specialists thought we should be arguing for. Drawing on the frequent meetings I had with our minister, and with our MAFF person from the Permanent Representation in Brussels (UKRep) alongside, I had to assess what was being proposed, feed in advice on priorities and tactics, perhaps adding suggestions as to where we could make alliances with other member states to improve our chances.

The value of this for me was that I built up a broad picture of the whole range of MAFF's work that related to Brussels. I had also to learn how to explain matters of agricultural policy to non-experts. I have described this as an insider's civil service job but there was an outward-facing aspect, even if 'outward' here meant out beyond the walls of MAFF only as far as the world of Whitehall and Westminster. Because I was the only person at my level with the overview of agricultural matters, which were generally very technical and often followed a contorted course, I was in demand to speak on agriculture at meetings of one kind and another at senior level in Whitehall: ambassadors' annual conferences, conferences and consultations with top people from other member states, and with officials from Sweden and Austria who were at that time preparing to join the EC. Some events of this kind were in those delicious country houses which HMG maintains at Ditchley Park or Chevening, others in the Locarno Room in the Foreign Office which has more than a touch of grandeur. I was very often the only person at such events to be drawn in from what the Foreign Office refers to with a touch of disdain as 'the home departments'. This was because agricultural policy in the EC and the cost of it held a unique place at that time in the UK government's concerns with the EC. I became the voice of MAFF at some top tables.

I was firmly caught up now, through the dominant place the CAP had in the EC budget, in Mrs Thatcher's campaign not just to get her money back but to reduce UK contributions to the EC budget into the future. In this campaign, the CAP was key. Mrs Thatcher had done her deal at Fontainebleau (1984), she had won a hugely worthwhile rebate on what the UK paid over each year (later partly given away by Tony Blair in the unsecured hope that he would get a quid pro quo from the French, which was not delivered). The EC had settled a new 5-year spending plan, budget discipline was in the air, and how to prevent the ever-buoyant CAP costs from breaking the new budget – that was the next challenge. During 1987 the Commission had produced a scheme for pegging costs for the main farm products when certain levels of spending were reached: 'stabilisers', as these arrangements were going to be called.

The House of Lords decided to examine and report on how effectively stabilisers might work. The House of Lords has often been regarded as making a negligible contribution to the efficient governance of the country. On EC legislation that assessment is wide of the mark. The Lords committees that scrutinise EC legislation are composed of some real experts, and the reports of these Lords committees were often among the most rounded and thorough assessments produced by any parliament in Europe. They attracted, and received, attention in the Commission. It was just my luck, then, that the Lords had set up their enquiry into stabilisers and fixed their timetable just before I started in post. They wanted – or rather, summoned – a team of officials from MAFF to give evidence on this, and it clearly fell to me to lead the team.

I did some homework. Then my star deputy (another Richard) pushed me to redouble my effort. Just as well. The day came, my first experience of sitting in front of that horseshoe of parliamentarians in enquiry mode. I was tense but well-prepared, and had to field questions for more than an hour and a half. All the evidence that we give to a committee like this appears in print, word for word. When I re-read what I said on that occasion it seems to me one of the clearest performances that I gave over the following five years or so. Is there a point here? Because I had come fresh to the subject and knew what I knew, but no more, my explanations came out as clear-cut and uncluttered. Maybe it was the Oxford weekly essay drill showing its benefits too.

In 1987-88 Mrs Thatcher was at the height of her powers. Her mastery of the operation of government was complete. If she was involved in a policy she knew all the details, up to the minute. There was hardly a higher priority for Mrs Thatcher at this time than squeezing the EC budget. Spending on the CAP was by far the largest chunk of that budget, as she well knew. So we, MAFF, were in her sights and I was in one of the posts meant to have the whole picture. When Mrs T's Private Secretary Charles Powell came on the phone with a question to me, I had the sensation of being within an arm's reach of a high-powered electricity cable. One false move and you'd be dead. I was not alone in this. Ministers were similarly affected. Mrs T had no qualms about making life uncomfortable for them. They needed to know their details. If she decided to dispute the line a minister was putting forward, she was quite capable of matching the minister's reading of his brief, and then out-arguing him. Quite often we would sit with our minister (in 1987-89 John MacGregor, one of the most intelligent we had had, though not the most finely-tuned politically) for ten minutes or so before a Cabinet meeting. He would seem to have absorbed all that we had to say, and to be comfortable with the line of advice, but his very last question before going out of the door would be: 'Is *she* going to be happy with that? What will *she* say?' Said with more than a note of nervousness in his voice.

There has never been a prime minister in my experience, before or since, who had such a comprehensive grip on the business of government and who could, as the Germans say, durchsetzen, she could make her views felt. She made mistakes, some big ones as time went on. But her grasp of what was going on in her areas of interest and her ability to intervene to good effect raised standards right across the government machine. We were all on our toes; in an electrified state – it's the most apt image.

1987-88 was also probably the time when Britain was at the heart of Europe, more than ever before or since. The Single European Act to which Mrs Thatcher signed up in 1986 spurred the EC on to 'complete the single market', and this was formalised in the Single Market 1992 programme. It has never yet been completed but 1987-92 was a period of progress on a broad range of subjects (goods more than services). The 1992 programme was put under a new Commissioner, hand-picked by Mrs Thatcher, Lord Cockfield. Economically Britain had a major interest in seeing the single market completed. Politically Mrs Thatcher was putting her formidable weight behind it. Operationally it was being driven by a British Commissioner.

The vaunted Heart of Europe policy went only downhill after that. Under John Major as our next prime minister, with opt-outs from the social policy secured ('game, set and match') in the Maastricht Treaty 1992; under Blair, after he had revived the slogan, with opt-outs from the Euro and Schengen; under Cameron – same slogan, weird choice of partners in the European parliament, yet more marginalisation. Given Mrs Thatcher's claws-out relationship with Brussels, given that it was her aggression towards Brussels which caused her colleagues to drive her out of office in 1990, it seems paradoxical to say this but if Britain ever came near to being at the heart of Europe I would put that in the late 1980s.

The Single Market was part of my job. The EC through the CAP had woven its web around a large number of MAFF divisions but there were others that had barely been touched so far. Now that a firm target date (1992) had been set for completing the single market and negotiations were being given new impetus, this changed. We started to look closely at our range of work on food standards, animal and plant health, all of which might be affected. It fell to me to sift through the field, all subjects quite new and strange to me, and to make the divisions aware of what the single market might mean for them.

On food, it would mean replacing a mish-mash of different standards set by this or that member state (Germany on beer, Belgium on chocolate, France on pretty much everything) with a single standard agreed at Community level. Britain had an economic interest in achieving progress here. The food manufacturing industry was strong in Britain, and keen to export, but our companies ran into some major difficulties exporting their products to other member states, most of all to France. The French were adept at using their national standards to protect their domestic food and drink manufacturers against imports. The Commission had made a faint-hearted effort to get the member states to agree EC standards for a certain number of products, but progress had been slow. The proposal on chocolate had been under discussion for more than a decade, Belgium flatly refusing to agree that the kind of chocolate made by Cadbury's and much loved by British consumers could be described as chocolate at all. Here was the most vivid illustration that, for food products, Community regulation could be good for Britain.

When we turned our attention to animal and plant health, the position was reversed. Britain's geographical position as an island meant that our trees, plants and animals were free from various diseases that occurred, and that farmers and growers had to battle against, or live with, on the continent. Logically enough, we wanted to maintain our relative freedom from disease. We had operated restrictions on imports to Britain and had done so for many years. The view on the continent, however, was that Britain should loosen many of its restrictions and allow movement of plant and animal material subject to checks, proportionate to the risks we were afraid of. This was the point of view taken up by the Commission. Our vets and plant health experts were deeply reluctant to go down that road, fearing that it could only result in higher levels of disease, at economic cost and, for some diseases, risk to human health too. As a matter of history, and looking back now, I think we have indeed had to suffer higher levels of plant and animal disease through the loosening of import controls that the single market forced on us; perhaps more harmfully on plants than on animals.

The one disease threat that we saw as in a category all on its own was rabies. Britain had had a rigorous ban on movement of dogs in and out of the country for nearly a hundred years, to prevent rabies coming into the country. This had proved very effective, its effectiveness possibly enhanced by comprehensive education of the public to live in dread of rabies. Graphic tales were told to us as children of the uniquely horrible death that rabies caused. Now, faced with the pressure of the single market campaign, at government level everyone was clear that this had to be a Red Line. On rabies, we would not be moved. Relaxation of plant health rules, OK, let's see how it goes, but on rabies we needed and were going to hold on to our total ban.

Even this issue was seen differently on the continent. Recent advances had been made in suppressing rabies in wildlife and the disease was in retreat; in fact, more commonly found now in Switzerland than in any EC country. It was time for the British to change their rules to a system more proportionate to this diminished risk.

While I was in my EC post we maintained our 'give no quarter' position. When John Major took over from Mrs Thatcher as prime minister and had the Eurosceptics snapping daily at his heels, the red line under rabies grew thicker. To concede to the Europeans and put our lives and our children's lives at risk was unthinkable; an absolute no-no. However, to pursue this topic to its conclusion, I must record with trepidation that after I had moved to the Cabinet Office, in direct defiance of an explicit instruction from No 10 not even to discuss the matter, I had very discreet talks one-to-one with the director general of the single market directorate in the Commission, who happened to be British, about possible moves we might make. Then another four or five years later, with Tony Blair as prime minister and the politics of Europe in a quieter phase, I was back in MAFF responsible for drawing up a Pets Travel Scheme under which dogs (and cats) would be allowed to move in and out of Britain on condition that they had been vaccinated against rabies and were micro-chipped to make them securely and individually identifiable. Helene Hayman as Minister of State and I as lead official worked up this scheme and piloted it into action. It resulted in a small step change in human happiness for those who wanted to move dogs, in particular, backwards and forwards between Britain and other countries. Ambassadors and their lady wives purred. I was warmly congratulated by the Agriculture Commissioner's chef de cabinet, whose particular cause for satisfaction, I learned, was that he could in future take his own Austrian hunting dogs with him to the Yorkshire moors for his annual trips to shoot grouse. The scheme has been in operation for twenty years now (2018) with no mishap. But if rabies ever did break out in Britain it could be terrifyingly difficult to stop. The urban foxes with which British cities are riddled, London most of all, would prove elusive and lethal carriers.

GATT

There was a separate part of my job which moved to a slower timetable, and to which I did not have to give close attention at the beginning. This concerned the negotiations on world trade. Since 1995 there has been a World Trade Organization (WTO) which, as the name says, organizes negotiations on world trade, and polices the rules on world trade. But from the late 1940s through to 1995 this work was done by a similar but lower-status organization called the 'General Agreement on Tariffs and Trade' or GATT for short.

GATT was, as the WTO now is, based in Geneva in Switzerland, in a rather dumpy 1920s office block in a prime position on the shore of Lake Geneva. Occasionally there were Geneva meetings that I needed to attend. More often I took part in regular meetings held in Whitehall to discuss where the UK stood in relation to what other countries wanted. These meetings, which touched on the responsibilities of several Whitehall departments, might have been chaired by the Cabinet Office but were actually chaired by the Department of Trade and Industry (DTI). Reasonably enough, because DTI had experts in the largest number of the issues that came up. Their deputy secretary, who presided, was rather obviously possessive of his role. It put him on a par with a Cabinet Office deputy secretary, and he took pride in that.

Alongside the range of issues that DTI looked after, there was discussion on agriculture. This was the largest of the issues that sat outside DTI's range of responsibilities, and it was considerably more complex than any of 'their' issues; complex in terms of the rules operated by the countries big in agricultural trade, and complex in terms of politics.

We were in the early stages of a new GATT 'Round' – Round being the term given to the periods of negotiation that tended to run for years at a time and to conclude with a package agreement on reducing barriers to trade. This current Round had been launched in 1986 at a meeting in Uruguay – so it was The Uruguay Round. For the first time in the history of GATT, a serious attempt was being made to tackle barriers to trade in agriculture. Previously that had been treated as just too tricky as well as too highly contentious. But a group of countries with major economic interest in exporting agricultural products, led by Australia, had decided to be bold, and to put up a challenge to the countries they identified as protectionist, the largest among them the EC and the US.

Agriculture was by no means the only area of trade rules at issue in the Uruguay Round but it was a 'first' that it was on the agenda at all, and the effort of tackling it was one reason why the Uruguay Round lasted from start to finish for 11 years. (It was in the end productive.)

All this is preliminary to saying we were in new and unfamiliar territory, where those with expertise from previous GATT negotiations did not feel confident of their ground. The traditional UK stance of being simply and straightforwardly in favour of reducing barriers to trade (always a touch hypocritical, in relation to our imperial past) did not work; here, on agriculture, we were now locked into a Community which was by any definition pretty protectionist, and a majority of its members were entirely comfortable with that. If the UK were to have any impact it would have to be through exercising artful influence on the EC from the inside. This was a new game, bringing new tensions.

During my first year on this patch the main work we did was of a very technical kind. The Australians (it was a set of Australian university economists) had invented a mathematical formula for reducing the very different ways in which governments, US and EC in particular, supported their farmers, to a set of numbers that could be compared with one another: Producer Subsidy Equivalents (PSEs). This was a completely new way of looking at things, and was quite a breakthrough. It suddenly became possible to discuss changes by steps in the various different systems whereby agriculture was supported – changes that while different could be treated as equivalent to each other. This seemed to open the way for a mutual reduction in cosseting farmers. In due course it provided the key to some historic ratcheting down of trade distortion on agriculture, but in this early phase in 1987-88 the experts on all sides were still crawling over the Australian idea and deciding what they thought of it.

GATT meetings are generally held in Geneva but every two years or so there is a gathering of ministers hosted by one of the member countries. Two years on from the launch of the Uruguay Round, ministers were to meet to take stock of progress, in Montreal. Our minister, John MacGregor, was to go, with me and the youngest of my assistants in support. I felt I was skating on thin ice. My attention for the past year had been mainly focussed on the internal EC issue of CAP reform and cutting the budget – and for reasons already given I had had to make sure I was 100% up to speed in that area. I had left GATT and the technical work on PSEs to my assistant. So I had very little idea what to expect from the ministerial meeting or how to guide John MacGregor, if I needed to. He seemed unworried by that. He was clear as to the main objective: the UK favoured liberalisation of trade. He took me with him for a chat with the Chancellor of the Exchequer, then Nigel Lawson. My main impression was of how small compared with his television image Nigel Lawson was, leaning against the mantelpiece.

We flew off from London to Montreal on 3 December. This so happened to be the day on which Edwina Currie, then Minister of Health, made remarks about salmonella in eggs which triggered a health scare, and uproar in the farming industry. 'Most of the egg production in this country sadly is now affected with salmonella' she said, in a TV interview. Leave aside just what foundation there was for her saying it, the repercussions for us when we arrived in Montreal were... interesting. You have to picture that we were quite a large UK delegation. The British did not take GATT lightly. In the lead was DTI's Secretary of State, Lord Young, closely supported by the deputy secretary Christopher Roberts, proud of his position and poised to steer the British contingent with a firm hand; perhaps a dozen DTI officials under his command. The non-DTI element consisted of John MacGregor, he too a Cabinet minister, me and my assistant, there to deal with the uncomfortably awkward subject of agriculture.

The first thing that happened on the morning of our arrival, while we were settling into the room in our hotel that had been equipped as our office, was that MacGregor was summoned to the phone for a long talk with his permanent secretary, Derek Andrews, about Edwina and her egg statement, while the fax machine which DTI had installed so that Lord Young could keep his finger on the pulse of the British economy started to churn out reams of briefing from MAFF on the 'egg crisis'; yards and yards of it. Lord Young took all that in his stride, but resentment among DTI officials grew. Here they were to make a uniquely purposeful UK contribution to stiffening the EC line on liberalisation of trade, their equipment had already been hi-jacked by MAFF, and MAFF's minister was giving his entire attention to some tin-pot local flutter – to do with *eggs*? All hope of cohesion in the delegation seemed dashed at the outset.

So there was this. For MAFF it was by any standards a serious turbulence, and there was also quite a lot of public money at issue. Looking back, it was dealt with in London, principally by Derek Andrews, with great competence. All MacGregor could really do from Montreal was keep in touch, and apply pressure for Edwina to be disciplined.

The second thing that happened, after we had been in Montreal for a couple of days and ministers had sat in session for a few hours, was that Lord Young announced to us all that his daughter was about to have a baby and he was going home to London to be with her. This was a hammer blow to Christopher Roberts. His act was falling apart. Lord Young left us. The next morning at 8 o'clock we had a delegation meeting, following our usual schedule, to plan the day ahead. Christopher positioned himself at the table as if to chair the discussion. John MacGregor conscientiously arrived on time. It took only seconds to detect that he, as a Cabinet minister, was not in any way happy to be treated by DTI's official as if he were a member of the team under his command. Christopher's antennae were not quite sensitive enough. Some sharp words had to be exchanged, MacGregor had to lay it on the line that in Lord Young's absence he was now the head of the British delegation. He would be happy to be briefed on matters outside his normal area of action, but he was now in charge. Christopher swallowed hard.

As the week went on, there were a few more sessions for ministers but for much of the time discussion was between officials, picking over this and that contentious issue. When it came to agriculture, Christopher Roberts was happy to leave it to me. All the more so as a couple of times the discussions on agriculture dragged on well into the night. Agriculture experts were well known to be seasoned to that but Christopher wanted to keep his regular hours. After one of those night-time sessions I went back to my hotel room around four or five in the morning and was getting into bed when I heard a sort of moaning and scratching somewhere just outside my room. I opened my door cautiously, to see a woman with Inuit features, obviously very drunk, stumbling along, propping herself against the wall as she went. I and John MacGregor and his private secretary had rooms close together, his more or less opposite mine. To my horror this drunken woman came to the door of MacGregor's room, opened it and stumbled in, closing the door behind her. My immediate suspicion was that we might have some form of terrorist on our hands. These were times of IRA attacks. The bombing of the Conservative party in conference in Brighton had happened not long before. But the situation might be less threatening... I went to the private secretary's room and we consulted. She slipped into MacGregor's room and came back saying he wanted to deal with the situation himself! He did so, and no harm in the end was done.

The same could not be said of the egg crisis, which did harm in equal measure to the British egg industry, to the Treasury (in compensation payments) and to Edwina Currie whose ministerial career ended there. She, however, showed remarkable powers of reinventing herself, as novelist, TV talking head, and close companion for a time to John Major.

No lasting harm was done to GATT and the Uruguay Round through those distractions that befell us in Montreal. A sequel meeting of ministers was held at the Heysel Stadium in Brussels two years later, an even more bleak scene than Montreal in chilly December drizzle had been. Negotiations were not ripe. Progress that was eventually made on agriculture required, on the EC side, that the EC should decide for itself how to reform its system before signing up to reductions by all parties. No French government would ever submit to reducing support for farmers under transparent pressure from non-Europeans, least of all the Americans, or Australians – les Anglo-Saxons. That scenario took more time.

So the only significant part I played at the Heysel, as I remember, was to hide in a corner, posing as a doorman, in a session of EC member states which had been restricted to one person per delegation – so sensitive was the matter judged to be. My furtive part was to take notes of that discussion and slide them out of a door to a waiting colleague from UKRep who turned them into telegrams back to London to keep HMG informed. Those dark arts of filtering information in and out of tense tightly controlled negotiations – we British did that perhaps with more derring-do than others. The story of John Kerr hiding under the table at one of John Major's summit meetings, which may sound far-fetched to the uninitiated, has the ring of truth to me.

By mid-1991 with the Uruguay Round stretching way ahead into the future and a new phase of CAP reform taking shape, my time in this post was about to come to an end. It remains only to mention that seismic changes were taking place further east in Europe, with the fall of the Berlin Wall and the collapse of communism. John Gummer's dash to Berlin to ride the tide of euphoria is a story I tacked on to my chapter about Berlin. In Whitehall, we struggled to absorb the magnitude of what was happening and what impact it would have on the EC's policies. The best brains from all around Whitehall sitting in sessions in the Cabinet Office wildly over-estimated the speed with which the two parts of Germany would knit together, and badly miscalculated the way in which German views on, inter alia, the CAP would be changed. Not for the first or last time we misjudged the strength of Germany's commitment to France and essential French interests.

This post was the basis for my being appointed a few years later to the post at the Cabinet Office which we come to in chapter 11, and the basis for my being appointed when I had run out of options in MAFF to the post in DTI which we come to in chapter 13. So, important career value had been building up for me from these four years in EC Group. Whether I added value to the work to the same extent that the work delivered value for me is not so easy to assess. A management consultant might look for the value of the decisions I took, but decision-taking was not my primary role. My contribution was the coordination in-house of complex and constantly shifting strands of business, the application of judgment, and the explaining outside, in and around Whitehall and Westminster, of complex issues to non-experts. Explaining the essence of complicated issues is perhaps not a bad basis for decision-taking. How well I really did in my explaining role can be partially assessed from the printed record of House of Lords committee proceedings. It felt at the time as if I had matched up to some testing occasions.

10

FISHERIES

In the summer of 1991 I was moved from the post in EC Group that I have been describing, to become head of the ministry's Fisheries Department. This was a move decided for me. When it was put to me I protested a little, arguing that I and the ministry would gain if I could stay where I was through to the conclusion of the GATT Uruguay Round negotiations. But the response from higher authority was that those negotiations might run for a lot longer yet, and that view proved right because it was another four years before they ended, with a deal and the creation of the World Trade Organization in place of GATT. The wisdom of management.

The Fisheries Department of what was then MAFF (later Defra) had a long history and was still treated as just a little separate from the ministry's main business, that of farming and food supplies. The head of the fisheries department was known, quaintly, as the Fisheries Secretary. This was the title that I now inherited.

The London-based fisheries staff occupied offices in Smith Square, in Nobel House, that were unusually attractive. They had been originally built for ICI. When ICI was formed as a company in 1926 it took in Nobel Industries Ltd, a specialist company making dynamite and gelignite founded in Scotland by the famous Alfred Nobel who made a large fortune from oil and donated some of that to endow the Nobel prizes, for peace and scientific discoveries. Nobel Industries Ltd gave its name to Nobel House, part of Imperial Chemical House, built in the late 1920s on the north bank of the Thames as a monumental headquarters for the new composite company. This building had some state-of-the-art technology and some touches of supreme elegance. These included a lift plated in special alloy, reserved for top management; some eighth-floor offices with fine vaulted and decorated plaster ceilings and, a floor or two below this, some more modest rooms panelled with limed Austrian oak. Into one of those I now moved. From my windows I had a stunning view of the

Thames between Lambeth and Westminster Bridges. This made quite a change from the sturdy 1950s offices in Whitehall Place which I was leaving behind. My trusted secretary Val moved with me. This made the transition easier for me. She and I puzzled out the new job together. Val had an office next to mine, equally beautifully panelled, which she shared with the secretary of the Chief Inspector of Fisheries.

The change of work was refreshing, if daunting at first. There was a much larger management challenge. I was in charge of several hundred people: four or five 'divisions' of policymakers all based in Nobel House; an inspectorate whose two or three senior managers were based where I was but with the rest, a hundred or so, spread all around the coast of England and Wales (my writ did not run in Scotland) at fishing ports. Most important was an internationally respected group of scientists, about 100 in all, experts in fisheries conservation and the marine environment. Their work centred on a large laboratory at Lowestoft on the easternmost headland of the Suffolk coast (housed partly in a former Edwardian Grand Hotel and Palais de Danse), with three smaller laboratories in Essex, Dorset and North Wales. Along with the management responsibilities, the context of work was as different as it could be, the Common Fisheries Policy instead of the Common Agricultural Policy, and an absolute maze of domestic UK rules and regulations. The style of doing business in Brussels and the nature of the UK industry and its leading personalities were all different too.

I can remember that for the first week or two when I started – it was fortunately August, holiday season, with activity in London and Brussels at a low ebb – Val and I spread out papers in little piles along a long table, and puzzled over them. It was hard to know where to start, what to do.

In the nature of Whitehall work, events soon solve that sort of question. When it comes to a committee of enquiry, the lawyers assume that no official ever acts, or should act, without complete understanding of what he or she is doing, and after careful assessment of the options. If only. Quite commonly, action has to be taken under time pressure, whether or not you fully understand what you are doing. This is all the more true when you are new to a job. You assess what is needed as best you can, and rely heavily on advice from those around you; your colleagues and maybe outside advisers. If your superior seems to know what is wanted, you go with that. If it is for you to decide, you take advice from your team, and maybe from people outside the team; trying always to keep in mind that the outsiders who present themselves as your advisers will be acting in pursuit of their own interests, quite probably working against the interests of others (in fisheries this was regularly so). You learn by trial and error whose advice to rely on, whose to mistrust and question. The quality of your decisions improves as time goes on. Fortunately inside a government department there is, normally, a fair degree of team spirit and collective responsibility. Officials among themselves, Ministers too in good times, are not trying to pin down responsibility for every action on any one individual. We reckoned to carry each other along and to make headway by collective effort. If each official refused to associate him/herself with every decision that they did not fully understand, or fully agree with, business would come to a grinding halt.

Certainly in my first few weeks as Fisheries Secretary I leaned heavily on support from above and below. From above? I was the senior adviser on fishing matters to the minister responsible, at that time David Curry. I was I think for the first time in my career in the situation of being responsible for advising a minister who knew more about it than I did. David Curry had been in his post for a year or two. He was a fast learner (a former Financial Times journalist, and a member of the European Parliament before he was elected to Westminster). He was a congenial person to work with. He could be quick-tempered and sharp-tongued (I can match that), but he was understanding of my need to get up to speed on a wholly new subject, and gave me some leeway to do it. We pretty soon formed a comfortable working partnership. In this we were very much helped by David Curry's private secretary, Stephen Hunter. Stephen had come into the administrative civil service by a scientific route quite closely related to fisheries. He had done a doctorate on Great Skuas at South Georgia; he had the look of an arctic explorer, bearded and a bit weather-beaten; and he went down well on our visits to fishing ports. David Curry and I had equal respect for his abilities, and as Stephen and I shared a serious interest in birds we became good friends and have kept in touch ever since. He, his minister and I got on well together.

What the work was like

Working on fisheries could be depressing. I am sure if I had stayed at it for longer I would have found it so. There is much to grieve about.

Humans have been greedily running down the stocks of fish, and mammals, in the seas around Europe and North America since the Middle Ages. The early descriptions of the abundance of fish, and marine life, are almost unbelievable to read now. They show how much has been lost, some of it beyond the point of no return; species have been driven to extinction. Fish can, sometimes, build up their numbers again from very low levels. But sometimes they can't, because we and our over-fishing have upset the balance between species too much. This process of over-exploitation of fish in the sea which has been going on for centuries is still going on, and accelerating. The hunt for fish is driven by the human appetite for fish, powered by technology which advanced by leaps and bounds in the twentieth century, and is made almost impossible to bring under control because of the freedom that fishermen have out at sea, and the keen competition between fishing nations.

Is the picture any different with farming? Over the twentieth century there were huge advances in technology for agriculture: the power of machines in combination with vast application of chemicals enabled farmers worldwide to produce far larger quantities of food than ever before. Whole new areas of the world were taken into agriculture, by clearance of forests and draining of wetlands. This process certainly had its damaging side. In the UK we record, and regret, the loss of bird numbers, butterflies, bees and wildflowers from farmed land. This may not be quite irreversible but there is not much reason to expect that intensive technology-driven farming will ease back. We need the food. And measures taken to make farming more friendly to wildlife are only marginal – literally, in most cases a matter of tweaking the margins of fields – and have so far produced results in terms of more wildlife which can only with a touch of generosity be described as marginally successful. Yet that picture of intensive agriculture and its impacts is not wholly depressing, because the output of food is very positive. There are people who think that we cannot continue for much longer to extract so much food from the land; that the land will impose a day of reckoning. And their view *may* turn out to be right. But so far, so good, in terms of food production.

Whereas, going back to fish, all the signs are negative, all the indicators are at amber or red. The number of fish in the sea is getting smaller; the individual fish caught by fishermen are smaller; with just a few local, short-lived exceptions. Marine life is being wrecked – notably by the effects of heavy nets being scraped across the sea-bed (beam trawling). Birds that feed on fish are beginning to decline (after a century when some species did extremely well out of the waste thrown overboard by fishermen at sea). The vast quantities of plastic that find their way into the sea are killing birds that swallow it, and probably harming birds and other creatures in more insidious ways too. We are turning the once fabulous variety and quantity of life in the sea into nothing more than a soup of jellyfish.

It is all downhill for the fishermen too. Farmers get fewer, as fewer can produce more. Fishermen get fewer and fewer, and struggle to produce as much fish for the table this year as last. As the fish get fewer they support fewer livelihoods. This is reflected, certainly in Britain, by the state of fishing communities around our coasts. Fishing ports that one hundred and two hundred years ago were places of drama, with a strong sense of community, and some money – like Lowestoft, a hub of the east coast herring industry – now an empty harbour. Yarmouth, a few miles up the coast, the same – except that it has an excellent little museum 'Time and Tide' which commemorates how life was when herring fishing was at its height. Hull and Grimsby were home to fleets of deep-sea trawlers which conducted major operations around Iceland and off North Norway. The cod wars of the 1960s more or less shut them down. Hull, when I visited, had only three to four large trawlers left. Smaller ports like Fleetwood and Hastings are just vestiges of what they once were[1]. Brixham in Devon is holding its own. Newlyn in Cornwall, livelier, thanks in part to one dominant entrepreneurial family; but shifting from one target species to another, the fish unable to keep pace with the power behind the fishing.

---

1 As an aside, in the fishing port of Polperro on the south coast of Cornwall is a renovated old fish market hall which was officially opened by me on 17 June 1992. The plaque on the wall recording this ceremonial act has been well tended and the building looked to be in active use when Poppy and I revisited in July 2017, 25 years on. This plaque is the most durable record of my career.

Does this sound depressing? I visited all these places in the course of two years' work and they were sad places, with their history and their atmosphere of places that had known better days. To this the fishing industry added an atmosphere of permanent internal warfare. Much more than the farmers, the fishermen were constantly warring among themselves: groups using different sized boats, and different types of fishing gear, chasing after different types of fish, working at different distances out from the coast. These groups cut across one another, one group working at the expense of another. So some of the time of officials and ministers was taken up listening to grievances, adjudicating between warring factions, trying to devise rules that would protect the smaller from the larger operators and allow each to have a slice, or some crumbs, from a cake which was getting smaller and smaller.

One answer to the conservation of fish lies in science, and fisheries scientists. We were very well served with scientific data on three levels. We had, as I have mentioned, a large number of our own scientists at our own laboratories; they were in theory a UK resource but Scotland had its own; then each EC country with fishing interests had a similar system, and the data from these countries was drawn together for the EC as a whole by the European Commission; and over and above this was an international organisation, the International Council for the Exploration of the Seas (ICES), which had a long history and a high reputation, and they too had a staff of expert fisheries scientists who vetted all the data passed to them by the wide range of their member countries, and they assembled it year by year into the most authoritative overall picture of the state of fish stocks.

All this data, of very high quality, was designed to be the basis for governments, the people in control of the fishing fleets, to take decisions which would prevent over-fishing. There were two fundamental reasons why this didn't happen. Firstly, fishermen have voices and votes; no-one spoke up for the fish. Secondly, fishermen out at sea are very difficult to keep under control. It was not completely true that no-one spoke up for the fish. The scientists did – but they trod carefully. They were wary of pushing their arguments too hard in case decision-takers disregarded them altogether. Conservationists also spoke up for the fish, and environmental NGOs including the powerful bird NGOs have stepped up their pressure for a better deal for fish. I think their lobbying has become stronger and more effective in the past 20 years than it was at the time when I was Fisheries Secretary. Last but not least Prince Charles through his Sustainability Unit at Clarence House has done excellent work in highlighting the problems and testing out solutions here and there in the world, though he has prudently steered clear of taking on the EU. His work again has I think gained in strength and effectiveness more recently. I was certainly not aware of it in the 1990s.

This is the big picture. Most of the time in our day-to-day work we were struggling with more detailed issues: specific bits of the Common Fisheries Policy, the European system for pegging back a dozen competing fishing fleets by means of a vast web of rules and regulations on size and design of nets, limits (quotas) on total numbers of each fish species that could be caught and landed.

Some of the rules were more easily enforced than others. There was always the difficulty of keeping track of what fishermen were doing out at sea. Instruments for recording where boats had been, and where they had been fishing, was just being tested, making use of GPS satellite technology, which was not at that time in widespread use as it is now. Alongside this was a fair amount of straight cheating by the fishermen: concealing of catches, falsification of records, selling on the black market. Accusations of cheating were always fiercely contested. But going to sea to catch fish has a very long tradition of attracting tough people who value their freedom, and respect for the letter of the law and for fine-grained rules and regulations is not what draws them into the job.

David Curry and I went about our work with evidence all around us that the EC system as it was, was not doing enough; and that tougher measures were needed to conserve fish stocks. David Curry tried to run ahead of the pack, by imposing some home-grown UK limits on the number of days each boat could spend at sea in a year. There was logic to this approach but his efforts showed up the problems one country runs into if it tries to run ahead of what the rest are doing, in an area of economic activity which is already subject to European law. We spent a lot of time on the legal difficulty of running home-grown rules alongside EC rules. And there was a great deal of anger from the fishermen that 'their' minister should be making life harder for them than it was for their competitors.

The UK has run into this difficulty a number of times in its membership of the EC/EU. Over beef in the 1970s, over agri-environment in the 1980s/1990s. Sometimes, the bright ideas that we pioneered were in due course taken up and stitched (sometimes for better, sometimes for worse) into the fabric of an EU system. But there were no prizes for having the bright idea and going out in front. On the contrary.

As for the idea of limiting days at sea, I am not sure whether it was ever seriously taken up for the CFP, but in 1991-2 we gave ourselves a lot of trouble trying to pioneer it. Trouble in the sense of hours of work with lawyers, and in Parliament; trouble in the sense of taking flak from the fishermen. David Curry and I attending one major annual conference of English fishermen came under fire from flour bombs. It was a new experience for, I think, both of us. Luckily the fishermen's aim was not much good – and eggs would have been harder to brush off.

When we were not in argument with English fishermen we were in argument with Scottish ministers and officials. I had not, up till then, worked in any job where conflict with Scotland was so real. It was not without reason. By the 1990s the Scottish sea fishing industry was markedly bigger than the English; long distance trawling, up to the Arctic off Norway, was going strong from Peterhead and Fraserburgh. Scotland had also a fish farming industry not matched in England. By the early 1990s salmon farming had sprouted along the west coast of Scotland and on some of the islands. The total value of all this activity may not have been great but it was creating jobs in remote places where there was little else to do, so it mattered politically. There was running tension with Norway over the price at which farmed salmon was being sold, and constant claims from our side that the Norwegian firms were being subsidised, and were therefore 'dumping' their produce on the British market. There was tension with Norway over rights of British (but mostly Scottish) trawlers to fish in Norwegian waters too. The Scots ministers and companies in Scotland were on the sharp end of these issues, but the constitutional position in 1991-2 (this was pre-devolution) was that the government at Westminster, i.e. MAFF ministers and officials, led in international discussions on fishing matters. When we went to Brussels for EC meetings a Scottish minister would always come with us for a Council of Ministers, but David Curry was in the lead. This caused usually only mild tension.

The most acute tension I can remember was when I had to appear before a House of Commons committee on some fishing subject, and my counterpart from Edinburgh insisted on sitting beside me and sharing in the answering of questions from MPs. There were two problems about this, one a matter of substance, and one of style. On substance as far as I remember we did not actually contradict one another; it was more that when I had said something that dealt with a question my Scottish friend wanted to have his say too, even if he was simply saying much the same as I had. It was perhaps his style which made me more uncomfortable. The habit at Westminster then as now is for civil servants to preserve a degree of formality when appearing in front of a parliamentary committee: the 'servant' part of civil servant has a touch of significance here. Habits in Edinburgh then as now were really quite different: ministers, Members of the Scottish Assembly, civil servants – all much on a level, and pulling together, against a common enemy down south. My friend beside me brought the Edinburgh style of operating to this Westminster occasion, talking more informally and chattily than I would. Taken all together, the MPs (as some told me afterwards) found it amusing to watch the mis-fit between us. It was symptomatic, though, of a constitutional arrangement over fisheries which did not fit the facts, and which devolution subsequently re-set.

Meetings of ministers of fisheries were held less often than the meetings of agriculture ministers. The major event of the annual calendar was a meeting at the very end of the year, to agree quotas for the year ahead. The annual process of collecting data on the current state of fish stocks, and the timetable for meetings of scientists first at EC and then international level to comb through the data and formulate advice to governments on what the safe levels of catch would be, pushed the crucial meeting of EC ministers right up close to the end of the year. It was nearly always the very last meeting of ministers of any variety in Brussels before Christmas. The fishermen's leaders all travelled to Brussels and stayed in hotels close to the Council of Ministers building. The group from each country expected 'their' minister to call on them while the negotiations were in progress, so that they could expose him/her afresh to their special pleading. So there was some time pressure and a touch of drama. But decisions were always reached in the nick of time; by stretching scientists' advice a bit, thereby giving more to the fishermen, at the expense of the fish. (In corresponding situations on agriculture it would be more for the farmers at the expense of taxpayers.)

Ministers met at one or two other times of year; one of these a so-called 'Informal'. These Informal meetings were usually held in the country that was currently holding the Presidency of the EC. The one that sticks in my mind was held I suppose in spring 1992, hosted by Germany. This was quite soon after west and east Germany had been reunited. The German minister wanted to show us... what? His new possessions in the east? This was a man who believed that Danzig (Gdansk, a city lying deep in Poland since 1945) should still by rights be in Germany. How do I know? He sat next to me as he held forth about that to one of his colleagues. Germans do assume that no-one else understands when they chat to each other in German. However, for public consumption the reason was to show us the scale of economic problems in the former east Germany.

We were to travel to the Baltic coast, and to the fishing port of Stralsund, opposite the island of Rügen. It is hard to imagine today, but there was no fast means of transporting a group – we were probably about 60 in all, ministers each with a senior official and private secretary, and the hosts – to that area. Our host had opted for flying us into Lübeck and taking us on from there in two huge Russian military helicopters. Two big egg-shaped khaki shells. Comfortable, they were not. We sat strapped to the outer metal shell; vibration and noise; conversation impossible. The helicopters flew low over the ground, so when you could get to see out of a window you caught glimpses of countryside, roads, villages, all looking much as they would have looked 60 years before. Untouched at best since the 1930s or less fortunately since the 1940s, showing the wreckage of war. We were on a voyage back in time.

Stralsund: what I remember most clearly is a visit to a fish processing plant, where various tinned fish products were being made on ancient dilapidated canning machinery. It all worked but the question our German hosts kept coming back to was: who will buy these products? We didn't know, and the Germans had hardly digested the situation, but the answer was: soon no-one would. These factories were finished. We were seeing the start of the collapse of the old East German economy, once the pride of the Soviet bloc. Now nearly all swept away.

We crossed from Stralsund to Rügen, the island of Caspar David Friedrich and the most famous white cliffs east of Dover. The place where we were all put up for a night was a hotel – but more than a hotel. It had been a holiday retreat and safe house for the communist party bosses up until a couple of years earlier. It was set in large grounds that had been rigorously protected against any intrusion by citizens foolish enough to want a glimpse of their rulers. We heard guard dogs baying in the surrounding woodland at night. Had anyone told the guards that the regime had changed?

This was a vivid insight into the dereliction that the Soviets had in part purposefully perpetuated in Germany as punishment for war, but also the hollowness of the economy that they thought they had installed there to serve them.

Familiarisation

I said that I wanted to go out on a fisheries protection vessel. Partly because I do like going to sea, however uncomfortable the sea conditions may be, even though I am not immune from sea-sickness (any more than Nelson was). But partly – and this was my 'official' reason – because the fisheries protection operations came under my responsibility; they were part of my command. I had made a practice as Chief Regional Officer in Wolverhampton of dipping as widely as I could into the activities of the staff who came under me, and I was wanting to do the same in Fisheries. You cannot otherwise complain if your staff make light of any attempts you make to influence how they go about their job, and feel able to pull the wool over your eyes when it suits them.

The main work of fisheries protection at sea, out to the limits of British territorial waters, was carried out in the 1990s by Royal Navy minesweepers, the ships and their crews being assigned to this work for a year or so, between other duties. These days the ships used by the Navy are specialist 'River Class' vessels, but at the time I am writing about they were minesweepers. The captains and their crews found it an interesting alternative to their regular naval work. It guaranteed constant activity and time at sea. There have been times, not so long ago, when fisheries protection was primarily about protecting British fishing vessels from assault by or interference from vessels of other nationalities. In the 1960s, around Iceland, that is very much what it was about. By the 1990s the work was as much, if not more, about policing of the rules of the EC's Common Fisheries Policy; the limits on the sizes and quantities of fish caught, and the types of fishing gear allowed. So really fisheries protection was more about prevention of fishermen from overfishing – protection of fish from the fishermen – than about protecting of fishermen from each other. But both types of work could come into the day's duty, and the Navy quite relished it.

I let my interest be known, and one afternoon I travelled down to Brixham in Devon and stayed in a little sea-front hotel recommended by the local Sea Fisheries Inspector. The next morning came, the weather was doing nothing in particular, I walked to the harbour where I was to be picked up. Now, it became clear after an hour or so that the captain of the minesweeper that I was to join had an agenda. He had a man from Whitehall in his sights and he was going to test that man's seaworthiness – to the limit. But standing on the harbour side waiting to be picked up I had been given no reason to suspect this.

The minesweeper was moored offshore. An inflatable manned by a couple of sailors was sent in to fetch me and take me on board. The tide was quite low, so when this inflatable came to the harbour wall, it was several feet below those of us standing waiting. The sailors switched off their motor, or it cut out. They were a little too energetic in trying to restart it. It spluttered and immediately cut out again. Now anyone with experience of a small petrol engine, on a garden motor mower for instance, knows that it is quite easy to flood the motor. There is a stage when it is better to pause for a few minutes than to keep pulling on the starter cord. Our sailors missed their moment for pausing, kept pulling, and the fumes of petrol from an unmistakeably flooded motor floated up to us on the harbour wall. The group of people which had consisted of me, the Sea Fisheries Inspector and not much more, gradually grew in number. This was becoming interesting: two sailors in uniform having trouble with their boat. Embarrassment set in down there; the sailors radioed to their mother ship for help; and a second inflatable was sent over. The little crowd of by-standers had a laugh or two, at the expense of the Royal Navy. The day had not started well for the Captain.

I was welcomed on board the grey minesweeper and given a quick look around, and a briefing on the plans for the day. The ship meanwhile moved off to sea. The plan was to head out to the middle of the English Channel (which is fairly wide between the coast of Devon and the coasts of Normandy and Brittany opposite). It was expected that we would there find a mixture of trawlers, of British and other nationalities, to check over. After an hour or so it was declared time for lunch, and I was shown to the Captain's dining room. He, his two or three senior officers and I sat down at a comfortable dining table, and a chicken curry was served. We were by now well out at sea. The sea was by no means rough but we were definitely riding what is technically known as a 'swell' – broad rolling waves, so that our ship was rising and falling, rolling slightly with the waves, in a regular rhythm. And chicken curry? I was beginning to detect the agenda.

The Captain, after some polite opening remarks, turned the conversation fairly quickly to whether all this was a new experience for me. Had I ever been on a naval vessel before? Seeing a need to look after my reputation, I said after a pause for effect: 'I think the first time was in 1946'. Now, this Captain will have been around 30, his officers about the same; so, born around 1960. I don't think I looked to them as though I had been born in the 1940s. They clearly judged my claim absurd. From the sceptical looks on their faces I could see that I needed to explain. So I told them the story of how I had travelled down to Devonport to meet my father on his return from the Far East at the end of the war; and of how I could just remember being taken to play with the ship's dog. This, my mention of the dog, though I did not know it, was proof to them of the validity of my story. That's right, they gasped, the Navy was indeed allowed to carry dogs during wartime, a measure to keep the troops happy. That had been a special relaxation of the rules; an exception from the strict prohibition on carrying dogs on ships that applied before and after the war, because of the risk of rabies.

This was something of a reverse for the Captain and his plan – rounds 1 and 2 to me – but he didn't let up. After lunch, my tour of the ship continued with a visit to the engine room. This involved much climbing up and down ladders and over bulkheads, with the chicken curry feeling rather restless, not at all helped by the smell of engine oil everywhere.

I may by now have looked a little pale. Anyway the Captain stepped up the pressure. The ship had arrived in our target area; various fishing vessels were in view; it was time for action stations. His proposal – but I don't remember being offered any alternative – was that I should join a boarding party which was to go from our ship across the water to a nearby beam trawler, go on board and check its catch for compliance with the rules.

I was lowered with two sailors into the inflatable, which seemed a lot smaller and more fragile out here in mid-Channel than it had done at the harbourside, and we chugged across open sea towards the trawler. It was not far, but far enough for the skipper of the trawler to see us coming. Beam trawlers have long poles which stick out either side, from which the mouth of their gigantic net is spread out under water when it is being trawled. Then when the time comes to haul in the net, the beams slowly swing together alongside the boat, drawing the mouth of the net towards the closed position. As we came close to the side, words were exchanged between our crew and the skipper, to the effect that 'you can come aboard if you want, but I am about to haul my nets so you'll have to watch out'. Boarding the fishing boat involved the three of us each choosing our moment to jump from our inflatable; no gang plank or ladder or anything like that, and two boats moving up and down at different rates on the waves. (We did at least have lifejackets.) Once on board we were left to make what checks we wanted on the fish already in the hold. I was a mere spectator while this inspection was made. My self-control was at full stretch now, under assault from the combined smells of fish and diesel, and the mid-Channel swell. I can't remember much from then on, except that I survived, chicken curry still in place all the way back to Brixham. The voyage back to port was a blur. But I reckon I won the battle of the day.

This, however, was a tame experience by comparison with what some of the fishermen themselves went through. The picture I have given of our fishing ports is of run-down operations and former glories. The English deep-sea fishing fleet had indeed shrunk from hundreds to about half a dozen vessels by the 1990s, shared between Hull and Grimsby. But they did serious fishing. I went on board one super-modern trawler in Hull, a large ship with bridge and control room high above the water. We were shown the state-of-the-art radar equipment with which the ship could track down shoals of fish in deep water. Looking around, I noticed a window cracked from one side to the other and I asked how that had happened. 'Oh, a wave' the shipowner said. Now, we were high above the water, and the windows on the bridge were clearly of reinforced glass. I could not quite understand. 'It must have been an exceptionally high wave.' 'No, no, the ship rolls, it will have rolled on its side and come down on the water, but they right themselves.' '!' Fishing in seas as rough as that is not for the faint-hearted.

Pushy neighbours

Some of my lively experiences were contributed by the Spanish. Spain's entry into the EC was still fairly recent and the terms of their Accession agreement had included restrictions on where the Spanish could fish for a number of years. The Spanish people have a vast appetite for fish, and to supply this there is a large fishing fleet – the modern-day Spanish word for it is 'armada', and the ship owners are 'armadores'. Foreseeing the potential of this fleet to hit the shared fisheries in EC waters hard, the other member states had imposed restrictions. Note: the very opposite of the approach they had taken when Britain joined in 1973, when the Six had moved smartly to set up in advance a common policy which would oblige the UK to let their fishing fleets make inroads into the rich fishing grounds in the seas around the UK.

Spain was on the prowl. I found myself on the receiving end of a charm offensive from my Spanish opposite number. He, fittingly, was a larger-than-life character who would not have been out of place on the poop deck of a Spanish galleon: Rafael Condé de Soro, from an elite Spanish family (his brother held a senior post in the Spanish diplomatic service). He radiated energy and had a vast appetite for food and drink; both.

I first met him in Madrid where on one occasion I remember we started work in his office around 11 or 12 and worked through until 4 or 5 before breaking off – for lunch. Spanish eating hours come as a jolt for us northern Europeans.

On another occasion I and, I think, my Scottish counterpart were both invited to see the home of the Spanish deep-sea fleet at Vigo, on the coast of Galicia. This involved stopping off at the cathedral of Santiago de Compostela with its terrifying censer swung lethally on the end of what seems like a thirty-foot chain. At Vigo we were taken out on a Spanish fisheries research vessel for a sail up one of the Rias Baixas. The main point of this seemed to be to eat and drink. Sherry and shellfish and crustaceans were served from mid-morning, in unlimited quantities – but this was only the preparation for lunch. At some point we were decanted and taken round the fish market and harbour at Vigo. The size of the boats was staggering. These were bigger than anything I had seen in Britain, where we have only the left-overs of a once powerful deep-sea fleet on Humberside and at Peterhead. The vast extent of the market was staggering too. These were ships, ships not boats, that roamed the Atlantic north, south, east and west to gather fish for the consumers of Madrid.

Our day –or was it two days – ended with a dinner at which fishermen were present. My buccaneering counterpart Rafael Condé ate and drank freely. We all peeled off to bed very late, but at breakfast next morning it was clear that our Rafael was none the worse for wear and had indeed been up hours before us, down on the market continuing discussions with 'his' fishermen.

That man was a force to be reckoned with – and backer of a fishing fleet that caused us considerable trouble as it progressively turned its attentions to British waters. I only once saw Condé a little confused, when I took him to Shetland. As we drove across the mainland of Shetland, with views of the sea opening up now to the left, now to the right, the indents and voes coming and going, he seemed genuinely bemused. I guess because Spain has a square sort of geography. If you are on the Atlantic coast the sea is always in one direction, if you are on the Mediterranean coast it is in the other direction; pretty much in straight lines. In Shetland it was here, there and everywhere. This seemed to be a new experience for him. (Then he had not been in the Falklands!) Being fogbound at Aberdeen airport was probably a new experience too. We were able to give him that twice.

For a time in 1992 the Navy received quite a battering from the French, but despite the Navy's earlier attempt to humiliate me I was firmly on their side in that episode. It was England against France – a continuation, really, of the Hundred Years War.

The epicentre of the trouble was Guernsey. For the most part there is an agreed 'median line' all down the English Channel; the boundary between UK and French territorial waters, agreed and recognised by the two countries, and in international law. But some time during 1992 a group of French fishing boats working out of ports near Cherbourg, on the Cotentin peninsula, had taken to fishing in a small area of sea known, because of its shape on the map, as the 'haricot' or bean. This bit of sea in our view belonged to Guernsey and therefore ultimately to the UK. But the French fishermen had started to contest this, and were regularly coming in and fishing there. The Guernsey authorities decided that enough was enough, but did not have the strength to push the French out. It needs to be explained that Guernsey and the other Channel Islands each have their own little fisheries inspectorate and protection service and, in normal times, carry out for themselves the enforcement of the local fisheries regulations, which each island makes. But the UK Government is ultimately responsible for safeguarding the Channel Islands against foreign attack (unsuccessfully when the Germans invaded in WWII); and as part of this the UK gives back-up to the islands' fisheries protection service if ever it is needed. It was needed now. So we sent at first one, and by the end three, RN minesweepers to deal with the incursion.

It was not easily dealt with. The French fishermen whipped themselves up into collective excitement, as French fishermen and farmers very readily do. This led, after a bit of posturing, to quite a serious international incident. A Royal Navy training vessel put in to Cherbourg on what was intended as a goodwill visit, planned some time before. This went badly wrong when a bunch of the local fishermen stormed on board and trapped the unfortunate trainees below deck, and took charge of the vessel for several hours. Now this was an insult to the Navy; lèse-majesté; not a matter to be shrugged off.

We had counsels of war in London. We first had to make quite sure of our legal position. Did the contested bit of water really belong to us or to France? The place to go to check this was the Foreign Office Legal Department, where charts are held to show the precise limits of our territorial waters. We found the relevant map of median lines in the Channel, and I studied it carefully with the Foreign Office legal adviser. It was fascinating. The 'line' was made up of many different stretches of line, each stretch dated, recording when agreement had been signed and sealed between Britain and France over many many years, painfully slowly. The earliest bits of dating went back to the middle ages, other bits to the seventeenth and eighteenth centuries, and there were interludes which matched the long periods when Britain and France were at war. When it came to the position around Guernsey, there were lines on the map, with the haricot sitting on the UK/Channel Islands side of the line, though it was not crystal clear that the line around the haricot had been sealed by any treaty agreement. However, it did look to be ours.

Ministers had to discuss what action we should take. I attended a tense discussion in a small room in the House of Commons, between the minister of agriculture and fisheries, then John Gummer, and the minister for war. John Gummer, keen as ever to get stuck in, suggested that now we had a minesweeper or two on station we should simply ram any offending French boat and send it packing. The War Minister went slightly pale: 'God, no!' he said, 'Do you know what the hull of a minesweeper is made of? Fibreglass, so as not to set off mines. In any collision with a fishing boat, it would be the fishing boat that would come off better.' So that bright idea had to be rejected. We settled for a cat-and-mouse approach, until one of our minesweepers could corner the most flagrant offender (a boat named Calypso), board it and make an arrest.

By now we had three – the full fleet – of minesweepers at Guernsey. And the Navy was out to settle the score. A week or so passed. Then one day... I was on my way home from London to Bedford on the train. We did not, in those far-off days, have mobile phones. The phone rang at home and Poppy picked up the call. It was the captain of one of our minesweepers: I have the Calypso in my reach. What do you want me to do? Poppy had to tell the captain that I was expected home soon, and he would have to hold on for his instructions. I don't think he had to wait long, but then my instruction to him was to give me a few minutes to prepare the way. Relations between the French and British governments were really quite brittle by now and it was essential to avoid springing any surprises that might upset relations further.

So I lifted the phone and rang the office of the French fisheries minister, and asked to speak to his chef (who by then I must have known quite well). I gave him this short message: I am ringing to inform you that we are about to arrest one of your fishing vessels, the Calypso, in Guernsey waters; I am not asking for any reaction from you, simply giving you the information. That message given, I rang back to the captain of the minesweeper and instructed him to go ahead and make the arrest. Which he did. The Calypso was taken in to St Peter Port in Guensey, where I think the skipper was given a fine, or they may have detained his boat and sent him back home without it. I can't remember. Anyway, everyone soon calmed down. And is the haricot still treated as Guernsey water?

Moving on

This brings us close to the end of my two years in Fisheries. Over my last few months in the post, I gave much time to a review of the fisheries research programme. There was a need to cut costs. I looked thoroughly at all the research that was being done at our four laboratories; partly at my desk in London, partly in discussion with the top team of scientists at Lowestoft. It was not easy to piece together quite why the scientists were doing all that they were doing. I hope I can say it without the comment seeming either lofty ('the two cultures') or malicious: it was ever the case that when I tried to puzzle out the fundamental relationship between the work being done in MAFF's laboratories and the reasons why the taxpayer should be paying for it – it was not too hard for the scientists in charge to blind me with science. It was the same later when I engaged with the veterinary laboratories.

I think I was on quite firm ground with the conclusions I drew from this review of what was going on in our fisheries labs. It appeared to me that some rather expensive work was being done on what you might call 'deep blue seas' research. That is to say, some fairly abstract projects about the influences on numbers of fish in the sea, work which was costing a lot in part because of the extent to which it needed to be done out at sea, on research vessels. It was expensive to keep these vessels at sea, and the scientific work that needed to be done in the finite amount of time these ships spent at sea was the most expensive work in the programme. The work which mattered most to us was the quite practical work of monitoring the size of the stocks of fish which were most sought after by our fishing fleet: monitoring the number of fish in the sea, where they were, and how their numbers and sizes were changing from year to year. Going back to the origin of our Lowestoft laboratory at the very beginning of the twentieth century, this had always been the main work. It still mattered most. There had been a quite understandable drift from this towards high-end theoretical questions. For the most intelligent and deep-thinking of our scientific team, those were more interesting questions to work on than the collection of data about fish numbers. But did we really need to be spending so much taxpayers' money as we were? I concluded, not.

So the report I prepared recommended not axing, but reducing, some of the 'blue seas' work. Now, before I had had time to deliver my report and put it into action my next job change came up. I moved out of MAFF on secondment to the Cabinet Office. As one of my last acts before moving, therefore, I handed in my report but had to leave it to my successor and others to decide what to do with it. I know for sure that, to the director and deputy director at Lowestoft this came as a betrayal. It seemed to them that I had acted in bad faith, drawing information out of them about their research programme and then using it to hit them with cost cuts. The cuts I had recommended were, I think, put into effect, though I was not consulted about that. I can remember keeping a copy of my report in a drawer in the Cabinet Office, fully expecting that I would be called back to MAFF to join in a discussion about my proposals. But that didn't happen.

There is no pleasure in telling this part of the story until we come to the after-effect, and what I count as a happy ending. One consequence down the track was that the deputy director at Lowestoft, a fine scientist for whom I had much respect, concluded that his future lay elsewhere. It was he who probably felt his wings clipped most by the cutting back of theoretical research work. Some two or three years later (and when he had missed being appointed to the director post), he upped and moved out of government, and became professor of oceanography at Southampton University. This was a post which actually suited his talents better. It gave him more freedom to do theoretical research, his career as a scientist flourished, and his quality was recognised by his being appointed a Fellow of the Royal Society. I was pleased by this, and I think he and I were able to put the ill-feeling over that review episode behind us when, more than ten years later, I included him in a Consultation at St George's House, Windsor, where we debated reform of the Common Fisheries Policy and he made an authoritative contribution to our gathering.

11

CABINET OFFICE

1993-94

In July 1993 I moved from Fisheries to the Cabinet Office. I had put my name forward for the post of deputy head of the European secretariat, a job which called for wide and deep knowledge of the European Community (it became the European Union only on 1 November 1993). There had been a little competition, I had seen off three or four other candidates, and was looking forward to stepping into a job for which I felt – as the head of the secretariat who appointed me also felt – I had the experience needed. This turned out to be a big change in type of work (bigger than I knew), and with it came a change of scene.

The Cabinet Office presents a stylish face on to Whitehall, the white stone pillared facade which stretches from the end of Downing Street to Dover House, the Scotland Office. This Whitehall frontage of the Cabinet Office was designed by Sir Charles Barry who had by then already designed the Travellers Club in Pall Mall, and went on to design the rebuild of the House of Commons after the 1834 fire. His Cabinet Office was completed in the mid-1840s – but it is only a facade. The building behind is a mixture of rooms large and small, halls and corridors, with bits of the fabric dating back to the early 1500s. You know you are walking with history from the moment you step through the front door.

Passing in from the street you go almost immediately up a flight of steps to a long corridor which runs back between two plain walls. The wall on your left is of brick dating from the Tudor period. It is a remnant of the old royal Palace of Whitehall which Henry VIII made the chief residence of his court in London and a major scene of fun and games. The part of this palace where the Cabinet Office now stands was the sports area. The wall in the entrance corridor was the west wall of the Great Close Tennis Court. Nearer to the front door, to the right, is another piece of Tudor wall, preserved behind glass now, the wall of a Small Tennis Court. The building came to the end of its life as a royal palace after King James II was deposed. Briefly in 1688 James had used it as a prison for the future Queen Anne and Lady Churchill. It was then for a few years a private home for the Churchill family. The whole palace burned down in 1698.

From then on the site was made over to the nation, and it has been at the heart of government ever since. It became a home for the Treasury, designed by William Kent, leading eighteenth century architect who went on to do major work for the prime minister Lord Walpole at his great private house in Norfolk, Houghton Hall. At the far end of the Tudor entrance corridor[1], just to the right, is a large conference room which was part of Kent's Treasury building. Now 'Conference Room A', it was designed in the 1730s as the Treasury's Board Room. It is still in routine use by ministers and officials, fitted out with a square of modern tables arranged around a huge square wooden table which was part of the original fittings, together with a gigantic throne-like chair from which the First Lord of the Treasury presided. Walpole sat here.

A little further on, towards the back of the present-day building, facing Horse Guards Parade, is the Cabinet Secretary's office, an elegant squarish panelled room, less ancient but just as awe-inspiring. It is from here that the Cabinet Secretary pulls the strings which draw all the various activities of government together; in theory, and by and large in practice.

On the next floor up, the room I knew best was a long elegant high-ceilinged room facing on to Horse Guards Parade: 'Conference Room C'. This room was for many years used by officials for their key discussions of the week on European business. The main furniture was a great long oval table around which 25 or 30 people could be seated. For our more complex discussions we needed that number of places and more. The room was ideal for the purpose, the only drawback being that in the months of May and early June the military bands practised intensively for the Trooping of the Colour on Horse Guards, below our windows, and the vigour with which the bands played could blank out our

---

1 This Tudor corridor was the place where, some six or seven years later, I was handed Tony Blair's personal copy of the Report of the BSE Enquiry, without his knowledge, a few days before it was published, so that I could have a preview and check whether I was about to be sent to the Tower. After a day or so, satisfied that it was not that bad, I met my collaborator in St James's Park and handed the report back to him in a plain brown envelope. In the best traditions of the British secret service.

Euro-discussions for minutes at a time[2]. Rather sadly, when Michael Heseltine was made deputy prime minister, just after my time in the Cabinet Office, he latched on to this room as ideal for his personal use, and even more sadly it was judged that the room was too large even for his expansive self-esteem, and the room was divided into offices for him and another minister, thereby wrecking its elegant proportions.

At the levels above these stately conference rooms, the Cabinet Office becomes a maze of little stairways and passages and offices of varying sizes. It is hard to say which floor my own office was on, because of all the stairs up and down. It was not large but not the pokiest. It had a view of sorts out to the rear of the building. One drawback was that it was within very clear earshot of the clock over the archway between Horse Guards and Whitehall. This clock strikes every quarter of an hour, with a clear sharp chime, utterly destructive of concentration, I found, when one is working against tight deadlines, for instance writing the minutes of Cabinet.

Dropping back down to ground level, close to the Cabinet Secretary's room was the way through from the Cabinet Office to the house next door, 10 Downing Street, barred by a green baize-covered door through which a very restricted number of us had permission (and the required code) to pass.

The long history of government on this site, and the variety of rooms that we worked in, were not just wallpaper to me. It was a consolation on the days when the work seemed overwhelmingly difficult, as it sometimes was, to breathe deeply and feel that, whether on top of the business or not, you were part of the long series of people who have struggled with the effort of governing Britain from this place.

---

2 This room had a balcony overlooking Horse Guards Parade. With permission, I took the family in one Saturday in June 1994 to watch the Trooping of the Colour. We had a much better view from this balcony than anyone in the stands below us. From that extra height we could make sense of the patterns of the guardsmen's complicated manoeuvres, which are not clear at all from down at ground level. We were enjoying this privileged experience thoroughly until an ebullient colleague intruded on our balcony (there was another one) with his children in tow, and proceeded to jig about and make loud conversation. It was no time at all before we heard hammering on the door of the Conference Room, and in burst a security man, who told us off in no uncertain terms, for 'distracting Her Majesty' – 'we were lucky not to have been picked off by one of the snipers positioned on the rooves around the parade ground'. Privileged experience soured. Thanks, A C.

It is a very British muddle. 10 Downing Street is much the same; a mix of state rooms and offices varying between middling and poky. In total contrast to the regal gilt and glitter of the French equivalent, or the bright and gleamingly modern German equivalent. Short on grandeur, our offices at the heart of government help (along with the shouty Westminster parliament) to cut down ministers' pretensions.

What was my new job about? The Cabinet Office is home to an assortment of different tasks, some of which belong there because they span all parts of government, such as efficiency in the working of the civil service, or control of government data or standards in public life; some of which are tacked on because they don't have any obvious home elsewhere in government. However, the core of the Cabinet Office work, and the essence of what the Cabinet Secretary does, is to support the Prime Minister and all his cabinet ministers in their running of the government in an orderly way.

This means taking care of the business which is passed up to Cabinet for discussion, making sure that the problems are only passed up if they really need to be; and that those which need to be are prepared and explained so that ministers can focus on the essential points that they have to decide. It is also the essence of the way in which the Cabinet Office handles this business, following a system which has been evolving since 1916, that ministers (or their officials) from all those parts of government which have an interest in a problem are informed in time to have a say, if they want to, before decisions are taken; and that the same ministers (or their officials) are informed about decisions once taken. So the producing of clear records (minutes) of meetings in quick time was a key part of our work here. The purpose of handling things in this way, which may sound rather cumbersome, is to tie all cabinet ministers in to complying with decisions that are taken – collective responsibility. Many other governments have much larger prime minister's offices than we do, and these countries are often surprised at what a small number of people our prime ministers have to support them. But there is not much point in giving a prime minister a large team of expert advisers at his or her beck and call to supply high quality advice and help in taking high-class decisions if the rest of the government can ignore the PM's decisions, either because they don't know about them or because they simply don't feel committed and may have different priorities. Greece over the

1980s and 1990s was an excellent example of a prime minister who was well supported by personal staff but unable to achieve much in practice because he had no levers to pull, no linkage to make his ministers act on his peerless decisions.

The Cabinet Office system, then, is designed to bring about decisions to which the whole government is committed, and will act on. Of course it doesn't all work smoothly all the time, but that is the purpose.

Where did I fit in? The preparing of business for Cabinet in the way that I have described is handled, day to day, by small teams of Cabinet Office officials, 'secretariats' (there were four of those in my time), reporting to the Cabinet Secretary. He calls together the heads of each of these secretariats or their deputies once a week to discuss what business they think should be put to Cabinet that week, and for the coming three to four weeks, and to slice it into a manageable programme. They each write a very short brief for the prime minister to have in front of him at the weekly Cabinet meeting, so that he knows in his role as chairman what questions to ask, and has some idea what his ministers are talking about.

Every few weeks it fell to me to be one of the four scribes taking minutes of the Cabinet's meeting. For the minute-takers, Cabinet meetings fell into two halves: for the first half the discussion was about domestic affairs, in the second half it was matters foreign and European. The minute-takers worked in pairs and the pairs changed over at half time. So I and my foreign affairs counterpart always slipped into the Cabinet Room with discussion already in progress, and sat down as unobtrusively as possible at the end of the long oval Cabinet table, notebooks in front of us, pens at the ready.

I witnessed no dramas in John Major's Cabinet meetings. He chaired quietly and politely, treating his colleagues with respect (what a contrast with how it all was under Margaret Thatcher!) and discussions seemed pretty inconsequential most of the time. The meeting once over, we were working to a tight deadline to produce our bit of the minutes; which meant reducing our notes of not necessarily coherent or meaningful discussion to a short bland impersonal piece, which had to be clear, and conclusive (if the prime minister had not drawn a conclusion explicitly we had to write into the record what follow-up action was needed and by which department). Also the minutes had to give nothing away about which minister had said what. All for one and one for all.

Our little pieces were sped down to the Cabinet Secretary who moulded them together, and by about tea-time the job was done, lapidary minutes sent round to all members of Cabinet. They were almost never challenged.

One of the four secretariats deals, or dealt then, with European Community business and only European Community business. Very little of the subject matter in this area actually went up to ministers to decide in Cabinet. Fortunately, because the Cabinet Secretary, Robin Butler, was visibly uncomfortable when it did. The issues tended to be complex, frequently unfamiliar to him and the timetable for decisions was always dependent on the timing of meetings in Brussels, not under his control and not amenable to his otherwise orderly scheduling of the agendas for Cabinet. Robin seemed pro-European in outlook but over the whole of his long and glittering career I could see no sign that he engaged closely with the substance of European business. This was sadly quite typical of senior people all across Whitehall, very many of whom I found through to the end of my career deeply ignorant of how the EU worked, and positively averse to getting to know about it. Mostly, however, the European issues were discussed and problems resolved by officials below ministerial – and Cabinet Secretary – level, and the fairly small number of problems that could not be ironed out by officials among themselves were generally passed up to a sub-committee of Cabinet chaired by the Foreign Secretary. Cabinet Office then wrote the brief for the Foreign Secretary, pointing to possible compromises, and I or one of my colleagues would sit beside him to help where needed.

In total, the volume of European business that needed to be discussed by officials was large, and never-ending. The officials' discussions were chaired (except for two specialist areas, trade and agriculture) by the Cabinet Office. The core of my job as deputy head of the European secretariat, was to chair many such discussions, and to attend many others alongside the head of the secretariat (a rather austere man called Geoffrey Fitchew, who had worked in the Treasury and the European Commission). So I spent part of nearly every day chairing a meeting, sometimes two or three in a day. That might sound boring, it might sound simple. It was anything but simple, and only occasionally boring.

The subjects changed all the time. Some came to us because the department concerned had very little experience of the EU, and wanted or needed advice on what to do. Those were the easy cases. Others came because the subject clearly might affect departments other than the lead department; our meetings gave those others a chance to comment and see whether they had objections, which would need to be weighed against what the lead department wanted. The lead department in such cases might well take the line that they knew best, and be resistant to interference by others. Some subjects needed to be discussed because they raised legal questions. The most sensitive question of all, at this time, was whether a new policy or line of action involved 'an extension of Community competence', in other words would we be going along with an extension of the Community's and in particular the Commission's powers? John Major's Conservative government had running difficulty with its Eurosceptic members of parliament. We were under instructions to be on constant watch for any creeping extension of Community powers, and to block energetically – even if there might be a benefit for the UK on other grounds in the policy proposed. And lastly there were cases where the European secretariat took the initiative in calling for discussion, for instance where some new problem or turn of events raised the need for new thinking in Whitehall; the Cabinet Office here in its role of making sure that the government formulated some policy, any policy, in response to the new situation.

Our aim was to make sure that all aspects of a subject were covered in the course of a meeting of an hour or so, and to end on clear conclusions as to what should be done next, and by whom. It fell to me at the meetings I chaired to make this happen. The meetings didn't run themselves. Some of those at the table might be only too happy if no clear conclusions were drawn. There was no scope at all for the chairman to sit back.

What with the constant change of subject matter, the difficulty of the subjects, and quite often the difficulty of achieving consensus, this job was more consistently mentally stretching than any other I did, before or after that. Not the most stressful; that was to come later, with BSE. Maybe not the most influential either. Cabinet Office has pride of place at the centre of government. Those who work there have a wider view of government than those who work in departments with a single mission. They are picked for their ability. But the nature of our input, on European subjects at least, seemed to be to shape and sharpen ideas for others to use in the front line. A main thrust of our work was helping our front-line negotiators to achieve deals that best served British interests and to spot and head off attempts by other EU countries to push ideas that would bring the UK more cost than benefit. Attempts were afoot at that time to grow a whole raft of social policies that John Major's government viewed in that light. As so often with our EU work, there was more to do by way of damage-limitation than in pursuing positive initiatives. I did not feel I was very often turning the ship of state in a decisive new direction. All that said, the work here was most demanding of concentration and brainpower.

There were two things which took the edge off the difficulty of it. One was the very high quality of the little team that I had to support me; four young assistants whose job it was to sniff out, before one of the meetings that I had to chair, what it was about, and then to write a chairman's brief – for me – analysing the problem, explaining possible complications that might need to be explored in discussion, and (crucially) suggesting a set of conclusions. These would not always be so much answers to a problem as next steps that the lead department (and possibly others) should take to influence the EU in line with what we wanted; tactics and game-handling could crucially affect how much we achieved. If the map in my chairman's brief did not always match the way discussion actually ran, it was nonetheless invaluable to have it at hand as a check that I had not been side-tracked from the points that mattered. The briefs came with a bundle of source documents, they could be bits of legislation or correspondence, all of which might be relevant once the meeting got going, and had to be at least skimmed through, so that you knew what you had got. Preparation for the meetings took up hours of time in the course of a week, and mostly I did it on the hour-long train ride between London and Bedford – against the rules, because many of the documents were highly classified. But there was no other way.

The other comfort factor was the star quality of many of the other officials. This job vastly widened my range of contacts around Whitehall. The departments for which EU business was significant tended, quite rightly, to put their brightest and best people on to it. The inner circle of the European operation consisted of No 10, Foreign Office, UKRep Brussels, and Treasury, including Treasury Solicitors. The senior posts on this circuit are generally occupied by highly able people but during the 1980s and early 1990s it was a golden age: Britain was fortunate in having on the European front line some exceptional performers by any standards. John Kerr and Michael Jay (successively later Heads of the Foreign Office); Rod Line in No 10 (he became our man in Moscow, later Chilcot Enquiry); Juliet Wheldon at Treasury Solicitors, the most lucid and nimble legal brain (sadly she died young); David Bostock at Treasury, rough-tongued, hard-nosed, razor-sharp, a loyal servant of British interests and exploder of compliant diplomacy (later our man on the European Court of Auditors). The quality of the exchanges between these giants was not just high, sometimes dazzling, often (thanks to John Kerr) highly entertaining. The scope for sloppy thinking – or relaxing – was very narrow indeed.

I had my share of rising stars on my own little team. John Grant, within five or six years our Ambassador in Stockholm, then Ambassador to the EU; and Mark Lyall Grant, whose career went on to tricky posts as our High Commissioner to Pakistan, later to the United Nations.

High-class coordination was the aim of our game. The quality of coordination as carried out by the UK was recognised in Brussels and in other European capitals as a strength: a high degree of consistency between one part of government and another. But it had its downside. Our method forced our front-line negotiators to be clear from an early stage what their main negotiating objectives were, but this resulted again and again in our negotiators stating, and letting everyone else know, what their objectives were. The French, our acknowledged equals in ability to coordinate, were adept at keeping their ultimate objectives under wraps until, often at a late stage in a negotiation, they would suddenly unveil a key demand, take everyone else by surprise, catch the UK locked into a position, and win ground. We could be flat-footed where the French could be adroit and artful.

Meetings were the staple of my working week but not the whole story. Our prime minister had in No 10 a very small staff of his own to call on (Tony Blair changed that), and the Cabinet Office secretariats were the first port of call when he needed someone to explain a problem or sit in on a meeting to record the discussion. I was called over a couple of times in that way, to take part in little meetings about the conclusion of the Uruguay (trade) Round, and about the appointing of the next head of the European Commission, to succeed Jacques Delors.

On one occasion I was one of four or five advisers on European affairs

whom John Major called in for a private horizon-scanning discussion over sup-
per in the small panelled dining room in the heart of No 10. Major had for
the evening the top brains of Whitehall including John Kerr and Michael Jay
around his table. They gave him their most lucid and expert analysis of where
things stood on the fundamental business of the EU. I forget exactly what, but
post Maastricht, post German reunification, tectonic plates were shifting. All I
remember is that as these giants of Whitehall put forward their very best analysis and guidance, in all its subtlety and ingenuity, John Major's eyes glazed, he
looked increasingly like a sick parrot. He didn't want to know. With his government limping precariously along, harried all the way by the Eurosceptics,
the 'bastards' as he not so very privately called them (some of the same names
still with us 25 years later: Bill Cash, Iain Duncan Smith, John Redwood), he
had zero appetite for the subtle games his European advisers were trailing before him. He smelt death.

Other times, there was trouble-shooting to do. It could be of an interesting kind. At this time, Central European countries were picking themselves up
amid the ruins of communism and some were turning their thoughts, or just
beginning to turn their thoughts, to a future where they would move into the
orbit of the European Union; perhaps even become part of it. Some thought
the way in would be quicker than it turned out to be. One country which was
keen to talk to us – to someone from London – was Romania. We had some
preparatory correspondence with the splendidly named Napoleon Pop. I can't
remember his exact position, but he was our trip fixer. It was decided that I together with John Macgregor, a counsellor at the Foreign Office, would make a
visit to Bucharest, and that we would couple this with a visit to Budapest, since
Hungary was keen on getting closer to the EU too.

Our mission was very ill-defined. Go and talk to them, was about the extent
of it. We flew into Bucharest via Vienna, on a local Romanian airline which
Poppy had made me promise not to use. We were put up at the British Ambassador's residence for a couple of nights. In the morning we were launched,
with very little preparation, into a vast hall where some 75 Romanian officials
were seated along two sides of a long table, expectantly – but expecting what?
We had translators, but there was little need. Conversation was quite possible
in English. We talked about how Community business was done, the respec-

tive roles of member states and the Commission, our methods of organising ourselves, and so on. We must have talked about other things too. There were questions. There was a lunch break in which John and I were taken to a back room and treated to what was clearly intended to be a choice meal of delicacies – but at home it would have seemed just about good enough for the bird table; hardened bacon rind seemed to be their ultimate delicacy. You had to feel sorry for our hosts. The press reported on our visit, and I still have a couple of cuttings from Romanian newspapers which I have not fully finished decoding.

Two things stick in my mind about the reception at the Embassy afterwards. I thought I had washed and changed quickly for the evening but in the ten minutes that it may have taken me John Macgregor had done the same *and* was downstairs ahead of me, coolly sitting playing the piano. There, I thought, are some diplomat's skills. The reception was a scene that we came across again and again in these immediate post-communism years: a very uneasy mixture of people in the room, old guard and new guard; the new guard keen to explore with us what life was like in the west, old guard eying their compatriots suspiciously, and us coldly.

Budapest was a total contrast. Twenty-five years further forward, I reckoned, in the state of the national economy and in the state of mind of leading individuals. We met a group in the Hungarian parliament, the building which sits on the Danube uncannily resembling the Houses of Parliament on the Thames. It was an easier encounter for us than it had been in Bucharest, talking to people who were much more tuned in already to the EU and how their country would need to change to qualify for membership.

I had an encounter with Ukrainians of a similar nature to the one we had had in Bucharest, only this was in London, in the Cabinet Office. A group came to visit, at their request. There must have been around 15 of them. I ought to have counted. As in Bucharest, the old guard and new guard were clearly distinguishable, and here they came to open and harsh disagreement with one another in front of us: X does not speak for Ukrainian government, that is not what we think now. We explained our system of cabinet government, and they struggled to understand. What was the point of this 'cabinet', this college of ministers? Why didn't the prime minister simply exert control?

That meeting ended with a moment of alarm (for me), because the group burst out of the meeting room we had been in and scattered in all directions through the office. Given that we had clearly had some unreconstructed communists among us, I had visions of being called in by security for a severe reprimand. These visitors were at best an unreliable lot. We scampered down to the front door to see whether they were finding their way out, and bit by bit they turned up, but since I didn't know exactly how many they had been I was nervous for some hours that we might have undesirables still roaming the office.

On a more peaceable note, we ran seminars for the Swedes and the Austrians at around this time. They were, with Finland, very close to becoming full EU members. Feedback from our events at Ditchley Park, Chevening and elsewhere was always favourable. They found the British more open and helpful to talk to and less prescriptive than the French or the Germans, both of whom in different ways had lectured them on how they wanted them to behave.

There has not been much mention of MAFF in this story so far. MAFF had been deeply involved in European Community business from the time of British accession in 1973 and for all of ten years before that. Agricultural policy bulked large in the European Community system. It still does, but it was even more dominant through the 1970s, 80s and 90s. Expenditure on farm support was taking up three quarters of the total EC budget, and it was the budget cost that we British tended to fixate on. Agriculture was also for a very long time the only real common policy, and it was that aspect that other member states were more keen on; the CAP was the glue that held the fledgling European Community together. All member states took part, and it permeated their lives. There was international trade policy too, the other big common policy, but that didn't involve spending big money and didn't have the visible impact that agricultural policy had.

Because the CAP was big, costly, complicated, and generated constant arguments, the British civil service needed people who knew all about it, who could understand and challenge what was going on. This drew MAFF into the game of high-level negotiations from the 1960s, and by the 1990s MAFF had an almost unrivalled grasp of the EU system, along with a network of contacts, and experience of tactics for bringing UK influence to bear, for achieving UK objectives or – even more important on this front – for thwarting the objectives of others.

One consequence was that MAFF was not in need of day-to-day advice from the Cabinet Office on what to do and how to do it on the Brussels front. In the 1990s, with Community policy seeping into more and more areas of government, an increasing number of other departments did need that sort of help. MAFF however came regularly to the Cabinet Office table for the weekly Friday morning discussions of high-level business, Council of Ministers and European Council business, because on issues at this level there were links to be made between what we wanted on agriculture and what we wanted on other things; priorities to settle; inconsistencies to be avoided. But in large part MAFF got on with its Euro-work, running its own in-house coordination meetings weekly.

A repercussion of that, which I noticed in my Cabinet Office meetings, was that when I did need a MAFF representative to join a discussion on a specific issue, say the dumping of farmed salmon by Norway, or a food standards topic linked to other single market business, the people fielded by MAFF showed up rather lamely against their counterparts from other departments; not very good at presenting their case in context, and giving the distinct impression of being protective of their patch. I think that was symptomatic of a house attitude that grew stronger in MAFF from the mid-1980s onwards; an attitude of 'we know what we are doing, we don't need our hands held by the "centre", and we are not keen to submit to pooling our thoughts; trust us and let us get on with it'.

There was one underlying reason for the secrecy with which MAFF operated in the upper reaches, which was not openly stated. Deals obtainable in the major CAP negotiations were almost always worse than what the British government wanted, worse in the sense of more expensive for the UK taxpayer, and therefore worse than the Treasury would consent to. This being so, either the UK should have blocked, or rejected, deal after deal in CAP negotiations, which would have meant being sidelined from major decision-taking over time, and losing the purchase needed to secure specific UK interests in the food and farming sectors – or indeed any influence at all. (This was our farming policy now, we had no domestic options left.) Or else MAFF negotiators had to cut the best deal they could and present it as a fait accompli to the authorities at home. That became the regular pattern from very early in our EC membership: doing deals, and riding out the criticism from the Treasury and others. Up to a point the 'centre' became resigned to this. It became MAFF's house style. Perhaps, though, MAFF could have won a higher degree of understanding if the underlying reasons had been aired more openly more often in Cabinet Office discussions.

As it was, the set-apart pattern of behaviour did not endear MAFF to other departments, they came to be seen as a poor team players. It bred, over time, a degree of mistrust which took its toll in the end. There was open and undoubted admiration from the stars in the Foreign Office and UKRep for the skill with which MAFF threaded through the maze of agricultural negotiations and helped to deliver successive CAP reforms; first Mrs Thatcher's budget deal and then the reforms of the CAP that the new budget disciplines forced on an unwilling 12. But as MAFF's 'trust us' attitude hardened, it took the edge off that admiration. It came to be a barrier between MAFF and the 'centre' and – just as a minister who has disdained to make friends among his party colleagues in the tearooms can find himself unceremoniously dumped when his policy gets into difficulty – so when the going got rough for MAFF in the later 1990s over food scares, then BSE, then foot and mouth disease, MAFF too came to be friendless; knives came out; support from the centre which could have made life easier was withdrawn; and the severely wounded body was dismembered, MAFF surrendering food policy to the new Food Standards Agency, then wholly despatched and replaced by Defra in 2001.

All that lay in the future at the time I am writing about here, but the seeds were there by the mid-1990s.

Any local inefficiency in relations between MAFF and the centre was put in the shade by the disruption caused to John Major's government by the Euro-sceptics in his Conservative party. He had started out as prime minister with the pious objective of putting the UK at the heart of Europe (the first of several British prime ministers to hoist that standard early in their time in office). The Eurosceptics saw to it that Major could achieve no such thing. One specific way in which this impinged on business with which I was involved at the Cabinet Office was over the selection of a new President for the European Commission. Jacques Delors, who had been larger than life and influential in this position for a decade, was coming to the end of his time. There were no rules for the selection of his successor; it was done by wheeling and dealing between member states, back-room manoeuvres. An obvious front-runner was the prime minister of Belgium, Jean-Luc Dehaene, who was ready, willing and pretty well-qualified to take the job. He was invited, or invited himself, to London for as it were a job interview, to talk to John Major; and I was invited to sit in on their meeting. We had only one or two of our ministers, I think, in the Cabinet room. Discussion was affable – John Major was generally affable, Dehaene jocular, full of bonhomie – but inconsequential. John Major's mind was made up beforehand. Dehaene wore his federalist views on his sleeve. He would take the Community further in the direction of a superstate. For fear of the Westminster Eurosceptics he had to be flatly ruled out. We had to find someone else. This view was conveyed to the other governments and after the matter had stewed further a new, fall-back, candidate emerged: Jacques Santer, then prime minister of Luxembourg. One virtue he had over Dehaene was that he was not so well-known, in particular not well-known to the Conservative Eurosceptics. So they had less on him, ergo less against him. He was in effect, if not a nonentity, a grey man, a not very eminent éminence grise. (We should of course have known that in the veins of every Luxemburger runs a strong streak of federalism.)

Now, we had the real good fortune in these years to have a Briton as top civil servant in the Commission, the Secretary General, David Williamson, one of the brightest stars Whitehall has ever contributed to the European 'project'. David exploded at the thought of Santer being imposed as his boss. He found it all but impossible to envisage the Commission operating effectively with Santer at its head, and he all but resigned. Anyhow, the time came for decision. The appointment had to be made by the European Council. I was deputed from the Cabinet Office to fly out with John Major and his Foreign Secretary, Douglas Hurd, to the meeting in Brussels. Santer was duly approved. The vignette that sticks in my mind is of a little press conference afterwards, in a backroom of the Council building; John Major confidently telling the journalists that we had got an excellent outcome, while Douglas Hurd, body half turned away, legs crossed, signalled as clearly as could be 'I am not anything to do with this'. And on the plane back home – we had to land at Alconbury near Huntingdon for John Major – the mood was subdued. Eurosceptics saw to it for many many years that the UK was never a convincing full member of the European project. Despite many successes that should be attributed to British influence in particular policy areas – budget discipline, the single market, enlargement to the north and then the east, even some pieces of CAP reform – euroscepticism repeatedly pulled us back to the sidelines.

To end on a less heavyweight topic, one of the minor tasks for the European secretariat was to encourage more Brits to join the European Commission, and the other EU institutions, and to give those who had got in the feeling that London valued and cared for them. Over time different schemes had been run to stimulate more applications both from inside the civil service and from other occupations and professions. All had fallen flat. It was an uphill struggle from the very beginning to attract British people to go to Brussels. The quality of those who got in at the beginning, in the early 1970s, was variable. That, I found, was still reflected some 30 years later, as I worked with some of that generation when they were coming to the peak of their careers. One bar was the level of proficiency in other languages which the Commission – rightly – requires. For many continentals that is an easy hurdle to clear. The Brits are let down by the weakness of our modern language teaching, along with their general apathy. As a result, up to the 1990s (but not for long after that) the best people 'we' got into the Commission were people in mid-career in the London civil service, already showing their ability (which the Commission wanted), who could be shoe-horned in past the language requirement; 'parachuted', in the Brussels jargon. The brightest and best of all British exports, David Williamson, who became top civil servant of all in the Commission, Lord Williamson on his retirement, went in by that route. But the active and effective unions to which career Brussels civil servants belong had ensured that parachuting was completely banned by the time of my secondment to the Commission ten years later.

Returning to everyday life in the 1990s, I and my team were supposed to ginger up young applicants, and this was not an area where successes were easily scored. We also aimed to keep a friendly eye on those who had got themselves in. My personal role on this front was to pay what was patronisingly called a 'pastoral visit' once a year to the different institutions – Commission, Court of Justice, Council of Ministers, European Parliament – to talk to British members of staff, to give them a fresh update from London on issues that might be of interest to them, and to get feedback including any complaints. I only did this once. We had a meeting in Brussels, quite well attended but rather tame. Most of those who came were well settled into their EU careers and, as I found out when I worked inside the Commission myself, the staff there are highly unionised and the unions exceedingly active on their behalf, pressing grievances of all kinds. So the interest of our British nationals in looking to Whitehall for any help over their terms and conditions of work was minimal at that stage. Though there were one or two professional moaners.

From Brussels I went on down to Luxembourg. This involved a journey by road in an UKRep people-carrier. The road from Brussels to Luxembourg varies in quality, and there are stretches where it winds through the hills of the Ardennes. It was midwinter. The journey down was slow and I think we arrived late. Only a handful of my flock turned out to receive their pastoral care. On the journey back it began to snow and our vehicle struggled. In the end we were making such poor progress that we pulled into a service station for an evening meal of cheese rolls and coffee. As with my other Cabinet Office experiences, this one was lifted by having good company. Nigel Sheinwald, then a rising star, head of chancery at UKRep, was with me; full of bounce and brilliance. (He was, within ten years, UK Ambassador to the EU, and then to the US.) That was an excursion to remember. Net impact on Britain's representation in the EU institutions – near zero.

Towards the end of 1994 I was invited to return to MAFF on promotion to deputy secretary, an offer I was hardly likely to refuse – though life for me and the family over the next five years would have been entirely different if I had. But deputy secretary was one of the three top posts in the department under the permanent secretary. I had expected to stay in the Cabinet Office for another year or so, and would have been happy to do so. As it was, I took away with me my much enlarged network of contacts all across Whitehall, and a training in leading purposeful discussions and in bringing together the right set of people to explore a subject from all angles. Those skills served me well for the next ten years in London and Brussels, and for ten years beyond that in the work I did for St George's House, Windsor Castle.

12

BSE: MUCH LIKE A WAR

1995-2000

T he job which came next changed the rest of my working life and left its
mark beyond that. I had no idea of what was to come. One day in October 1994 I was invited over from the Cabinet Office for a conversation with the
permanent secretary at MAFF, now Richard Packer. He put it to me that one
of his three deputy secretaries was retiring at the end of the year, and he would
like me to take over the job, Head of the Food Safety Directorate. I had only a
vague idea of the range of work we were talking about. It was certainly the area
of MAFF work in which I had least experience. But it would be a promotion,
and any further promotion was far from guaranteed at the level I had then
reached. I had no hesitation in accepting.

I then had one or two conversations with my predecessor before he retired.
He was of little help in giving me the picture. He was on a steep run-down to
retirement and I don't know that he had understood the essentials of his job; or
maybe he had side-stepped them. The clearest advice that I picked up from him
was to take all the hospitality I could from the big food manufacturers. He had
had a keen appetite for that. He left me next to no organised handover notes.
The day of his retirement came, he disappeared from the scene, and I found
myself immersed for the next five years in highly technical subjects which I had
never dealt with before and never dealt with again afterwards. This was to be
a self-contained compartment of my career. I don't expect the story will make
pleasant reading.

The range of work I had to deal with was very wide, so wide that it can't be
summarised. I have to list the main elements:

- Food safety and science. This spanned food hygiene, food standards and
authenticity, additives and contaminants (including radiological contamina-
tion), 'novel' foods and processes (such as the inclusion of additives claimed to
boost health or energy), consumer relations, standards for animal feed, and last

but not least coordination of food emergencies. [I had at least some experience of that from my Chief Regional Officer days.]

- Animal health. This spanned control of diseases in farmed animals (where BSE was the dominant active concern), animal welfare, meat hygiene, and oversight and guidance of the State Veterinary Service through the Chief Veterinary Officer.
- Plant protection, and agricultural inputs – this was another way of describing the regulation of fertilisers and chemicals used on farms; policy for organic farming; health and safety for farm workers.
- Farming and the environment. This was added to my responsibilities after six months, and consisted of developing policies for farming to protect and enhance the countryside and to reduce pollution from farm operations.

Time has passed and public concerns have shifted in some ways since the 1990s, but not a lot. It is not hard to see that the subjects I was now taking charge of included many about which people worry, and feel strongly, areas where consumers feel at risk and expect government to protect them. What exactly is going into their food; what chemicals have been applied on the farm, are we eating them and if so what are they doing to us; is our meat being handled hygienically from the slaughterhouse to the butcher's counter or supermarket cold cabinet; is harmful radiation being used to preserve food; is organic better for us, or not; can't farmers do less harm to birds, bees and flowers in their fields, and to the look of the landscape; can't animals be treated better on farms and when they are being moved around from farm to farm or farm to slaughter? I was going to be deep in subjects on which public concerns run strongly, most of them science-based. My lack of scientific training was not helpful.

As for disease, there is an underlying level of diseases of farm animals to be kept under control all the time (as with humans), and then occasional major outbreaks of highly contagious diseases like swine fever or foot-and-mouth or bird flu, that can cause the death of large numbers of animals or birds in a very short time and call for the destruction of further large numbers to stop the disease. And then there was BSE. Much of my activity over the following five years was centred on BSE. But for the first few months my time was taken up with other matters.

I had started the job in mid-December, hoping for some quiet between Christmas and New Year to sort my ideas out. Events stopped that. In the week after Christmas 1994 there were some violent incidents in demonstrations against the transport of live animals. Campaigners had been protesting for some time that farmed animals – cattle and sheep – were being exported from Britain to the continent by land, sea and air in harsh conditions. This campaign all of a sudden flared up, starting with the incidents just after Christmas, and there followed a well-coordinated campaign concentrated at three points of export: Coventry airport, and the sea ports of Brightlingsea (Essex) and Shoreham (Sussex). Furious crowds gathered at these places at the times when consignments for export were expected, blocking the way for the transporter vehicles and causing considerable chaos and damage in the towns.

Public disorder that disrupts normal traffic quickly concentrates ministers' minds. I had been here twenty years before, back in 1974 when Welsh farmer protests over cattle coming in from Ireland led to me being summoned before the home secretary. MAFF's minister in 1994, William Waldegrave, wanted top-level attention given to sorting out this new disruption. I found myself spending much of my time for the next six months putting together and carrying through a plan for tighter European rules on the transport of animals: the maximum length of time for which they could be transported without a break, the amount of space they should be allowed, the provision of water on board and food at stopping-places. Moving the issue up the EU agenda and generating support in other countries for new tighter rules was uphill work. In most other European countries the public are much less concerned than in the UK about how animals are treated, if they are concerned at all. Support was not easy to find. We did best in Sweden. It seemed that there was some public sympathy but also, the country had only recently joined the EU and I think their agriculture minister was rather pleased to be able to join in a campaign with the UK, a large and longstanding member state. In addition, we learned that the Swedes were manufacturing a luxurious new type of animal transporter with all mod cons, so they will have seen a commercial interest in forcing other countries to upgrade.

The negotiations were very time-consuming, involving trips to Stockholm, Dublin, Brussels and Luxembourg. But at the end of six months we won agreement to the changes we were after at the Agriculture Council in June 1995.

I was aware all through that time that in terms of the other business I was meant to be looking after this was all something of a sideshow. There were much more serious things going on. But the protesters over the welfare of animals in transit had succeeded in forcing their issue high up the political agenda and it required high-level effort to bring it under control. Waldegrave was duly thankful.

The next priority for me was meat hygiene. We were in the middle of a major change in the way meat hygiene was policed in slaughterhouses. The established system in the UK had been that local authorities at district council level each employed some meat hygiene inspectors who went the rounds of slaughterhouses and meat plants. There were 176 such local authorities; the standard of enforcement varied around the country and was known to be pretty unsatisfactory in some areas. The European Union had strict and detailed rules on how such work ought to be done. The Commission was not at all happy that the British system matched up to requirements. MAFF with the Department of Health had therefore been developing plans for a national meat hygiene service since 1991, and this was due to be brought into operation by summer 1995. It now fell to me and my staff to get it to the starting line.

Setting up the new service was fraught with problems. Taking work away from local authorities and giving it to central government was unusual and the local authorities were not inclined to make that easy. The meat industry were worried that a new stricter system would mean higher charges (local authority charges had varied). In particular they saw higher costs looming in the EU requirement that slaughterhouse operations must be supervised by a qualified vet. The local authority inspectors had had some special training, but not to university level. Vets would command higher pay. The meat industry were well aware that they could find sympathy among politicians if they argued that this was a case of EU rules imposing unnecessary costs, so they played on that aspect and found ready support from Eurosceptic MPs. The government of John Major was constantly at risk of its legislation being defeated by Eurosceptics and that was the case here. MAFF ministers were alert to the danger and gave commitments in both Houses of Parliament that they would keep the cost of the new service as low as possible. Then there were management problems for us to overcome, the hardest of which was moving 711 staff coming from 176 different previous employers with a variety of different pay rates and conditions of employment on to one unified system – without levelling up to the highest-cost solutions. This was an administrative headache.

From June 1995 when the animal transport problems were laid to rest, it was the Meat Hygiene Service (MHS) which took over as the main call on my time. Setting the level of charges to industry, in the teeth of their running opposition; pressing the MHS management to clamp down on their costs; recruiting the number of qualified vets required – they had in the end to be recruited mostly from Spain because vets trained in Britain had no knowledge of meat hygiene work; handling the consequent protests from industry that the Spanish veterinarians aroused; sorting out a single set of hygiene standards for the country as a whole – these matters were difficult and time-consuming.

Alongside the welfare of animals in transit and the creation of the MHS, there was an ongoing and very grave animal disease problem: BSE. I was well aware that this was occupying much of the time of some of my staff. It was soon to reach the level of a national and international crisis but it was not at that pitch in the summer of 1995, and I did not give much of my thinking time to it. It was acutely complicated and I could see, and was confident, that I had key members of staff who were fully up to speed on the matter, working directly and much of the time to the chief veterinary officer and the permanent secretary, both of them equally up to speed. With that high-level team and high level of competence, my efforts were more productively focussed on keeping other parts of the business under control.

However, as the year went on I was called in on strategic meetings about BSE more frequently. I was still struggling to make sense of the discussions, which were deeply technical and in scientific terms that I did not understand. But two things slowly became clear. First, the performance of the Meat Hygiene Service was closely bound up with the control of the disease BSE in cattle, and the minimising of any risk to human health that BSE might pose. Second, the assumption that BSE, whilst virulently infective in the cattle population, was not a threat to humans – an assumption which had been firmly held for some years on the basis of respectable scientific reasoning - was beginning to look less secure.

I knew where I was with the first of these issues – up to a point. One of the features of dealing with BSE was that it was a new disease about which scientists were continually learning. As a result of new findings, the controls in slaughterhouses that had seemed sufficient up till then needed to be changed and made more rigorous in 1995. This called for more intricate work by MHS staff – and pushed up staff costs. Industry resistance stiffened. At the same time there were repeated instances of slaughterhouses failing to work to the new more stringent standards. This fuelled fears, in private and in public (because the press were now following closely), that BSE was still being recycled into the cattle population. It is time to step back and explain more about the nature of BSE.

BSE: a very short introduction

BSE: bovine spongiform encephalopathy. A spongiform encephalopathy is a disease of the brain that turns it spongy. BSE was seen in cattle for the first time in the 1980s. It was unheard of before then, not that it had been waiting to be discovered; it appeared to be a new disease. For new diseases to emerge in farmed animals is not so unusual. The State Veterinary Service with staff throughout the country has a system for collecting and pooling information on diseases including those not previously recognised, and a system for referring unexplained data to the government's Central Veterinary Laboratory (CVL) for analysis. This system swung into action rapidly when the first cases of BSE were picked up, in 1984-5.

It took until 1987 for the CVL to work through possible explanations. In the meantime the disease spread rapidly throughout Britain. The animals affected were mostly dairy cows. The impact was dramatic and distressing. Cows lost their balance, began to stagger and then fall to their knees. Pictures of cows in this miserable state became a frequent sight on TV. Within a short time hundreds of cattle were going down with the disease every week. It was fatal in every case. There was no known cure.

The veterinary scientists were working intensively to discover the nature of the disease, what had caused it and how it was being spread. The nature of the disease was relatively easy to pin down. The brains of the cattle that had died, when analysed under a microscope, were seen to be riddled with holes, giving them a spongy appearance. This seemed to show that BSE – as it was now going to be called – was one of a family of brain diseases already known which had a similar effect on the texture of the victim's brain. Related diseases included scrapie in sheep, and in humans CJD (Creutzfeldt-Jakob Disease) and kuru – but kuru is a story better kept for another time. All were fatal in every case.

This gave BSE a forbidding quality. Fed with the horrifying pictures now regularly being shown on TV, the public was growing alarmed. What if this BSE disease could affect humans? Most of us had been eating beef at one time or another. The vets continued to work on the question of what had caused the disease; where it had come from. It seemed most likely at that early stage in the mid-1980s that BSE was indeed related to scrapie since that was a disease of the same nature, with similar symptoms, and was occurring very widely in sheep on UK farms. Scrapie had been known in the UK sheep flock for over 200 years. No attempt had been made to stamp it out because sheep are cheap, and it had never been shown to have any ill-effects on humans. Nor had it got into cattle up till then, but perhaps some slight mutation had occurred that enabled scrapie to 'jump the species barrier'? That seemed a reasonable possibility.

Following that line of thinking, the vets took comfort from the fact that scrapie had never infected humans. They concentrated their researches on the question of how BSE was being spread – it was spreading rapidly through the cattle population – and how the spread could be stopped. They made the important finding, which has stood the test of time, that BSE was being spread by means of animal feed, compound feed that contained remains of cattle and sheep, technically known as meat-and-bonemeal (MBM). Some people were furiously critical on learning of this. They denounced what they said was an obviously unnatural practice: feeding animals to animals, tantamount to cannibalism, calculated to generate disease. Yet in fact the incorporation of animal remains into animal rations had already been practised for more than 50 years without any harmful effects. The purpose was to add protein to the feed mix. Protein from other sources that an animal would never come across in nature are regularly added to compound feed. The Danes feed fishmeal to their pigs though pigs are not natural fish eaters (and the fish the Danes use would be better left to sustain Scotland's sea birds). So denouncing MBM as an affront to nature did not really help to explain how BSE had come about.

One possible explanation, the scientists considered, was that the process by which MBM was manufactured ('rendering' was the technical term for it) had been changed not long before; in simplest terms continuous processing replaced processing in batches, and the temperature had been turned down. Perhaps this is what had allowed infection to get through? Quite a lively industry of commentators and critics was growing up, and they turned fierce criticism on government for having allowed this lax practice to develop. But in fact the rendering companies had made the changes one by one quite some time before, and because of advances in technology; nothing to do with government regulation.

In the end – and this is running several years ahead – the conclusion was that BSE quite possibly started with a spontaneous genetic fault in cattle, in a single animal, creating a condition akin to scrapie but not actually derived from or caused by scrapie; that it had then spread and been multiplied up through the unlucky accident of the remains of the first affected animal being used in the manufacture of MBM and so getting into animal feed – following what was normal and long-standing practice. This theory best fitted the geography and pattern of spread of the earliest cases of BSE when all the evidence from the early years had been studied closely, delving back into case notes from before the disease had been clearly recognised.

However, the veterinary scientists were on the right track in thinking that animal feed was the 'vector', the route by which BSE was being spread. They recommended on the strength of this that all protein from either sheep or cattle should be immediately banned from inclusion in cattle feed. That ban was promptly put in place: 1988. The number of cases – now running at 500 and more each month – did not immediately drop. An immediate effect was not expected. In common with other such diseases, BSE was taking some years to develop into acute and visible form; some four to five years was the average in cattle. But four years on from the feed ban the number of cases (by then running at more than *3000* each month) did indeed fall away sharply. The feed ban had been working.

A further piece of explanation is needed. BSE in common with other encephalopathies affected the central nervous system, i.e. the brain and spinal cord, but the infectivity did not spread into muscle meat. The 1988 committee of scientists recommended that animals which had shown visible symptoms of BSE or died of it should definitely be kept out of the human food chain and destroyed. A second and more specialised committee went further, in 1989, and recommended that the brain and spinal cord of seemingly healthy animals should, as a precaution, be removed in slaughterhouses; treated as 'specified risk material', and not allowed into the manufacture of animal feed or into the human food chain. The advice continued to be that the muscle meat of animals not visibly affected should be safe to eat.

Over time further laboratory work showed that the infectivity was being found in some additional parts of the animal (but still not in muscle meat) and those findings were the basis of the tighter rules that we had to bring in in summer 1995. Unsurprisingly such revision of the rules and restrictions, based on new advice from the scientists, further undermined public trust, whereas to the experts it was only to be expected. We were dealing with a previously unknown disease, the nature of which was unusually complex, and scientists only learned about it bit by bit, by meticulous research. The experiments they needed to conduct did not produce instant results. Some consisted of injecting BSE into other animals, mainly laboratory mice, and BSE which took on average four years to develop in cattle developed more quickly in mice, but not instantly. So those closest to the scientists were not surprised that new findings emerged over time. But to the general public it appeared that government did not really have a grip; ministers were repeatedly shifting their ground. This undoubtedly fed into a wider loss of public confidence on food safety matters.

A further piece of explanation will help in understanding what happened later. This involves going one step further into microbiology. BSE, in common with other spongiform encephalopathies, is not spread by a germ or a virus. It is not contagious in that way. The disease works by deforming molecules of a certain protein (prion) in the brain, causing it to change from its usual shape; and then the deformed protein is able to contaminate other protein particles causing them too to go out of shape, and that is how the trademark holes gradually develop in the brain. Now germs and viruses can be destroyed by heat. Material thought to be carrying infection can normally be sterilised by heat treatment. Not so material in which BSE infection is present. The malignant protein is almost indestructible. Heat treatment is certainly of no use against it. This quality of the infective agent made the control of BSE significantly harder. The rules on removing infective parts of a carcase, the specified risk materials, were all well and good, and practical as well, until it was later learned that even the most microscopic scrap of specified risk material left in the part of the carcase going for animal feed was capable of perpetuating the spread of the disease.

It became apparent from 1992 onwards when the 1988 feed ban should in theory have stopped BSE in its tracks that the measures were not being as effective as they should in theory have been. Slapdash operation in some slaughterhouses may have been one reason, hoarding by farmers of pre-ban stocks of feed another; but the sheer impossibility of cleaning every last particle of infective material – from carcases, from vehicles carrying material to the renderers, from the renderers' production lines was at work too. BSE was beginning to show nightmare quality.

The story moved on. In the latter part of 1995 there were concerns that the slaughterhouses were falling down on their job of keeping the specified risk material out of the human and animal food chains. I have already referred to this in describing the problems the MHS had to struggle with in its first months of operation.

There was also a concern, which built up only slowly, that BSE might, contrary to belief up till then, be a danger to humans. Suspicions came from two directions. Government veterinary scientists had assumed from early on that BSE had most probably sprung from scrapie, and would behave like scrapie in all respects including not harming human health. That was a comforting thought and, human nature being what it is, our scientists probably clung to it a little more firmly than they should. There was perhaps also less fluid communication between groups of scientists inside and outside government than there should have been. Laboratory work gradually began to show that BSE was passing to some other species of animals that had never contracted scrapie, and also that it was being found in parts of the cattle anatomy that scrapie had not reached in sheep. BSE was beginning to look less than 100% similar to scrapie. This should have set warning lights flashing.

From a different direction came news that a handful of young people had contracted and were dying of CJD. CJD had been known for a long time as a disease in humans, affecting the brain and killing in every case. It showed up quite by chance in a very small number of people around the world each year, always in older people; or it could be accidentally and tragically passed on in hospitals, by transmission of infected tissue or blood from someone affected to another, otherwise healthy person of any age. Because BSE and CJD looked to be closely related diseases, the 1988 recommendations had included advice to watch out for any signs that CJD was showing up in any way at variance with the pattern of the past, for instance in younger people. Therefore the news that was coming through in 1995 of some cases of CJD in younger people did set warning lights flashing. The chief medical officer told MAFF's permanent secretary (Richard Packer) that he was uneasy about this. Department of Health and MAFF together turned to the committee of eminent scientists that had been formed specifically to advise government on BSE – SEAC: the Spongiform Encephalopathy Advisory Committee (set up in 1990) – and asked them to focus on the new evidence. If BSE did turn out to be passing from cattle to humans, the situation would change utterly.

The members of SEAC were medical, veterinary and research scientists of deep expertise. They were working at the frontiers of knowledge. They approached the question cautiously and meticulously, and took several months to form a conclusion. Over that time further cases of CJD in younger people came to light. Evidence was building up. By February 1996 SEAC was moving towards a conclusion but, as some members were not present each time they met, they checked and rechecked their collective view. By mid-March they felt ready to say that in their view the new variant of CJD in young people (brains showed a slightly different pattern under the microscope) had most probably been caused by eating beef infected with BSE.

This brought matters to the brink. Making this news public would clearly convulse public opinion, and have repercussions internationally, not just on trade but on Britain's reputation. The prime minister was informed. SEAC was pressed to say what new steps they would advise government to take. That would be an absolutely essential component of the public announcement that would soon have to be made. SEAC worked up their advice overnight and next morning a highly unusual meeting took place, SEAC members face to face with the prime minister and his Cabinet. Momentarily, methodical and clear-headed scientists and desperately tense and anxious politicians sat across the table from one another.

Within hours the politicians were making statements in Parliament. It is time to return from the realms of analysis to the arena of action.

The world changed

Between 3.30 and 4.30 on Wednesday 20 March 1996 Stephen Dorrell, secretary of state for health, and Douglas Hogg, minister of agriculture, made statements in the House of Commons about BSE. Mr Dorrell reported the latest opinion from SEAC: the most likely explanation of the (by then 10) cases of CJD in young people was that they were linked to exposure to BSE through eating beef before the specified bovine offal ban of 1989. He added SEAC's conclusion that the risk from eating beef in 1996 was likely to be extremely small. Mr Hogg explained that on SEAC advice MAFF would require all beef animals more than 30 months old to be deboned under MHS supervision, and would ban all MBM from any species of mammal in all forms of animal feed.

Our world changed at a stroke. This was no exaggeration. Our principal finance officer came into my office while the statements were being made in Parliament, and I remember saying to him that this meant the end of the ministry of agriculture as we knew it. So it did, though the end came slowly, in several blows. That, however, was a small parochial concern compared with the fury and hysteria which took over inside and outside government and raged for many weeks. BSE was the top story on radio and TV and on the front pages of every newspaper. Inside government there was a meltdown of the normal ways of conducting business; at the highest level ministers ran hither and thither, meeting several times a day, sometimes in this or that committee, sometimes in none. There was often no time to report the conclusions of one ministerial group before another had met and reached conclusions going off at a tangent from the previous one if not flatly contrary to it. I have given this chapter the heading 'Much Like a War' but I don't think such chaos would have been tolerated in wartime.

Both among ministers and the general public there was intense anger trained on MAFF. In most people's eyes a major food scare and the department of government responsible for food safety were as one. A danger to human health had been declared, and the ministry must have been sitting on information. Indeed wasn't that what people had been suspecting ever since John Gummer had been challenged to feed a beefburger to his daughter back in 1990? Much fury was directed at MAFF. It was written all over the faces of the ministers I saw daily – except that of MAFF's senior minister, Douglas Hogg. This equating of MAFF with the problem of BSE was a superficial reaction. It did not survive the painstaking analysis of a public inquiry four years later. But it was never dislodged from the public mind, nor from the minds of some at the centre of the Whitehall machine.

Those then were the atmospherics, from the day of the twin statements in Parliament. Inside the offices of MAFF the atmosphere was different. We were locked down in intense activity. Office hours became longer and longer. Easter was cancelled for us that year. Officials and ministers carried on as usual through the Easter weekend. I did not get home again in daylight until daylight had lengthened at the very end of April.

The activity was on two levels: practical and political. At the practical level there were problems in all directions demanding immediate solutions. Protecting public safety was the top priority. This meant putting into action SEAC's advice on taking special precautions with cattle over a certain age. It was quickly decided to go one step further and keep these older cattle out of the food chain altogether. There was a surge of ideas for going further and slaughtering whole swathes of the British cattle herd, which had to be sifted and evaluated only to be discarded as disproportionate.

Public consumption of beef had not surprisingly dropped sharply after the 20 March announcement. What was surprising was that it started to pick up again quite quickly; much more quickly in Britain than it did on the continent where, by any reckoning, the risk from eating beef was vastly lower. But in the short term there was a large amount of beef with nowhere to go – other than into cold storage.

Some specialist operations were hard hit. The renderers, a vital outlet for waste products from the slaughterhouses, found themselves unprofitable overnight when, on SEAC advice, MBM could no longer be sold to animal feed compounders. They had to be subsidised for a time. Slaughterhouses were hit by the sharp drop in consumption which meant no butcher needed nor wanted any fresh stock for some weeks; and they were hit because they were holding stocks of beef from the older animals which were suddenly barred from consumption.

All these were new problems out of the blue, calling for innovative solutions which had also to be cost-effective. Fortunately there was one clear head amid the turmoil. Richard Packer seized each problem in turn and solved it in quick time. If it had not been for his long experience of agricultural markets, incisive mind, steady judgment and speed of decision-taking, there would have been real chaos to add to the general hysteria. It was his finest hour. Very little has been written by way of praise for MAFF officials and their handling of BSE so I think it is time to put on record that in this first torrid phase of the crisis Richard Packer saved the day, several times over; in the first few weeks by constructing the schemes to protect the public and keep the beef market ticking over; and then a few weeks down the track in working with his European Commission counterpart to point the way forward from the deadlock into which anti-Europeans in Westminster propelled the government.

Douglas Hogg to his great credit worked seamlessly with Richard Packer and the officials, turning his powerful legal mind and giving his (less powerful) political support to the actions he was persuaded were needed.

Meanwhile at the political level I was sent out each day to represent MAFF at the discussions which other ministers insisted on having, mainly in the Cabinet Office but sometimes in the House of Commons, in the room of the Deputy Prime Minister, Michael Heseltine. Heseltine could hardly bring himself to speak to me, such was his barely controlled rage at the turn of events. Others were more civil. But these meetings smacked of displacement activity. They were not materially helpful to what needed to be done.

They were least of all helpful on the European front. The first reaction from continental countries to the sight and sound of public panic over BSE was, quite unsurprisingly, to ban all trade in beef from Britain. As seen from the continent theirs was a wholly proportionate measure to protect public safety in their countries while the new situation – which had been sprung on them without any prior warning – was assessed. In Westminster this 'beef ban' provoked a furious reaction, led of course by the Eurosceptics. John Major's government was dragged in their wake. In Brussels the Commission were making their own attempt to find some firm ground in the sea of fears and emotions into which the UK announcement had pitched them. They came up with the idea that what was needed was a 'BSE eradication plan' to which EU veterinarians and then their political masters might subscribe to. They looked to the UK to have first shot at this.

MAFF set about it. The idea grew and gained ground. But it took time, and ministers were intolerant of the time it was taking. There was insistence in Westminster that this whole problem of the beef ban must be resolved at the very latest at the next European Council or Summit, scheduled to be held in Florence in late June. Desk work in London was going too slowly. A team of high-level emissaries must be sent round Europe to rally support for the UK position.

So, one Sunday afternoon at the beginning of June an aircraft of the Queen's Flight took off from Northolt with the Foreign Secretary, Malcolm Rifkind, the Minister of Agriculture, Douglas Hogg, their two private secretaries, and Andrew Cahn from the Cabinet Office and me on board. We were to visit as many of the 14 capitals of the EU member states as we could in the space of a week. We touched down in ten or eleven, I think (missing out Denmark, Sweden and Austria). The atmosphere in the cabin of our plane was difficult. Malcolm Rifkind barely spoke to Douglas Hogg and I don't think spoke to me throughout the week. The cabin attendants, possibly quite well drilled in attending on dysfunctional groups, did their best for us; the very best were the fresh scones with strawberry jam and clotted cream served on days when we were in the air at tea-time.

Our little delegation was received coolly in most places. We were seen by German ministers in Bonn (the German government had not yet completed its move to Berlin), and by President Chirac in Paris. I had the mild thrill of walking with Douglas Hogg up the famous front steps of the Elysée Palace and being shown into a first floor room where Chirac awaited us. He graciously took our provisional BSE eradication plan from my hands, and listened courteously as Hogg set out our position. The sight of Britain in deep trouble tends to bring out a touch of warmth in the French. There was a moment of comedy in Rome. We were about to be shown into the presence of the Italian prime minister in the Palazzo Chigi. A pair of enormous panelled doors – they seemed about 20 feet high – swung gently open for us to enter. Rifkind's mobile phone rang at that instant and he stepped back into a corner of the ante-room to take the call. It was his prime minister with some last-minute instructions. There was an awkward pause while the Italian prime minister and his team peered at the open doorspace, wondering where their British visitors had got to.

In Madrid or Lisbon, I forget which, there was a lively car cavalcade. In most places we were driven through the streets of the capital fairly calmly but a few governments gave us full-scale security treatment: escort with flashing lights, screaming sirens, outriders. A performance of that kind had near-fatal consequences in Dublin. We were travelling back to the airport from our meeting with the Irish ministers. Our convoy was taking the special precautions against attack that consist of cars swinging from side to side in S patterns, the principal cars holding a relatively straight course while the escort cars weave from side to side in front and behind to fend off any overtaking. We were travelling in this fashion down O'Connell Street at something like 60 miles an hour, taking up three lanes of the road, when two young girls stepped out of McDonald's some way in front of us and started to walk across the road, sipping milkshakes. They caught sight of us, stopped and stood motionless in our path, still sipping their milkshakes, as our convoy sped past them weaving as it went. Steady nerves! It was their salvation.

At the end of the week, ten or eleven capitals under our belts and no nearer at all to wringing any change out of the EU position, we headed back over London; over London and on up to Edinburgh. Rifkind, pulling rank, insisted that he should be dropped off home in Edinburgh first, before the rest of us were landed back at Northolt.

This was a memorable and colourful week, but of no real consequence. While we had been jetting round Europe, Richard Packer had been working with his opposite number, the Agriculture Commissioner's chef de cabinet, on a more solid form of the eradication plan. It was their version which came to form the basis of an agreement – of a kind – at the Florence European Council two weeks later.

Over the remainder of 1996 and into 1997, the focus was partly on developing and refining the domestic schemes already referred to, and partly on discussions on the European front. One particular call to arms was when the European Parliament, which then had less power than it acquired later under the Lisbon Treaty, called for a UK minister to appear before their committee of enquiry into BSE. Douglas Hogg refused to go, playing the Conservatives' habitual line of disrespecting the European 'Assembly'. Richard Packer was nominated in his place, and astounded the MEPs with truculent responses to their accusatory line of questioning, telling them at one point that in effect BSE had been 'an act of God'! This took the wind out of their sails.

So we limped on into the spring of 1997 when, in the May Election, Tony Blair ushered in a 'new dawn'. Did BSE have a decisive impact on the Conservatives' defeat? Significantly Kenneth Clarke in his memoirs chronicling that period makes no mention of BSE. He lays principal blame for the election defeat on the divisions within the party over Europe. Seen in that light, BSE did no more than show up the weakness. BSE events showed up the collective brain failure from which a sect of the Conservatives were suffering: chronic aversion to Europe. This disease smouldered on for twenty more years before flaring up virulently over Brexit.

New government – new expectations

Not all changes of government are as difficult for the civil service as the change from 18 years of Conservative rule to the arrival of Tony Blair's Labour government turned out to be. Whitehall civil servants were widely keen to see a new government in 1997 and to respond to new ministers' ideas. The Labour ministers coming into office did not see it like this at all. They were convinced that they would be dealing with civil servants irremediably steeped in Thatcherite thinking. They did not expect to be able to shift that, nor did they want to work with it, so they came ready to work round it. This hindered effective engagement between government and civil service, certainly in the upper reaches of Whitehall, for some long time. There were exceptions. Bernard Donoughue (whom we met in chapter 6), now appointed as MAFF's minister in the Lords, recognised me and treated me as someone he knew he could work with. He passed that view on to his boss, Jack Cunningham, and as a result I enjoyed easier relations from the start than did Richard Packer.

The Blair government came in with the general idea of turning round many policies, and of acting on many of the wishes of their voters. One message they had got loud and clear from the voters (specifically from the professional lobbyists on behalf of consumers) was that food safety was not safe in MAFF's hands. So there was a plan from the outset to set up a new food agency which would take over food safety and standards. As for BSE, well, the Blair government would mend fences with the EU, put Britain back at the heart of Europe, and get the beef ban lifted in short order. Blair had this as one of his personal targets.

Accordingly two activities which bulked large for me over the next three to four years were negotiations in Brussels over the beef ban, and negotiations with the Department of Health over creation of the new Food Standards Agency (it was to report to Health ministers). Then from the beginning of 1998 through 1999 a very large amount of my time went on responding to the BSE Inquiry which Labour set up.

Unlike many EU discussions the negotiations over the beef ban were not for the most part carried out in committee but between a small team of Commission officials and a small team from the UK. On most occasions I led for the UK, with our deputy chief veterinary officer on one side and an official from Northern Ireland on the other. Our best chance was to start with a concession for Northern Ireland where the number of BSE cases had been lowest. Across the table sat, for the Commission, the German official who rose to notoriety when he led the talks with the Greeks on the crisis in their economy: Horst Reichenbach. He was fair with us, but he had no room to make any concessions for some long time. We were sent home again and again to come up with cast-iron evidence and more refined proposals – for extremely limited concessions. So frequent were my trips to Brussels over this period in 1997-98 that the *Financial Times* published a profile of me under the heading 'Classical scholar who lives out of a suitcase'. It often felt like that. Gratifyingly my efforts, though they were slow in bringing any returns, were at least recognised in London. I received a couple of hand-written thank-you notes from Tony Blair and one from Clare Short as Secretary of State for Northern Ireland.

Negotiations over the creation of the Food Standards Agency were less physically exhausting since no travel was involved, but they were no fun. The

Department of Health officials were icily polite but could barely conceal their pleasure at taking food safety work out of our hands. The case for doing so was never very clear in objective terms. Changes in machinery of government do not often rest on logical arguments; more a matter of responding to some general public mood or political preference with touches of window-dressing. I recalled a consumer conference that I had attended in Swansea in summer 1995 when I had been openly mocked by the consumer leaders present for daring to mention MAFF and food safety in the same breath. Our credibility had been shot well before the BSE crisis broke. Richard Packer spent some effort trying to argue against the creation of the food agency, to no avail; he merely strengthened the feeling in the upper reaches of government that he was 'part of the problem'.

The new agency when it came into operation made a very good job of turning the page on what had gone before and creating a wholly new approach. It made a point of operating with a high degree of openness, holding its Board meetings in public and making freely available information about new threats to food safety at a very early stage. Past practice would have been (as with SEAC and BSE) to make very sure of data before releasing it. The Food Standards Agency deliberately set out to test how the public would react to being told about threats in the offing and clouds on the horizon. On the whole their approach seemed to have been met with a more mature public response, less febrile than it was in the early 1990s. Perhaps this was the way of the future. Whether it would have stood the test of BSE-vCJD in 1995-96 is another matter.

During this time a particular safety issue that fell to me to handle was the use of organophosphates (OPs), in particular their use in sheep dip. There were two angles to this. It had been argued for many years that OP sheep dip had harmful effects on farm workers; that regular exposure to sheep dip resulted in damage to the central nervous system. Then one particular campaigner produced a theory that OPs were the root cause of BSE. The available data from medical research did not seem to support the first line of argument, while the second failed to recognise that a fully satisfactory explanation for BSE had by now already been given. Argument rumbled on and in the end I was asked to chair an interdepartmental committee to draw together all (all) relevant information from every corner of Whitehall. These turned into some of the largest meetings I ever chaired. Thirty or more specialists gathered round a gigantic table in an elegant room at the top of Nobel House and said their piece. At the end of several meetings we were still unable to see firm pointers to a link between OPs and nervous disorders in shepherds, let alone BSE. But the knowledge that we were taking this fresh hard look at the evidence reached the campaigners and some of them were grateful to us. It led to the one and only occasion when I was singled out for mention by name in the House of Lords. The Countess of Mar, who had championed the cause of the OP campaigners, when she learned that I had moved on from MAFF, voiced the regret of the sufferers that I had been taken off the case.

By 1998 the BSE crisis was subsiding and life, though still very busy, felt more on an even keel. Animosity between the UK and the other EU member states had abated. The New Labour government had sent out conciliatory signals on first taking office. Very early on they had declared that they would pay greater respect to the European Parliament than their predecessors had done. This was largely symbolic, but influential. I saw the warmth of the reaction from the other side, as I happened to travel with Jack Cunningham when he paid a visit to the Parliament in Strasbourg; his first, and the very first by any serving British minister for over 18 years. The excitement in the Parliament was tangible. Jack Cunningham basked in this and played the crowd – and caused anguish to his private secretary by hosting a celebration dinner in one of Strasbourg's more expensive restaurants, where the number of our guests grew uncontrollably and champagne flowed to all and sundry.

There was a Tony Blair factor at work too. Tony Blair enjoyed enormous popularity among British voters at the beginning, and he enjoyed quite some popularity on the continent too. He was a young leader, highly articulate, he spoke quite good French! Other member states were envious. Blair was everyone's idea of a fresh start. So attitudes towards Britain swung round markedly.

It all helped. The number of BSE cases was falling steadily. The number of vCJD cases had risen, but not dramatically. Lifting the beef ban was the main focus for us, and the negotiations, though difficult, had settled into a pattern. Perhaps life really would return to normal before much longer?

But then came the BSE Inquiry. I had had no experience of being caught up in a public inquiry. I don't think any of us had. At a stroke, it added an immense new workload. It took a little while to grasp that we were, each of us who had been involved with BSE in any way (prior to the March 1996 announcement), going to have to spend days and weeks reading back through all the written records of what we had done, meetings we had attended (even in a listening role); and would have to prepare detailed statements of evidence summarising all that as a basis for the inquiry to cross-question us. Any thought of life returning to normal had evaporated. This was hard going. We were each going to have to tread carefully – anything we might say could be used against us – and it was unclear in the early stages what the inquiry would be driving at.

This became a doubly stressful period. On the Brussels front we were straining to make further progress in lifting the ban on exports of beef from Britain. We hung on every decision or vote in the veterinary and food safety committees that decided our fate. Each scrap of news had to be flashed to No 10 which was equally avid for progress and chafing at MAFF's failure to deliver. On the home front I was having to squeeze more hours out of each day so as to pull my story together for the inquiry. I put immense pressure on my secretary Debbie, who felt it but stood up to it – and stood up for me through thick and thin. This was a friendship forged under fire, and we remained firm friends ever after.

For the inquiry, in line with government practice each of us in a senior position was provided with free legal advice. Richard Packer and I had a pair of skilled solicitors from the elite law firm Allen & Overy, the senior of our pair uniquely for a solicitor also a qualified QC. They were of great help. In my case though there was one drawback. The terms of reference of the inquiry meant that it would be looking exclusively at the period up till the bombshell announcement of 20 March 1996; at everything from the first emergence of BSE in the 1980s up till then, but at nothing beyond. The drawback was that I had mostly played a passive role in BSE decision-taking prior to March 1996. I had had other pressing things to do; active on the Meat Hygiene Service, but that was tangential to the main subject under investigation. My lawyers did their best to draw out significance from the bits that I had done, clearly feeling that my evidence seemed slight in relation to my seniority and the prominent part I had been playing more recently; but they struggled, and advised from time to time that if I could not depict my part more dynamically then I might be vulnerable to criticism.

The inquiry showed little recognition of how the civil service works. There was a running assumption that if you were present at a meeting you had subscribed to the conclusions, and that to do so you must have fully informed yourself about every aspect under discussion and fully satisfied yourself that you agreed with the conclusions. You could be held responsible. They seemed unaware that in civil service teams some people are more actively involved and more up to speed than others on one thing; and some may be primarily occupied with other, also highly, important issues. I held back from saying at any point that other things had been more pressing for me in the winter of 1995-96 than BSE, albeit I had haunting memories of serial lapses in the Meat Hygiene Service, each one hot news, and of leaving the front door some mornings with the latest horror story ringing out from the Today programme behind me, braced for an emergency debate in Parliament to be called that afternoon. BSE had been for other people to lead on.

All that said, I suffered no worse than those around me when the inquiry report came out, in the autumn of 2000. Publication stirred up the whole dreadful saga in the media again. The press burrowed for content to put under their preconceived headlines about 'The Guilty Men' but the inquiry had been sparing with criticism and the rather generalised points that they made did not support sensational newspaper stories. Nevertheless public association of BSE with the ministry that handled it lived on.

From the start of the New Labour government there were hostile pressures on Richard Packer. He had displayed formidable qualities at the height of the BSE crisis. It would hardly be an exaggeration to say that he single-handed saved operations from complete meltdown. What followed, for him, had a touch of Greek tragedy. His supreme strengths worked against him when the government changed. His total grasp of the BSE situation, and the pride he took in having extracted his country from the worst of it, was less than welcomed by his new masters. Incoming ministers rarely take kindly to a head of department who seems to know all the answers better than they do and to have a reason for not running with each new idea they come up with. That was part, part, of what came into play now. There were other darker forces too. Richard Packer had a sharp brain, and a sharp tongue and sharp elbows. Over his several years at the top he had had bruising encounters with a spread of people highly placed inside and outside Whitehall. When the going got tough for him, he could not call in allies within the Whitehall system to rally to his support. (Douglas Hogg had found himself similarly placed with his fellow MPs for similar reasons back in 1996.) To those outside government working in the world of industry it was self-evident that BSE had been a corporate disaster for which responsibility lay with MAFF, and that a head or two should roll for it. With the BSE Inquiry in full swing RJP was naturally resistant to giving ground to critics that could have been construed as admission of past fault. He stood his ground, with adamantine firmness. But with the inquiry's work completed he was finally pressed to take early retirement. He left the stage in early 2000.

He was not immediately replaced. It fell to me to keep his position warm until a successor had been appointed. So for three or four months I was acting permanent secretary. I dropped a few stitches but there were no disasters. I made an appearance before the Public Accounts Committee – one of the harder tests that is thrown at permanent secretaries – and was complimented at the end by the committee chairman, David Davis. Then I too was moved. Two reputations tainted by BSE.

I felt a strong desire to put BSE behind me and in work terms I was able to. But the nightmare lingered on. BSE the cattle disease had receded. There was light at the end of that tunnel. But vCJD? The number of cases in young people had risen by the year 2000 to around 150. Each case caused deep distress to the family: a young life cut short. Some of the families wrote to us in personal terms, angry. In the public mind there was an inalienable link between this disease and the ministry which had 'hosted' it. Still, 150 cases was low compared with the 185,000 cases of BSE in cattle and low compared with the projection of epidemiologist-in-chief Professor Anderson who had told us to be prepared for up to 500,000 cases of vCJD in humans. Was there light at the end of this tunnel too?

We could not be so sure. The reason lies deep in genetics. In short there is a place in the human genetic code where a person has two amino-acids in combination; with three possible combinations, two of one, two of the other, or one of each. All those who have succumbed to vCJD at a young age (with just one exception) have the combination that just 37% of the population have. The other 60% or so of us have combinations which may either (let us hope) give us immunity, but may only give us greater resistance, and just postpone the onset of the disease. We might have a longer incubation period. One of the most respected medical experts on CJD warned years ago that this meant there could conceivably be a second wave of vCJD cases still to come, that would break when those with the more resistant genetic make-up succumbed in later life. Now, 20 years on from March 1996, thirty years on from the time when the disease was probably picked up by those in whom it has so far emerged, can we see dim light at the end of this tunnel too? The uncertainty has not yet gone out of my mind.

13

INTO A WIDER WORLD

2000-2003

Friends and colleagues who knew me in my time at MAFF sometimes express surprise that I am a member of the Travellers Club in Pall Mall. They knew that I travelled innumerable times from London to Brussels, and occasionally to other countries of Europe. But isn't the Travellers Club for more serious travellers? My travels around the European Union would as a matter of fact have been more than sufficient to meet the rules of admission to the Travellers, but the next few pages will explain that I have travelled the world much more widely than my work in MAFF ever required.

My time at MAFF came to an end in the summer of 2000. A new permanent secretary had been appointed, Brian Bender from the Cabinet Office, with a mission to overhaul what was widely regarded by others in Whitehall as a failed institution. I could conceivably have dropped back into the post that I had occupied before my four months as stop-gap permanent secretary but I had been in that post for more than five years, all of them traumatic, and even if I had been willing to go back I think strong pressure would have been put on me to leave. I was part of the past.

It was lucky, then, that just at that time a post became vacant in the Department of Trade and Industry (DTI) which would suit me very well: Director General of World Trade Policy, a deputy secretary post. Unexpectedly, Tony Hutton who had been doing the job for three years and might have stayed longer was offered a post at OECD in Paris as director of their personnel department. He was well qualified for that, having done the equivalent job for five years at DTI, and he was not going to refuse to work in Paris on an international civil servant's salary. I had worked alongside his predecessor, Christopher Roberts, in the Uruguay Round of world trade negotiations so I had a track record; I knew at least some aspects of the job, and could offer a close knowledge of the problems of trade in agriculture, on which international negotiations repeatedly founder. DTI knew me, I knew them, it took only a brief exchange of letters to persuade the Cabinet Office that it would solve a problem if I moved across to DTI to take Tony Hutton's place. It would get me out of Brian Bender's way, and save the cost of sending me into early retirement. DTI's permanent secretary, Michael Scholar (ex-Treasury), made me feel welcome.

This deal was done and dusted during May, but Tony Hutton was not leaving for Paris until September. So I had three months in which to do not much else but read my way into the trade policy work and attend one or two meetings alongside Tony. This was far too long for a hand-over. Tony's staff prepared folder after folder of briefing material on every aspect of the job, all much too detailed to be really useful. Done with good intentions, but what it showed was that this trade policy team had not had to brief a new boss from scratch before. Tony had worked in that area earlier in his career, and his predecessor Christopher Roberts had done the job for many years.

There was an important meeting in Brussels once a month which I would be required to attend, a meeting of the heads of trade policy from each EU member state with the Commission's trade policy team. Trade policy was a subject area for which the Commission had 'full competence' - as was agriculture. So I was familiar with the constitutional position. The broad lines of policy were settled, and adjusted from time to time, by the Council of Ministers on advice from the Commission; the Commission were responsible for managing day-to-day business in line with ministers' instructions, on behalf of the member states, and responsible in particular for handling negotiations with countries outside the EU. There were many such negotiations in progress at any one time. The Commission guarded jealously their leading role in this, and (not altogether surprisingly) resented it when individual member states struck up dialogue with countries with whom they were negotiating. From the Commission's point of view, the proper channel for member states to use to feed in their views on the day-to-day conduct of business, and for the Commission to use to feed member states as much information as was good for them on the progress of tricky negotiations, was provided by formal meetings with member state officials which they held every Friday; throughout the year on one Friday a month at senior level – the level which I would attend – and on other Fridays at the level of deputies. The requirement for the Commission to hold these meetings was enshrined in the Treaty: it had been in Article 113 of the original Treaty of Rome, and this became Article 133 of the revised Treaty now in force. So the committee was commonly referred to as 'the 133 Committee', and old hands still often slipped back into calling it the '113 Committee': Full Members, or Titulaires, for the senior level, Deputies for the lower level.

These Friday meetings together with much emailing and phoning around that went on in between meetings amounted to a constant stream of communication between Commission and member states about where the problems were and how they should be dealt with. Those who criticise the Commission for being unelected, out-of-touch and high-handed are generally ignorant of how close this linkage is, on trade as it is on agriculture.

The monthly meetings of Full Members were to be a fixed part of my timetable once I started the job. Tony invited me to sit in with him at the last of these meetings that he attended, in July, so that I could be introduced to my future collaborators, and get the flavour of the discussions. I was mildly surprised. The pace of discussion was slow and stately, there did not seem to be any pressing need for decisions, discussions ran to time, and the timetable allowed for us all to adjourn for a two-hour lunch provided by the Commission, at which one or two sensitive issues could be aired, and Château Haut-Batailley flowed freely. This was, as I found out over time, a fair sample of a Friday 133 Committee: low tension, gentle pace, compared with what I had been used to in MAFF. But I am perhaps getting ahead of myself. That was July and I did not take up the reins until September. More about the nature of the work will emerge as we go along; more also about the extent of travelling, which I promised would feature in this part of the story.

Tony's parting advice to me was that my new secretary of state, Stephen Byers, would be going to India in a few months' time and I should make sure that I was taken with him. That sounded interesting. I did not realise how tricky it would prove to be.

September came and went without incident. I am not sure that I had any contact with the secretary of state but I got to know his minister of state, Richard Caborn, who took some interest in trade policy and was keen to push the case for launching a new Round of WTO negotiations. That was the big issue at the time. An attempt had been made only a year previously, at a meeting hosted by the US in Seattle, but had broken up in failure when the US had pushed their own interests rather too hard – and NGOs had caused a riot. So I sat in with Richard Caborn when he had meetings with his opposite numbers, the trade ministers – from France (in London) and Sweden (in Stockholm) in these my early weeks.

There was a tradition that the country holding the EU presidency hosted one meeting of the 133 committee at a place of their choice, so once in every six months the regular Friday meeting left Brussels. France held the presidency in the second half of 2000 and hosted our October meeting in Bordeaux. This was done in fine style. Our French colleague Jean-François Stoll was a stylish operator, and well-connected. The main event, once routine business had been done, was a visit to the fabled Château Margaux. We had a conducted tour of the cellars, where alcoves with the most precious vintages were sealed off behind iron grills; faded cobwebby labels going back to the 1860s and 1850s. Then followed dinner with the châtelaine, the owner of Château Margaux. She was Greek in origin, fluent in French, and her conversation was a blend of French combative style and Greek κέφι – high spirits. We were seated at round tables, eight or ten to a table. I felt honoured as a newcomer to be included at the hostess's table. There was, however, an element of challenge to this. Conversation turned to the differences between the range of wines on offer on the shop shelves in France and Belgium – French wines completely dominant – and the much wider variety of wines from around the world on offer particularly in Britain. I got nowhere with my line of argument that this was a good thing: a wide choice to meet consumers' tastes. No, shrieked our hostess, c'est une vraie invasion! France should be protected from this invasion of abominable foreign products. There, in a nutshell, was the difference between France and Britain on free trade. Sharpest over agricultural produce, like wine; but sharp too on a handful of other issues like 'audiovisual' – shorthand for protection for French films and TV. Jean-François Stoll had engineered a high-class introduction for me into one of the perennially sensitive points of trade policy.

A few weeks later Richard Caborn went on a visit to South Africa, and I went with him. We flew to Pretoria where we had a meeting or two with their highly-regarded minister for trade, one of the very few Anglo-Saxons in the post-apartheid government, and then we attended an event arranged by the locally-based British officials to promote sales of British products. Caborn treated the various members of the government whom he met with great familiarity, referring to them all by their first names rather than titles, including Thabo for Thabo Mbeki, the then prime minister; and reminding them at frequent intervals that he and some other New Labour ministers had been active campaigners against apartheid. I did not notice that his tone of familiarity was mirrored on the other side. Ministers in the New South African government were feeling the weight of responsibility for steering their country along the tricky path of reconciliation.

This was my first and is still my only visit to southern Africa. My handful of first impressions did not amount to much. Being driven in official cars on main roads with light traffic (in contrast with India), long lines of Africans – workers, or out of work? – walking endlessly along the side of the road. A distant view of the monument to the Great Trek. Fears about street crime in Johannesburg – and home crime everywhere, barred gates, guns under pillows. We had a brief brush with the dangers of Johannesburg when the First Secretary with whom I was riding suddenly ordered our driver to stop, and to take his car straight back to the High Commission, leaving us to order up a taxi for the continuation of our journey. My colleague explained that he had become fearful that our official driver was intent on taking us into a threatening part of town. Last impression: at the main trade promotion event, held in a marquee one evening, the electricity cut out and we were plunged into darkness but after a moment the audience broke into song, a low, slow and melancholy African hymn-like song.

Flying back up the length of Africa overnight at the end of this visit, I looked out at the vast stretch of complete darkness below us, and mused on what very large parts of the world there were about which I knew nothing. But this was changing.

Near to the end of the year, in mid-December 2000, and at short notice Bill Clinton made a visit to Northern Ireland and then delivered a speech to an invited audience at Warwick University. This was to be his last appearance anywhere outside the US before he handed over the office of President to George W Bush. Clinton enjoyed ecstatic publicity in Northern Ireland; he had been active in the peace process. I was among those invited to the Warwick event. I was nowhere near the front row but it was impossible not to be struck by the magnetic power of Bill Clinton's personality, to feel the charm. He exuded it, he played the audience, he radiated. At the end, Big US Security ensured that none of us, no-one, could move before the President had been safely whisked heavenwards. The long delay meant that I missed my evening Eurostar to Brussels and would be late for the 133 committee next day. No harm done. Our Brussels staff made sure that the reason for my late arrival was understood by all. When I walked in late, I might have been wearing the mantle of Clinton myself. In those far-off times, EU colleagues were fascinated by the closeness between the governments of London and Washington. I had brought a frisson of the special relationship into the staid Brussels meeting room.

Stephen Byers's trip to India, the trip that Tony Hutton had said was essential for me, did not come about until January 2001. This, like Caborn's trip to South Africa, was to be part government-to-government talks, part trade promotion. We were accompanied by a group of British businessmen with deals to settle and problems to discuss. On every trip to India we were instructed to challenge the super-high tariff that the Indians imposed on Scotch whisky to protect their own production of whisky of a lower grade. So the Director of the Scotch Whisky Association came with us – a retired diplomat whom I had last met as UK Ambassador to Belgium during the BSE crisis.

I had never been in India before. I was not a keen reader of the National Geographic, nor had I spent any time studying travel brochures and dreaming of holidays in India. From the moment we came out of the airport at Delhi I hit a wall of surprises. I was simply amazed at everything I saw. 'I have never been anywhere so different!' I exclaimed, in naive astonishment. The variety of costumes, the colour, the noise, the richness of smells, the chaos on the roads – but somehow things miss each other. Animals everywhere. I knew to expect the Brahmin cattle, but not the pigs and goats along the roadsides, nor elephants as part of the taxi system. And this was just along the main road from Delhi airport to the city.

We must have arrived on a Saturday because we then had a free day before any of our meetings started. This was unusual. It was very rare to have free time scheduled into our travel plans. But it appeared that Stephen Byers wanted to have a day to spend with the lady who was travelling with him – to whom I was never introduced. In any event he made clear that he would not be needing his private secretary or me; we could amuse ourselves for the day. We were all staying together in the high commissioner's residence, a spacious colonial building of the finest style, designed by Edward Lutyens, and rated among the very best of the rich and varied stock of British diplomatic buildings around the world. The house has a large garden, rich in birds. One of our high commissioners in the 1950s wrote a beautifully illustrated book about the birds in this garden month by month through the year. We could have settled for spending our free day here, and we would have been well looked after by the staff, headed by the major-domo who was dressed resplendently in pukka Indian servant's No 1 ceremonial uniform, complete with turban, sash and ornate frock coat.

But the private secretary and I felt a need to get out and see India. With the high commissioner's help, plans were made for us to go to the Taj Mahal and then on to other sites. Now it is not so well known, but I experienced it several times, that the weather in Delhi is really wintry in the first half of January. For a short season the chill comes down from the Himalayas, the temperature on the streets and in the offices (which have no heating) falls to around 4 degrees; local people go around swaddled in long thick scarves; and there is dense fog which only clears towards the middle of the day. The airport is regularly closed by fog up till lunchtime.

This hit our travel plans. We were put on a train to Agra, the roads being too dangerous in fog. The train crept along at a walking pace or not much more, obstructed by people and animals all along the line. We drifted through fog, with little sense of motion, but a sense that our day was slipping away from us. Cups of sweet milky tea from the chai wallah didn't do much for us.

Our reward was to see the staggeringly beautiful sight of the Taj Mahal just as the morning mist was lifting, the outline at first indistinct but coming into focus as it emerged from the mist, more and more detail coming into view as we watched. Black kites started taking to the air and sailing close around the exquisite contours of the building. We spent some time being guided through and around the mausoleum and gardens before linking up with a driver who then took us on to Fatehpur Sikri and the Mughal fort. The roads were now rated as safe on the British diplomatic scale, as the mist had been replaced by bright sunlight. But it was my first experience of being driven across country in India – terrifying all the way.

We arrived back at the high commissioner's residence quite late in the evening, not that Stephen Byers seemed at all bothered by that. He was quite pleased to have his private secretary back, but paid little attention to me. So it continued. The next day we made a call on the Indian trade minister, a fragile elderly man who came dressed in flowing robes. We held a session with the contingent of businessmen who rehearsed for us their various aims and concerns.

Duty done in Delhi we took off for Hyberabad where a large business conference was being held; a major annual fixture organised by the two leading Indian business confederations, and attended by many foreign visitors apart from us. My memory of this (which may have faded) is that the central event was an evening reception held out in the open, after dark, at the hill-top palace which had once belonged to the Nizam of Hyderabad. We were much further south now and the night air was warm. Stephen Byers was keen to meet the Chief Minister of the region (Andhra Pradesh), called Chandrababu Naidu, who was highly regarded (in Britain) for his effectiveness in putting through economic reforms. Once that encounter, which didn't amount to more than a brush-past, had taken place I wandered off around the palace grounds. The lights of Hyderabad glittered all around, below the hill-top. I found my way to a dilapidated outhouse of some kind where I found two full-height paintings, of King George V and his queen, Queen Mary. There they leaned against the outhouse wall, under cover but not much protected from the weather, not defaced or slashed, just cast aside as unwanted relics of Empire – or maybe originally kept as a precaution against restoration of the old regime?

In early March I was back in India again, not this time accompanying a minister but as part of a delegation with a mission to discuss problems which the Indians were saying stood in the way of launching a new WTO Round and must be solved first. For the UK government the launch of a new Round had become an important objective. It was an objective shared by the EU as a whole but Britain was working harder for it than some others. We might perhaps be able to use our 'special relationship' with India to help shift some of their objections. So I with my closest colleague from the Foreign Office, Michael Arthur, at that time the FCO's Economic Director in London, whom I had known by then for some 10-15 years, and a senior lady from the Department for International Development, had teamed up to see where we could get to. We had three sessions over two days with my Indian counterpart. We seemed to have made progress but then he was pulled back, and we finished up without agreement. Were we misguided in thinking there was any special relationship between us and the Indians? Yes and no. The Indians certainly at government level are determinedly independent and resistant to any hints of being pushed around by the British. On the other hand we do understand one another. We have a language in common and understand one another when we speak it. (Many Indians, it has to be said, speak English better, with a larger vocabulary and more variation of style, than most native English speakers.) My French counterpart (Jean-François Stoll) said in an unguarded moment that the French, keen as they are to do business with India, are jealous of two advantages the British have over them: we understand Indians when they speak English (the French struggle) – and we like their food! In addition to those basic points, there are the numerous personal ties between Indians in India and Indians living in Britain, and a huge flow of exchange visits particularly in the weeks around the end of the year. Through this we have a fine-grained understanding of the background to each other's positions, on trade and the economy as on many other matters. The British have certain advantages in dealing with government-to-government business – but we drift at our peril into treating this as a legacy, and an entitlement, of Empire. That, it is not.

My particular business in Delhi on this occasion completed, or rather left incomplete, I was scheduled to go on my own to Pakistan for talks with Pakistani officials in Islamabad, and from there to fly across to Cairo to link up again with Michael Arthur for talks with the Egyptians.

It is only two hours flying time from Delhi to Islamabad but it hits you immediately that you are arriving in a very different country: very Muslim, very military. Long prayers to Allah Akhbar were played on my Pakistan Airways plane before take-off. The journey was split into two flights, with a stop in Lahore. The British honorary consul turned out here to greet me, and take me to the VIP lounge. His name was Fakir Saheed Aijazuddin, but he could have been a retired English army officer: six foot six, lean and fit, wispy grey hair, and a cut-glass Sandhurst accent. Thoroughly charming, very correct, and clearly well-connected with the men of power and influence in Pakistan. In between giving me quick-fire accounts of Pakistan's government, his own family history

('We've been in Lahore for 14 generations') and a summary of a book he had just published about Pakistan's role in putting Nixon and Kissinger in contact with Chairman Mao, he would leap to his feet and greet someone coming into the lounge with 'General, I must introduce you to our British visitor, Mr Carden, a junior minister'.

It was by now clear that I was being given red-carpet treatment. With only a touch of exaggeration, the Pakistanis were treating this visit by a senior British official as a significant warming of relations after a period when their country had been cold-shouldered by Britain and the Commonwealth for the rigidity of their military rule. I stumbled as best I could through a testing situation.

Landing at Islamabad and walking across the tarmac, the first thing I saw was a couple of light planes with UN colours – there to patrol the border with Afghanistan. We were not far from a war zone here.

I stayed at the high commissioner's residence, to find that he was a former submarine officer turned diplomat, and his First Secretary an ex Scots Guards officer. So, military matched against military. No doubt our men were a fair match for the locals, but so very different from our men (and women) in Delhi.

The talks next day proved to be a roller-coaster for me. I was entertained to lunch by the top tier of government officials including a permanent secretary who introduced himself by saying 'I gather you are a John's man?' and the governor of their central bank who tested my knowledge of economic affairs to the brink. It must have been evident in the lunch conversation that I was well out of my depth. A session with my real opposite number, their senior man on international trade talks (Gulrez Yazdani, who now lives in Bedford) came as welcome relief.

At the end of the afternoon I was put back on a plane. Now this was meant to be the start of my journey to Cairo, travelling completely alone. I am sure my secretary who had booked my flights had very little idea what she was doing. She had booked me for the first leg of this journey on a local flight from Islamabad to Peshawar. Peshawar is in the North-West Frontier province of Pakistan, 30-40 miles from the Khyber Pass, in the so-called tribal areas. In my secretary's favour, it is a place that has become much better known since, than it was in early 2001. From Peshawar I was to fly on an Air Pakistan flight scheduled to stop at Al Ain in the United Arab Emirates (where I was to pick up my connection to Cairo) before continuing on to Abu Dhabi. Now why would a large airliner fly a full load of passengers from Peshawar to the Gulf?

The flight from Islamabad to Peshawar was on a small 30-seater aircraft which flew low, giving good views of the countryside. The passengers were all subdued, watching the sun set against the curve of mountains.

The plane going on from Peshawar to the Gulf was a full-size Airbus, fully booked. I had been squeezed on as a late addition. The arrivals hall was one simple shed, the departures hall another. When I walked into the departures hall I saw in a flash that I was the only European passenger. The hall was full of men (no women) in tribal costumes of all kinds, sitting, squatting, some praying on mats in little screened-off areas; most sitting quite quietly. They began quietly and shyly to cast glances at me. I was creating general surprise, and I felt my share of it. There was much smoking of strong cigarettes. I wished I could take some photographs of this richly exotic collection of travellers but sensed that that would not be well received. So I sat making a few notes, keeping my head down. Around me sat my fellow passengers, some in turbans, some in loose fitting head gear that spread around their shoulders, some in tight fitting embroidered head cosies, others in caps like deep pan pizzas. Some with the faces of Pakistani – or Afghan – tribesmen, others looking every inch like Arabs from Arabia.

Take-off was preceded by prayers over the sound system on the plane. There was a lot of jostling for seats but everyone was careful not to jostle me. I had no feeling of threat, just total amazement. How did I come to be here? There was a delay, then an announcement which I didn't fully understand but from which I gathered that we were to be diverted via Karachi – well south of the route we should have been taking. Now the background to this, which only emerged later, was that we were all travelling as luck would have it at the very time when, in Afghanistan, the Taliban were orchestrating the demolition of the Bhamiyan statues of Buddha. That act, as news of it emerged, caused international consternation and, rationally or not, airspace over Afghanistan was closed for a time. It was closed to us that night. For our flight trying to get to the Gulf and for me trying to get to Cairo, it caused a huge detour. Our plane took off in the end and we landed at Karachi, my fellow passengers now all agitated, vocal, and clambering about between the rows of seats. The plane needed to refuel. This was all done quite briskly, but my connection at Al Ain was tight. I could see that I was more than likely to miss my flight to Cairo. I made contact with the pilot, the one and only person on the plane who I was able to communicate with, and he agreed, it was a risk, but he would see what he could do. On we went, me with the tribesmen who were bound, it was now clear, for Mecca, for a Hajj. As we descended towards Al Ain two hours late our pilot told me he had seen the flight to Cairo taking off into the night. He advised me to stay on his plane to Abu Dhabi where I would have a larger choice of alternative flights. So I did, and spent a few night hours in the very elegantly decorated Abu Dhabi airport lounge before taking a flight to Milan and from there on to Brussels. I had given up on Cairo. I would have arrived too late for the planned programme of meetings. Instead I arrived in time for Friday's 133 meeting, greeted with warmth and curiosity by colleagues because news had spread of my disappearance off the radar somewhere out from Peshawar.

The next month or two were quieter. In April I went to Switzerland for a meeting of the 'Evian Group'. This was an annual gathering of policymakers, opinion formers and academics from around the world, for the purpose of promoting the cause of free trade and open markets. Named I suppose after an original meeting at Evian, across the lake, it was generally held in Montreux on Lake Geneva. The self-appointed leader of the meetings was Jean-Pierre Lehmann, a professor of international political economy at the IMD business school in Lausanne. He was totally dedicated to the cause of free trade. He had founded the Evian Group and held it together by a combination of charisma and outstanding zeal for the cause.

Britain has pretty consistently supported the principle of free trade and we consistently worked to promote it in the ranks of the EU, pulling against the protectionist views of France and the southern member states. So the leading official on trade policy in London was expected to attend 'Evian'. That apart, it was an excellent networking opportunity. Leading trade officials from distant countries in Asia and North America were there, as was the head of the WTO.

These were good times for supporters of free trade and open markets. Major changes in that direction were taking place in the world economy. India had started on a process of economic reform in the early 1990s, gradually dismantling its system of high tariffs on imports and elaborate state subsidies for industries of all kinds. China was moving strongly in the same direction, working seriously to qualify for membership of the WTO. There was, too, much evidence that the moves India and China were making to open up their economies were having beneficial effects for them: India's growth rate was around 8% a year, China's if anything a little higher. It was reckoned, by 2000/2001, that hundreds of millions of people in India and China had been lifted above the United Nations poverty line by these economic changes; still desperately poor but lifted out of extreme poverty. The large NGOs that worked to improve lives of those in extreme poverty around the world such as Oxfam, Save the Children and CAFOD, had all come to the view that free trade was helpful to their objectives; they directed their fire against conspicuous unfair trade practices – above all the farm subsidies paid in Europe and the United States. Each of these NGOs now had their own specialist officers for trade policy, who kept a close eye on the positions that governments were taking, and on the progress or lack of progress in international trade negotiations. These trade specialists in the NGOs were people with whom I had regular meetings in London, and I had high regard for several of them. Old hands at trade policy tried to dismiss them but like it or not they were serious operators.

If all this liberalisation and economic progress in developing countries was going to have adverse effects on workers in richer countries, that was not yet showing through. It was assumed that specific industries in the UK would take a hit, as work was switched to Asia where it could be done more cheaply. The Labour government under Tony Blair and Gordon Brown firmly favoured free trade as helping to relieve poverty worldwide, whilst promising government support for specific industries at home that ran into difficulty as a result of it; help not in the form of protection against imports or subsidies for failing industries but, for workers who lost their jobs, help to retrain and relocate. Patricia Hewitt once she became Secretary of State for Trade and Industry in the summer of 2001 was articulate in taking that line. As MP for a constituency with a very large number of voters of Indian origin, she had an interest in seeing both sides of the issue. The idea that free trade, globalisation, might have much more widespread adverse impact on populations in Europe had not yet emerged; not in Britain, though it was already stirring in France.

Later in April it was the turn of a new presidency to host a meeting of the

133 committee away from home. Sweden this time and they chose to take us to the island of Gotland, in the middle of the Baltic. This was an eye-opener for all of us except possibly our colleague from Denmark. Gotland, we learned, had a fascinating history centred on trade. It had been a flourishing staging post at the height of the Hanseatic League. Ships criss-crossing the Baltic between Russia, Germany, Poland and places west – Sweden and beyond – had needed to put in at Gotland to take on fresh food and water. Then, as ships became more powerful, and as trade between Hanseatic ports subsided, somewhere around 1600 Gotland was by-passed, its usefulness gone. By the time the modern Swedes began to take interest in it again, they recognised the value of preserving this survival from the past, and they have conserved it well. The main city, Visby, is a medieval walled town that has survived as if in a time capsule, rich in medieval buildings. The rest of the island is peppered with medieval churches, 93 of them. I was so taken with discovering this piece of Europe about which I had known nothing that I took the family back for a holiday that summer.

On 7 June 2001 there was a general election following which Stephen Byers was moved from DTI to the Department of Transport, Local Government and the Regions. I was glad : I had found him more difficult to work with than any other minister in my whole career. It was not that he was actively difficult but that he seemed not to want a working relationship with me of any kind; nor with most of his other officials. He lost my respect conclusively over the following episode. I had been called to his office to explain some piece of upcoming business, and took with me two of my leading assistants, Rachel and Caroline, so that they could contribute to the discussion. Entering his office I introduced them, saying in a few words what each of them did, and its significance in our trade work. Byers stared down at some papers, never lifted his head and, after a short but significant silence, said coldly: 'What is this meeting about?'

Byers was replaced at DTI by Patricia Hewitt, and Richard Caborn by Liz Symons. In a new twist to the structure of government, Liz Symons was appointed both as trade minister in DTI and as a minister of state in the Foreign Office. This gave the Foreign Office more of a basis for taking close interest in our trade policy work than they had had before. It raised questions about whether they might take the subject over entirely. That would be an easy step. Trade policy work was handled by the ministry of foreign affairs in about half of the EU member states, so there would be no serious mismatch there. Was DTI about to surrender to the FCO?

This question would play out over the remainder of my time in DTI. But now it was time to take flight again, first to Washington and then to Brasilia. This was, I think, my first trip to Washington since taking up post. The Commission's Director-General for Trade, Peter Carl, explicitly asked me *not* to go. He had a range of issues under discussion with the Americans and feared that the UK, with its tendency to go its own way and play on its (rather good) contacts in Washington, would complicate his job. Advice from my staff in London and Brussels was that I should ignore Peter Carl, and the message from Washington was that I would be welcome. So I went. I was becoming pretty used to long haul flying and to the schedules that embassies imposed, but I always found travelling east to Asia much easier than travelling west, to America. I find it much easier to wake up early and get started than to stay up late and keep going after normal bedtime. The embassy in Washington regularly planned a programme for officials arriving mid-afternoon from London that included a dinner-discussion, requiring one to stay at least half awake until what would have been well after midnight at home. I hated this. The only way to cope was to refuse all offers of alcohol on the flight out. On this my first visit to Washington it was not helpful that my deputy, travelling with me, was well dosed with alcohol by the time we landed, and made at best a slurred contribution to the evening's proceedings.

From Washington I was scheduled to travel on my own to Brasilia, changing planes in Miami and Sao Paolo. It was my first visit to Brazil and my first encounter with the extra pain imposed on government visitors through the seat of government being situated in the middle of nowhere – two hours' or so flying time from either of the two major cities where international flights all arrived.

Flying into Sao Paolo in the early morning, I had to wait two hours for a connecting flight to Brasilia. There I was received by our relaxed and courteous ambassador Roger Bone. I was put up in his beautiful ambassador's residence surrounded by sub-tropical trees and flowers, and joined there to my complete surprise, and the ambassador's, by my counterpart from the Department of International Development who had been sent to shadow me. Brasilia is a cross between a university campus and a sculpture park, landmark buildings sprinkled around with wide open spaces between them. Impressive in its way, but it falls short of making a coherent impact.

My talks with the Brazilian officials centred on the prospects for WTO talks in the autumn, and the chances of getting agreement on the launch of a new WTO Round. This continued to be the big issue. Brazil with its fast-growing economy and major place in agricultural trade was just beginning to emerge as a heavyweight player on the WTO scene. My visit happened to coincide with a strike by government workers. There were protests outside several of the buildings where I was trying to hold serious talks. These protests took the form of mini-carnivals: hours of merry music – but loud! – and dancing. It was a most effective way of making business inside the offices hard to conduct, whilst the high-spirited merrymaking of the 'protesters' seemed quite effective in deflecting hostility and discipline.

Summer holidays (and our family visit to Gotland) over, the pace of business quickened. At DTI we now had the two new ministers, Patricia Hewitt and Liz Symons; also a new permanent secretary. Michael Scholar had sadly left to become President of St John's College, Oxford. His successor, Robin Young, was keen to make his mark.

On trade policy, all talks were concentrated on the possibility of launching a new WTO Round that autumn. Liz Symons was reading her way into the subject but had not yet taken part in many face-to-face discussions with other countries. She did however have a good feel for whether a negotiation was ripe, and ready to bring to a conclusion, as she had spent the main part of her career in the world of trade unions; she had been top official in the union for senior civil servants. She had no hesitation in telling me and Michael Arthur that this negotiation felt to her unripe.

My round of travels kicked off briskly in September, with day trips first to Budapest (Hungary was not yet a member of the EU, but active in the WTO) and then to Rome for a bilateral with my Italian opposite number. Italy's stance on trade issues frequently differed from ours but their man on the 133 committee had been in post for many years, he was a veteran of 133 business, so I hoped to sway him a bit in our favour by paying court to him on his home ground. A 5 am start from Harpenden on each of these days, and home to bed.

Friday saw an informal EU trade ministers meeting in Bruges. On Saturday I took off at tea-time, flying alone to Bangkok. There I linked up with a number of European colleagues, officials and ministers, for an onward flight to Hanoi where we were all to take part in a formal meeting of European and Asian trade ministers. British ministers had decided not to attend, so I was to 'fly the flag' for the UK. I stepped off the plane at Hanoi and to my surprise was steered to a red carpet, presented with a large bouquet of flowers by a Vietnamese official, in a blaze of flash-lights; then into a big black Mercedes flying a large Union Jack on the bonnet. This car, accompanied everywhere by a police motorcyclist riding in front, was my transport throughout my time in Hanoi. I had come of age as a trade ambassador!

The police outrider who swept the streets clear in front of me with a blue flashing light was something of an obstacle to tourism. There was no escaping him – and a security man who stuck to me like a limpet when I was out of the car. I had fleeting visits to Ho Chi Minh's tomb and the president's palace, and appreciated the streets of elegant French colonial houses in the city centre – no sign of bomb damage here or anywhere else. The atmosphere was of a firmly communist country, under strict police and military control, although that was soon to change, as I saw in two subsequent visits. Our business consisted partly of a large formal committee meeting, in which the EU trade commissioner Pascal Lamy did most of the talking for the EU side. But part for me was a one-to-one meeting with Vietnam's trade minister, for which my car conducted me with due ceremony across the town.

That day's business completed, I set off to fly to Tokyo, which involved changing planes in Ho Chi Minh City, previously known as Saigon. The date was 11th September, the year 2001. By the time I arrived in Saigon it was around ten in the evening. I went into the departure lounge, waiting for my flight to Tokyo. The lounge was almost empty. The barman called across to me in great excitement: 'Watch breaking news, watch breaking news!' and there on the CNN screen I watched the second of the hijacked airliners fly into the second tower of the World Trade Center in New York. This was a shattering thing to see – in any case, but especially as I was about to get on a plane. I have never been so grateful for mobile phones. I rang home, spoke to Poppy, and we swift-ly agreed that Saigon was not the best place to be if the world was about to erupt in turmoil. Tokyo would be better.

I flew into Tokyo after very little sleep. The flight took five hours but I and my colleague flying with me were so electrified by what we had seen that sleeping was far from our minds. There was consolation in flying down over Japan in the early morning and having a fantastic geographer's view of the coastline up past Osaka, and an absolutely perfect view of Mount Fuji in the light of the rising sun.

We came into Tokyo through the early morning rush-hour. On the streets, people were only just catching up with what had happened in New York and Washington. Our ambassador had been up all night in frantic discussions. Not surprisingly the business I had gone for – a long round of meetings with Japanese officials, then dinner with the ambassador and 40 businessmen – was overcast by events.

My next impression of 9/11 was flying into Heathrow early the following morning to see the airport carpeted, everywhere except the key runways, densely packed with planes of US airlines, all grounded, as they were for some days. It was one of the two images of 9/11 that are fixed in my mind: that barman in Saigon, and Heathrow turned into a parking lot for hundreds of US aircraft.

Doha

The attacks in Washington threw trade policy into turmoil. Was it now going to be possible to proceed with plans for a WTO meeting of ministers, scheduled to be hosted by Qatar in Doha? Were hopes of launching a new WTO Round now dead? There was turmoil over this in DTI for a start, and warfare spread between departments in Whitehall. Liz Symons, tending to apply her sense of realism, came out vehemently against. The state of the world was just too fraught; there was no point in going ahead. Michael Arthur and I tried in vain to calm her. World leaders on both sides of the Atlantic came out rather fast with the contrary view that it would be best to proceed; countries of the world must show that they could pull together.

Liz Symons shifted her ground: worthwhile it might be, but too dangerous in Doha, an Arab state, no great distance from Afghanistan; and moreover Osama bin Laden's tapes had been broadcast to the world by Al Jazeera (Doha-based). This point of view was shared by all trade delegates world-wide. The US was building up to open war with Afghanistan, and had a major military base outside Doha, and Qatar was teeming with immigrant workers, mainly from Pakistan. Let's meet anywhere but Doha.

In the search for alternative cities to meet in, two emerged: Geneva and Singapore. By mid-October there was high expectation that the meeting would be moved, but decision came there none. Within DTI, ministerial fire was turned on me, for not 'gripping the issue'. WTO member countries across the world said, this is a decision which only the US and UK can take; they are in the frontline of military action. In Brussels the Commission said, we can't judge the security risks; of all our EU member states, it is the UK which has an embassy in Qatar and renowned security services.

The Qataris upped the ante, challenging doubters to say why Doha was not a safe place to meet. The FCO blinked first, sent a man to Doha who returned saying all seemed fine. The US then sent in Vice President Cheney who, against our expectations, told the Emir of Qatar they'd be happy to come.

So Doha it was to be. Concerns then turned to what protection we would have. The FCO was by now so committed that they wanted no further questions asked about personal security. The security services had spoken. But my staff – and our ministers – were in a state of mounting unease. We would need to take a delegation of 20-30 people including some junior staff. These were people for whom normal life was commuting to London and sitting at an office desk. They were vocally unwilling to spend a week in a war zone. With DTI ministers' support I challenged the edict from the top of the Foreign Office and paid a call on an office in an unfamiliar part of the Old Admiralty building facing on to Horseguards Parade. We extracted – but only a day before we were to take off for Doha – agreement that we could have two Scotland Yard personal protection officers for our delegation of home civil servants for the duration of the conference.

The conference went ahead and we were in Doha for a week in early November. On the flight out, one of our protection officers sat next to me all the way. Our plane made a scheduled stop at Bahrain and we had a short time in the lounge there, to admire displays of the local black pearls, and lots of stately Arabs exuding wealth. As we got back on the plane the protection officer murmured to me that I had better not tell my staff but news had reached him that the Americans had just shot dead someone acting suspiciously at the gate of their military base on the outskirts of Doha. I kept this to myself.

At first sight Qatar is akin to the surface of the moon. A great spread of desert out of which sprouted, in the last ten years of the twentieth century, a crop of office blocks, smart mosques and hotels, all in a very limited area on the coast; white and cream against the bright blue sky - normally bright blue, though for part of our week in November it was overcast and a few drops of rain fell. A very few palm trees and no grass except in straight lines where the ground is drip-fed by irrigation pipes. With vast fields of oil and gas, money flows out of the ground into the hands of the extensive ruling family. Much of the work of keeping the wheels of the Qatari economy turning is done by immigrants, guest-workers, from Pakistan and elsewhere.

For an entire week we were cooped up all but permanently inside a security compound thrown around a huge conference centre and a couple of hotels. The Qataris made a show of tight security with plenty of machine guns on display, and a scattering of anti-aircraft guns at a few checkpoints. Individual security guards on each floor by the lifts seemed mainly to be dozing, quite often plainly asleep. Inside the conference centre bodyguards were assigned to a few key characters. The US Trade Representative Robert Zoellick was conspicuous because wherever he went he moved surrounded by two concentric circles of security men, immensely tall Qataris in flowing robes forming the outer ring, his own US security team, themselves no dwarves, only just visible on the inside. For the UK we had our team of two from Scotland Yard. With all the foreign workers inside as well as outside the conference centre, of many different origins and (as my security guard admitted) subject to no form of vetting, I am sure a determined aggressor could have blown us all up if he had tried. But we came through; nervous but unharmed.

The conference itself, with all this tension, was productive. It was the tense state of world affairs and relations between nations that made it as productive as it was. With hindsight the deal done was done under duress and for that reason it did not stick. But that is running ahead.

WTO ministerial conferences consist of a few plenary sessions, all 160 or so delegations in one large meeting hall, and much longer stretches when the

INTO A WIDER WORLD

key negotiations are being driven by about twenty delegates handpicked by the chairman of the conference and the head of the WTO between them, to represent the largest interests and key points of view. These select few are shut away in what is always called the Green Room, often for hours if not days at a time. While they are hatching the plot, the rest occupy their time talking to each other, maybe negotiating on specific problems, maybe working out deals for the future. From time to time the Commission, who represent all the EU member states in the Green Room process, need to drop out of that and check their lines with the member states. This can be another time-consuming process, and while the EU countries with the Commission are haggling among themselves the larger process is stalled, and the other countries of the world have to occupy themselves as best they can. For the UK as a member state of the EU, much of the delegation time was spent either on talks outside the mainstream – Patricia Hewitt at this conference gave considerable time to talking with Commonwealth developing countries – or on using dark arts to get inside information from the Green Room participants. I was practised in the latter from Uruguay Round experience, and the contacts I had been building up around the world over the past year now became valuable. Every so often, when it seems that the overall process is close to a conclusion, progress is stalled either by France or India holding out for a special interest. In the course of the Doha event we hit blocks of both kinds. It always is either France or India.

The daily routine for us at Doha was that we opened our delegation office at 7 each morning and had a meeting of the full delegation at 8. With ministers from three departments (DTI, FCO and DfID) and officials from these departments plus Treasury, we numbered around 30 in total. I was designated leader of the official team. At the morning meeting it was for me to summarise the latest state of the talks and to orchestrate plans for what ministers and officials should aim to do in the day ahead. For Patricia Hewitt this was often a meeting or two with Commonwealth counterparts, Liz Symons talked to other trade ministers (and made an excursion to pay court to Sheikha Mousa, the third and most forceful of the Emir's wives). As and when the Commission felt a need to call their member states together, the top 3-4 of us had to be there. Those sessions could go on for hours and the EU showed no compunction about keeping the rest of the world waiting.

By the end of a week of this process a deal had taken shape. It was designed to reflect the changed balance between the four richest parties (US, EU, Canada and Japan), who had dominated all previous such deals since the founding of GATT in 1948, and the developing countries the largest of whom, through their strong economic progress in the 1990s, now accounted for a significant share of world trade. The deal aimed to reflect pressure too from the smaller developing countries who, though not effectively coordinated, had begun to express more focussed demands and, with NGOs acting as amplifiers, to make their voices heard. The background of fear and tension against which the Doha conference was held influenced the largest and strongest WTO players to give more ground to the arguments from developing countries large and small than they would otherwise have done. The mission statement for the conference was that the world must pull together. As a result the deal on the table in the final session included strong commitments to future steps to help smaller countries participate in international trade, and obligations on the richer countries to cut back on their practices that hit developing countries adversely – first and foremost the EU and US systems of subsidies for agriculture. When the deal was judged ripe, the Qatari chairman of the conference called a plenary session. This had its flutter of drama because India, not for the first time, refused to agree with the rest. WTO deals have to be done by unanimity; there is no majority voting. It took, as I recall, several hours of pleading, the Indian minister withdrawing for private conversations and arm-twisting, and a call from London, before the chairman finally brought down his gavel. Deal done.

Patricia Hewitt was well pleased, as she had (along with Gordon Brown and Clare Short) put her weight behind more generous terms for developing countries. She was entitled to feel pleased because she had cut an influential figure during the conference. Pleasing Gordon Brown was, too, a useful thing for a minister in Blair's government to do. Sadly, as noted above, once the international tension subsided, the richer countries' will to help developing countries also subsided, many of the thorny problems grew thornier, and 15 years after that Doha conference the Doha Round has not been brought to a conclusion. It never will be. The most solid and lasting decision taken in the week was to admit China to the WTO, and thereby to the international rules-based system of international trade.

Carrying on – at odds with DTI

No sooner had we returned to London than Robin Young and his ideas for DTI began to impinge on me. He presented a plan for recasting the top of the department under three or four broad themes, with trade policy and coordination of EU policy brigaded together under a broader economic heading. For me this scheme involved taking on additional responsibility (the EU coordination) – not a problem – but also, it appeared, taking my place under a supremo for the broader economic block of work. Subordinating myself to someone who would stand between me and the permanent secretary after I had performed at higher levels for six years by then – that would be conspicuous downgrading. I remonstrated. Robin Young was adept at side-stepping head-on argument, so I did the same. His vision for me was that I should become an office manager of a larger staff and delegate more of the front-line work of representation and negotiation to staff below me. Not only did I not have a direct deputy who could have made any impact on the trade talks which, as we have seen, were universally at top official or junior minister level, it was not my vision that I would spend the last year or so of my career managing an assortment of DTI staff and tasks. I had been hired to do the trade ambassador's job, was doing it rather well, and intended to stick to that. There was a stand-off between Robin Young and me. Patricia Hewitt to whom I looked for support in return for the support I had given her at Doha would not get involved – a quite proper position for a minister to take on a matter of personnel management. I calculated that if I pressed my case against Robin any further I would be shown the door marked early retirement. Not being ready for that, I settled for ignoring his new reporting structure and getting on with the job as before, now dividing my time between trade policy and EU representational work. Fortunately I was acquiring a really able deputy on the EU side – someone who has subsequently risen to a key role in planning for Brexit (2017).

We moved into 2002. It would shorten this story if I could say 2002 brought more of the same, but there are more novelties and surprises still to come.

Early in 2002 I took up an invitation from the Hong Kong government to spend a week as their guest. This was the second time in my career that I was on the receiving end of a government hospitality scheme. The programme arranged for me was to include some meetings with senior officials of the Hong Kong government and business community, some accompanied visits to their institutions such as the Legislative Council, some guided tourism, and a little free time.

Perhaps the first thing to mention is that my flight out to Hong Kong was the one and only long haul flight I have ever (so far) made in economy class. That was not the fault of my hosts, who had booked a club class seat for me. In the departure lounge at Heathrow the airline made an appeal for a club class passenger to accept a downgrade to economy in return for a cash payment of something close to £1000. This seemed rather attractive. Unusually, I was not going to have to do business for HMG immediately on arrival, sleep was not of the essence, nor was HMG paying for my ticket. I took the cash with a clear conscience, stretched out on a vacant row of three seats at the back of the plane and slept rather well. The money paid for one of two cataract operations that Poppy had to have that spring.

Hong Kong was a mixture of experiences. I remember a rather frosty session with a domineering set of business leaders, exciting visions of the skyscrapers that curve around Victoria Harbour (and have multiplied since my time); explanation of the role of the LegCo and rules for elections to it – which did not square with my reading of the Basic Law. I earned grumbles from the Foreign Office for a paper I wrote on return, expressing doubts as to how the promises of democracy made by the UK on handover in 1997 were to be fulfilled, with the rules of election to the LegCo as they were. One of the highlights was a helicopter trip for the group of us on the hospitality scheme that week all round the borders of Hong Kong island and the New Territories. Another highlight for me was a walk with a university zoologist on the Maipo marshes. He knew exactly where to take me to see a flock of 70 Black-faced Spoonbills – around 10 % of the world population. He knew too where there was a gate in the high frontier fence between Hong Kong territory and the People's Republic of China, through which he said he had a permit to go for research purposes. We went through together and surveyed the mudflats of the Pearl River for a short time. I was tempted to take a picture of the old woman trudging across the mud, dragging a sort of sledge loaded with her catch of shellfish. However, what with memories of British birdwatchers arrested from time to time for taking liberties with security zones in foreign countries and uncertainty as to whether my zoologist guide's permit extended to me, I kept my camera in my pocket. Lastly I used one of my free afternoons to take the short boat trip from Hong Kong to Macao where I wandered happily around the streets of time-worn Portuguese colonial houses. This scruffy part of town felt more like home than the high-rise glitz and pushiness of Hong Kong.

During that March I made a brief visit to Moscow with Michael Arthur; to Toledo for a meeting of EU trade ministers, accompanying Liz Symons; and to Ditchley Park for a conference on the world economy. April took me back to Montreux for the annual 'Evian' meeting, and to Seville where the Spanish presidency hosted a meeting of the 133 committee. Although we were not at the end of April the daytime temperature in Seville was reaching 37 degrees, and the nights were warm. Evening drinks in the courtyard of the Alcazar in warm air, with darkness falling and a full moon rising...

On this occasion, as on very few others, I hired a car and got up early the day after our meeting, and took myself off to the Coto Doñana. It was further to drive than I had allowed for, but I reached El Rocio by eight in the morning, and stood bemused that there was absolutely no-one on the streets at that time. But this was the deep south of Spain, life went on late into the night but did not kick off early in the morning. My time was far too short to do more than dip around in the publicly accessible areas of the famous nature reserve but I saw a sprinkling of the birds which make it famous, and returned to Seville and the flight home well pleased – cheerful enough to write some annual staff reports on the flight back to London.

In May I attended a small bilateral meeting with senior German officials at Chevening, and in July joined the UK-hosted annual trade policy confer-ence at Wilton Park. Sessions at Ditchley, Wilton Park or Chevening always involved lively discussions, high quality debate and high quality networking in the homely style of an English country house, that is to say, with passable food and sleeping quarters, the most superb public rooms and, through the windows, views of entrancing parkland grazed by well-bred sheep and cattle.

I think the nature of international trade policy work will be clear by now. There was a running conversation between the trading nations of the world, large and small. Something like a cat's-cradle of conversations, with the more protectionist countries trying to pull the threads of the cradle their way, the more open-market countries pulling the threads in the opposite direction; each faction some of the time restating well-worn arguments simply in order to counter-balance the noise from the other side. The countries which, by the twenty-teens, had become well-recognised as 'emerging', big, developing countries were at the beginning of the century just beginning to make their views and interests felt. A larger cluster of smaller developing and least-developed countries were pitching into the conversation too, greatly helped by some NGOs, and winning sympathy and support for their special interests from a few, but not many, countries in the rich western world. The UK under the Blair-Brown government was one of those few.

By autumn 2002 I knew that I had only six to eight months left to me in this job before I hit the Whitehall retirement age, fixed at 60 in those days. In the last part of this narrative I shall focus selectively on the places and characters that made a particular impression on me. There were some more mundane activities going on in the background.

There was a trip to Washington in September into which I stitched a meeting with Oxfam. The main story of what I did with Oxfam and why comes in the next chapter. In Washington on this occasion I was invited to join a demonstration on Capitol Hill to highlight a recently-published Oxfam report on poverty among coffee growers. I imagined that there would be a big event with lots of American razzmatazz. We gathered on a lawn in front of the immense Capitol building in strong late summer sunshine – just ten people to start with, joined by a slow trickle of more, and a few school children in fairtrade T-shirts. At the appointed hour a congressman, a Guatemalan coffee grower and Bianca Jagger stepped forward and spoke into the single press camera, Bianca Jagger speaking best. A few autographs were signed. And with this Oxfam's message had been projected to the American people.

I moved on to Ottawa for a day and a half of talks with Canadian officials, whose views were in most respects close to the UK's. Just two hours' flying time from Washington, Ottawa contrasted sharply. The air was fresh, the streets were wide and clear, there was water of rivers and lakes all around. The city had a northern feel. Some parts could have been in the Baltic but so many buildings showed Victorian influence, a cross between South Kensington or St

Pancras and Scottish baronial that the overall impression was more Inverness than Helsinki.

Our talks went smoothly and left me with an hour to cross the river to the very fine museum of Canadian history and culture from the times of the 'first people' to the twentieth century.

Late in the autumn I made a trip to Greece, for which I needed no encouragement. But it came at a price. The programme arranged for me, which had to fit in with a political event a day later, was to start with a meeting with our ambassador in Athens at 8 am. However, on the evening before that I was needed in London to host a meeting of EU member states at which my good friend Tom Jensen, at that time Denmark's ambassador in London, had promised to make the speech of welcome. I had coaxed him into doing this and could not let him down. Luckily (or not) there was a BA flight to Athens that left about half past ten in the evening, the next to last flight out of Heathrow before the airport closed for the night. This enabled me to hang on in London for the reception and still be in Athens before breakfast. Not much sleep, but the sight of the acropolis at dawn was reinvigorating.

All that day I had a succession of meetings in government offices, ferried from one to another in a heavily armoured car (a British diplomat had been shot dead in Athens not long before). Then at teatime I joined the group for the weekend conference and we were whisked away on a hydrofoil to the little island of Hydra. The conference was part politics, part government policy. We were twenty a side, Greeks and British, and a mixture of career officials, politicians, academics and journalists. Roger Liddle (No 10) and Melanie Johnson (then a minister at DTI) provided the political element on our side. The politicians of the left sought common ground, we aired some economic problems, and enjoyed the very special atmosphere of Hydra. So close to Athens, it is a world apart: no motor traffic, everything that needs to move is moved by mules or donkeys or human muscle power. Vividly Greek.

At the beginning of March I was detailed off to lead a little team to Taiwan for trade talks, not about high policy but a menu of problems which we had over trade with each other. I was told this would be a tricky mission. Taiwan has a peculiar international status as a breakaway state from mainland China. In its early days in the 1950s when it became home to the Chinese government

244

in exile, expelled by the communists and led by Chiang Kai Shek, it basked in the approval of the Americans and their cold war allies. More recently, as mainland China has grown in strength, the Chinese have put pressure on other countries not to recognise Taiwan as a legitimate state, not to undermine China's long-term aim of taking Taiwan back. Towing China's line, Britain did not officially, diplomatically, recognise Taiwan – and still doesn't. But Taiwan has a strong economy and there is valuable two-way trade between us. So I was to carry out some repair work on the machinery of trade without falling into any traps that the Taiwanese might lay for me in the area of diplomatic recognition.

The Portuguese when they came across Taiwan island at the time of the great explorers named it Ilha Formosa, because of its great natural beauty. I did not see any of that. Taiwan is a destination favoured by bird tours, but I didn't see any birds. We stayed firmly in the town of Taipei, which I found very scruffy.

Our talks started early on the morning of our arrival, with a series of British business people explaining their problems and grievances. The crunch came on the morning of Day 2: formal talks at the Taiwan Trade Ministry. My little team of three did battle against a home team which ran up to 30 at one stage. We had to give some tough messages, about cheating and forgery (of everything from CDs to soap powder). I was by now confident in this role and had strong support to right and left. We held our own, and we escaped alive – but had to pay a price at a gruesome dinner that evening. Our hosts' idea of fun was competitive downing of large glasses of top quality French wine, interspersed (from their side) with toasts to the ladies of the party (we had three, they had none) which veered into more and more brazen suggestions...

My impression of the coarseness of Taiwan was cemented. The one bright point was, earlier that day, a snatched visit to the museum which houses the treasures spirited away from the Imperial Palace in Peking, the Forbidden City, in the 1940s. Looted? Who are we to criticize? The museum is a treasure trove and we had the benefit of a VIP guide who, in one and a half hours, led us through the whole of Chinese history from 4000 BC, picking out in each gallery a handful of things for us to savour. That was a wonderful privilege, all the more appreciated by my colleague Susan who was Hong Kong Chinese by birth.

Of the short visit to Tokyo that came after, one memory is of a very small earthquake. The floor of the cafe we were sitting in suddenly went all liquid. Another is that I tried my best to deliver a tough message to the Japanese officials and public on their super-protective system of import controls on agriculture. I was conscious that this was probably my last opportunity to take a shot at a system that stood out as the high point of protectionism in an era when even the EU was moving towards more open trade, even on farm products. I gave a prepared interview to a Japanese journalist but I went on too long. I doubt if he printed even a word of my carefully constructed critical arguments.

It was in March 2003 that Blair led Britain into the Iraq War. There were some tense meetings in Whitehall. Among the ministers I was working with the mood that we just must stand by the Americans ran strongly: they came to our aid twice when we British were in terrible danger, we simply have to stand by them now. This sounds highly simplistic in the light of everything that came afterwards, but I remember that as the dominant mood.

Michael Arthur and I set off at this time on a joint mission, first to Brazil, then to Mexico, then to Barbados. As we waited in the Heathrow departure lounge for our flight to Rio, Michael and I watched Blair making his speech to the House of Commons appealing for MPs' support for going into this war. The trip to Brazil meant a long overnight flight and then the painful add-on of two more hours up to Brasilia. After an afternoon of recovery time, we had two evening dinner-discussions with a long day of talks in between; then back into the air for a dawn flight to Sao Paolo and a long, long, flight up to Mexico. Brazil is vast. Central America is a snake of land over which our plane took a straight northerly course, giving us views of the Pacific and the Gulf of Panama, then the Caribbean, then the Pacific again. We flew into Mexico City over two sharp-topped little volcanos.

Mexico City made a change from the high-rise cities of East Asia from which I had just come: buildings limited to two or three stories because of the high risk of earthquakes. In the one full day we had here, the programme of meetings left no time for sightseeing. My main memory is of gazing out of office windows – concentration flagging? – across the city to the ring of hills that surrounds it, and enjoying the splashes of colour provided by the many jacaranda trees that were then coming into flower.

Now nearing the end of two weeks in which I was covering around 22,000 miles, I felt my energy ebbing, and so I took the last of our stopping points, Barbados, as my swansong. In any case the main business to be done was for Michael, doing Foreign Office pastoral duty. Barbados brought the number of countries I had visited for DTI business to 32. There were trade talks for me to do here, but the main significance was a personal one: for the first time I was setting foot in the Caribbean, where my father had worked and made money, and which for him and my mother had been familiar territory in the 1950s and 1960s. Their world had gone – though the era of sugar plantations and cricket pitches was still lingering on here in Barbados.

Within a few weeks – after one more lightning visit to India – my time at DTI came to an end. DTI management expressed their frustration at the way I had breezed past their management reforms by attempting to dismantle my office during my last afternoon. Literally. A team of workmen arrived and started to unscrew the partition walls of my office around me. I sent them packing. Open plan could wait until the next day.

14

WITH OXFAM IN INDIA

2003

I was in Hyderabad and then Delhi in the first week of January 2003 on DTI business. The weather was cold in Delhi, and there was fog. As regularly happens in early January the airport was closed for half the day, and flights were all taking off late. Once my DTI business was completed, I took off again for Hyderabad, this time to link up with an Oxfam team. This was to be a continuation of my week's secondment to Oxfam which had started in the autumn of 2002 with two days in Oxford, being briefed at headquarters in Summertown and attending a meeting of their governing Council, followed by a few hours in Washington, taking part in a little demonstration on behalf of Guatemalan coffee growers. The Council meeting in Oxford had been an interesting experience; much more hard-hitting than the Council meetings of the RSPB which I was to get to know later, and my only close encounter with Sriti Vadera, then on Oxfam's Council, who acquired quite some power and influence under Gordon Brown. Bianca Jagger had contributed her stardust to the Washington event. But it was the coming few days in India that I had been looking forward to most.

Everyone knows of Oxfam for its work on famine relief and response to disasters. But there is another quite distinct side of their work, which they refer to as 'livelihoods'. The aim of that work is to strengthen the position of the poorest people in developing countries; to strengthen their ability to run their homes and manage their finances, and make a living; and where they are employed in factories or on the land, to strengthen their position in bargaining for improvements in their pay and working conditions. This was the work I was going to see on the ground. I was to spend the next two to three days in the company of two people from the South India livelihoods team.

Landing an hour or so late in Hyderabad, I was picked up by taxi and taken to a hotel, through the night scene of this city of five million people. It was mid-evening, business was in full swing. We drove through intense traffic, the road packed with cars, tuk-tuks, pedestrians and cycles. Every inch of the road space occupied. Driving here is an art-form: how to never let a splinter of space open up between you and the vehicles in front or to either side. Just an inch seems enough for a wheel, of a bicycle or a tuk-tuk, to insert itself and complicate the next move. Turning across the flow of traffic requires infinite patience, as you nudge aside the ungiving push of traffic, the criss-crossing pedestrians. There are no collisions. Of course nothing is moving at more than a snail's pace, but the temptation to ram a way through must sometimes be terribly strong. Everyone is creeping their way with much patience, and a degree of alertness.

The next morning I was taken to the Oxfam office, which I would never have found on my own: down a back street which seemed to be leading nowhere, up some stairs and past a landing on which a couple of sweepers seemed to have made their home. There I met Nupur Kukrety, the very young lady in charge, and her assistant Nishant. They with a support staff of ten (more washers-up and sweepers than aid workers) were responsible for projects all over South India. Much of this my first day went on discussions in the office, about weaving and textiles, and coffee growing. A little group of associated workers came in and talked about agriculture and where India could gain if Europe's Common Agricultural Policy were reformed, if the EU exported less skimmed milk powder to India, and if European consumers had less picky rules about food safety. It interested me to hear from those getting the rough end of all the protective rules and standards that increasingly sensitive European consumers have been fighting for over the past ten years.

Then in mid-afternoon the three of us, Nupur Kukrety, Nishant and I, took a flight to Bangalore. I expected a wave of heat on landing there, as it is some distance south from Hyderabad, but no, this is India in winter, Bangalore was quite foggy, though pleasantly warm at 24 degrees. More bright lights and chaos on the roads.

The day was not done. We drove straight from the airport to a meeting of women employed at a scatter of textile factories in the suburbs of Bangalore. The point of the meeting was for the Oxfam team and their local associates to hear from the women about the ways they were being treated – or maltreated – by their employers.

The meeting was taking place in a school hall which we had difficulty in locating. We had to keep stopping and asking the way. It did not help that neither Nupur nor Nishant spoke the local Indian language, and most of the streets had no name on them. When we found it, the little hall in a primary school was much fuller than expected. There were perhaps 150 women, aged around 20-40, a few with their children in tow. The meeting was being held after dark. It was between six and seven in the evening. Almost everyone there was speaking the local language, which only two people in the Oxfam group could speak. Just a few were able also to speak Hindi, which Nupur spoke.

Discussion was only just getting going, and it was taking time. One by one, very cautiously, women came forward from the audience and stories came tumbling out, a few sentences from one, a few minutes from another. How pay slips are falsified, hours of work extended, production targets ratcheted up and up, leave and Sunday pay withheld. The women are entitled to pay rises after five years in service, but are routinely sacked after four years and some months.

The women are plainly terrified of being reported to their employers. Again and again they press for reassurance: you are not taking our names, are you? I daren't take any pictures, though a few people take pictures of me. The background is that union activity is wholly forbidden. The meeting taking place could all too easily be treated as an unlawful assembly. I cannot think how much time and quiet persuasion it must have taken to make this gathering happen at all.

After about half an hour the trickle of stories dried up and the meeting broke into smaller groups. With one of the interpreters I attempted conversation with a few of the women workers. They are all fascinated that I am there. They are torn between hope that it can make a difference and terror that news of the meeting will get back to their employers. After a little more time they begin to slip away, and we gather that they have not even told their husbands where they were going; they must now get back to cook an evening meal and behave as though nothing had happened.

For us, Nupur, Nishant and me, it was a thoughtful evening meal in a backstreet restaurant after that. These are situations, conditions of work, that conscientious western consumers suggest cracking by means of a boycott of this or that product or brand. That would not be Oxfam's choice. The factory work is invaluable for the women we have met; it is invaluable to have a little bit of money of their own, however little, however hard earned. These are social conditions that have to change from within, by the same slow process as working conditions for children, women – and men – were changed in Britain over two hundred years of social campaigns and legislation in parliament. It is hard to envisage the pitiful conditions that we had been hearing about that evening changing other than by social pressures from inside India, locked down bit by bit in legislation. The protests of concerned consumers in the West need to be channelled with more care.

The next day in Bangalore started with a visit to a factory making shirts; not T-shirts but up-market Hugo Boss and Louis Vuitton shirts for the western market. The factory floor was clean and bright but the pace of cutting and stitching was intensive; signs of gruelling targets. We met the owner, who was very switched-on and politically correct – but quite possibly as ruthless as any, once the monitors and observers were off his scene. We went on to a series of meetings at a smart management college, improbably located on the outskirts of Bangalore, in an expanse of open ground, some of it occupied by a camp of squatters under the trees, here and there a cockerel and a pig or two scratching around, but with smart new buildings in various states of construction; Bangalore expanding before our eyes. Here Oxfam staff told me more of the scope of their livelihoods work. First, of their plans cautiously, very cautiously, to draw the employers of the textile workers into treating them better. Then came more about the workers on the coffee plantations in the Western Ghats. How market collapse had brought the old mountain estates to ruin, and the coffee pickers almost to destitution. Behind this was a new arrival on the international market: Vietnam. Vietnam had then just recently moved into coffee growing and was depressing world prices with large quantities of pretty poor quality beans, of no interest to more discriminating coffee drinkers but irresistibly cheap to the blenders and the manufacturers of instant coffee who make up a large part of the market.

Then another flight, back to Hyderabad. I was pitched into an evening of confusion, and some alarm. The Oxfam team dropped me at 'my' hotel and disappeared into the night. My hotel proceeded to deny my existence even though they had my laundry from two days before, and my suitcase. After a long argument they sent me off by car through the hysteria of mid-evening traffic right across town to another, distinctly basic, hotel. I had absolutely no idea where I was now. No-one seemed able to produce a street map of Hyderabad. I chose not to be too alarmed at being abandoned in unknown territory, and went to sleep.

Next morning after what seemed like hours of waiting, and a lot of failed attempts to ring mobile phone numbers, I was very relieved that Nupur and Nishant turned up. Relief all round that they had tracked me down.

Then came the last and greatest adventure. We were to go and see handloom weavers in Nalgonda. Nalgonda? A district about 60 km from Hyderabad, or it may have been 60 miles, to the south east. It took us more than two hours to get there. For two thirds of the way we were driving through ribbon development and hardly ever out of sight of people. India teems with people! The driving was slow because all along the way we were running up behind ox and buffalo carts, men pushing carts by hand up hills at a snail's pace, wayside cows (one dead, waiting for the vultures – but no vultures are left – and the kites); pigs and goats. There was of necessity a lot of overtaking on this two-lane road, and evidence of some fearsome head-on collisions. All along the way, a riotous mixture of vehicles ranging from heavy trucks highly painted with slogans and pictures, some of them hand-made with metal plates patched together; ancient buses of the peculiar Indian design, simply bins mounted high off the ground, some of those with people hanging on from the outside; through to tiny three-wheeled tuk-tuks, puttering along; and then the handcarts and foot traffic.

The village that we were to see was surviving entirely on weaving. The land around being too poor for farming, everyone who lived in this village was involved in weaving. It was like going back to a weaving town in England as it would have been in the mid-1700s, before any form of mechanisation had been introduced; before the Spinning Jenny, and pre-Arkwright. Each house in the village, each family, was a weaving 'business'. The 'houses' were tiny cottages with bare floors; just a ground floor, no upstairs; either two or three rooms to a house. All members of the family had parts to play. The father sat at a loom positioned close to the floor, sitting 10-12 hours a day with his feet dropped into a pit dug into the ground; mother spinning the yarn; son or daughter dying the yarn to fit the pattern of material to be made, or arranging the dyed yarn in the correct way to go on to the loom.

The two or three families I visited were excited by our visit. My photographs show this. I heard later that they were thrilled with the copies of my photographs that I sent back to them through Oxfam. Quite a different situation here from the terrified women at that furtive meeting in Bangalore. These villagers were living in the simplest possible conditions but they were earning their keep. They did not look poverty-stricken nor unhappy. The houses all looked spotlessly clean, and the families appeared to be talking with pride of their techniques and their skills. What they were producing was high-quality sari cloth. We were told that it took three full days to produce cloth for one sari, and from what we were told about the price they were getting per sari I reckoned that they could not be earning more than about £25 a month for the whole family.

It was a journey back in time – and how could such methods survive in the twenty-first century? The Oxfam team were doing their best to help these handloom weavers to get a better price for their cloth. But the signs were very unhopeful. Nupur took me with her to a department store back in Hyderabad where she had arranged a meeting with their buyer for textiles and clothing. The buyer, a lady, was not unsympathetic but what she had to say to us was pretty negative. The problem was that there was so much variation in quality between the output of one household unit of production and another. The department store really could not cope with such variability, even by putting the saris on sale at reduced prices. It simply did not fit their style of business and what their customers expected.

I do not know how much headway the team made with their efforts on behalf of the handloom weavers. I could see their patient, cautious and sensitive efforts on behalf of the factory workers bearing fruit in the long term. My picture is that it will be a very long haul to improve factory working conditions in India, but that sustained pressure from inside Indian society is the key to progress; pressure from concerned customers in the West a potential support, provided it is applied with restraint.

Overall my time with Oxfam left me full of admiration for the quality of their livelihoods work. The skills and dedication of their staff on the ground were deeply impressive. It increased my respect for the leading campaigners, the senior UK-based NGO staff who were engaging with me at DTI over trade policy, and with DfID over our international aid programmes. I would in future give all the more weight to their views, knowing that they were basing their arguments about working conditions, and the impact of rich country policies on the markets in developing countries, and the adverse impact of those, on information coming to them from colleagues who had intimate first-hand knowledge of the conditions of the very poorest people in the countries concerned.

I was not required by DTI to report on my secondment to Oxfam nor did I volunteer to do so. I have to doubt whether any of my DTI contemporaries who spent five days with this or that industry or business sector could have claimed as great a return on their experiences as the leap forward in understanding which I gained from my extended 'week' in the hands of Oxfam.

15

BRUSSELS FROM THE INSIDE

2003-05

So I had reached retirement age. But I did not feel in any way ready to retire. What next?

'How will he manage? He has always been so busy with his work. I am worried that he won't cope with retirement.' —Rosie

'I cannot believe that you will be short of offers of employment. My main advice is that you do not commit yourself to too much too quickly. I found that retirement is like furnishing a new home. You are tempted to fill all the space straightaway but if you do so you subsequently regret some of the pieces you first committed yourself to.' —Robin Butler

Retirement opens up big new possibilities. Compulsory retirement opens them up compulsorily.

This sounds like an obvious point but it is a point that probably made a big difference for me. Many people choose when to retire. If they are self-employed they can go into retirement at a time best for them. People who have run a business and made money sometimes decide to retire at a very early age, maybe in their 40s. This seems a great waste of talent. People working in a large organization are quite commonly given the option of taking 'early retirement'. This is certainly a regular occurrence in the services, civil and military, which have a narrowing pyramid of senior posts and routinely thin out their numbers to avoid having to carry older people for whom they have no need. Their ideal is that the less talented people should peel off into early retirement, though in practice they tend to lose a proportion of more talented people who are confident of making their way in the wider world. Some of my contemporaries in the civil service took early retirement around the age of 50. Some of those went on to do challenging and interesting things and make adequate money. Some didn't.

There are serious professions in which you find people who have run out of interest by the age of 50. I know dentists and doctors who were clearly bored with their work by that age. Some of them retired early or would happily have done so. One doctor I know seized an offer of early retirement at 50 from work as a GP and went on to spend the next ten years devoting his time to bird-watching in Norfolk. He took pleasure and gave pleasure in that field. But how sad. Not only a waste of all that expensive medical training; sad that the demanding work as a doctor was no longer throwing up enough interest for him. If I had taken early retirement at 50 I would have missed out on the most interesting things in my working life. It is, I suppose, a feature of the home civil service, and the diplomatic service too, that you have no sooner proved yourself competent in one complex, difficult post; you are moved onwards and (with luck) upwards, to something different and even more difficult. There is never any shortage in public affairs of hard things that need careful management and problem-solving skills. For people prepared to work hard at continuing to learn and take on new challenges, interesting new openings just keep coming.

Events shaped the last 10 years of my career in Whitehall, pretty drastically; and continued to shape what I did in my retirement.

In the year when I reached the age of 60, that was still the compulsory age of retirement for Whitehall civil servants, whatever level they had reached in the organization. The system changed not long afterwards and if I were reaching the age of 60 now I would be able to choose whether or not to stay in the same occupation. I have little doubt that I would have tried to stay somewhere within the London-centred UK government organization – the medium in which I had grown and flourished for the previous 30 years.

But that was not an option for me. I approached 60 knowing that I must find something new to do – or fall by the wayside. I consulted widely. I wrote letters to a large number of people in a wide variety of positions and occupations: former work colleagues, politicians – former ministers with whom I had worked, friends in various walks of life. Ostensibly I was asking for their advice, and they gave some, but I am sure I was rather hoping that one or two might come up with job offers.

BSE-blight presumably weighed in here. The larger part of my career had been in MAFF, involved with the food and farming industries. My time in

MAFF was, by the time I was coming up to retirement (2002), overshadowed all too strongly by the catastrophe of BSE which had put MAFF on a war footing since March 1996 and me in the front line. Since 2000 (when I moved from MAFF to DTI), the news had been dominated by the public enquiry into BSE. Lord Phillips' report came out in October 2000, with its generalised criticism of a raft of former MAFF ministers and senior officials, me included.

I, and my closest colleague at MAFF, Richard Packer, were not regarded as flavour-of-the-month on the job market. Companies wanting a name that might bring them power and influence in Whitehall – let's face it, one principal reason companies have for putting former top officials on their payroll – were not going to home in on me. Nor did they.

However by 2003 I had coming up to three years of presiding at the top of a different kind of work in a different government department; Director General of World Trade Policy in the Department of Trade and Industry (as it was then called). This was something different for the job market to weigh up. Less fortunately, expertise in world trade policy, and the interaction of governments in the World Trade Organization, as important as it may be for the world economy, is a rather rarified skill, and the niches for it in the private sector are few and far between. Of my immediate predecessors in that DTI post, one – and he was more expert in the field than any UK official before or since – had found a home in an American law firm, where he stayed happily and I suppose lucratively for a good ten years. The other had gone off to be HR director at an international organization, the OECD in Paris; a serious post in a delightful city, but it had come his way more because of his earlier position as head of HR in DTI than because of his more recent trade policy experience.

So there I was, towards the end of 2002, casting around for advice and weighing up the possibilities. People retiring from the upper reaches of the civil service commonly like to attach themselves to a business, as a non-executive or even executive director, to make some money. I had had a brief taste of work in a food company, as non-executive director of Golden Wonder Crisps when it was part of Imperial Group, in the 1980s. My impression was that senior staff in a company like that had to spend much of their time watching minute aspects of the costs of production, or sales margins, and making minute adjustments to those; rationally enough, because profits can be massively affected by fine-tuning of that kind, to produce small margins of advantage over competitors. But from what I had seen the scope for more strategic thinking, which was more interesting to me, was very confined – and confined even in large companies to a very small head office team. I could not feel that my way forward lay in that direction (and anyway I had BSE blight working against me).

Others choose to go into, or back into, academic life. My recently acquired grasp of trade policy, and of the economics and realities of international trade, was sufficient to make me interesting to the International Relations Department of the LSE for a couple of years. But that is jumping ahead in this story. Other things happened first. I gave only brief thought to going back to my subject of real academic expertise, classical Greek, and the field of my post-graduate studies: Greek papyrology. One of my contemporaries from Professor Lloyd-Jones's master classes (1966-67) had done just that. Leonard Ingrams, brother of Richard Ingrams (of Private Eye fame), switched from papyrology into merchant banking as a young man, and on retiring from his banking he went back to papyri. He was preparing a new edition of some fragments of Greek poetry when he died all of a sudden at the wheel of his car, driving home from Glyndebourne.

The Greek papyri are full of interest. They have opened up the subject of ancient Greek in a dramatic way. For hundreds of years it appeared that the stock of literature, history and science that had survived from the ancient Greeks through the middle ages to modern times was what it was, and could never be added to. Then suddenly excavations in Egypt by British archaeologists, some of them from Oxford, between about 1880 and 1920, had thrown up vast quantities of papyri (old paper) from the sands of Egypt. Much the largest part of this material, though it had come from the sands of Egypt, was written in Greek. For a thousand years from the death of Alexander the Great, Egypt was administered by people who spoke Greek, first under the Ptolemies and then under the Roman empire. The administrative classes spoke, read and wrote in Greek not only for their work but in their homes.

Nearly all of the papyrus recovered had already been torn up at the time it was 'lost'. The places where most of it was found had been town rubbish dumps. Much smaller quantities had been used as wrapping for mummies. This 'paper' had generally been used on both sides; first on one side for works of literature,

then when that literature went out of fashion re-used for more everyday purposes, like letters to the family, or accounts, or shopping lists. How very useful
that people in those days wanted to make maximum use of their paper (it was
expensive) and good that they didn't have shredders. The torn fragments were
shipped back, lovingly wrapped, to museums and libraries in Britain, Germany
and elsewhere in Europe, and a little to America. The quantity excavated in that
period, now 100 years ago, was so great that it is still being worked through.

There is fascination in the challenge of deciphering and puzzling out the
scraps, and much to be learned from what is on them: whether works of literature (on the front side) or details of everyday life (on the back). I was encouraged, by Poppy among others, to go back and pick up this tricky art. But, partly
because I had been keeping half an eye on the subject all through the Whitehall
years, I knew how much new work had been done, some of it by those who had
sat with me in the Lloyd-Jones master-classes. It would cost me years of close
and painstaking study to bring myself up to speed, to the point where I could
be sure of adding in a worthwhile way to the mountain of scholarship. I could
have done it, but only at the price of shutting out everything else.

While I was weighing up these different ways of using my retirement, a
suggestion came to the rescue. Peter Carl, director general of the international
trade side of the European Commission (DG Trade), the top Brussels official
with whom I had been working closely in my three years in DTI, tentatively
asked whether I would like to join him as an advisor, for a year or two. He may
have known what he had in mind, but I am certain that I didn't know how
this assignment would work out. Peter Carl, though, I knew as a commanding
figure on the European trade policy scene, also a man of exactingly high standards, and he did nothing without weighing and measuring his alternatives with
scrupulous care; he was not given to unpremeditated precipitate action. It was
both reassuring and interesting for me to think that he might think I might
add value, working with him inside the Commission. Also it would solve a
problem.

Working out how to put this idea into practice was not at all straightforward. It was quite unprecedented for the Commission to take in someone of
my seniority (it was then, and I broke new ground; but one or two others later followed where I led). There is a regular scheme, of long standing, for the

Commission to take in officials from national governments and from outside government on loan for two or three years: 'detached national experts' as they were known. But these are normally people in mid-career, not at the point of retirement. They are 'detached' from an employer to whom they return after their two or three years in Brussels. On the British side there are rules governing what work retired senior civil servants can take up, and a committee in the Cabinet Office makes judgements on this; and also rules on how much a civil servant can earn from a new public service appointment without the earnings being deducted from pension payments.

I was not inclined to go down the path of high earnings from a business appointment but equally I wanted to be careful that I was not going to lose any of my hard-earned pension. The small print of going into the Commission on loan had to be examined with care. In the event we had to summon up some creative interpretation of the rules on both sides. At the Brussels end, DG Trade's personnel officer Bruno Pragnell was a great help. He had a good personnel officer's reassuring bedside manner. He told me much later that he was under firm instructions from Peter Carl (he who must be obeyed) to make the assignment work. This involved some elastic application of the Commission's requirement that the official on loan must have continued financial support from the organization in the home country from which he/she is being loaned. DTI was stoutly resistant to the concept of loan. As far as they were concerned I was going into retirement when I reached the age of 60 and they were wholly averse to treating me as being on loan, with the implication that I might exercise a right to return. That looked to them like entering into a fresh financial commitment to me. Their position in turn met with a response from the Commission (February 2003) that was not encouraging: 'First and most importantly I must stress that a formal retirement from DTI will present insuperable problems for any possible detachment. The Commission's Decision [in effect a law] states categorically that the persons covered by these rules shall remain in the service of their employer throughout the period of secondment and shall continue to be paid by their employer'. Reconciling these two bureaucratic positions was achieved by my creative argument that the terms on which DTI *were* prepared to go forward with me, namely a contract whereby they would make regular payments to me, related to my previous salary, and would commit to keeping up those payments for as long as I was on 'detached' service with the Commission, amounted in effect to my being in a 'clearly defined, stable working relationship'. I would not be an employee of DTI, but then 'employee' was not a term used in the Commission's rule book. Their rules talked of being 'in service'. Could we not regard the contractual terms on offer from DTI as being 'in service'? This, under Bruno Pragnell's sympathetic hand, seemed to do the trick. It might seem a trivial point to have argued about but winning this argument, on a technicality, opened the way to two satisfying years of living mainly in Brussels, experiencing the European Commission from inside its engine room, contributing my accumulated experience, and making new friends.

Once the terms of the contract had been hammered out, I had to turn to the practical problems of where to live, and how much to come and go. William was still at school, and just coming up to A levels, so Poppy would have to stay and keep our Harpenden home going for some time to come. I stopped work with DTI at the end of April 2003 and I was to take up post in the Commission in mid-June, so I had less than six weeks in which to find myself somewhere to live. I made two or three exploratory trips to Brussels, and used an agent who specialised in finding accommodation for British officials. It did not take me long to get the measure of her method. She would propose four or five places to be viewed in a day. Each of her menus would include some distinctly unappealing places within the price range I had stipulated, and one much more appealing place priced above my limit. The snags with the cheaper places were not always clear at first sight. My discoveries came at the price of walking the streets around the apartments she had taken me to until I had spotted the night club, open till 4am, or the strong-smelling restaurant kitchen vented towards the apartment upstairs. And it rained hard on all these house-hunting days. The going was not easy.

How did I finally choose the place that became home from home for the next two years, and the family who became our 'Belgian family' for years after that? A combination of luck and persistence. Rue Goffart is in Ixelles. Laure and her husband Damien had restored two floors at the top of their six-floor, late nineteenth century house in rue Goffart and created a spacious two-floor apartment or 'duplex' which Laure had furnished with a quirky mixture of battered antique pieces of furniture and fittings from Ikea. I think I met Laure only on my return for a second look at this apartment. She made a welcoming impression. Not until later did I appreciate that, along with the apartment, I was renting an honorary place in the family too. The accident of this choice made a big difference to the next two years. I had a home to come back to in the evenings, and Poppy when she began to visit more often was equally welcomed as a friend of the family.

There were some unfamiliar formalities to go through. I had to register with the police, who required my name to be shown on the street door where I lived. I had to register with the health service, and became a member of the Fédération des Mutualités Socialistes du Brabant. There were things that took some getting used to, like the challenge of climbing from street level to my front door: 83 steps, no lift. I lost a stone in weight within the first few months and then remained fit to climb those stairs several times a day. For my visitors it was always a struggle.

Ixelles is in part a fashionable area, down beside the Etangs d'Ixelles, lakes flanked with elegant Art Nouveau houses in finest Brussels style. Then from the lakeside Ixelles goes uphill, the streets become narrower, the houses older, and the community changes. At the top is a little square, Place Blyckaerts, and off that runs the rue Goffart.

The houses up here are tall and shabby, the population multi-ethnic, North African around the square, more Congolese a mile along the ridge into the district of Matongé. The shabbiness is entirely at odds with the shiny modern, glass and steel 'European Quarter' where the EU institutions have their offices, or the green and leafy suburbs with their spacious villas where the majority of Eurocrats and diplomats live. How had I come to choose scruffy Place Blyckaerts? Poppy was shocked and depressed at first. Likewise the smart senior officials with whom I worked in DG Trade thought it a bizarre place to have chosen. But to me the mix of people on the streets had a familiar feel, I had no wish to isolate myself in some diplomatic compound for these two years; and as Poppy and I found over time we were getting to know the side of Brussels where the Belgians, the natives, keep themselves at arm's length from the euro-community which has stolen a chunk of their city; and, keeping themselves to themselves, have a lively and interesting time.

The family in rue Goffart became our home from home, looked after us well, and shared their interests with us. I could shut my front door at the top of the house when I wanted to, but from time to time I was pressed into joining the family in the kitchen or the garden for a drink or a meal. Slowly we came to know one another. Laure dealt in objets d'art, but also assisted Damien in his business. Damien ran a computer software business from a house at the end of the garden – a proper house on two floors which would once have been the coachman's house – where he employed a team of high-powered IT experts. The leading light was a Russian and there were others from eastern Europe. The business was seriously lucrative. In the main house, we had a succession of cleaning ladies also from the east, one from Poland, one from Moldova. Laure had a penchant for taking in people, let us say people whose papers were not in good order, and then helping them to establish themselves in Belgium. So there were dramas from time to time when one of those she was helping seemed to be running out of road. Laure had outstanding success with the woman from Moldova who has settled in Brussels, established a family around her, and whose two daughters flourished at school and grew into socially well-balanced citizens of the west. Céleste, daughter of Laure and Damien, showed her parents' robustness in resisting the parental prejudice in favour of French over Flemish (a preference which runs strongly in francophone Brussels) and firmly insisted on taking one year of her schooling in a Flemish town outside Brussels. Gloom settled over the household for a time over this, but Céleste emerged none the worse. Isidore, much younger, showed his independence by falling down several flights of stairs and breaking nearly every bone in his body. But he survived and seemed none the worse for that experience.

Joining the trade policy department in the European Commission after working for three years as head of trade policy in London – that sounds like 'more of the same'. It was actually very different.

For a start I now had no management responsibilities. At most (but not all the time) I had a secretary. For the past twenty years management had been – or was meant to have been – a major part of my duties. (No amount of management training ever turned me into more than a mediocre people-manager.) Now I was a 'detached national expert', outside the management structure of career Commission officials; and as a special adviser to their director general I was doubly detached.

This was a plus and a minus. One or two of the permanent officials who were enthusiastic about my arrival on the scene wanted to see me shake things up. They encouraged me to take a stand and insist on being given a more formal role, integrated into the top management team. That was not going to happen. Very quietly, other colleagues intimated that I would do best to tread carefully. Of the half dozen directors who reported directly to Peter Carl, there was one, just one, who resented my coming and would have firmly fought off my being allowed a more managerial role. Right would have been on his side. The Commission's rules (and the institution is strong on rules) draw a sharp distinction between the officials who are established, career Eurocrats, there because they have passed the formidable 'concours' (entrance exam), and those who are on loan, as I was, from one or other member state, taken in on a temporary basis because they have some useful specialist knowledge or skill to add to the mix. The former are the 'fonctionnaires' and they are jealous of their position. In my view, reasonably so.

The fonctionnaires are a talented lot, and generally have the edge on the national experts, particularly in their ability to work fluently in several languages and to mediate between different national interests. This is a key part of what the Commission exists to do. Taking a different route from the United States, and at odds (as I found) with the way Asian countries work when they negotiate together, the European Community/Union opted from the outset to make it possible for national officials and ministers to have all their formal discussions each person speaking his or her own language. Professional interpreters see to it that the proceedings of formal meetings – everything everyone says – is simultaneously translated for everyone else around the room, in many languages. But Commission officials exploring differences of opinion and mediating between them informally need to be able to talk to national officials, or ministers, in their own languages. They need to be clever and they need to be linguists.

Other aspects of the entrance exam in which Commission officials have succeeded are not so hard to master; the history and politics of Europe and the ways of working of the European Union's institutions – all that is easy enough to swot up, with a little study time. It is the facility with languages over which British applicants have struggled ever since the beginning, and the position has not improved at all over time. We simply do not have an effective system of language teaching, nor do we have anything like the same day-to-day exposure to foreign languages that is common experience for people living in continental countries.

Leaving aside this built-in British inability at languages, I found the general level of intelligence of the senior Commission officials I worked with was high, and I did not begrudge them their pride in the status they had achieved. That did, however, set a clear limit to my own personal standing in DG Trade. Once I had taken the measure of the cross-currents, I concluded that pushing myself forward could have made life briefly more interesting but could lead to my being ejected and packed off home in quick time. There was too much interest in being inside the Commission. I decided to settle for the terms on offer, and not to overplay my hand.

My position as special adviser to Peter Carl of itself gave me a good avenue for exerting influence. I had his ear. I could offer him my opinions on whatever I wanted. He turned to me for advice when he wanted to tap into my deep knowledge of agricultural policy, or my ability to interpret British ways of thinking.

The trade arrangements for agriculture are particularly complicated, not easily understood unless you have studied them closely or, as I had, grown up with them over many years. The politics of agriculture are equally complicated, and cannot be wholly understood in terms of economic interest. Both in Europe and the United States agriculture has been supported by governments over many years with extremely complex arrangements and the governments, under political pressure from farmers, are vigorously resistant to change. Time and again in the process of trying to reach comprehensive trade deals the Europeans and Americans had fallen foul of each others' cherished agricultural interests. For the leading trade negotiators here in Brussels now, as I had previously experienced in London, the stumbling block of agriculture was very frustrating and hard to understand. So Peter Carl periodically invited me to explain issues to him that he, formidably intelligent and well-versed in trade policy as he was, had not been able to unravel for himself. Of course he had his experts in the house who could explain those issues to him after a fashion, but to a man they all had difficulty in taking an objective view of the European position; they had been reared to defend the CAP. In turning to me Peter was trying to get the measure of where there might be more room for movement, for accommodation with the trading nations outside Europe, than he was hearing from his in-house staff.

I produced for him one or two in-depth analyses of which I was quite proud, in particular of the CAP's sugar regime, then coming up for review. I gave him some perspectives on policy in London and links with the Commonwealth countries. From my supplying advice on such topics it was a short step to my being given a place on the little team then working out first ideas for an EU-Canada trade agreement. We are hearing now, in 2017-18, that that agreement took five to seven years to negotiate. That could be true in some formal sense but we and the Canadians were exchanging views and discussing first thoughts well over fifteen years ago.

One member of that little team was a young Spanish girl, Lorella, at that time still at an early stage of her career. She was put forward to defend some of our ideas in an internal Commission meeting with her counterpart from DG Agriculture. She invited me with my greater knowledge of agriculture to back her up. I have seldom been in a meeting of any kind where two people went at each other so fiercely. Those two fought like cats: the one Spanish, the other Irish, they hammered out their argument in French but it lost nothing in cut and thrust through their both speaking a language other than their own. It was a dazzling display, surpassing anything I have seen in Whitehall.

That was an eye-opener, but I found the same later on several occasions. Different parts of the Commission argue ferociously over their positions before agreement is reached on what they, the Commission, will put on the table for member states to grind over in their turn. The rigour and quality of those internal Commission discussions impressed me.

As for Lorella, her fluency in French was as nothing to her fluency in English – she spoke it about twice as fast as a native English speaker; Spanish speed; and she was a quick and lively thinker too, hard to keep up with. In the Whitehall system someone of her youth and ability would have been tried out on several different areas of work in quick succession, and promoted. Movement is regularly slower inside the Commission and promotion comes much more slowly. Lorella, disappointingly, 15 years later has still not broken through to the senior level. She was the liveliest of the 'desk officers' that I had the luck to mentor. This mentoring, passing on of experience to eager young people, was the most satisfying aspect of my work at the time.

My perspective on the Commonwealth led to my being included in the Commission team for one or two talks with ACP countries – the African, Caribbean and Pacific countries, many of them Commonwealth members, with which the European Union has favourable trading arrangements. These ACP arrangements were at that time going through a thorough overhaul. One meeting I attended began with half an hour or so where the two groups, a handful of Commission negotiators and a dozen or so ACP ambassadors, assembled and mingled. Mingled, as it turned out, was what we didn't do. I moved around, talking to several of the ACP ambassadors and then, when I linked up again with the Commission colleagues, was quizzed by one of them asking me with evident surprise how I knew the people I had been speaking to. It clearly seemed to her very strange that I should have been speaking, at ease, with people I had *not* met before. This was not the only occasion when I found that not just the Commission's own staff but officials from member states too at these ACP meetings either, possibly, did not have the idea of making informal conversation at diplomatic gatherings, or else had particular inhibitions about doing so with coloured people. My suspicion is, it was the latter.

Peter Carl used me as a trouble-shooter, and as a leader of 'missions' which played to my previous experience from London. Hence he sent me twice to India. On the first occasion I was one of a team of officials accompanying the President of the Commission, then Romano Prodi, to an EU-India Summit. I gave a speech at a conference in Delhi, sharing a platform with the Indian finance minister. My speech came after one by Chris Patten, then Commissioner for External Relations. He struck the audience as too relaxed, de haut en bas, and was slated in the Indian papers the next day. In my speech I adopted a different tone, delivered some straightforward messages about what we wanted from the Indians on trade, and happily got a better press reaction. The following day came the formal government-to-government 'summit'. We were a small delegation. The Italian prime minister Silvio Berlusconi was meant to come with us, as Italy then held the Presidency, but to no-one's great surprise he pulled out at the very last minute and nominated his junior foreign minister to attend in his place. She was unknown to all of us – and history has forgotten her name. It was not the very competent Italian lady, one time foreign minister, who is now (2018) High Representative for Foreign Affairs for the European Union. There have been some very competent Italian foreign ministers, and some very adroit ones. The lady sent to us by Berlusconi was not of such quality. She did however understand her instructions: strict instructions given to her by Berlusconi as she stepped on to her plane in Rome. She was *not* to allow the Commission to lead the delegation; Berlusconi would have done so had he attended, and she was to do so in his place. This did not play well. Prodi, unassertive in normal circumstances and almost always mild-mannered and polite, was not inclined to let this relatively unknown junior minister from Italy lead what were quite important discussions with India. (The two of them were from opposite ends of the Italian political spectrum. This was unstated fuel for the fire.) To settle the matter the Indians told us their prime minister was not going to sit opposite this unknown Italian; he would treat Prodi as in the lead for the EU. Argument had raged between Prodi and the Italian lady in the delegation's hotel the night before. It broke out again as we entered the conference room. In a corner, to start with. The prime minister of India came in with his little team, they took their places on one side of the conference table, and waited for their European guests to seat themselves opposite. They waited in mounting amazement as Prodi and the Italian minister stayed huddled in a corner of the room, rowing animatedly. At long last the EU team sat down, disagreement unresolved. Each time it was the turn of the Europeans to speak, Prodi and the Italian minister cut across each other, snatched words from each other. The performance was a disgrace. No wonder if the outside world finds it hard to take the EU for a serious performer when it comes to foreign affairs.

For the second of my DG Trade trips to India, after some business in Delhi I went down to Mumbai and spoke at a gathering of Indian business people convened by the EU's local trade office. This is an event that sticks in my mind because, after speaking and fielding questions for a couple of hours, I became thirsty and unthinkingly took an open glass of water from a tray – and suffered acute stomach disorder for about six weeks afterwards. A more substantive reason for remembering the occasion is that it is when I first met Professor Poonam Kumar. Poonam had been in the audience in Delhi and wanted to pursue the discussion. She picked up contact again when I was back in London a year or so later and, for a time, we worked together. But that comes later.

Another stage on which I was launched was EU-ASEAN. ASEAN stands for the Association of South-East Asian States, a regional organization bringing together ten countries of south-east Asia - but not China. It included Vietnam and Myanmar. It was agreed, partly because the director and head of unit who might otherwise have dealt with this business were heavily loaded with work on the 2004 enlargement of the EU (the accession of the eight former communist countries of central Europe, with Cyprus and Malta), partly because ASEAN conducts its business in English, that I should lead the Commission's team for an upcoming round of discussions with ASEAN, and I did so for my full two years. This was in direct contravention of the aforementioned rule that a detached national expert should not exercise command over the fonctionnaires. I carried it off without encountering any revolt from the delegations I led. For ASEAN the country in the chair at the time was Vietnam, a country I had visited before (I witnessed the '9/11' attacks from the departure lounge in Ho Chi Minh City, aka Saigon, airport). We had to prepare an agenda for a high-level meeting on trade. This involved some discussions in Hanoi and some, I think, in Luxembourg, before the high-level meeting itself, again in Hanoi. The Vietnamese team that we worked with was very efficient and their lady leader both efficient and gracious. So there was no real difficulty in doing what we had to do. The difficulties for me such as they were came in welding unified positions out of a scatter of member state views – herding the EU cats – and then, as the action in Hanoi shifted from the officials at my level to their superiors, a degree of formality and prickliness. The seniors on the Vietnamese side were dubbed vice-ministers but these were communist officials, part of the communist apparatus that still ruled the country. However, any difficulties they caused us were as nothing to the shock-waves when the representative of Myanmar took the floor; dressed in full military uniform and speaking in loud, bombastic voice, – I can't remember what his speech was all about but he injected an uncomfortable militaristic note into the proceedings; a hard-line warrior giving us a taste for how the Myanmar system was then. Has it softened somewhat since?

Being in Hanoi three times in five years gave me a rare view of a country going through rapid development and the speed at which things were changing. From such simple indications as the ratio of pedal bikes to tuk-tuks to automobiles on the streets, you could see the general level of prosperity rising. After our events in Hanoi had passed off successfully I had one further overseas mission in the ASEAN cause. It was the turn of the Europeans to host a meeting and the Irish held the EU Presidency, so the meeting was held in Dublin, in a hotel on Malahide Bay to the north of the city. The Irish of course ensured a calm and relaxed atmosphere, and the Asian visitors clearly enjoyed the experience of being in Dublin and in Ireland, a first for them all. For me, the first was that I was able to fly Poppy over to join me at the end of the meeting and we stayed on to visit our great friends who live there, the first and only time in my career of official travels when I did not have to speed on to the next official engagement on the very next plane out.

It would be wrong to read into that that the Commission ran a more relaxed system for its staff than does the British government. It is a criticism commonly made of the Commission by the British press and public, that the EU is colossally wasteful of member states' money. My experience of their system from the inside was quite the opposite. Their rules for official travel are in several respects tighter than those I was used to in London. Use of taxis is all but forbidden, and a very convincing explanation is needed before any taxi costs are reimbursed. An official on an overseas visit is formally required to take the next plane home at the end of a meeting. The rates of allowance for time spent overseas were thrifty compared with London's.

In other ways too, the Commission runs a tight ship. There are not the armies of clerks and executive officers that exist (or did until recently) in Whitehall to support graduate staff in positions of responsibility, and who do... not all that much. At or above the level of head of unit (roughly Grade 5, or assistant secretary in old Whitehall terms) an officer in the Commission has a secretary. But below that, staff are left to do all their own typing (as has by now become normal in London too), copying, distribution of papers and keeping of records. The upside of this is a considerable saving in staff numbers. The downside is that the central record-keeping, on which a bureaucracy relies, is weak. The junior policy-makers all keep their own personal records and whilst there is in theory a central filing system I never saw any evidence of, or use made of, it. I'm told improvements were made not long afterwards.

I did for most of my two years have a secretary, who acted as my guide to procedures and did some of my chores for me. This was a gesture to my special status. I didn't keep my secretary very busy and I could not see that the senior staff kept theirs busy either. But these secretaries were a pleasant bunch (all the more so for not being over-stressed) and I saw it as valuable, particularly for me in my tricky position, to cultivate them and treat them with respect. In return they helped me. My first secretary was a quiet Danish girl, Bettina, rather withdrawn, not given to saying much. We worked in French as well as English. I don't think she ever saw the point of working for me. However, when she left and had had a baby she sent me a very touching little thank-you note for the baby clothes we gave her. She was followed by one who was determinedly idle and a notorious malingerer. (I was, by then, expected to pay the price for having been well looked after earlier.) She was not the only one of her kind to take the Commission for a ride.

The staff overall were strongly unionised, and for the most part left-leaning; the centre of gravity of political views was in the range Guardian to Libération reader. Not a day went past without a flier from one or other of the several staff associations dropping into my in-tray. Some were protests about member state pressure (generally led by Britain) for economies in levels of pay or pensions. Sometimes there were protests about the increasing use of the English language. English had gained ground with the accession of Sweden and Finland ten years earlier. By 2003 the Commission was working increasingly in English for internal purposes, though partly still in French. By 2004 French – which had been *the* working language inside the Commission from the 1950s through to the 1990s – was to all intents and purposes dead. It was the 2004 enlargement which killed it. Of the ten countries that joined in that year, Cyprus and Malta used English for post-colonial reasons. For the eight central Europeans, a poll was conducted. It showed that for each their first preference was their own national language, with Russian second (for post-colonial reasons), German third (for historical reasons), English fourth – and French came fifth. I have a vivid memory of an internal DG Trade meeting chaired by a seasoned senior official who was French. He led off in his lucid, easy-to-follow French and discussion started up. But our chairman had clearly detected some fidgeting around the table because after five to ten minutes he asked 'Are we all happy to continue this in French?' Hands went up, quite a few, for switching to English. It was, I felt, a historic moment. French simply no longer worked as the common language for Europe. Now that Britain is moving towards leaving the Union, there is talk of reviving French as the main working language. I cannot see that as feasible. But increased use of English was seen as carrying with it a stream of economic opinion, through *The Economist* and *Financial Times*, which jarred with the collective preference of the staff, they being as said left-leaning, statist, and solidly in favour of the 'European project'.

I had some sympathy with the resistance to English being used as the dominant language to work in, insofar as the dominant use of any one language does bring with it a distinct limiting of the range of opinion and style of debate. Against that, there is no doubt that the number of languages spoken in Europe, and used as of right in the conduct EU business, 22 at the last count, carries with it huge costs for interpretation at meetings and translation of discussion documents and laws. It was shaming in a way to find that for ASEAN purposes their ten member countries each with their own national language, or several, happily work together using English, with no call at all for translation. Yet the European system has allowed our wealth of languages to continue if not to flourish. The practical need for one common working language has resulted in English becoming, for now, the language of choice.

The English spoken and written, for working purposes, inside the Commission was a flattened-out version of real English, sprinkled with numerous bits of jargon and slightly out-of-tune grammar, much of it traceable to French. This gave me added value in the ranks. Much of the work that I did was with 'desk officers', up-and-coming 30-35-year-olds with a subject to look after. They were not all finding it equally easy to adjust to the fairly recent requirement to draft their policy papers in English. So, along with the more substantive help I was able to give, they were always pleased to turn to me for advice on use of English, and for me to run my eye over their drafts. I learned to ration my corrections to the places where it mattered, so as to make the meaning clear. If the meaning was already unambiguous, even if the language was stilted, not what a native English speaker would say, I left it alone. All the same I found that when I wrote, or gave a talk, in my natural style, it met with a flutter of appreciation.

It was then, and probably is now, quite rare for these Eurocrats struggling with the English language, to be able to measure themselves against the real thing. I found exactly the same when I came up against real stylish French, as written by Pascal Lamy or one of our senior colleagues, Pierre Defraigne; or a stylish piece such as Prodi produced (in Italian) when he rather touchingly wrote a personal Christmas letter to all members of the Commission's staff. French certainly suffered in just the same way as English when used as the common medium of communication; bureaucratic French, used second-hand by people who were aiming no higher than to say what they meant without ambiguity, became drained of life, without style and without feeling.

The Commissioner for Trade for most of my time there was Pascal Lamy, a man who can absolutely not be accused of lacking in style. A master of his complicated subject, a canny negotiator, lucid when expressing himself either in French or in English, he was a star operator. His successor, when the Commissioners all changed in the autumn of 2004, was Peter Mandelson. When he arrived he was unfamiliar with the intricacies of trade policy, but he was a fast learner. I had to warn Peter Carl that he was going to be up against a political operator and power player of a high order, not averse to scheming and manipulation. I warned Peter Carl to tread carefully, not to overplay his hand with his new master, master of the subject matter though he himself was. I warned in particular against getting caught in the crossfire between Peter Mandelson and Gordon Brown (of which I myself had had a little experience before leaving Whitehall). Peter sadly did not trim to these warnings, or not sufficiently. He fell into the trap that I had seen one or two top officials in Whitehall fall into over the years: that of taking the view that they know best about their complex and technical area of business, and understand it all better than their incoming political master; attempting with too heavy a hand to steer the newcomer; provoking the newcomer to assert who is boss.

There was a difference of view between the two Peters which Mandelson turned to his advantage. The issue was whether the EU should put all its efforts into backing the multilateral system of rules on trade, through the World Trade Organization, and do all it could to support the Doha Round, or should put at least some of its effort into developing preferential trade agreements with some individual countries or groups of countries. Peter Carl's view was that as a matter of principle the multilateral trade system was better for the world economy, and for the EU economy, than piecemeal agreements could be. I shared that analysis and did my bit to persuade doubters inside DG Trade that it was the better way to go. But doubts were growing at that time, inside and outside the Commission. The Doha Round had been launched in November 2001, within weeks of the 9/11 attacks on the US, and in that very tense time for international relations the member countries of the WTO had closed ranks and signed up to a deal which in calmer times they would not have done. By 2004 it was becoming clear that differences of interest between developed and developing countries were going to make action on the Doha terms extremely difficult, and progress was slow. Meanwhile, quite a number of the EU's trading partners were making preferential deals with one another and it was becoming harder and harder to argue that the EU should not see what it could do in the same line. It is none too clear to me, looking back now, that Peter Carl's view was the wrong one; but he fell foul of Mandelson by trying to close his Commissioner off from tapping into the different views held by the staff; Mandelson was far too acute not to notice that there was a debate from which he was being excluded.

It is little consolation to be on the right side of history when the final years of a fine career are in the balance. Peter Carl found himself on the move, not long into Mandelson's tenure, transferred to Environment, which he claimed was a perfect fit with his personal enthusiasms. That perfect match lasted quite a short time. He left the Commission to become an adviser to the French Minister for the Environment, but that did not last long either. For a time he reappeared in Brussels as a consultant – the fate of many top Eurocrats who don't seem to know how to retire.

I have painted some of the strengths and weaknesses that I found in my varied two years inside the Commission. I end on a note of praise for those I worked with. Difficult it certainly is to run an organization smoothly with staff drawn from twenty countries or more, and all those different national traditions of public service. The Commission seemed to me to do its job more than effectively, despite that. Talent on the whole rose to the top, rather too slowly, but talent rose and some of it was talent of star quality. Those who couldn't or didn't want to match up to the exacting demands of the job were allowed to trail along, not disciplined much for their weak performance, but not detracting much from the collective performance where it mattered. Some of the very best work I saw was in the briefing pack produced for Mandelson as new Commissioner: an encyclopaedia of notes on all aspects of his job, clear, concise notes as well-crafted as the Whitehall equivalent, rather better on the whole for brevity and penetrating analysis. Of the talented 30-35-year-olds, several have remained good friends and I wish them all well as they plough on with their careers. We British, if Brexit goes through, will soon have no part in it all.

It is gratifying to be able to end also with a note of praise for me from the Commission. Pierre Defraigne was in formal terms deputy to Peter Carl but in reality of high standing in his own right, having been chef de cabinet for an earlier Commissioner. He and I had a long-running debate on the future of the European Union. Giving evidence (in Brussels) to a House of Lords committee on 11 March 2004, he was asked by Lord Wright: 'Have you any thoughts about British performance that we ought to bear in mind in writing our report?' Defraigne's reply was: 'On trade matters the British civil service is absolutely outstanding. I think that is the real reason why we have Richard Carden here [in the Commission]... He has retired but we hired him as a special consultant and we have asked him to perform a series of special missions... It is an old tradition to have a first class expert.'

In my valedictory message to the top of the office as I left the Commission, I sounded one clear note of warning: be careful how you use your strength. I praised the high quality of work produced by a high-powered team and a well-drilled machine. The danger I warned of was that the sheer strength of the DG Trade operation threatened to open up gaps between the Commission and its member states on the one hand, and the EU and the non-EU countries with whom it did dealings on the other.

The risk then as now comes not simply from a concentration of high-powered people in the upper reaches of the Commission. It is ingrained in the work the Commission has to do. The brightest and best brains in the Commission, at least on trade and agriculture, lived in a permanent state of negotiation one way and the other. They lived and breathed negotiation. It became part of their mind-set. On every issue where the EU has to take a common position, that has first to be worked out in hard negotiation between the Commission and the member states. The end-product of that process is often a complex and nuanced position, an amalgam of member states' wish lists, which the Commission then has to try to hold together in any subsequent negotiation with outsiders. This can project the EU as over-complicated, over-bearing and rigid.

The risk against which I was warning was that the sheer ability and agility of the Commission staff left a good many member states struggling to keep up, and the majority of the EU's trading partners trailing way behind. This ability-gap was liable, I said, to alienate the partners EU and non-EU. As I delicately phrased it to my DG Trade bosses then: 'the analytical power gives us the ability to formulate negotiating positions of a subtlety and complexity which only the most sophisticated of our trade partners can keep up with'. I was studiously understating my point. I had seen when the EU was overhauling its trading arrangements with developing countries in 2003-05 that the African and Caribbean countries had indeed felt cowed and brow-beaten when the Commission presented them with a complicated new system for grouping them together by region. Typically well-worked out in advance, the EU came across as high-handed, and this provoked ill feeling.

The Commission staff are not good at seeing themselves as others see them. One of the most formidable negotiating machines in the world can be just too clever for its own good. We see more than a touch of this syndrome in the 2018 negotiations over Brexit.

16

BRITAIN AND EUROPE: OBSERVATIONS FROM THE CUTTING EDGE

1970-2018

The European Community came into being in the 1950s, grew up into a working organization in the 1960s, and Britain joined in 1973. Nearly all my 35 years of work in the public service that came to an end in 2005 were involved, mostly very closely, with this 'Europe': the European Economic Community which turned by steps into the European Union; the 'European project'. Now in 2018 Britain is drawing away from the EU towards the yawning uncertainties of Brexit. Do my experiences have anything useful to offer?

The period I worked through confirmed that Britain was uncomfortable with the European project from the outset. Its effort to adjust to the European system was stressful, acutely so for the first ten years; and as time went on, instead of settling into the mainstream as it might have done at some points, Britain called for one opt-out after another. The more the project moved towards closer union – the mission statement in the Treaty of Rome to which UK politicians had persistently turned a blind eye – the more our governments felt impelled to insist on exemptions. Until Britain stood clearly on the margins.

It is too much to expect that my experiences can answer the question: what went wrong? When I have drawn out the points that seem to me to emerge from a review of the 45 years that Britain has spent 'inside', and my close involvement in it, my observations will undoubtedly provide fuel for both sides of the debate. I can only describe what went on in the engine room; my experiences as one of always quite a small band of officials working at the cutting edge, taking part in the work of constructing and operating a unique supranational system. My observations will chart the particular difficulties that Britain had with it and how we attempted to surmount them.

* * * * *

When I heard Edward Heath speak at the Oxford Union in the early 1960s, I was attracted by what he said about joining the European Community. His message was upbeat. He was not the first British politician to advocate Britain joining. Harold Macmillan had done so, but Macmillan was a voice from the past for us teenagers and a figure of fun, lampooned weekly on the new satirical television programme 'That Was The Week That Was'. Heath had been leading the team that made the first serious but unsuccessful shot at getting Britain in, in 1962. He had fought in the 1939-45 war, and the ending of wars between the countries of Europe was for him, as for the founders of the European Community, a fundamental argument in favour of the project. For the previous 250 years Western Europe had suffered again and again from conflict between France and Germany, with Britain sometimes involved and sometimes not. Creating a system with the purpose of making it impossible for those two countries to go to war again seemed of the utmost importance. Heath was not the only leading politician to think so – but most of the others were on the continent, not in Britain.

The majority opinion in favour of joining, for the British, was entirely about economics. By the early 1960s it was clear that the economies of France and even more of Germany were performing better than Britain's, and the French and German people were enjoying the benefits. Britain was continuing to stutter along economically, industrially; the pound had been devalued by 14% in November 1967 (bringing the spending power of my student grant down with a bump in Berlin). The view gathered strength on the British side that our industry and business would benefit from the 'cold shower' of being thrown up against higher-performing neighbours. This view would be criticised ferociously in the context of the Brexit debate (2018) as betraying a lack of confidence in Britain and Britain's ability to go it alone. In 1970 when Heath, by then prime minister, led Britain into the EEC we were a country that did lack confidence in itself, in economic terms at least. And for quite good reason. Things were bad and got worse. By the mid-1970s the UK had to crawl to the International Monetary Fund for a loan. The country was bankrupt. Constant clashes between organised labour and their managers and the government were dragging the British economy further and further behind. It was not clear then and it is not clear now how we expected joining the EEC to save us, but we did.

In line with the strong but vague admiration for France and Germany, we young civil servants starting our careers in the 1970s were encouraged to go and learn from our French and German counterparts. I was sent on a short visit to ENA, the hot-house in Paris that schools France's top civil servants, to hear about the French statist system of government and the easy passage between their high-flying civil service jobs and captaincy of state-run industries. We went also to the staff college in Bonn. The Germans were seen more as a model for decentralised national government, and for long-term investment decisions, and their cooperative system of management in industry (Mitbestimmung) was in black-and-white contrast with the permanent warfare between unions and management that had become the norm in Britain. Their system worked for them. Why not for us? Neither the French statist system of government nor the easy cooperation between banks, management and workers that delivered so well for the Germans in actual fact caught on in Britain. But the 1970s were years when there were high hopes that the economic success of our neighbours would somehow or other rub off on us.

* * * * *

The most immediate impact of our joining the then Economic Community, the Common Market, was on agriculture. This caused friction between us and the original Six. It touched raw nerves on both sides. Agriculture had been one of the most difficult areas of the negotiations over our entry, and one of the last to be settled. On the British side, the problems were two-fold: impact on the price of food in the shops, and impact on long-standing trade with Commonwealth countries. It is hard now, fifty years on, to appreciate just how much concern there was on both these issues. For the Six, the concern was that they had agreed among themselves with difficulty a common policy for agriculture (CAP) – apart from coal and steel and atomic energy the only policy that they had at that stage. They knew that the British had a markedly different idea of how best to support farmers, involving lower prices to consumers and a higher cost to taxpayers. They were braced for the British to try to unpick the CAP and they were determined to stand firm against that.

Our terms of accession allowed us five years of transition to the full CAP, five steps of raising prices on the home front and bringing in higher charges on imports, which were expected to discourage our imports from the Commonwealth and switch us into buying more (higher cost) produce from inside the EC.

A year after we joined, the Heath government fell and the Wilson Labour government which replaced it demanded a renegotiation of the terms of entry. So Britain's commitment to EC membership already seemed wobbly, pretty much as predicted by De Gaulle when he had refused to let us in the first time. One leading and stated aim of the Wilson renegotiation was to create openings for the import of more food from the Commonwealth – Caribbean sugar, New Zealand butter and lamb – and to create options to support farmers at home by deficiency payments rather than the Community's preferred system of pegging prices to farmers, and consumers, by taking surplus off the market into 'intervention' stores. The renegotiation was short and sharp, less than a year, and was followed by a referendum on the results. The government's pamphlet recommending to voters that they should support the results and vote in favour of staying in the EC on the new terms is interesting to look back at. It was divided into 15 sections, agriculture coming top of the list, ahead of such less contentious matters as political cooperation and parliamentary sovereignty.

My experiences from that period taught me some early lessons both on how the Community operated and how the British government handled the misgivings which the British public had about it. I was pitched into an area of action which turned out to be highly important for Wilson and his renegotiation and his referendum result. The story is told in my chapter 6. We were made to suffer through long days and nights to secure any exception from the EC norm. At each stage, our issue and our special demands were dealt with as part of a package in which other member states had demands of their own. The Six held together against the British plea for special treatment, the Commission dealt with us with steely determination, and we learned the painful lesson that if in this Community you do hold out for special treatment you end up paying a price, or rather two prices: you have to subordinate your key demand to other objectives you may have alongside that, *and* you have to concede to a variety of demands that other member states may have – or may introduce, seeing their opportunity, in order for the end-result to be a package from which gains and losses are spread in some sort of rough balance all round.

During this episode I spent more time in the negotiating rooms of Brussels and Luxembourg than in my office in Whitehall, but when I was at my desk a part of the work was to draft replies for our ministers to give to parliamentary questions (PQs) about the state of the beef market and what impact the CAP was having on it. The public and their MPs on their behalf were deeply suspicious that we were being sucked into the CAP system. Was the CAP going to make the British housewife (no qualms about using sexist terms in those days) pay more for the beef British farmers produced, and was it going to make us pay more for beef imported from outside the EC? The answer should clearly have been yes to both questions, taking the long view. But as it happened the world market went through a very exceptional phase and just for a short time prices on the world market shot up above prices in the EC. Everyone knew that this was a blip and would not last. But we crafted replies to PQs that put maximum emphasis on the here and now, and slid disingenuously round the longer term prospects. For us junior civil servants it felt uncomfortable though not exactly dishonest. The government's pamphlet to voters on the outcome of the renegotiation was able to draw on this little episode to suggest the prospect that the CAP was capable of sheltering EC consumers from upsurges in world prices. The situation has almost never arisen again – and we didn't expect it to. Here then was an early lesson in how a British government can cloak the uncomfortable features of Community membership, and divert public concerns by the artful use of smoke and mirrors – and the help of pliable civil servants. It was a lesson in presentation of a kind that came my way a good many more times.

As for the severity of treatment meted out by the Six, I think it came as a surprise to some of us. France was known to have been very guarded about letting Britain in, and highly protective of the CAP, but were the other members of the Six not broadly sympathetic at political level? Were they not looking forward to the added weight that they expected Britain to contribute, with its worldwide connections and reputation for administrative skills? We were learning that any such friendly feelings of a political kind found no place when it came to negotiations on practical matters. There the game was cut-and-thrust, each for himself, high alert, strong nerves, stamina. The prizes went to those who could play this game best. The French were high-class players.

* * * * *

When I came back to MAFF from the Treasury in 1979, Thatcher's Conservative government had taken over from Callaghan's enfeebled Labour government and the order of the day was cost cutting. Cutting public expenditure on the home front, but the budget of the European Community must be cut too. The cost of the Common Agricultural Policy which anyway took up the largest part of the Community budget had ballooned in the 1970s. This above all must be cut. So MAFF was once again centre stage for delivery of a key government policy for Europe.

Coming from the Treasury where looking for cost savings had been the essence of my work for two years, I slid easily into the Thatcherite mode. Not so the chums across the Channel. All across the European Community (then 12 countries) farm ministers and their civil servants were directing their efforts to getting more money out of the CAP. It was the perfect example of a group spending more than they would each spend individually – the shared bill at the restaurant. The blame for high spending could not be pinned on any one member state. The majority of states were in any case net beneficiaries of the Community budget unlike Britain which paid in much more than it got out. So their finance ministers were relaxed. Not so the British Treasury.

It was even better than this, for the farm ministers. A complicated system of artificial exchange rates special to farming, known as green rates, had been constructed so that real exchange rates – with the high inflation of the 1970s some member states were devaluing their real rates all the time – did not automatically take effect on the payment systems of the CAP, the intervention prices that underpinned market prices. A devaluation of any national currency would put up the amount due to a farmer in that country for a tonne of grain or butter, because the support prices were set in a notional currency for all member states, based on a basket of real rates. Thanks to the green rate system these increases which should have come about as and when the national real currency sank in value were delayed but then – wonder of wonders for agriculture ministers – a minister could ask at a Council of Ministers meeting for collective agreement to move his green rate closer to the real rate; and then he could take home to his farmers a price increase and present it as if they owed it to his benevolence and negotiating skill, not to the weakness of their country's national economy. It was a marvellous era for agriculture ministers. CAP costs rose and rose, mountains of grain, beef and butter and lakes of wine were built up at Community taxpayers' expense.

By around 1980 the Commission had become clear that somehow or other the lid must be put on. But they struggled against the spendthrift mentality all across Europe. The arrival of Thatcher on this scene was not altogether unwelcome, at least not to the Commission. This was for me the first encounter with a situation that I ran into again, with CAP reform, and with trade policy and the issue of liberalisation of trade. The Commission needed Britain and the British position on cost-cutting or free trade as long as Britain was at one end of the range of opinion among member states and not off the scale altogether. The Commission found it helpful if Britain was articulating the case for change and pulling the centre of gravity of member state opinion in the direction it needed to go. However, for British influence to be of any help in these situations our views needed to have at least some support among other member states. This point was for a long time not well understood by the Treasury, nor by the high priests of trade policy in Whitehall. On cutting the cost of the CAP we officials in MAFF found ourselves needing to face both ways, professing in Whitehall a degree of acquiescence in unrealistically stringent (off the scale) instructions from Treasury, then shading the line down to make it digestible, and of practical impact, in Brussels. Here was an area where a degree of subtlety was needed by those operating at the cutting edge – and a degree of economy with the truth on the home front.

Up to a point, then, Britain's call for cuts in farm spending in the early 1980s chimed in with the need that the Commission had begun to see clearly for finding ways to put the brakes on. But Britain's need went further. We wanted, and needed, not just to cut CAP spending in total but to cut our share of it. This put us at odds with all other member states, because if our share were to be cut others would have to pay in more; and the Commission saw no interest in assisting us.

Yet Thatcher and her case for 'wanting her money back' had a very strong basis. The formula agreed when we joined (not the only bad deal done then) was at odds with our relatively small farming sector and the relatively high imports from non-EC countries. It took Thatcher five years of ferocious and bitter campaigning to wrench a better deal, at Fontainebleau in 1984. Over that time there was a high degree of animosity to Britain in the upper reaches, though it did not much affect day-to-day business at the levels where I operated. And it passed off. An illustration that, at that stage anyway, the mood towards Britain could change really quite quickly. At that stage in 1984 the Six had been wrestling for over 20 years first to trim Britain into shape to fit into their world and then to accommodate, to the absolute minimum, our demands for adjustment to the system. After Fontainebleau there was a collective sigh of relief that perhaps now at last Britain was in, and would settle down and contribute the strengths that many of them had been hoping and waiting for. Our influence had been diverted for ten long years into correcting an imperfect accession deal, terms set too harshly by the Six at the outset.

* * * * *

I returned to Brussels work in autumn 1987 after three years in the English countryside where I had been painfully embroiled in the introduction of milk quotas: a Europe-wide scheme to cut back the vast overproduction of milk which was put into effect with immense care and exactitude in the UK – and with careful inexactitude in Italy. By 1987 the British budget problem seemed to have been laid to rest. Britain with its continuing zeal to cut costs was now in the Community mainstream.

Cost-saving measures were pushed through at that time against considerable resistance from the countries for whom higher CAP spending was all good news, the Commission fighting with determination, grateful for the unswerving support of the British. Britain by then could have felt secure in the mainstream and settled to being one member state among 12. But Mrs Thatcher's ferocious independence which had been a vital asset in battling our share of the overall budget down to a more reasonable level became a mixed asset in the next phase. I recall a story told to us by friends in the Danish Embassy on one occasion around this time. It was Denmark's turn in the Presidency; they were chairing all the meetings of ministers. Their prime minister came to London on a round of visits to prepare a European summit. Denmark was one of our closest allies and their prime minister was trying to be helpful. He ran through his ideas for the forthcoming summit meeting with Mrs Thatcher in a meeting at 10 Downing Street. She had other ideas. Our friends at the embassy rang us a couple of hours later and said he had arrived back from No.10 in a state of shock, still trembling from the telling-off he had been given, and told his officials that he had not been treated in that way since his junior school. The Thatcher ferocity barred us from ever being 'at the heart of Europe' in her time.

Yet there were things that were going well for us. Most notably the Single Market campaign. The Single European Act (1986) opened the way for a whole range of proposals to remove non-tariff barriers on manufactured products but also on the standards for professions such as doctors, lawyers and architects, to be settled by majority voting. It was a very important breakthrough. The Commission declared a grand five-year plan to achieve decisions on 'completing the single market' – a complete set of rules for internal trade and the movement of people qualified to offer professional services – by 1992. In charge of this new programme of action was a British Commissioner, Lord Cockfield. UK manufacturers, traders and professionals were to gain from it on a broad front. I have given the picture in chapter 9.

There was a stream of new legislation, of course, and for those who regard all new laws coming from Brussels as undesirable, for whom harmonisation is anathema and the Commission the embodiment of evil, this single market campaign was all bad news. That view has, in Britain, run all too strongly and obscured the underlying nature of the exercise, from which British manufacturers and exporters and providers of professional services stood to gain. The point of the exercise was to replace, product by product, subject area by subject area, the existing variety of national rules by a single set of rules for the whole Community. Where previously the manufacturers of say telephones or office equipment had had to make to one standard for sale in Germany and another for France and a different standard again for Italy, the Commission's aim was to get agreement on one standard that met the essential safety or quality standards for all. The end result was fewer rules for a manufacturer or exporter to comply with, not more. A new standard emerging from Brussels took the place of several different national requirements. Trading became easier. This was intended to, and did, save production costs and led to an increase in the flow of goods and services across frontiers in Europe. More than that, EC producers could now make economies of scale and become more competitive with Japan and the US in non-EC markets.

It is hard to understand, looking back, why this was not regarded as a notable achievement by Britain – with the British Commissioner in charge – and for Britain, British operators gaining new markets on a broad front. It should have been scored as the first clear economic gain for Britain from membership of the EC.

There were admittedly downsides: aspects of the market opening which had drawbacks for farmers and growers, and public health. These elements could be grouped under the general heading 'disease' – and formed part of my work. Again the detail is in chapter 9. We had to take the rough with the smooth. Perhaps on one or two matters we might use our freedom, given Brexit, to revert to our previous arrangements. The pet travel scheme has run now for nearly 20 years without any mishap, but I still fear that we are living dangerously. Were rabies to slip into the country it could spread uncontrollably fast into London and other inner cities, through the dense population of urban foxes that we have sentimentally allowed to build up. The consequences could be dire. Perhaps after Brexit we should reimpose rabies controls as before?

Taking the rough with the smooth the Single Market must have brought large net economic benefits to the UK. It is strange that the benefits should have been so lost from sight that Brexiters now campaign for leaving the single market in order that Britain can be free to set product standards different from those adopted by the EU. Where is the advantage to British manufacturers and traders in that?

*   *   *   *   *

The single market campaign, 1986-92, was a period when other things were going our way in Europe, or at least going less adversely than they might have done, and British influence was behind this. The period roughly coincided with the Uruguay Round of GATT – international trade – negotiations: 1986-94. International pressure was brought to bear on the European Community to reform its CAP; to reduce its restrictions on imports and to curb

286

subsidised exports which had caused major disruption on the markets for developing countries in particular. This was a direction of change which the UK wanted and from our position inside the EC we gave it support and encouragement. Circumspectly, on the principle of staying within the range of member states' opinion or losing all influence over them. The Commission and the UK worked well together, first over hatching a set of reforms to the CAP (the MacSharry reforms of 1992), then brokering a deal with the other leading members of GATT. MAFF's minister John Gummer had an influential role in this delicate exercise. He was one of the rare British ministers who had a good feel for the subtleties needed to make British influence effective, in the agriculture sector above all.

CAP Reform, the Uruguay Round, and the enlargement of the Community all made progress in those years and British influence ran strongly in all three areas. It was, in my opinion, the period of our membership when our ability to influence was at its height. We had officials in key positions in London and Brussels who had, as I had, been thrown into European affairs early in our careers and had learned our craft in the years when exercising British influence was uphill all the way; learning how to operate in this strange new system, operating in the times when Britain had painful adjustments to make, and then working through the mega-battle over the budget and CAP costs when British influence was desperately hard to achieve. We had come up the hard way. Compared with many of our Community partners we were battle-hardened, and we had learned the dark arts of getting what we wanted by stealth and cunning as well as open debate; knowing whose ear to whisper in, at what stage. These arts served us well in that period.

As John Major's government ran its course, demanding opt-outs (at Maastricht) and fighting mis-judged battles (the blocking tactics over BSE), British influence took a downturn.

* * * * *

BSE was big. The impact of the disease on cattle farmers in Britain was severe at the time, though not as devastating for individual farm businesses as was foot-and-mouth in 2001. The costs to the British taxpayer were far higher: compensating farmers in the early stages, and dealing with the impact on a much broader front after the announcement that BSE could be affecting humans, cost between £3 and 4 billion, and the subsequent public inquiry in itself cost £27 million and more. The announcement in March 1996 of the possibility of transmission to humans had a sharp short-term effect on farmers' incomes, and on public confidence in food safety or more precisely on public confidence in government statements on food safety, and had a shattering and rather more long-lasting impact on our relations with the rest of the European Union: member states and Commission. For me in work terms BSE was big: I did almost nothing else for about four years.

However, the long-term effects of this catastrophe on Britain's position in the EU can be overstated. It seemed worst at the time. The feverish resistance put up by the Major government to the restrictions on trade imposed by the EU in the initial stages (1996-97) was an ill-judged over-reaction driven to a great extent by the Eurosceptic faction. With them at his heels John Major had no option but to give a bulldog performance to show he was not going to be pushed around by 'Brussels'. That did short-term damage, but the 1997 change of government soon put it behind us.

The Commission, they too driven in the short term by the need to manage panic reactions from some member states (and self-interested reactions from others), fairly rapidly moved from backing a total shut-down of trade to working with us in MAFF on restoration. If the path they set us took nearly ten years to traverse, to bring results through a clamp-down on the disease in ways other member states could understand, and restoration of public confidence bit by bit – well, ten years is about par for the course in restoring a brand after a catastrophe. Austria had a similar experience: pulling its wines clean off the market for a decade after Austrian winemakers were found to be routinely using diethylene glycol in their winemaking.

Did the Commission treat us with undue severity, or discrimination? Not really. Not every step they took, not every condition they imposed on us, squared with our more expert scientific understanding. But they acted to our advantage in supporting the reopening of trade when they judged the time was right, and slowly but consistently stepped up pressure on member states that still held out against restoration of trade; notably France. Without the Commission and the force of the European Court on our side, had we been fighting as a lone independent country, we would quite probably have had to wait as long for France as we had to wait for China – China lifted its BSE restrictions only in 2018. There is in Britain a line of criticism of the EU that the countries of Europe are so argumentative, so often quarrelling, that we would be better off out. My view is that the quarrelsomeness of the countries of Europe one with another is a strong reason for having a system of rules to keep the lid on these quarrels. Britain demonstrably benefited at times. Here on BSE was a specific example of the EU framework of law helping us, although there was next to no comment to that effect at the time.

* * * * *

The CAP loomed large in my career from 1973 to 2000. It is hard to identify positive points for Britain out of the Common Agricultural Policy. We certainly didn't join the Economic Community all those years ago for the attractions of its agricultural policy. By the early years of the 21st century the budget cost of the CAP had come down, even though it still took around 40% of total EU expenditure; its adverse effects on international trade and the markets of developing countries had been toned down too. British efforts had played a part but external pressure from the international community through GATT/WTO had counted for more. We could include in the balance sheet, on the positive side, the addition to the CAP of agri-environment schemes; subsidies to farmers to farm in ways more friendly to traditional landscapes and to wildlife. This was a British idea in origin that we succeeded in getting the EU to take up, or nominally to take up. Only really in the Netherlands were these subsidies used for what they were meant for. Most other member states drew the money and passed it on to farmers as additional income, with minimal conditions attached.

All in all it would be surprising if, given Brexit, Britain could not design a better agricultural policy for itself (better for the public interest and perhaps better even for farmers) than the CAP. Likewise on fisheries. (Blame for the deal we accepted on fisheries when we joined in 1973 ought to be equally split between the Six, for deliberately designing a policy from which they would gain so much at Britain's expense and introducing it just when the accession deal was nearly done, and Heath for passively accepting it.) The essence of my work on the CAP was damage-limitation. We workers in the front line took satisfaction from trimming budget costs here, tweaking the rules in Britain's favour there. Among experts on our own side we could score these as modest successes. To the non-experts back home, inside and outside government, we were tarred for working in an area that was by and large bad for Britain.

It therefore came as a welcome change when, late in my career, I moved on to international trade: five years in London then Brussels. Britain worked here as part of the EU pack. Member states were divided broadly into two camps: those who saw advantages in free trade and leaned towards making the EU rules more open, and those who were happy with the protectionist system for agriculture as it was and had no problem with protectionism for other industries too. This division ran more or less north versus south; the 'northern liberals' and the protectionist southerners, France for this purpose being firmly a southerner.

International pressure was brought to bear on the EU and its CAP during the periodic international trade 'rounds' – the Uruguay Round (1986-94) where I spent some time in the front line; then the Doha Round which I helped to launch in 2001. (That petered out with little result, but not before the EU had put on the table some commitments on curbing its subsidies for agricultural exports.) The conduct of trade negotiations was similar in some ways, different in others, from what I had been used to. The politics of agriculture were never far away. Many non-EU countries large and small, developed and developing, wanted the EU to allow in more agricultural imports and to cut out subsidies to exports. The EU, ever conscious that it would come under pressure to do this, resisted long and hard while exploring what concessions it could extract in return. That made for slow progress. A concerted and highly effective campaign to put pressure on the EU over agriculture was at the heart of the Uruguay Round, and that took more than eight years. The following Round, launched at Doha, soon got stuck, though not entirely over agriculture. Over fifteen years after that, multilateral negotiations (involving all trading nations of the world) languished and smaller-scale efforts at regional deals between pairs or groups of countries or trading blocs sprouted instead. For the

EU, whether negotiating with Canada or India or the countries of Latin America, pressure from the other side to open up on agriculture was a constant – only with Japan was the boot on the other foot.

The slow pace of trade negotiations is derided by the non-experts but the packages on which deals are done are immensely complicated, covering thousands of products in meticulous detail. The teams who negotiate these packages are formidably skilled. The UK now launching into this activity as a new player has a very great deal to learn. For the parties to the negotiations there is a balance to be struck between economic gains and political pain. Negotiators laboriously cross-check with groups representing sectoral interests and with their politicians as they feel their way forward – as cautiously as if the field ahead were sown with mines.

The European Commission, with their responsibility to act on behalf of the member states where trade is concerned, took endless care over this. I described in my chapter 13 the system of weekly all-day meetings supplemented by almost constant conversations whereby the Commission felt its way forward, balancing (balance again!) the various and sometimes conflicting views with which member states bombarded it.

The Commission played off the liberals against the protectionists when it suited, but they needed the liberals to be active and speaking with a strong voice. The Commission's house view was in favour of liberalising, though on agriculture only as far as the 'southerners' (France mainly) would tolerate, and on industrial goods never quite as far as the British were prepared to go. Britain was able to exert strong influence within the Community not just because we favoured free trade; so did the Scandinavians, and the Germans too where industrial goods were concerned (but see below). What Britain could add to this mix was ability to articulate the case for trade. Much of the EU discussion was conducted in English, but non-native speakers had more difficulty in stringing their arguments together in the cut-and-thrust of debate. The British being simply more articulate – and their ministers trained in the Westminster parliament to be quick in argument – supplied good ammunition for the Commission's negotiators; sound bites that they could remember and re-deploy. And Britain in the liberal camp was a fair match in weight (and nimbleness in argument) for France in the opposing camp.

There were times when the British weighing in on the liberal side tipped the scales. It remains to be seen whether the EU without Britain will maintain the same degree of openness or be pulled back by the protectionists. Perhaps it will stay liberal. Perhaps Germany, when collective guilt for Hitler has receded some more, will become more assertive and less beholden to the French.

Acute conflicts sometimes arose among member states and had to be resolved. The moments of highest tension would arise over agriculture. Differences of view between the protectionists and those willing to move could be staved off, and staved off for long stretches of time. The moments of truth came – and this only very occasionally – during sessions of international negotiations when a deal had been all but done and the EU *had* to decide exactly how much it was going to concede on agriculture. I have said that member states fell into two camps, more liberal northerners versus protectionist southerners. But in the last analysis, on these occasions when the EU was on the spot, when a hundred and fifty other members of the WTO were waiting for an answer and the hands of the clock appeared to be at midnight, the last member state to give in was France. Every time.

French reluctance to give in, put Germany on the spot; Germany for whom exports of manufactured goods far outweighed their farming interests. A moment would come when France would appeal to Germany to support it. The conversation was not always out in the open, though sometimes it was. But if France really wanted to dig in, rather than make an elaborate display before conceding an inch or two, then the French would turn to the Germans, confident that if France and Germany stood together they would not be overridden. This took us right back to the beginning of the European project.

* * * * *

The kernel of the original community of Six was reconciliation between France and Germany, bound together to start with by shared management of their coal and steel industries, followed by the common policy for agriculture. The bond between France and Germany has held through thick and thin. Over many years Britain often tried to prise them apart. On farm support and on international trade there were quite a few specific times and situations when we British, officials and ministers, thought Germany was poised to side with us against France, because economic interests – in cutting the budget, or opening up international trade – clearly pulled Germany towards our side of the argument. On crunch occasions, sometimes with visible reluctance, Germany finished up siding with France. In those situations Germany was acting against its economic interests, its behaviour was economically irrational. It was only to be understood if the bond between Germany and France was non-negotiable, unbreakable. To make sense of this in terms of national interests you have to appreciate that for German governments, successive governments regardless of political colour, it is an absolute necessity for their country to be a part of a community of countries *and* for unity between France and Germany to be an essential part of this. My experience all indicated that this was so.

We learned to understand this in Whitehall but we seriously expected that German behaviour might change after reunification. Specifically, on our analysis, German attitudes to farm support might change; the latifundia, the very large farms in the former communist regions, would be more able to run with less CAP support and to face international competition. Good prospects, then, for cutting the Community budget and for responding to international pressure for more liberal trade in farm products and foodstuffs. But Germany continued to stand by France on these issues. The Franco-German lock remained unbroken. At the level of routine business the exchanges between their civil servants and the frequency of meetings between their ministers are in a different league from anything Britain or any other member state went in for. If there is a special state-to-state relationship anywhere in international affairs, it is the bond between France and Germany.

This has been good for all of us. Wars between France and Germany in the twentieth century were ruinous – ruinous to them and all their neighbours. Those wars certainly bankrupted Britain and opened the way for the United States to lever the British Empire out of existence. It may be that war between the countries of western Europe is now a pretty remote possibility. But the episodes of war in the former Yugoslavia and between Russia and Ukraine and Georgia, and Russian pressure on the Baltics, show that the danger of war is not all that far away; and wars can spread. To have total lock-down between France and Germany is a big prize, and despite the passing of time the lock seemed to me to be as robust as ever. Historians may record this, and not the contorted economic policies (the CAP, the Euro), as the most important achievement of the European project.

But the European project can't be boiled down to that one essential point. An elaborate system of economic and political cooperation has been built up over 70 years to achieve unity first between the core six nations including France and Germany, then the progressively larger number of countries who have chosen to ally themselves with the project, for a variety of reasons. Most of the later joiners have gained in some way – putting dictatorships behind them, for the most part, and making large gains in economic prosperity. For Britain the gains were never so clear. The British economy picked up from the low point of the 1970s, but it was Thatcher's policies not the EC's wot did that.

Britain so it seems is taking a break. That might not cause much of a set-back to the project in the short term. The 27 members whom we would leave behind might well choose to pursue the present course, more or less. If pushed to take decisive further steps towards political and economic union, some might peel off. But the majority could well persist even though the road will be hard. In fifty years time? Various worlds are possible. Maybe Europe will go down the road of Alexander's empire, and split into several successor empires, one to the north, one to the east; possibly northern € and southern €? That would not necessarily vitiate the founders' ambition of maintaining Europe as a force in the world. We'd just need to ensure more friendly relations between our sub-empires than Alexander's diadochi managed.

17

ST GEORGE'S HOUSE

1980s - 2017

June 20 and 21 2017 were very hot days. I spent them in Windsor Castle, facilitating a conference about the future of farming in the UK after Brexit (leaving the European Union). Most of our discussions were held in the Vicars' Hall, a barn-like medieval room with a ceiling of timber beams – and no air-conditioning. The outside temperature rose well over 30 degrees on both days. Yet the participants kept their minds fully on the subject, and the final session was the liveliest and most productive of any that I can remember.

This was a conference hosted by St George's House, where such gatherings are called 'Consultations', for reasons that I shall come on to. The participants at this one were some of the top people from the British and Northern Irish farming world: practising farmers, staffers of farming organizations, leading lights from the National Trust and the RSPB, and leaders of four farming charities whose work is to provide advice, support, and homes, to farmers who fall on hard times and have to give up their businesses. Maybe two thirds of the participants here knew one another well and would meet frequently at other events; the remainder were new to each other. Some had been to St George's House before and knew what to expect; some were there for the first time, much impressed by being inside the Castle, working in a place dripping with a thousand years of English history.

This was typical of events that I was involved in once every year or two from the year 2000, and in which I often played a leading part. More of that but first, what is 'St George's House'? It is a house, a spacious Queen Anne building right next to St George's Chapel, the royal chapel that dominates the lower part of the huge area enclosed by the castle walls. Around the chapel on three sides there are houses from various periods of history: stone houses of a piece with the castle walls for the military knights, grace-and-favour residences, that is, for distinguished old soldiers; accommodation for the troops who guard the castle; a horseshoe of half-timbered houses for families who work in the castle;

a half-timbered house for the organist and practising rooms for the boys who sing at the services in the chapel, and more spacious stone-built houses for the Dean and Canons, the little team of clergy who perform the daily chapel services. And there is St George's House. This last was gently decaying and looking for a new use in the middle of the last century. The Dean – the senior churchman in residence, who is close to the Royal Family – suggested to the Duke of Edinburgh that it could be put to use as a conference centre of a particular kind. And so in 1966 it was.

The concept with which the Duke and the Dean started was that this house could be turned into a hostel for groups of people with positions of responsibility meeting to discuss problems and concerns in a secluded and private setting. It was always part of the plan that some of these people should be groups of clergy in mid-career, stepping back from their day-to-day work to think more reflectively about the problems they had to deal with, and to discuss them with others in similar situations. Alongside this was a more vague idea that the House could be useful as a place where people from various walks of life with various responsibilities could come and discuss social issues, current or foreseeable, and argue over contentious topics removed from the pressures of publicity or public attention. It was in one sense an innovative idea for adapting the College of St George, which had on the whole been facing inwards, and concentrating on its operation of chapel services, to face outwards and offer something to society outside the castle walls. This being a time (the 1960s) when society in Britain and beyond seemed to be going through rapid change and difficult adjustments.

Over the fifty years since the House was founded, the service it offers to clergymen has continued. Clergy courses still make up perhaps a quarter of the annual programme. However, the function as a place for secluded discussion on contentious topics has grown and flourished, and has come into focus. A sample from the programmes of the last couple of years gives some idea of the wide range of Consultation topics:

- Relationships and wellbeing in public policy
- The ethics of big data (with the Royal Statistical Society)
- Charting a new course for youth services
- Electoral reform (with the Economic and Social Research Council)

- Consultation for Her Majesty's Lord Lieutenants (an annual gathering)
- Digital living: getting the most out of digital society
- A roadmap for tackling childhood obesity
- Civil society and the state: the role of charities in campaigning
- The role of virtue in the professions
- Freedom of speech and universities.

Some of these Consultations were one-off, some were linked in short series over a year or so, and there were topics that were dealt with again and again. Farming was one of those.

Over time I learned what lay behind the choice of the word Consultation rather than Conference for the gatherings at St George's House. Whereas a conference very often takes the form of a string of speakers delivering their views from a platform to an audience which may get only a few minutes here and there in the programme to raise questions or discuss the views expressed from the platform, St George's House events were so arranged that everyone present had a chance to, and was encouraged to, express their own views on the subject in hand and to probe the views of others. A small number of speakers would deliver prepared talks but they were encouraged to leave at least half their allotted time for questions and discussion, and there would nearly always be sessions where those present were split into smaller groups with only a very light steer as to what they should discuss. The aim was for the members of the groups to engage with each other, pooling views and picking views apart. The present Warden, Canon Hueston Finlay, likes to describe the purpose as being to encourage 'high-level disagreement'. Behind this is the idea that the House wants to be a safe place where people who disagree can have searching discussions with each other over what they disagree about. Maybe they will still disagree after this but they are likely to take away a clearer understanding of their opponents' points of view. This may not always result in conflict resolution, but even conflict calming is a worthwhile outcome.

How did I become involved? My first visit to St George's House, prompted by John Holroyd when he was head of HR ('Director of Establishments') at MAFF, must have been around 1981-82. The Warden of the House then was Sir Hugh Beach, a retired general with a distinguished career behind him, and tall distinguished bearing. He guided the House in a gentle and fatherly manner. I do not have a clear memory of anything else about that occasion. We were a group of 25-30 young people, in our twenties and thirties, fished from a wide variety of occupations. This was one of a series of 'Windsor Meetings' the aim of which was to put together 'future leaders' from various walks of life to analyse the key issues facing society, and to speculate ten years or more into the future, in a loosely structured debate. We did this for two or three days. It was all very pleasant. I am sure we didn't come to any conclusions of any value. I ought probably to have kept in touch with some of the other participants but I didn't. My focus at that time was very firmly on work in Whitehall and Brussels. The future in my perspective was the future of Britain in Europe and the future lines of development of the European Economic Community (as it was still being called). That was intensive work and left no room in my mind for idle-seeming debate about the future of society, or of the world. According to the warden who started this series of Windsor Meetings: 'Their discussions were always stimulating and their reports insightful, but the ultimate benefit was the realisation that they had a responsibility to help shape the society which they were likely to inherit.' Fine words.

It was quite a long time before I went to St George's House again. When I did, it was with a much clearer purpose. I think I may have been invited to a Consultation in the late 1990s where food safety was one of the topics. I certainly attended one in January 2000, with Richard Packer. The subject was agricultural policy: 'Can future farming come closer to public aspirations?' Richard was coming to the end of his time at the head of the ministry of agriculture and was by turns uncomfortable and impatient with the discussion here, which to his mind was indulging in impractical, unfounded ideas which had long since been evaluated and rejected by the more rigorous processes of Whitehall.

Not long after that, in December 2002 and May 2003, I was invited back again for a pair of Consultations which had a specific purpose: 'Establishing a Future for Agriculture'. The heading told only part of the story. In August 2001 Tony Blair's government had set up a Policy Commission on the Future of Farming and Food, with the instruction to advise the government on... The remit took up seven lines of print but in short the call was for ideas on how to steer farmers in Britain towards relying less on subsidies and learning to make more money from the 'market place', by producing what consumers want. For most forms of business this would be a pretty obvious message. But farmers had been heavily reliant on subsidy for half a century, and since 1973 well fed on subsidies by the EU's Common Agricultural Policy. The Blair government aimed to chisel away at CAP spending, and at the protectionist charges on imports from outside the EU. Alongside this they needed a positive message for British farmers on how they were to survive with less nannying from the state.

In most other EU countries the farmers and their unions fought vigorously against the very idea. In Britain, attitudes were different. Farmers were not wholly against. But there was a need for a new push to win farmers round for actually changing their ways of farming in line with the Blairite message. Blair's ministers were lucky to find an ideal man for this in Don Curry. Don, recently knighted for services to agriculture and a few years later elevated to the House of Lords, was a man whom I had known for a long time through his role as a leader of the meat industry. I got to know him much better through our meetings at St George's House.

He led those two Consultations in 2002 and 2003, road testing the conclusions of his Policy Commission and working to carry the leaders of the farming industry with him. He made steady progress not only because the conclusions were right for the time, and fell on a set of people already half persuaded. A good part of the success came from Don's charisma and power to lead. Size helps. He is a tall man. A Northumbrian tenant farmer, known to former colleagues for lifelong commitment to the collective good of livestock farmers and so to some of the poorer parts of British farming. Quietly spoken, transparently honest, persuasive. Backed by a team of heavy hitters on his Commission from the food, farming and environmental organizations, he made a lasting impact.

These then were two occasions when the House served a serious role in bringing about change. From then onwards, those who decide the annual programme of events for the House were receptive to ideas for further Consultations on farming. I had by now left the ministry of agriculture for international trade at DTI and then the European Commission. But the House kept in touch and I was invited back to speak on three occasions in 2004-06, at Consultations essentially about agriculture. I found these much less satisfactory. The organisers claimed connections with Don Curry's approach and purported to be looking into different aspects of that: the influences on UK farming of consumer demand, overseas trade, and government support. There was some logic behind the selection of topics but the leaders of those discussions had their own agenda. They leaned towards promoting soft ideas like minimising air miles, buying food from local sources, growing food by organic/biological methods – ideas that needed hard scrutiny, to distinguish the good and the bad impact that they can have on the environment as well as on meeting food needs. I got used to my attempts to introduce hard facts being described as 'reductionist'. This, as used by those who did not respond kindly to their cherished ideas being challenged by facts, was a term signalling strong disapproval. It was a plea to allow emotion and wishful thinking an equal place in the debate alongside science and economics. I, coming from the culture of evidence-based policy-making in Whitehall, did not take happily to that climate of discussion.

Shortly after this I had retired from Whitehall and the European Commission. I was doing a little teaching at the London School of Economics and a period of consulting with Poonam Kumar's think-tank based in Mumbai, and when the House asked me whether I could give time to organising some more food or farming Consultations for them, I willingly agreed.

It is now more than ten years since that time, and looking back I can distinguish two distinct phases. The first phase ran from 2007 to 2012. In that period I played a leading part in designing and running five Consultations. I had a clear idea by now as to the kind of discussion for which the House was particularly suited: debates on topics on which there were serious differences of opinion, where senior people brought together in retreat in a safe place, removed from press and publicity, could argue over their differences without 'grandstanding'; not necessarily reaching new conclusions but gaining more understanding of and respect for each other's positions. In selecting my topics I was in part reacting against those rather soggy discussions of 2004-06, and the tendency for the same coterie of participants to turn up each time, as of right. The topics I chose were:

- climate change and British farming (2007)
- genetic modification (2009)
- food policy with devolution (2009)

- food and health (2010)
- fisheries (2012).

Each occasion turned out differently. From the discussion of climate change two things stick in my memory. The keynote speech was given by the chief scientist from Defra, whose idea of a presentation (I experienced this twice) was to project a powerpoint presentation of nearly 40 slides, all closely printed with diagrams and text, whilst giving a quick-fire talk - from a different script! Very testing for his audience. My overall impression from the two days of discussion was that climate change could have quite a benign impact on farmers and growers in Britain: warmer summers, longer growing seasons, more CO_2 in the atmosphere making plants grow better. There would come a time of reckoning but initially farmers in Britain would gain a bit over their competitors in the southern parts of Europe where high temperatures would hit harder.

On GM, I proceeded in the knowledge that Prince Charles, in whose back yard we were operating, had firm ideas – against. But the subject seemed ripe for the sort of debate which St George's House could do well. Public concern had been stirred up in Britain later than in other European countries, mainly in reaction to heavy-handed attempts by American multinationals to force the pace. Public fears were being constantly fanned by the popular press, but were perhaps less deep-seated than on the continent. Nevertheless, concern had taken hold to the point where scientific arguments were no longer getting a hearing. Perhaps a Consultation could throw some light.

We had good scientists who took us through the differences between genetic modification and the use of genetic markers or gene editing to assist conventional selective breeding; through the past and possible future forms of genetically modified farm crops, the advantages they could have either (as mainly up till then) for farmers or (projecting into the future) for consumers; and the varying uptake around the world. Controversy ran strongly. Those with the strongest convictions departed unconvinced. I felt I had learned a lot, and that my friends from Rothamsted research station (Sir John Lawes' old farm in Harpenden) were telling a persuasive story.

Food policy with devolution was an event of a different kind. It sprang from my own experiences in Whitehall. As devolution took hold, from 1999 onwards, the food and farming departments in the four 'territories' of the UK began to develop divergent policies. It was of course inherent in devolution that they should do so. But when it came to food safety, policy differences were liable to undermine public confidence in government and agencies of government. Confidence had taken a severe knock in the 1990s and the prime need now was to rebuild it. I had seen that contact between officials in the four different administrations was sporadic, sometimes deliberately centrifugal. Our Consultation aimed to bring the key people on food policy together for bridge-building, in a setting where those from the devolved administrations might feel less pressure to assert their independence than in Whitehall.

For food and health I had brought in some really first class speakers but I came memorably unstuck with one of them. She was from the US. I favoured in general having one or two speakers from other parts of the world, to provide challenge for, or just to widen, UK-centric ideas. The lady in question came with recommendations. Maybe I had not done sufficient research into her background. She treated us to some homespun anthropology and a theory of differences between 'racial types' which most participants found uncomfortable, even rather shocking. One, a respectable Oxford-based health specialist, broke into this talk and shouted out loud that the US guest speaker ought never have been invited. Then in an attempt to row back a bit he specified that he was criticising not her but the organizers of the event. Me.

My second phase overlapped with the first, running from 2010 to 2017 or so. By chance, in 2010, a topic was served up to us: the Future of England's Uplands. A commission set up by government had been looking into this and was close to the point of reporting but then government cut off nearly all its funds. There was concern that the work done should not be lost. St George's House decided to host a Consultation to firm up the conclusions and help to put them into practice. This was an event of another different kind. We were picking up work done by other people; the agenda was pre-set, and those who had led the commission had to form the core of the participants, but we expanded the cast. I stepped back from the leading role and deferred to two or three of those who had led the earlier work. We tried hard to steer discussion round over two days to a firm menu of action points, with each action assigned to a person or organization to take it forward. The outcome was a year or so of focussed activity followed up by a second Consultation at Windsor, and a more conventional conference at the Newton Rigg agricultural college at Penrith.

From that time on I took a deliberate decision to stand back from the leading role I had played between 2007 and 2012. It was more than ten years since I had been actively involved in policy work on food and farming, through MAFF. I had kept up with a few friends who still worked there but my links in the food and farming world were not as good as they had been (most people I had worked with having moved on into new jobs) and my understanding of the policy issues was dangerously dated. So I looked to build a team who could take on the active work under my guidance.

The first Consultation that I helped to deliver on this basis was about bringing more young people into farming. There is a longstanding problem over bringing new entrants into the farming industry. You need a large amount of money to buy a farm in Britain. Even to start off as a tenant farmer you need capital. How do you build up the experience to make a success of your own business in an ever more technical and competitive sector, when farmers employ fewer and fewer paid assistants? We wanted at least half our participants for this event to be 'young' people (farmers are generally classed as young up to the age of 40, though for many elderly farmers slogging on into their 70s or beyond the son in his mid-fifties is still the 'young man'). A few senior figures from the farming industry were clearly required, including one who had just written a report on the subject. But we wanted the young to be there in sufficient numbers that they would not feel any pressure to bow to the opinions of their elders. They, the young, should take ownership of the conclusions. This was successful beyond our expectations. Through one or two accidents, more than half of the participants who turned up on the day were the younger ones. They sparkled with energy and self-reliance. They took charge of the event and ran with it, producing some encouragingly self-reliant conclusions. The spirit by and large was: do not assume that we need much help from legislators or regulators, give us a few new openings and sources of advice and information, and we can deal with the situation. It was a thoroughly upbeat event.

The warden over the past ten years, Canon Hueston Findlay, and his programme director Gary McKeone have been happy with the food and farming Consultations that I have led or orchestrated. They have indeed been flattering about how those compare with the other Consultations in their annual pro-gramme. It is not for me to pronounce on that but I know what my formula for success has been. For the five Consultations that I designed and ran between 2007 and 2012 I aimed to pick subjects that were alive and in the news. Some of them subjects on which opinion was strongly divided (GM) or where there was a high level of concern but the evidence and arguments less than clear (Climate Change, Food & Health), some where there was a straight clash of economic interest (Fisheries). Subsequently there were issues where there was clear analy-sis and pointers to action, but a need for a push forward to make things happen (Uplands, New Entrants). My aim was to home in on a problem of real prac-tical importance both to people operating in the food or farming or fisheries sectors and to the wider public.

In designing the programme and selecting participants my first step (draw-ing here on my Cabinet Office experience) was to bring to the table not only leading decision takers from organizations with a direct and obvious interest, but some who might be indirectly affected or could have relevant experience that could make for a more rounded conclusion. I tried to walk all round the chosen issue, to be inclusive in who we invited, to include in the mix of par-ticipants one or more people who held views 'outside the box'; all the more so if the central topic was one on which there was a settled government poli-cy, when I used purposely to include people who would expose that position to challenge. Conversely where there was a clear tide of opinion at odds with government policy (as had been the case on GM, and on organic food/farm-ing), I would include those who could spell out and give the rationale and ev-idence (economic or scientific) behind the position taken up by government. For some events I was lucky to draw in Allan Buckwell, a university professor of economics who worked towards the end of his career for farming organisa-tions, a man who had no fear of challenging either government or the farmers, and had a real flair for stoking up, and summarising, debates.

For any given topic it is possible to draw in people from varying levels of seniority or eminence. The present warden of the House is fond of stating that St George's House aims to nurse wisdom through high-level disagreement. I took my tune from that, and aimed high with my invitations. One of the weak-nesses of the period I have criticised, 2004-06, was that the level of participants had drooped. The leaders themselves came from rather narrow fields. I used my past position of seniority in Whitehall to lever people senior in other fields to join us at Windsor and this was, I am sure, one part of my success in the early years. I knew top people, they felt encouraged that an event in which I had a leading part might be worth their time, and we could get a good cast-list together. The situation of the House, inside Windsor Castle, had its influence too. People however hard-pressed they are for time find it hard to resist an invitation to spend a couple of days inside the Castle. The result was debates between people who had power and influence in their own areas, a broad view of the issues and of what might be achieved in the real world – and the ability to enact change if they were persuaded of the need. All this helped to move us on from the dreamy wishful thinking that had been a feature of the earlier phase.

One other guiding principle for me was to have a mix of participants who had been at the House before, and others who had not. There had been a period when Food & Farming Consultations had attracted a loyal following of old faithfuls, and a rather cosy consensus. Fresh participants livened discussion.

Once the cast list had been assembled, design of the programme was simple enough. We aimed for one or two speakers at the beginning who would give a solid authoritative account of mainstream opinion or alternative opinions, the centre ground, with concise presentations of the facts, or key evidence, or key arguments. Then participants were encouraged to radiate out, first in plenary debate and then in smaller groups. The programme always included some group work. Nudged sometimes by a little light facilitation, these sessions often brought in new ideas that enlarged on the opening presentations.

I was always conscious – I had sometimes to remind myself to break old habits of allegiance to government – that St George's House had a leaning towards challenge. We had for many years a Consultations officer on the staff of the House, Sue Pendry (wife of the Queen's private groom, Terry Pendry, who is frequently pictured in *The Times* riding alongside the Queen), and she had special affection for the farming series. She would come up with ideas for speakers and participants from outside the box and I made room for some of her suggestions, aware that I was working for the House, not they for me. I did not in every way run with the spirit of the House but certainly tried to temper my ideas of rigour with the wider sympathies shown by the permanent staff.

Lastly a word about the nature of the discussions. It was our aim to make sure that by the end of the event all participants whether expert or non-expert, new or old, had had their say. This is of the essence of a House Consultation and what makes those Consultations different from a conventional conference. We tried actively to draw out views from everyone present and to reflect their views as the debate was drawn together. No-one was too eminent to be challenged, no-one too minor to be listened to. Making sure that the shy were drawn in and the pushy kept under control required a modicum of action from the chair, but chairing was generally light touch.

Did it all add up to much? There were those events that did result in some specific practical actions: on the Uplands and New Entrants. There were some from which most participants seemingly departed with the views they came in with (Climate Change, GM), though I personally felt better educated at the end on these topics, so possibly a few other people did too. On Food and Devolution we closed some gaps in the ways in which the machinery of government was working, and that had needed doing. On Fisheries, a wholly new topic for the House with a wholly new cast of participants, our main achievement was in relationship-building. We gave the leaders of the various factions in the English and Scottish fishing industries a chance for some quality time with the relatively new director general of fisheries in the European Commission. Relationship between the top official in the Commission and the handful of leaders from the British industry was very important to both sides, and we were giving a chance for the parties to get to know each other in a safe setting. Two British members of the European Parliament with formative influence on fisheries policy were with us too. At this event relationship-building was the key contribution we were making.

Did all the above mean a lot of work for me? I still find that those who meet me at 'my' Consultations assume that I must work full-time at Windsor, be based in the Castle, or spend much of my time on these events. Even in my most active phase with a Consultation every year or occasionally two in a year the work I have described was very spread out. It may in some years have added up to six weeks or so; not more. Preparation always started at least six, ideally nine months in advance, principally because once the design was agreed you needed to pin down the lead speakers a long way ahead. The diaries of such people fill up. It was my habit to visit all our speakers in person to take them through what we were looking for and to explain the form and style of the event – which, for many, was different from what they would be used to. This part of the process took up some time but opened interesting doors for me, into universities and research establishments for example. I would then keep in touch with the speakers and sometimes put them in touch with each other as the event came closer. It helped the speakers to know roughly what direction their counterparts would be coming from, and helped to make the programmes more coherent.

That recipe seemed to stand the test of time. The Consultations I generated were judged good-to-excellent by the Warden and his colleagues responsible for the programme of the House, and by many participants. I have left until last the magic of Windsor, the power exerted by the place where all this happened. I have said just a little about the atmosphere of working in the Castle. For people who are at St George's House for the first time it can be an amazing experience. The way we programmed our Consultations, there was not time to indulge in amazement for long before getting down to work. We looked to the atmosphere to put people in a higher level of animation, and it does that.

St George's House sits right up against St George's Chapel. In terms of the way Windsor Castle is organized, St George's House and its programme of activities, including the Consultations on food and farming, come under the 'College of St George'. This college was founded in 1348 by King Edward III. There is an absolutely continuous line that can be traced from that date to the present day, and this continuity is very much alive. It comes in for frequent mention in the daily chapel services. Four times a year the Evensong service takes the form of an Obit – a service of commemoration of all the college's benefactors. The Military Knights attend. After the standard prayers for Evensong have been recited, the Dean stands up and reads the Commemoration of the Founder, Patrons and Benefactors. This goes on for some time. The recitation of kings, queens and members of the royal family begins with King Henry III. The Black Prince gets a mention. There is a long list of Knights of the Garter and various others. Then, 'lastly we remember.. those who in more recent centuries have given their substance to aid the College... Among Kings and Queens we name King Henry VIII...' In more recent centuries! A delicious reminder of the continuity and stretch of history that this site has seen. Having once passed Henry VIII, the catalogue of benefactors canters to a fairly brisk close, finishing with mention of a handful of twentieth-century characters with more familiar names.

St George's Chapel is among other things home to the Order of the Garter. At every Consultation I have been to, the programme of discussions pauses for an hour from five till six in the afternoon so that participants can if they wish go to the Evensong service. Those attending the service sit in the back row of the choir stalls. The wooden panels behind each seat are covered with brass plates engraved with the names and short histories of individual Knights of the Garter going back for hundreds of years (in all there are 800 such plaques). High above the choir hang the heraldic banners of the living members of the order, each banner embroidered with emblems reflecting the name of the peer in a punning way (a rebus). In the floor in the centre of the choir is an inscription marking that the bodies of King Henry VIII and of King Charles I lie beneath there; Charles's head and body reunited, but only after some skirmishing with the constable whom Cromwell put in charge of the castle following Charles's execution in London.

The chapel is steeped in antiquity and we rub shoulders with antiquity elsewhere in the buildings we use. The House itself, dating 'only' from the time of Queen Anne, is a relatively young thing. The Vicars' Hall, which we use for all our main, plenary discussions, is late Tudor, Elizabethan, and the story is that Shakespeare's Merry Wives of Windsor was given its first performance in this room. There is no firm evidence but the dates fit and it is pleasant to believe it is true.

To one side of Denton's Commons, the open space between St George's House, the Vicars' Hall and the Chapel, is a much older building, up against the outer wall of the Castle. It doesn't look its age because the wall facing Denton's Commons is a Victorian facade, but behind that is a house on four floors, much adapted over hundreds of years, the earliest bits of which are the vestiges of a palace built here for King Henry III – so dating from the 1200s. We have Fellows' meetings in rooms where some of the original stonework can be seen, and I have regularly been assigned a bedroom at the top of this house where there is an acute risk of hitting your head in the night on the criss-crossing roof beams (I speak from hard experience). Behind St George's House is a set of very ancient rooms, 'chambers' built to house the canons and some still lived in by the canons and their families. In part of this complex which dates from about 1350 is a room that we sometimes use for group work, in which patches of a fifteenth century wall painting have been preserved; a painting that depicted St Catherine being broken on the wheel.

And talking of torture, on one occasion I had to move with all my participants from the Vicars' Hall to a room beneath the Curfew Tower, the tower that stands on the side of the castle facing Windsor Central station, the first feature of the castle that visitors see if they arrive by train from Slough. The room we moved into is best described as a dungeon, because that is what it once was. It is unheated, dark, and is little used. All stone, it consists of a central area with a high ceiling, and several passages radiating off, with much lower ceilings, and sundry instruments of torture still lurking in far corners. These, happily, seem to have found no regular use in the modern life of the castle, so they have been left where they were.

With all this antiquity around it is no great wonder that those who come to Consultations quite often feel blown away by working here. It is more surprising that we seem to succeed in keeping their attention by and large focussed on the subjects for discussion.

A high point of the year in the programme of St George's House events is the Annual Lecture, held in late June. A distinguished speaker is invited to address an invited audience of several hundred of the great and the good in St George's Chapel. The themes for this annual lecture vary widely and the quality of the speakers has varied too. It is unfortunate that the sound system is of poor quality, and this never seems to improve. So on the occasions when the speaker really is worth listening to, as for example Tom Stoppard was, the audience finds itself straining to hear. The reward is a drinks reception on Denton's Commons where one or two members of the Royal Family circulate and make conversation with the guests; most prominently the Duke of Edinburgh, until very recently. For the select few who are counted as having helped the House in particular ways, there is the additional reward of a dinner in the Vicar's Hall where, again, the Duke of Edinburgh regularly sat with us through the evening, until he was close to 95 years old. The Duke it was who launched the House into existence fifty years ago, and who has shown active interest in it over the years. How will it, and its distinctive brand of discussions, survive his passing?

18

BIRDS

My interest: how it started and how it built up

People often ask me how long I have been interested in birds. I have been in the habit of saying that it was Grandpa Ratcliff (mother's father) who got me started, when I was about ten. This still seems right, within a year or two. Grandpa had a copy of T A Coward's *The Birds of the British Isles and their Eggs*, volume I (only ever volume I), second edition. It caught my interest and I used to look at it when we were in his house. That book is on my shelves now. It is inscribed 'To H J Ratcliff with love from F G Ratcliff' (Grandma – Florence Gertrude). The second edition of Coward was published in October 1925, the year of their twentieth wedding anniversary, but their anniversary was in June, so perhaps this was a Christmas present. Anyway, after twenty years of marriage Grandma was in a position to know that birds were one of Grandpa's interests. Grandpa also had a pair of field glasses (we never called them binoculars in those days). He used to take me for walks up Pinner Hill, near where they lived, pointing out birds as we went.

Our family holidays moved on after four or five years from the Kent coast at Broadstairs to the West Country, first to Somerset in 1954 and then a year or two later to Devon. By that time I was beginning to take note of the birds we saw there that we did not see at home: buzzards, curlews and stonechats, for instance.

I did some DIY ringing of birds in our garden. When I was 13 or 14, in 1956 or soon after, I had started to keep and breed budgerigars. This involved handling the birds, and putting identifying leg rings on the chicks. From this I took to trapping and putting coloured rings on some of our garden birds. I had not been trained. I probably ought to have applied for a licence, but I just did it. I had a simple drop-down trap, and ringed mainly robins, blackbirds and sparrows. I kept a record of the birds that stayed around, and noted the ages they reached.

In 1956 I started at Merchant Taylors'. The school not only had a large expanse of playing fields where flocks of gulls gathered in winter and wheatears occasionally turned up on migration. It was also on the edge of a river valley which was rich in gravel. There are gravel pits strung out for miles along the Colne Valley between Watford and Uxbridge. One of the largest of these lay alongside our school grounds. It had been disused for long enough that vegetation had grown up along the banks and the company that extracted the gravel had left it with several islands – it was in a state that conservationists would fight for today. It was indeed very attractive to wildlife. Over the next year or two, wandering around in my lunch breaks, I got a good grounding in this lakeside wildlife. Water voles were an everyday sight. They have since become very rare. There was a good variety of water birds. Great-crested Grebes nested on the islands and I could watch their elegant and complex courtship display from close at hand. Occasionally a Water Rail appeared. At migration times Common Sandpiper visited for a few days, so I learned to recognise their sharp calls and their distinctive flight low over the water on stiff arched wings. Once a Hobby flew through – a much rarer bird then than it is now. This was all a big step forward from watching garden birds on Pinner Hill or in Northwood.

One keen birdwatcher, Martin, a year ahead at school and always several years ahead in bird skills, became a close friend and we regularly went out on birdwatching trips together. This partnership may not have started until 1957 or 1958. From then on, Martin expanded my range rapidly, both geographically and in variety of birds.

We went everywhere by bike. We were not old enough to drive. We did not need to cycle more than a few miles from school to get to other gravel pits along the River Colne, and some of those attracted larger numbers of ducks in the winter than our school lake, and different species. That was progress, but Martin knew of more exciting territory than this: 'Staines'. Staines was our shorthand for the cluster of huge concrete-sided reservoirs that lie just to the west of the built-up area of Greater London, and immediately to the west of Heathrow airport. New reservoirs have been added over the years. In the late 1950s there were three that mattered to us. The 'Staines' area also included 'Perry Oaks' – which I'll come to.

This area was 12-14 miles from home at its nearest point. We always cycled there and back, and cycled several miles further in doing the rounds of the reservoirs; and quite often we walked several miles to make a circuit of one of them. In school holidays this made a reasonably energetic round trip of 30 miles or more, but it was not unknown in summer time for us to do it after school, or after a morning at school.

The Staines area was another big leap forward for me and my interest in birds. I have been keeping bird notebooks since 1958, so I can give an exact date for my first visit to Staines. It was 2 January 1959. I can still remember the amazement and thrill of standing on the causeway that runs across the middle of Staines reservoir (the first and oldest of the 'Staines' cluster; opened in 1901). It was mid-winter. Large numbers of ducks were flying backwards and forwards between the two areas of water. The water is deep, more attractive to diving ducks than to dabbling ducks such as Mallard. There were Tufted Ducks and Pochard which I knew well by now, but also Goldeneye, Scaup, Goosander and Smew which I had never seen before. The last of these, Smew, breeds in the arctic and comes south as far as Scotland in winter, but only in very small numbers further south into England, and then it normally stays on or near the coast.

This was a first sign that the Staines area was an unusual magnet for birds. The huge expanses of open water edged by plain, bare concrete banks obviously had something in common, from a bird's point of view, with sea coast and shingle shoreline. Birds that are hard to find anywhere inland, and not easy to find along the east coast, would regularly turn up at Staines. I saw my first Snow Bunting here.

Across the road from the old Staines reservoir with its causeway across the middle that made it relatively easy to see everything that was out on the water was a larger reservoir, King George VI (1947). To survey this completely you had to walk right round it, a circuit of three to four miles, and we occasionally did that. One of the specialities that could be found here was the Black-necked Grebe, the daintiest of our five grebe species, only ever found in small numbers. Black-necked Grebes on King George VI were the subject of my first and only scientific note. With Martin, I watched two of them diving, and timed the length of their dives. When I got home and consulted the Witherby Handbook it appeared that our birds had been spending longer underwater than anyone had recorded previously. No doubt this was because the depth of water here was greater than the depth where they would normally be found. They favour shallower lakes fringed with reeds. I wrote up our measurements and the note was published (*British Birds*, March 1960, p.127).

These reservoirs take water from the Thames and hold it to supply Greater London. As the needs of London's population have grown, so too the reservoirs have multiplied. Several more have been added since the time I am writing about, each one bigger than the last. As a result the total expanse of open water in the area is vastly more than it was, and although birds probably occur in the same variety as before they are more spread out over a larger area, making them harder to find. More to the point, security has been tightened up and it would not be possible now to ramble at will along the banks as we used to do. These days it is easier to admire the spectacle through the windows of a plane on its way into or out of Heathrow.

Even closer to Heathrow airport was another of our hunting grounds, Perry Oaks. The rustic name seemed to have been chosen to throw you off the scent. This was a totally different type of habitat: a sewage farm. A sewage farm?! In those days there were some sewage treatment plants where the raw intake, let us call it, was purified up to a point in an enclosed process and then pumped out into 'pits', little fields separated by grassy embankments, where the product was spread out like mud and left for the weather to finish off the purification process. Sewage farms of this kind were hugely attractive to wading birds that would more normally spend their time on coastal estuaries, with the broad expanses of mud that they provide. These were in effect inland marshes. With technological advances and tighter health regulations they have all disappeared now.

Perry Oaks was one of the three most famous (among birders) sewage farms of that type; the rivals were Wisbech (Cambridgeshire) and Beddington (Surrey). This was a premier league bird habitat. We had to apply to the Thames Water Authority for a permit. With that permit we could wander all over the Perry Oaks plant itself and, since this bordered on Heathrow airport and there was no security fence between the two, we would sometimes take a short cut round the airport perimeter road, so saving a mile or two of the cycle ride home.

As to birds, I had my first encounter here with many species of wading birds that are common along the east coast but not much seen inland, and certainly not in the green and leafy outer London suburbs. I had never been to any of the coastal estuaries, and wetland reserves such as the RSPB has created all round the country in the last 30 or 40 years were unknown. Minsmere was in its infancy. The Wildfowl Trust's wonderful London Wetland Centre at Barnes had not been dreamt of. Mud apart, the banks around the pits at Perry Oaks were overgrown and attractive to common and not so common little birds (Bearded Tit, wintering Chiffchaffs), and must have been rich in voles. I saw my first Barn Owl here.

So these trips to the Staines area/edge of Heathrow were for several years *the* main way in which my range of birds grew, but by the mid-1960s aircraft noise became a problem. Aircraft had become larger and noisier, and flights more frequent. You could no longer hear the wading birds call – and call is the most reliable way of identifying some species of wading bird that look very similar. Also, security tightened, both at Perry Oaks and around the reservoirs, for good reason. Perry Oaks lived on for a long time, and I used to look wistfully at it through the windows of my plane on the days when the wind was coming from the east, and aircraft had to taxi to the far western end of the runway for take-off. It finally went under concrete when Terminal 5 was built, sometime just after 2000.

It was perhaps in 1960 or 1961 when, with Martin, I made my first bird-watching trip to the coast, to the North Kent marshes at Cliffe. We went by train to High Halstow, an isolated halt in open countryside, and then we walked and walked. It felt like miles and probably was one or two miles, made longer because we had to go through a series of field gates where the ground had been paddled to deep mud by cattle. It was an ordeal of mud to get to the shoreline. At long last we reached it and I was treated to another leap forward. It was not just a first acquaintance with some new wading species, real coastal specialities like Grey Plover; it was also an introduction for me to a wholly new kind of landscape, the wide open flat farmland and endless grey vista of water and mud, the Thames Estuary at its mid-winter bleakest. This is the landscape which Dickens describes at the beginning of *Great Expectations*. Indeed, the site he had in mind, at Cooling, is very close to where we were. At the end of some hours of exciting birding, the ordeal by mud had to be faced again; and then the long journey by train home across London.

Some of the satisfaction of that day came from the landscape, some from the birds. A new point begins to emerge here. My interest, by 1960, was not simply in seeing new birds. Other people in our group, including Martin, as they reached driving age, took to cars and made ever more trips to the coast, chasing novelty. I found less thrill in that and more in the surroundings where I was watching birds, and my interest also branched down a scientific track.

From 1958 I was keeping notebooks recording what I had seen, anything interesting about the behaviour of the bird, and detailed descriptions of birds I was seeing for the first time and found tricky to identify. We have now reached no. 25 in my series of these notebooks. I still have them all, going back to the beginning. Since they now cover a period of nearly 60 years, they are beginning to provide supporting evidence of changes that have occurred over that time. Birders professional and amateur keep up continued criticism of farming as the main reason why bird numbers have dropped in Britain since around 1970. When I look back through my notebooks from the 1960s, the species that catch my eye are Spotted Flycatcher, which I used to see in our gardens in Northwood, and Willow Tit which I recorded every time I visited Ruislip Woods – two species that have declined steeply and would not be found in those places now, but that is for reasons quite unconnected with farming.

Ruislip Woods, Ruislip Common, and the two golf courses that adjoin them, were favourite places for the family walks with our pack of Golden Retrievers. It was also good varied habitat for birds. The Red-backed Shrike had just, but only just, stopped nesting there (again nothing to do with farming practices; there was a widespread decline in the 1950s). There was a spectacular starling roost in winter. Two years running, one morning in mid-May I dragged myself out of bed at 3 am, taking a reluctant retriever with me, so as to be in place on Ruislip Common to record the start of the dawn chorus. Cuckoo was the first to strike up, at 03.57 one year, Skylark at 03.46 the year after, with Cuckoo joining in at 03.49.

From 1959 I was subscribing to serious bird journals: *British Birds*, and *Bird Study*, the journal of the British Trust for Ornithology (BTO) which I had joined. On a very small scale I took part in the BTO's nest recording scheme; also in a nationwide survey started in 1961, by a lady who lived on Pinner Hill, into birds killed by cars on the road – the very first stirrings of concern that cars were killing birds. Who cares about that now?

Martin was linked in to a group of very keen birders of similar age who spent all their spare time chasing birds that they had not seen before. Later they would have been called 'twitchers' but that label had not been invented then. By any standards they were keen, and also extremely skilled at identifying birds. One of them in particular went on to become one of Britain's topmost bird spotters, referred to with respect nowadays by the legendary Lee Evans, a man who aspires to get the top score in number of different bird species seen in Britain each year, and usually does come out top. This group of Martin's associates were impressive in their skill, for example, at identifying a bird flying overhead from its call alone, or the shape of its silhouette; or telling apart some of the small brown wading birds, a group of which have very few identifying markings and look identical to the uninitiated – but sometimes turn out under skilled examination to be extremely rare American cousins of birds common in Europe. Example: the Semi-palmated Sandpiper, which Martin and co picked out by eye at Wisbech sewage farm one day, mainly by the shape of its feet! It was always a learning experience to be in the field with them.

I was impressed by their skills but did not go down their road of rarity-hunting. By 1960 we had had family holidays in Devon and I loved the feel of the rocky coasts and wild seas. In April 1960 I took myself off for the first time to Lundy, a rocky island out in the middle of the Bristol Channel. This was the first of many visits I made over the next six years. I stayed on the island sometimes for a week, sometimes for a month. Lundy was (then) a bird observatory, one of a chain of stations around the coast of Britain with a warden in residence who kept records and organised visitors into contributing records of what they saw to the Observatory's 'log'. In autumn 1960 I was signed on as an assistant warden helping to walk the island every day, watching and recording.

This was regarded by Martin and co as rather a perverse choice. From their point of view, with their interest in notching up variety, the east coast of England was the place to be; decidedly better than the west coast. More birds on migration pass down the east coast, taking a short cut from Scandinavia or blown across the North Sea by accident, than move down the west coast. The chances of seeing something rare are greater. I understood that, but still firmly preferred the feel of being on a wild island, with wild weather never far away, with cliffs packed from spring to mid-summer with spectacular numbers of nesting sea birds; and I could be part of the observatory activity. In any case, rarities did occur, and when they did they might be very rare species indeed. Over the years Lundy has notched up the first records in Britain of some American birds blown across the Atlantic. My own first for Britain came from the opposite direction. I have told the story of the Bimaculated Lark in chapter 2.

Observatories attract some top birders. Lundy was less accessible than most, but during my times there I met several people who went on to make full-time careers out of birds, one as a university scientist, one or two others as wardens of nature reserves. I helped to ring migrating birds, and learned quite a bit about links between weather conditions and bird movements.

In 1962 I went up to Oxford, with my name linked to the identification of the Bimaculated Lark. If I *had* joined the university bird club, the Oxford Ornithological Society (OOS), I would have soon met some more fledgling professionals. I did not join the OOS and to this day I cannot understand why not. I can clearly remember going to a freshers' fair where all the university clubs and societies set out their stalls, and I can remember stopping at the OOS stand and talking to the members there. Lundy came into the conversation and I was treated with respect when I mentioned that I was one of the two people to have seen the Bimaculated Lark. News had only just got around. Why did I not join on the spot? Why was I not pressed to join, or followed up? If I had joined this society I would have met some future career ornithologists, Ian Newton for one. Ian became a good friend, but only forty years later, by which time he was Professor Ian Newton FRS, now one of Britain's most distinguished bird scientists, with a wonderfully clear style of explaining complex science to non-experts. He was at Oxford in the early 1960s, doing a D.Phil. I would have got to know him and his contemporaries, and some who had already started out on careers. The Edward Grey Institute in Oxford which specialises in research on birds 'in the field', i.e. in the wild, was the first of its kind, and still one of very few, to be integrated into a university. I can now only regret very much that I missed my opportunity to make those links at Oxford. It would have moved what was still only an amateur interest up to a more scientific level. Looking back now, I believe too that it would have been a good counter-balance to my academic work on the ancient world. But I can only suppose that on that day in October 1962 I was afraid that it would become a major distraction.

The upshot was that I did concentrate on academic work in my time at Oxford and did very little on birds – in term time. An occasional cycle ride round Otmoor which was, in the 1960s, a desolate area of marshy grassland, grazed by cattle. A few years later farmers ploughed it up to grow grain, and more recently the RSPB has spent years of effort trying to restore it to the wild state that I knew, a good home for Curlews and Lapwing. In the vacations I continued with a mixture of Staines and Lundy.

My time in Berlin (chapter 5) did not give much opportunity for birding but there were just occasional unexpected flashes of bird life: coming out of the Philharmonie – the city centre concert hall – in the intervals in spring time you were surrounded by the song of Nightingales; and walking with Ursula over her golf course at Wannsee I noted that Hobbies were flying around us, and nesting in the isolated pines.

Once work in Whitehall got under way (chapter 6) there was, again, very little time for birding. Even at weekends Poppy and I were kept busy with house-keeping and home decorating. But there was time at least to introduce Poppy to birdwatching. She was a fast and enthusiastic learner. We went frequently to the Suffolk coast in the three to four years that my mother lived at Skilman's Hill on the south side of Southwold; and when she and we moved to the Chilterns there were visits to Tring reservoirs, and some delicious early morning walks in summer around Coombe Hill and Ivinghoe. Grasshopper Warblers bred on the steep slopes, Whinchats turned up on migration in spring, Woodcock and Redstart bred in the woods at Ashridge. All those birds have become much more scarce now – but not because of farming.

From 1978 when we moved back into London, until 2002, my birdwatching was virtually at a standstill. We had our rural interlude in Shropshire, but Shropshire is not a good county for birds. It is too far from the coast.

Things only came alive again when the RSPB invited me to become a member of their governing Council. I shall tell that story separately. Enough to say here that the annual visits which the Council made to one part of the RSPB's empire after another introduced us to some wonderful places, and gave us a privileged view of the birds that the RSPB was trying to protect, guided by people who knew exactly where to find them, even including one or two birds that I had not seen before. I'll let the Capercaillie that we saw performing its courtship display in the forest at Abernethy, in the early hours of one May morning, stand as the example.

Retirement was now opening up for me. We moved from commuter-land and lived for seven months in a former mining area of Derbyshire, near Bolsover. This was unexpectedly fruitful for bird watching. Near where we lived were some disused open-cast coal mines which had been restored by the Derbyshire Wildlife Trust and transformed into excellent habitat, a mixture of open water and woodland. We joined the county bird club and the local RSPB group; and found that both were brimming with knowledgeable and enthusiastic birders. With their help we found interesting birds in attractive places, and took particular satisfaction in learning that the Pink-footed Geese which we had watched on the south Lancashire mosses, and on the north Norfolk coast, regularly passed over this bit of Derbyshire on their way from one of those areas to the other; passing east in autumn, west in winter. Place a ruler on a map between south Lancashire and north Norfolk and you see that the direct route for these geese took them over Bolsover. Eagle-eyed local birdwatchers recorded them here in large numbers, flying over.

From Derbyshire we moved to the Breckland area of west Norfolk, and settled for the next ten years on the edge of a famous shooting estate, at Hilborough. Sandwiched between this area that was rigorously keepered for game on the one side and a large area closed off for the army to practise manoeuvres with live ammunition on the other, we had by accident landed on a patch that was exceptionally rich in bird life. Some birds that had become scarce in other parts of the country, like Marsh Tit, were resident in our garden. Brambling and Siskin came to our feeders every winter. Spotted Flycatchers nested every year. One year we had three pairs of those. I guarded their nests fiercely but relaxed enough to invite a BTO expert to ring the young of a second brood in 2016. Stone-curlew nested just a field away from our house. But the jewel in the crown was the Hawfinch. This is a bird, common on the continent but very scarce and hard to find in Britain, so much so that I had never seen one (except in Sweden) when we moved to Hilborough. Two weeks after we moved in I was thrilled to see a mother Hawfinch feeding one of her young on our lawn. They have continued to drop in on us very occasionally at entirely unpredictable times, in most years once or twice in the breeding season and in 2018 two pairs fed actively on our drive every day for two weeks, picking up hornbeam seeds, and teasing us to find proof that they were actually nesting on our patch. One winter's day six dropped in and spent a few minutes at a drinking trough before disappearing. What with Hawfinch and Stone-curlew, Red Kites that have moved into the area since we did and now appear over our house most days, Bewick's Swans flying overhead on their way to and from Welney, and a Great Grey Shrike that stayed just up the road for several weeks one winter, in a spot which they have favoured over the years, this Hilborough garden has had bird interest 'to die for'.

What is so interesting? – and do birds really matter?

Now I have told the story of my interest started, and how it built up and ex-panded through contact with some specific people and places. Friends ask what is so interesting or important about birds that I and others give so much attention to them. Here is my attempt to explain.

Birds are everywhere, in town gardens, city centres, remote wild hills and mountains, along coasts and in ordinary, nothing-special countryside. Not everyone takes an interest in birds but very many people notice them some of the time. Birds do some interesting things. So do ants and bees, but you need to be quite specialised to understand the behaviour of ants or bees, whereas for birds you don't need to be specialised at all. You can get some enjoyment from just watching them coming to garden feeders, or carrying material for nest-building to a hedge or a nest-box; watching them from the kitchen win-dow or noticing how they follow you around when you are gardening. There are places nowadays where people with only the vaguest interest in birds, and no special training, can go to see a variety of birds, including some out-of-the-ordinary and even quite rare birds. RSPB reserves: that label 'reserves' makes some people think – wrongly – that these are not places for the uninitiated. They are ideal places for beginners. There are also the many varied woods and marshes looked after by county wildlife trusts. The Wildfowl and Wetland Trust (WWT) with ten special places for ducks and geese in different parts of the UK has created what is possibly the best place of all in the London area for people to go and see what a wide range of birds can be found in the middle of a huge built-up area, if only a suitable space is made for them. The WWT's London Wetland Centre at Barnes is like a motorway service station for the long-distance travelling bird.

Very many people (too many) have written about birds in a general way, trying to communicate to their readers how birds have given enjoyment to them. Simon Barnes, who was at one time the sports writer for *The Times* (and used to sprinkle his reports on Wimbledon or Twickenham with notes on the birds he had seen during the matches) wrote a book *How to be a Bad Birdwatcher.* That is quite a good place for a learner to start. Simon is clever at catching in a few well-chosen words what is distinctive about this or that type of bird. A quite different sort of book was written by Edward Grey, Viscount Grey, a hundred years ago. He described scenes from his long life of watching birds, and called his book *The Charm of Birds.* The title sounds old-fashioned now and his style of writing is of its time, but the stories are alive with the enjoyment he got from watching birds living their lives. He was Britain's Foreign Secretary at the beginning of the First World War and was solely responsible for very secretive negotiations between France, Germany, Austria and Russia in the months immediately before war broke out. He seems to have been able to take time off for bird-watching even at the height of that crisis. Might things have turned out better if he had concentrated harder in the Office? However, he left us a beautiful diary of the enjoyment that birds gave him throughout his working life. It is due for a revival.

Birds and landscape.

Birds can be watched in dramatic landscapes. But the landscapes that people appreciate for their beauty are not always the best places for birds. To take an extreme example the Lake District, which is perhaps the rural area in England most praised (since Wordsworth) and most loved (since Beatrix Potter) and most visited by tourists, is really quite poor for birds; relatively little variety, relatively few surprises. Some of the areas which are best for birds are places that no-one in their right mind would go to for any other reason, like Perry Oaks sewage farm on the fringe of Heathrow airport. But there are areas good for birds which have drama as landscapes as well. For example the long stretches of bare shingle on the coast at Spurn Head, Blakeney Point or Dungeness (the last has exceptional botanical interest too, flagged up by Derek Jarman and his garden). Or the wild windswept promontories at Portland Bill (with its historic prison), or the Lizard and Land's End, or the Mull of Galloway from which you look across the sea to the Isle of Man in the south and the coast of Northern Ireland to the west. These are wonderful places to watch sea birds or migration, awe-inspiring places simply to be at. Bird-watching can introduce you to pieces of Britain's scenery which are under-appreciated in this age when travel, for so many people, means getting on a plane and going to a far-away country.

My pursuit of birds has taken me to many of *the fringes of Britain*, which are not high on the tourist's list, but at least as interesting for their scenery and history as places that people would happily visit on excursions if they were on holiday in Spain or Portugal, or Thailand or Cambodia.

Who goes to the Isle of Sheppey, with its unruly prison and its candy-floss and fruit-machine resort of Leysdown? Poppy and I used to go to Sheppey every New Year's Day from Blackheath for fresh air and the sight of wild geese and birds of prey in profusion, in as wild a landscape as you can find within two hours of Central London. Bempton cliffs, where sea birds nest on cliff ledges, not far from the east Yorkshire wolds that have been refreshingly captured in paint by David Hockney. Orkney and Shetland are rich in history and breathtakingly wild scenery, but few English people other than naturalists go there or are remotely aware of what they are missing. Orkney offers early British history in a gentle farming landscape. Shetland with wild windswept moorland and spectacular cliffs has been outstandingly successful in taming the oil exploration industry; successful in making the oilmen design their on-shore installations to sit unobtrusively in folds of the hillsides; successful in extracting money from the industry and using it wisely to create public halls, sports facilities, museums and exhibition spaces that enrich life for the residents and for visitors alike. Shetland has a feel of modernity which was not there when I first visited the islands sixty years ago – when birds led me there. The seriously remote islands of Fair Isle and Foula have cliff scenery as impressive as anywhere in Europe.

Lundy was – was, and is no longer – a fringe of a special kind. Out in the middle of the Bristol Channel, with the mainland of North Devon visible on a clear day, but frequently cut off by bad weather and out of reach of the law, this island was for centuries privately owned, and was allowed to treat itself as another country. The owner in the 1950s-1960s was a London business man, Harman, who delighted in maintaining his island as a private fiefdom. The laws of the UK would I hope have applied if there had been a murder. But for most purposes no rules applied. The pub stayed open all day and as much of the night as customers wanted. The post office issued its own stamps. The farming ticked along in a primitive way. French (but not English) fishermen were encouraged to put in for shelter and come ashore in bad weather, and sometimes enlivened the bar for a day or two. When there was a need to import manual labour for a building project, the Harmans brought in a team from an Austrian skiing village, Alpbach, and the building site echoed to the sound of Alpine Austrian voices. Order, if not law, was maintained by a tall authoritarian 'agent', Arthur Gade. Not all the buildings had electricity and those that did had it for only a few hours in the day. It was like stepping back in time from the 1950s to the Edwardian era. At most twelve people resided and worked on the island, not counting 3-4 lighthouse men who manned the North and South Lights. There was a strong spirit of self-sufficiency, and only people with strong personalities stood this way of life: boatman, mechanic, shepherd, shopkeeper – those people stand out strongly in my memory. It is all different now. The island was bought in the 1970s by the National Trust who handed over the management to the Landmark Trust. They have 'improved' any buildings that can be let to holidaymakers and put a high price on them. Despite the prices, the holiday homes are booked for a year and more ahead. Coming and going at short notice must be very difficult now. I don't know how birdwatchers fit into the new gentrified Lundy. With great difficulty, I imagine.

Spotting your bird.

As you get further into it, bird-watching throws up new challenges. These become part of the interest. It is not always easy to spot the bird you are looking for. It is tantalising when the person standing next to you says 'It's over there. Can't you see it?' Out on the sea shore, or out in the middle of a bare field. You need to have some idea what you are looking for, and where to look. The Spotted Flycatchers in our garden are understated little grey birds, good at hiding away. Look hard in the branches where you have seen them before. They are creatures of habit, and they have favourite perches. Stone-curlew are perfectly camouflaged and need to be, because they live out in open fields and nest on the ground. If you know them, you can pick them out in a stony field by the little patch of yellow at the base of their beaks. Leaf warblers in woodland once the trees have their leaves are very hard to see, easier to pick out by their calls and songs. Wading birds on mudflats all look much the same until you are practised in picking out their slightly different shapes, and stripes, and speed of movement.

Good eyesight and good hearing are vital. So one of the challenges is to have keen senses – and to stay alert. As we get older, and sight and hearing go into decline, we lean on friends who have not yet decayed. David Tomlinson is one of my props now that I am in my mid-70s.

Identifying your bird.

Learning how to identify birds, how to distinguish one species from another, is a lot easier than it was 60 years ago. The latest field guides are enormously improved on those that we had in the 1950s, and unrecognisably better than the pictures in my grandfather's Coward (vol.1) from 25 years before that. Colour printing has become more accurate, the pointers in the text and on the pictures to the features you should look for get more sharply focussed with every new edition, building on the never-ending stream of observations by bird-watchers and biology scientists.

Some new inventions have reduced the need for human skills. Digital cameras and the discovery that they can be attached to a bird-watcher's telescope in the field to take instant magnified pictures – 'digiscoping' – together with the possibility of sending these pictures from a smart phone by email mean that bird-watchers don't now have to sit puzzling over the bird in front of them that they cannot identify. They can email pictures of it there and then to friends and get advice back in real time. In my early days you had to make notes in your notebook (not easy if it was raining) and hope you were recording the features that would lead to an identification later, back home. That was the way we had to record, and much later identify, the Bimaculated Lark (chapter 2).

Has that taken all the skill, suspense and fun out of identifying birds in the field? Not at all. It remains a challenge requiring you to go into the field on full alert, with all your accumulated knowledge at the ready. Most birds don't sit obligingly for you to train your telescope on them and digiscope them. They fly about. They fly overhead and only make you aware of them with a faint flight call as they are heading away from you and about to disappear. They pop out of a bush and pop straight back in again. You have to be ready to identify on the basis of incomplete views and short glimpses. You have also to be ready to write off a proportion of the birds you see in a day as unidentifiable. Many birders are reluctant to do that, and the result is that they claim sightings that may not be accurate. Those who compile the records of birds seen in an area, or a county, or the country as a whole, aim for accuracy, and want their reports to be authoritative, and they get to know which observers they can fully rely on and those whom they need to treat with caution.

I hope I am one of those who do not overclaim. I apply high standards of proof. Particularly if I have never seen the bird before, I am not satisfied by the person standing next to me, however skilled, saying 'that is what it is'. I want to know and see the features that make it the species it is. Even my best friends are sometimes wrong. With David, who is much more skilled than I am, I argued for what seemed like half an hour over a wheatear we had in front of us all that time. The identification turned on whether it did or did not have little patches of white on the outside of the base of its tail. Without them, it would have been a rarer type of wheatear that we had not seen on that trip; with them, a commoner type of which we had seen several. The diacritical patches of white were not apparent. It might not have had them, but I thought that for just a second I had glimpsed them, so I was reluctant to be persuaded that it was the rarer species. Time passed, no white patches showed, I remained sceptical and David got shirty. At long last the bird spread its tail more fully and there indeed were the little white patches. Poppy commented that I had been applying my training as a papyrologist. The skills are indeed similar. You must go on the basis of what you see, and no more; be ready to extrapolate from what you see, but only if that does not conflict with the evidence of your eyes.

Conclusion: for all the help that modern technology now provides, there is a high degree of challenge and fascination in telling one species of bird from another – on the basis of the skimpy evidence that birds often give us to go on.

A form of hunting.

Bird-watchers keep lists of all kinds. Life lists are the highest grade: all the species you have ever seen – in the UK, or anywhere in the world. There is special respect for those who have seen more than 400 species in Britain (out of the 600 or so ever recorded here). I once worked for a minister who was in that 400 Club. He was also the only qualified, licensed bird ringer in the House of Commons. People who list all the species they have seen anywhere in the world don't really attract respect until their tally gets up into the thousands; 7-8,000 out of the theoretical maximum of around 10,000.

Birders list the number of species they have seen in a year; in a day; in their garden; from the windows of a train; from the windows of their office (note to employers: try not to employ one of those). I confess to liking lists. I keep a year list and I frequently keep a list of the birds seen in a day. I did not keep a list of birds seen from my office but I did once hear a Black Redstart singing on the roof of the ministry of agriculture just off Whitehall, and that happened to be during the time of the minister mentioned above. His private secretary may have been surprised to receive an instruction from me to alert his minister to the presence of this Black Redstart on our roof.

All this listing injects a keenness to see something that you have not yet seen – on that day, in that year, in your life. A day list in particular makes you look more carefully at every bird that shows itself, and look harder for the birds that are not showing. My experience is that this makes you see more than you otherwise would. Listing does turn what might be a relaxed ramble with binoculars into a form of hunting, the critics would say, but it also means you detect a higher proportion of the birds that are actually there to be seen. Along with that it means that if you set out with hopes of a good score there will be days when you are disappointed. You can't count on every day being better than the last. When you have made all possible discounts for weather conditions, the known ups and downs of that specific season or year or habitat, birds are very capable of springing surprises. There are days when everything falls into place, all the birds you expect to see are there and half a dozen highly interesting extras turn up. There are other days when you can't find half the birds you know for certain to be somewhere around. They just don't show.

Birds as hunting can disappoint. The most recent of the three trips I have made to the wonderful wetland in northern Greece, around Lake Kerkini, disappointed us. We just didn't see nearly as many birds as must have been there. But then the amount of time when nothing happens must be a great deal worse for a fisherman.

Citizen science.

The notes and records kept by an individual birder are of some interest, as mine from 50 years ago are beginning to be. But records become much more interesting when they are pooled. Local bird clubs and natural history societies have always done that. Their annual reports made up from records sent in by lots of individual members give a useful picture of how bird life is changing (or not) in that area.

The British Trust for Ornithology (BTO) takes this to a whole new level, through wider coverage, more sophistication. The BTO organises surveys, some of which run year after year, like their Breeding Bird Survey, some of which are run for just one or two years, to gather information about a bird of particular concern, House Martin and Woodcock being recent examples. The BTO explains what information they want birders to collect, from what kind of habitat, between what dates or what times of day. Then it is over to the BTO's members, amateur birdwatchers, to collect the required information and send it in.

The BTO receives in this way a vastly greater amount of information than any team of professional researchers could collect on their own. BTO staff, who include trained scientists and statisticians, are able to analyse the data and draw conclusions from it about whether the population of this or that bird is changing, and to look for the reasons. This process is called 'citizen science', although the BTO and its members have been doing it since long before that label was invented by Americans. The BTO must be one of the most productive organisations in the world in the business of citizen science. It flourishes on the back of the vast army of birdwatchers in Britain.

Apart from the surveys already mentioned the BTO has published a huge, beautiful and fascinating atlas based on the results of bird ringing. The ringing of birds with little aluminium rings put on their legs has been carried out in Britain for more than one hundred years. The father of our next door neighbour in Norfolk, Harriet, was a passionate bird ringer, pioneered a method of catching Sand Martins for ringing, and became the public voice of the BTO for many years, a writer of books and articles, and frequent broadcaster: Chris Mead. The library at the BTO's headquarters in Norfolk is named after him.

Once a bird has been ringed, information can be gained about where it goes to and how long it lives, either if the bird is re-trapped later by another bird ringer or if it is found, and reported to the address on the ring. The information from birds ringed builds up only very slowly. The percentage of recoveries is very very low. But it *has* built up and we have learned fascinating things about the distances 'British' birds travel, where they get to, and how long they live. The BTO's *Migration Atlas* is a mine of all this information

Every ten years or so the BTO has organised a country-wide survey of birds of all kinds in Britain (and Ireland). Working to rules carefully devised by the BTO's experts, hundreds of birdwatchers walk through bird habitats of all kinds recording what they see. Their data is turned into an atlas of which birds live in Britain and where. By comparing one atlas with another, now that we have several produced 10-15 years apart, we have a picture that is based on very firm evidence of how the population of each species is changing, some up, some down, some spreading to new areas, others retreating from where they were. Thanks to advances in statistics the most recent of these atlases even attempts to assess not just where each species has been recorded but the density of its population.

Lastly, a recent innovation that makes use of the spread of home computers is BirdTrack, a system for individual watchers to record electronically, day by day if they wish, the lists of birds they have seen in this or that area. The data is instantly accessible to the BTO's analysts. From this they can derive more than just summaries of what birds are being seen where; they can produce in real time a day-by-day picture at spring migration time for instance, when birds are flooding into Britain from the south, of how Swallows or Cuckoos or the warblers are spreading gradually further and further north across Britain.

The mention of Cuckoos brings one last development to mind. Ringing has yielded fascinating information but, as mentioned, the rate of recovery is very low and at best we only learn a scatter of points at which our birds have been found. Using very latest technology birds, ever smaller species of birds, can be fitted with miniature radio transmitters or GPS chips from which we can learn for that individual exactly where it goes and how fast it travels, and for our birds that move out of Britain in winter just where they go; mainly to Africa. This technology is expensive (so far) and only a small number of birds can be tagged, as some Cuckoos and Nightingales have been. The most astonishing discovery made using this technology is that one tiny wading bird, the Red-necked Phalarope which nests in Shetland, migrates westwards across the Atlantic from the north of Scotland to America and spends the winter on the Pacific coast of Ecuador and Peru, the only bird known to migrate in the opposite direction to all other migrants when they leave the UK.

Professional science.

The study of birds is not just for amateurs. The BTO and RSPB each employ some scientists, the BTO to interpret the data fed in from their surveys, the RSPB to work out what steps to take to make the conditions on their reserves better for birds. This is science at the practical end of the scale. There is also a higher level of science, ornithology as a branch of biology. Quite a number of universities in Britain and across the world now support researchers and lecturers in ornithology, working on a wide range of problems from the practical through analytical to the abstract end of the scale.

As is the way with science now, the results of much of the scientists' work is published in the form of short papers, some on very narrow questions, and more and more these papers tend to have not one but three or four authors; researchers with different skills pooling their efforts. Fortunately for the amateurs and the general reader a few of those who have spent their careers on bird science step back, assess the bigger picture, and can write books which rest firmly on the latest scientific work but present the story in ways that the non-expert can understand. One of the best of these is Tim Birkhead who teaches animal behaviour and the history of science at Sheffield University. His *Wisdom of Birds* which he calls a history of ornithology tells how our knowledge of birds has built up over the past 3-400 years, and the people who have led the way. Darwin was a key staging point: the study of birds and the study of evolution have remained closely connected.

Another writer of this kind is Ian Newton, who was fortunate in working for most of his career in a government institute which allowed him to pursue research without teaching commitments. He is supremely able to communicate complex science in plain words. He has written important books for scientists on why populations of birds vary, and how species develop and separate off from one another. Those are heavy tomes for serious students but alongside those he writes with pellucid clarity books intended for the non-expert. His *New Naturalist* volumes on *Bird Migration* and *Bird Populations* are a joy to read, and his latest NN volume on *Farming and Birds* (2017) gives the definitive picture on a subject of very wide interest, at a time when the UK has a chance to write its own policy for farming for the first time in 70 years, correcting the aspects of the CAP that we have criticised for so long.

One of the most intellectually fascinating experiences I have had from birds was when in 2013 I attended a week-long conference of the European Ornithologists' Union, hosted by the University of East Anglia in Norwich. It was an impressive gathering of 350 bird scientists from 30 countries, mainly from Europe but there was a strong contingent from China. The range of topics discussed included the effects of forest management on woodpeckers, how kestrels are experiencing the cost of city living, the battle for airspace between birds and aircraft, and how birds can be saved from colliding with windows by architects understanding how birds see. The impacts of economic development and of climate change were recurring themes. I, as a non-scientist, was in a very small minority; most participants were career scientists. It was impressive to see such a large number of young post-graduate and start-of-career scientists based in universities across Europe and beyond, brimming with energy and enthusiasm for birds; keen minds unravelling ever deeper mysteries of bird biology and behaviour.

I was also struck by the key role of advanced technology. Quite a few of the projects reported had only been made possible by very recent technological innovations in the speed of photography, miniaturisation of cameras, and of location devices that can be attached to ever smaller species of birds.

Among the mysteries of birds, migration is maybe the one that is still part mysterious. Scientists have not fully unravelled it. How do birds find their way across the world without getting lost? Researches into metabolism can be fascinating too. How many people knew before we were told at this conference that some Bar-tailed Godwits migrate in one single flight from Alaska to New Zealand, a distance of 11-12,000 kilometres *and* that so as not to carry any spare weight on this desperately long flight the birds absorb into their bodies a large portion of their intestines before setting off (not needed, as no food is available during the eight to nine day flight) and regrow themselves when they land at the other end? By the way, no unfit birds survive.

The uses of bird science.

But I haven't yet really given the answer to the question: what if anything is so *important* about birds? All this observing and recording of birds, is it any more than an idle, fascinating but pointless pastime? Some of the data collected by the BTO and RSPB and their scientists' interpretation of their data is used either to persuade government of the need to take action; or to refine the action they are already taking for instance through subsidies to farmers to make their farming practices more helpful to birds; or turned into guidance for the RSPB's and other land managers on the reserves which they own. Farmed land has been made much more difficult for birds over the past 50 years, and there have been very large drops in the numbers of some species of bird which rely in particular on farmed land. This process started in Britain with the drainage and improvement of land to increase food production in the 1950s and 1960s, and gathered pace when Britain joined the European Community in 1973 and farmers suddenly received large increases in the prices for basic commodities. That led, within ten years, to farms specialising in arable or livestock in place of the mixed farming which had been common up till then, and which had given birds a varied food supply through the year. In parallel, steady advances in technology led to farm machinery becoming bigger and heavier and making quicker work of harvesting and sowing. At the same time use of chemical fertilisers and pesticides increased and became widespread. This last has resulted in a dramatic loss of insects from the countryside – essential food for birds of many kinds wiped out.

Scientists have unravelled for us the adverse impact that all these changes have had on birds. Scientists working with land managers have advised how best to reduce the negative impacts. In part the result has been legal prohibition on the use of the most harmful pesticides (DDT was top of the list). In part it has meant scientists working hand in hand with government departments to formulate schemes that encourage farmers to make slight changes in the timing of their operations or to farm the less productive parts of their land not for food but for wildlife. Agri-environment schemes, invented in Britain, have this purpose. Scientists have played a key part, Sadly, the evidence after 30 years of these schemes being applied and improved is that even in Britain where there is strong public support, and commitment from very many farmers, they have not done much to reduce the adverse impact on birds of modern farming. In many other countries of Europe, where commitment was less in the first place, the picture is that farmers take the money and do the minimum.

The efforts of scientists are not entirely wasted. These schemes will with luck, Brexit or no Brexit, move into a second generation, more sharply focussed. Ways to make the schemes more effective for birds are already clear. It is over to administrators, politicians – and farmers – to put that into effect.

Scientists' efforts have more impact when they are channelled into the management of bird reserves. These are areas of marshland or woodland or farmed land where birds have priority and the land is managed to produce the best conditions for birds. This does not simply come about by benign neglect. Scientists' input is essential.

So much for the contribution made by scientists who work at the 'applied' end of the scale. Their work is clearly aimed at helping birds. What about the scientists who work in universities at the 'pure' end of the scale, pursuing problems for their own sake, out of intellectual curiosity? Who do they help? What use is their work?

Apart from saying that we should never stamp out the pursuit of lines of inquiry for their own sake, we can, as it happens, point to a few specific results of scientific work on birds which have brought practical benefits to humans, even if that was not what the scientists set out to do. Studies on bird song, for example, have thrown up clues as to how humans learn speech, and findings from studies of song birds have led to dramatic advances in studies of the human brain.

Do we really need birds?

The examples of bird science throwing up discoveries that can be directly read across to humans are few and far between. Birds can however be useful to us as indicators of changes in the world around us. On the farming front they gave the first indications of the side-effects of some of the chemicals that came into use 50 years ago. DDT was shown to have clear and harmful impact on birds, but on humans too. Many other pesticides have been so effective at killing pests that they have stripped out important food for birds. Bird numbers fell. That concerned bird lovers but it did not take long for a second concern to emerge. The insects that pesticides were killing were also important for the production of human food; as pollinators of the flowers and crops that we need. We should certainly worry about the decline in insects, whether or not we care about the decline in birds.

So birds do us a favour as indicators of environmental change. Do we need them for any other reason? Some enthusiasts for birds argue that they are essential for our well-being; that birds, the sight and sound of birds, are essential to human happiness. The amount that has been written about birds (including here!) is evidence of the interest and joy that *some* people *can* derive from birds. Many people do. But it seems an exaggeration to move from that to saying that they are a key part of human happiness. I am sure many, perhaps most, people could live happily without them. A good many people find city life completely satisfying. The variety of human contact and culture available in a city gives them all they want. To the point where some of them complain on the occasions when they get into the countryside, that it is all green and pretty boring. For me, birds are up there with Beethoven and Caravaggio, with power to uplift our spirits, and to reward close study as well. We have to keep in mind that they have come to be what they are without human intervention; all the evidence is that they have very slowly evolved. We need to treat them carefully because we would not know how to replace them.

Ecosystem services.

Over the last ten years professional economists have been trying to develop methods of putting a monetary value on the benefits that humans get from the environment, apart from the benefits which already have a market value; most obviously that means food. The products of farming and forestry and fisheries all have prices which go up and down with changes in supply and demand, and the producers get a return from the market. But there are benefits that we appear to get for nothing, such as clean water and fresh air; or awesome land-scape or bird displays and birdsong; or less visibly the sequestration of carbon by woodland or peat moors or the sea. Economists are making some progress in their attempts to define the value of these things. It is a branch of economics that is bound to make progress. The aim is to make us all aware of what it would cost to get these benefits if nature, or land managers as a by-product of their other activities, were not providing them. The next steps are to warn us to take greater care of our environment – and maybe to put a price on some aspects of land management so that we pay for the environmental goods, or services, that we have been getting for free up till now.

I have included birds and bird song on my list above. But economists would not automatically think of including those items. There are other aspects of the environment which have stronger claims. Taking greater care of the environment sounds as though it ought automatically to be good for birds, but that is not necessarily so. Managing large areas for clean water or for carbon sequestration could result in large expanses of land, water, woodland or reed beds which, from the point of view of birds, could be monoculture – perfect for producing the environmental results desired, but severely lacking in the variety on which birds depend for year-round food supplies; from their point of view no better than the monocultures of crops grown for (humans') food. So it is for now questionable whether the movement towards environmental services is going to be of much help to our struggling birds.

Dawns

I'll round off on birds with some more notes on my personal experiences. It is well-known that dawn is an especially good time for seeing and hearing birds. They are hyperactive in the hour or so after dawn. If you want to catch sight of birds at this active hour, you must be prepared to get into the field at first light. That gets more testing as the days get longer. New Year's Day coincides with just about the latest sunrise of the year. Each year since we have lived in Norfolk I have started the year by going to a nearby woodland particularly favoured by Hawfinches. There are two trees out on their own in a paddock where Hawfinches can be relied on to appear at first light, to preen for a few minutes, after which they scatter and might be anywhere for the rest of the day. I have got to know within five minutes the time when the birds come to these treetops on the 1st of January, and so far they have not let me down. This little walk can be relied on to produce other birds of interest, active in the first light of one of the shortest feeding days of the year for them.

A special dawn outing was in the middle of April one year, just after Easter. Poppy and I had gone to a wedding in the far north of Northumberland, and stayed in a hotel near Hadrian's Wall. I spotted beforehand that this was going to be very close to an RSPB reserve, a piece of moorland on the edge of the Pennines particularly favoured by Black Grouse. These Black Grouse are much rarer and harder to track down than Red Grouse. They have picky habits. They are hanging on in remote parts of Wales and Scotland; in England the place we were close to is one of very few reliable Black Grouse areas left. It seemed worth making the effort. They are birds that come out into the open most often in early morning, for the males to display to the females, then they melt into the scenery and are much harder to find for the rest of the day. So I made enquiries, got advice on the best viewing point, and set off at 5 am two mornings running. Easter that year was ice cold. Tracking down Black Grouse involved standing as still as possible for an hour to an hour and a half, scanning the opposite hillside and listening. I got a few distant views, and an appetite for a large breakfast.

Another dawn effort was at Minsmere in Suffolk, this time at the end of April – dawn earlier. Poppy and I were staying in a pub on the edge of Minsmere's vast marsh, the 'Eel's Foot'. It was arranged the previous evening that a group of us would parade at Minsmere at 4.30 the following morning to walk and hear the dawn chorus of song birds. Out of bed at 4 am, a short drive through the woods with the car window open; Nightingales singing loud and clear in the stillness and darkness just before dawn. At the meeting point it was impressive to find that the 30 people who had signed up were all there, awake and ready to go. The morning was cold – and drizzly, and windy. The birds on the whole had the sense to lie in. As a dawn chorus of birdsong it was below expectations. But there were one or two compensations like a long close view of a Bittern – a brown streaky sort of heron, extremely well camouflaged; and then the extraordinarily rare sight of a Bittern flying up from a reedbed to see off a Crane that happened to fly over its territory.

Soon after that in the same year we were up in Scotland, at Abernethy, hoping to get a glimpse of a Capercaillie. This is one of Scotland's rarest birds. It looks something like a turkey – not small, but at home in dense pine forest where it lives on shoots and leaves and is rarely seen out in the open. Except when it is giving its breeding display – in May, soon after dawn. Then the males come out in the open, into forest clearings, to perform a weird display of puffing up, fanning their purple tails, tossing back their purple heads with a bright red marking on top. The first requirement for anyone to stand even a chance of seeing this is to get up early, and then to have local advice on where to go. And then it may be necessary to wait for a long time. We were on the point of giving up our attempt when at last we were rewarded with the full display.

I have mentioned already my teenage walks for the dawn chorus in May in Ruislip Woods, leaving home at 3 am. Once we get into June when the first light comes soon after 3 in southern England birds sing less; pairing accomplished and nesting underway. So the incentive for watchers to get out of bed with the birds rather fortunately falls away. Until the wild geese start to arrive in September/October, by which time daybreak has become less of a stretch.

19

BIRDS AND CONSERVATION

2003–2018

There was an element of accident about the three main conservation activities that I became involved with in my retirement. I was taken up in turn by the RSPB, the World Pheasant Association (WPA) and the Holkham estate in north Norfolk. It came about in the following ways.

RSPB

As I was coming to the end of my time in Whitehall, I was asked by the RSPB's chief executive Graham Wynne whether I would be willing to become a member of their council. Once I had said yes in principle I had to be interviewed by the chairman of council. This consisted of a sandwich and half pint in a bar off Victoria Street.

The RSPB's interest in recruiting me as an adviser and trustee – the two roles of a member of council – stemmed, I guessed, from my having been the top official in MAFF responsible for agri-environment schemes. To this extent their choice was misplaced. All the time that I had agri-environment schemes under my command I had been almost totally taken up with BSE. To my assistants who really did deal with agri-environment, Dudley and Sarah, I was notable for my neglect of them and their subject. If we talked for a few minutes on a Monday morning, it was a good week. When I occasionally chaired a meeting on their work, I drove it through at speed, cutting short the attempts they made to open up any exploratory discussion. Just keep to what we need to decide here and now. BSE won't wait.

If the RSPB ever learned the truth of that, they didn't show their disappointment. I did my best to deliver value for them in other ways, from the inside track in London and Brussels. One was to give guidance on how they should handle their discussions with ministers and top officials. The RSPB was in origin a campaigning organization, and campaigning zeal still came to the fore when they wanted change. Sharp and aggressive is not the best tone to adopt, particularly with ministers, and particularly not with ministers who are quite sympathetically inclined to the case you are arguing. We were, at this time, in the period of Tony Blair's Labour government. Quite a few ministers were keen to respond to organizations that they saw as having been repressed in the long years of Conservative government (1979-97). I knew from first hand that some of our ministers in MAFF regarded RSPB as representing a large slab of public opinion that had been cold-shouldered by the hard-hearted Conservatives. Eliot Morley was a self-confessed fanatical birder, but the other ministers on the MAFF team were moderately sympathetic to RSPB interests too. When I conveyed this to Graham Wynne he was doubtful at first but came round to seeing that RSPB now had a government which was its friend, and accepted that he and his team would do better to tone down the campaigning rhetoric and speak to ministers in a more friendly manner when presenting demands. Some of his deputies found that a difficult adjustment to make.

By the time I took up my place on the RSPB council I had made the move from Whitehall to Brussels. There I got to know and worked with the RSPB's specialists on the EU, and with BirdLife International, whose office happened to be just across the road from mine in the Charlemagne building on rue de la Loi. (BirdLife is an umbrella organization which links together bird protection societies worldwide. RSPB is, in formal terms, the UK partner of BirdLife on a par with partners in countries around the world, but RSPB provides a very large part of BirdLife's funding, so the relationship is abnormally close.)

I worked quite a lot with RSPB's Brussels-based staff on the EU Constitution which was then taking shape, and together we produced an analysis of the Constitution's good and bad points, seen through the lens of protection of the environment, habitats and birds. Our conclusion was that the good outweighed the bad. I put this analysis forward to the council. The chairman took some persuading to have the subject discussed at all. I pressed, and it was finally put on the agenda and discussed, very briefly. Council members showed little or no interest. In this they were no more than reflecting public opinion. The British press had been depicting the Constitution as a monstrosity. It was in due course rejected by voters in the core EU countries, France and the Netherlands. So the British were never called on to express any formal verdict.

However, I think the essence of our analysis was correct: that the EU gives stronger protection to the environment via the Birds and Habitats Directives (recently – 2016 – renewed) than a UK government can be relied on to do. This showed up for example in the nonchalant demotion of the environment in the priorities of the Cameron-Osborne government, and came to the fore as a sharp concern in the Brexit debate. Rightly so. EU laws have had a virtuous impact on clean air, clean water and nature protection in Britain.

Those then were two issues where I gave the RSPB the benefit of my inside track in Whitehall and Brussels. There were other issues on which they got the benefit of my analysis of topics they discussed. For instance the RSPB was initially all in favour of energy crops – crops grown as fuel for power generation – seen as renewable sources of energy, green, and all to the good. I was one of the first if not the first to point out in a council discussion that some of the crops being used in UK power generation were being grown in developing countries where they were being planted on land cleared of virgin forest. The damage done to the environment was huge. The forests being felled were some of the richest places on earth for biodiversity. My point was well taken and the RSPB policy changed.

The council consisted of 24 members (reduced to 18 after my time). This number included one or two amateur birders and one or two people chosen for their professional skills, in finance or the law. The others nearly all had scientific training, several as career university teachers of ornithology. I was the only example of the Whitehall generalist. To my mind, after 30 years in MAFF which had included some years working directly with farmers, I knew a thing or two about farming. I had been a manager of some very large groups of staff, so I had views on management. And I had years of experience in responding to ministers' demands for instant judgments on people, problem situations and technical work. My judgment, and presentation of a case to best advantage, had been tried and tested daily.

So when we sat round the council table listening to presentations by the senior staff on matters scientific, managerial or financial, I often had thoughts on the arguments being put forward, whether they seemed convincing, whether this or that aspect needed additional analysis. I knew equally well that a committee member who pipes up on every topic is a pain to his colleagues. But my training in being effective in committee had been of the highest order, and went back a long way. I rationed my contributions carefully. Even so, I sensed that the scientists on council and among the senior staffers did not understand why I thought I had *any* contribution to make either on scientific or on managerial topics. I should keep to my own zone of expertise: politics and government. Graham Wynne did not fall into that way of thinking, being himself a generalist and manager. But I don't think the chairman of council quite understood; Ian Newton, a professional scientist who had had a career path which had been mercifully light on management and rough-and-tumble debate and pressurised decisions. I think he thought I saw myself as a professional gadfly.

Those were the ways in which I made my input. What did I get out in return? I learned a great deal more about birds, and we got to visit some special places with experts as our guides. Poppy was often able to share in this. Together we made some lasting friends. Pam Pumphrey, for many years the leader of the RSPB's committee for Scotland, and her husband Matthew live and farm, in a small way, in Dumfriesshire. During our two years of futile house-hunting in Dumfries and Galloway we called on them for help and consolation. A year or two later Pam had to deliver some of her Longhorn cattle to Norfolk, not long after our move to Hilborough. She rang to ask whether she would be coming anywhere near where we had settled. Her delivery was to Cockley Cley Hall – not three miles from our new house! Since then we have made a joint expedition to Orkney and Shetland, and remain firm friends.

As to seeing birds in special places, once a year the whole RSPB council with a retinue of staff went on a progress in one region of the UK or another, for two or three days, with site visits and demonstrations of conservation at work. Over my five years we visited Cumbria, Kent, Dorset, Scotland (Abernethy and Forsinard) and Northern Ireland. I would not say that I can remember any deeply impressive presentations by members of staff. It was the birds that stole the show: Capercaillie displaying in the forest, Slavonian Grebes in breeding dress – and the fragile habitats that were being kept in good heart by the RSPB's efforts.

RSPB in my time on council was riding high. Graham Wynne was around half way through his time as chief executive, well into his stride, with a firm grip on his organization and quite a charismatic public presence. The organization is large: around 1500 full-time staff and an army of volunteers whose time adds up to the equivalent of another 500. The RSPB is one of the largest NGOs in Britain, second to the National Trust but probably ahead of nearly all the others. It is exceptionally well-funded. Annual income in my time was £120-140 million and it has risen since then. Remarkably, nearly £30 million of this came from legacies and even more remarkably much of that money was coming from bequests by people who had not been members of the RSPB in their lifetimes. How did that come about? One can only speculate. Are there many people with money who, as death closes in on them, summon their solicitors and say, I don't want my money going to the family, advise me what good cause it could go to?

Be that as it may, the Treasurer of the RSPB is not a post to keep you awake at night. It is something like being bursar of St John's College in Oxford. Michael Scholar enjoyed telling the tale of how, when he was being interviewed by the Fellows of St John's for the post of college president, he picked up on mention of a large new project and said, like the well-trained Treasury man that he was, that he would want to look at alternative options that the project might be squeezing out. There were puzzled looks around the table and then the bursar said: 'Income is not a problem for this college.' So with the RSPB. There must, you would think, come a time when the legacy income falls, but that may be a generation away. There is no sign yet. Income from government grants may fall, post Brexit. But then again it may not, if the government of the day gives higher priority to improving the environment than to the economics of farming.

The RSPB for all its very large staff does not seem to throw up many people of national status. Norman Sills, architect of Titchwell and Lakenheath Fen, is an undoubted first-class expert in watery habitat. Debbie Pain who moved from RSPB to the Wildfowl Trust blossomed into an authoritative conservation manager there, a fluent and persuasive speaker, and leader of a ground-breaking team rescuing the Spoon-billed Sandpiper from the very brink of extinction. But beyond those two...?

Is there something about the culture of the RSPB that stifles, or fails to fire up, its talented people? Many, especially the younger ones, have had university training to prepare them for careers in conservation. They ought to be good communicators, but that talent is thinly spread. Maybe the size of the organization is against it? It may have grown too large for its own good, or it may be past the peak of its life cycle. Certainly there are times when its appetite for buying land needs to be curbed. While I was on council the number of sites in RSPB ownership passed the 200 mark. There is no ideal number but the suite of reserves now includes a mixture of large, medium and small. There is a policy of developing and extending the large ones, so as to manage 'on a landscape scale'. The vast holding at Abernethy and the growing area of the Great Fen fit with this philosophy. But alongside this there is a long tail of small, some very small, reserves, some which have been held for many years, some showing signs of neglect. When we last visited Marazion Marsh in Cornwall, in summer 2017, we found a wetland so overgrown with bushes and high grasses that the pools famous for attracting vagrant waders from North America were now totally invisible. Is it not time for the estate to be thinned out?

One long-running concern for friends of the RSPB as well as its enemies centres on predation. Some of the birds that the RSPB works to protect on its reserves are subject to heavy predation. Their numbers are dwindling and predation may be – in some places clearly is – the major cause of the decline. This is most definitely the case with wading birds that nest on the ground, on wet grassland, where their eggs and chicks are very vulnerable.

Private landowners with game birds to protect routinely take action against various bird and mammal predator species, where it is legal to do so. One private landowner who has developed a special interest in managing reserves for ground-nesting waders has analysed the case in fine detail and published his conclusions: Philip Merricks, manager of Elmley National Nature Reserve (NNR) on Sheppey. The science is pretty clear. In areas that are particularly attractive to ground-nesting waders such as Lapwing and Redshank, predators are attracted too, and for them these are rich pickings. They will congregate, work in teams (Crows and Jackdaws have near-human intelligence), and the nesting waders cannot defend themselves. Philip's conclusions, supported by Dutch research, are that along with careful management of the habitat by grazing and control of water levels it is essential to keep foxes, stoats and weasels, crows and magpies at bay. Hedgehogs and badgers do damage too, but are under strict legal protection. Marsh Harriers find wader chicks quite tasty but they too are strictly protected. With them the action has to take the form of prevention or distraction, but where the law allows then tough measures are essential. That means killing.

The RSPB has a longstanding reluctance to kill. This is understandable. Of the thousands of members who provide its funds many, perhaps most, feel love for wild creatures. Many, probably most, are town dwellers for whom killing wild creatures hardly comes into their daily lives. Maybe the cat brings a dead mouse or bird through the door occasionally. But they do not expect the RSPB with its mission to protect birds to do any killing. So there is a wide gulf between the attitude of town-based bird lovers and professional managers of land in the countryside. The latter group, convinced (on good evidence) that protection has to involve some killing in the name of predator control argue that the RSPB staff should do more to persuade their members of the case. The RSPB has never been keen, many of the staff are individually averse, so when any anti-predator measures are taken they are never more than half-measures. Half measures do no use. So some vulnerable species struggle to survive on RSPB reserves.

The clearest indication was when the RSPB for some years managed a reserve adjacent to Philip Merricks' land at Elmley. On his side of the fence, with predators 'controlled', Lapwing and Redshank held their own. On the RSPB's patch, with half measures, they declined.

Some of us tried to have this issue debated in my time on the council. The chairman Ian Newton leaned heavily in favour of keeping off the subject and scientists on the council backed that position. Their guiding principle was not to launch discussion on any issue which might 'divide the council'. So a highly contentious and difficult matter in need of debate went undebated for a long time and when, after weeks of careful preparation, we had some discussion in council, it was not pressed to any robust conclusions. This attitude, the reluctance to have the debate, was quite strange to me. Debate on subjects where opinion was divided was everyday experience in Whitehall. What else did the Cabinet Office secretariats do but hear discord and try to find common ground between conflicting points of view? What else is the political world but a never-ending process of finding ways through differences of opinion? Why assume that because there were two points of view a debate would inevitably lead to a schism? Why not search for common ground and an agreed way forward? Perhaps that reluctance stemmed from a scientist's way of thinking, where mediation and compromise are not standard working methods.

So the RSPB muddled on – and still does – with some unsatisfactory and ineffective actions on some of its reserves, and with periodic attacks on other land managers for the ways they deal with predation. Outcome: damage to the RSPB's relations with farmers and landowners on a broader front.

There is one particular aspect on which the RSPB is right in principle – if not in its recipes for solving the problem. A small number of landowners, managers of grouse moors, continue to kill birds of prey that have been given the highest legal protection for the past 60 years or more. This has to stop. But it is a far cry from that to the killing of crows and foxes, stoats and weasels, to protect Lapwing and Redshank which, without firmer action, will soon be as scarce as Hen Harriers.

WPA

Those who know me are surprised when I say that I am a member of the World Pheasant Association (WPA), as I have been since 2008; even more surprised to hear that I was chairman of the Association for a couple of years. Where did this interest in 'world' pheasants spring from? What was it all about?

The connection started by chance. In 2007 we moved to Hilborough in Norfolk where our next door neighbours were the Mead household: Verity, widow of Chris Mead who had been a well-known bird ringer, broadcaster and writer on birds, and Harriet their daughter, well-known for her creative welding of scrap metal into amazing likenesses of birds and animals. At that time Harriet had a partner Dr Stephen Browne who was a career bird scientist. He was a supportive member of the WPA, supportive in particular of the association's paid director, Dr Phil McGowan. Stephen and I chatted from time to time over the garden gate, getting to know each other. One day Stephen asked whether I would be interested in joining the WPA, and becoming one of their council of trustees. Their chairman Dick Potts was suggesting they would be glad of my experience.

Now, I knew nothing of the WPA but I knew Dick Potts. He had a high reputation as an authority on the conservation of game birds – pheasants and partridges – on farmland in Britain. We had come across one another when I was in MAFF. He was in 2007-08 not only chairman of the WPA but the top man at the Game and Wildlife Conservation Trust. I regarded him as a serious person.

This was the second proposition that Stephen Browne had put to me, the first being that I should join him on Hilborough parish council. The WPA idea promised to be the more interesting of the two options. Accordingly, when I was invited to attend the next meeting of their council as a guest, I accepted.

The WPA has always been a small organization and its council is large in relation to its number of members. There may have been eight or ten around the table on that occasion, with Dick Potts in the chair. Dick's style of chairing struck me as all too informal, though I was soon to learn for myself that chairing the WPA's leading characters was like herding cats. Dick had some interest in what the WPA did, though it did not seem to run very deep. He handed over the chairmanship within a few months of my joining and disappeared off that scene. His deep knowledge of game birds and their conservation was channelled through the Game and Wildlife Conservation Trust, and he published a definitive book on partridges in 2012.

For my part I was accepted into the ranks of the WPA's governing council, seamlessly, by a vague process of election. The director very soon started turning to me for advice on how to bring the association's affairs into better order.

At this point it is best to explain a little history. The WPA was founded in 1975 by three or four men with shared interests in shooting, and in keeping exotic pheasants in captivity, breeding them in aviaries to display to their friends. This group of founding fathers all had wealth behind them. Their idea was to do something to preserve for the future the types of bird that they loved, in the wild as well as in captivity. Many birds of the pheasant family originate in the Himalayas: in northern India, Pakistan and Nepal, and in the mountains of southern China. Many of them are endangered in the wild, under threat from both agriculture and hunting by humans. From agriculture because the habitat they need is dense forest which is being steadily cut down, as in so many developing countries, to create more land for farming. From hunters because so many of the pheasants, partridges, quails and their relatives are tubby. They carry a good amount of flesh and are good to eat. In remote mountain areas villagers hunt them not for sport but to feed the family.

So these birds, many of them with complicated colourful plumage, much prized by collectors, are in need of human action to ensure their survival. From that the idea of the WPA was born. From the start, the interests of keeping birds in captivity and of conserving them in the wild sailed along in company. Of the founding members, one or two had keen interests in conservation in the wild, others had less. As time went on, the number of subscribing members in Britain and Ireland built up. By far the largest number of these were interested in breeding birds in captivity. Many of that group were not at all well off. For them the WPA offered a network through which they could exchange surplus birds for new ones, to enrich their collections.

As a force for conservation of birds in the wild, the WPA is a minnow up against much larger organizations such as the World Wildlife Fund or Flora and Fauna International or Conservation International (US), all of those with access to much larger funds. But the WPA has achieved a distinctive impact, using a distinctive approach. It focussed on a limited number of regions in, particularly, China, India and Nepal. It could not remotely afford to station permanent staff in those countries. Instead it worked by singling out local enthusiasts, young people at the beginning of careers as university scientists or zoo technicians; it helped them with training, advanced their education in their own countries and paid for one or two of them to visit Britain, in some cases for a university year. This was an exceptional opportunity particularly for young people from China in the 1980s. By a combination of luck and good judgement a sprinkling of those people who were given WPA help in their early years have gone on to make careers in conservation and are now in senior positions, with power and influence. Two senior academics in China feel much indebted to WPA for help they were given on their way up the career ladder.

This marriage of modest funds and UK expertise with local enthusiasm in regions where money and expert knowledge were in short supply met a need – at the time. Now, 40 years later, China in particular is much more self-sufficient. But a bond had been created.

Out of that grew various conservation actions on the ground. The most notable of all these was in the Pipar valley in the high mountains of Nepal, where a WPA initiative consisted of protecting rare 'tragopans' primarily through the education of villagers; educating them through the construction of schools and provision of teachers; then supplementing an all-round primary education with education in the value of conserving the rare birds in the valley. The Pipar project is a model of how conservation, in a region where people are poor and need food, has to start by convincing the locals that there is some advantage in it for them. Overall the number of projects the WPA has had a hand in has not been vast but they were carefully chosen and – as Matt Ridley, Lord Ridley, one of the association's patrons, once put it to me – 'boots on the ground' has been the hallmark. Action in the field, at low cost, money channelled through local activists.

As time went on the number of WPA members in Britain grew and most of these members were keepers of birds in captivity, on a small scale, as a hobby. Branches sprouted up in France, Germany, and Benelux too. Stimulated by the example of the WPA in Britain, they happily called themselves 'WPA' branches, though they have always been legally and financially independent. Their members were almost entirely bird-keeping enthusiasts. Interest in conservation action in Asia was very much a minority interest for all the continental branches.

Now coming back to my arrival on the scene and the hopes of what I could contribute, in Britain the WPA operates as a charity registered with the Charity Commission. It was important to make sure that the WPA (UK) complied with the Charity Commission's rules, which had recently been tightened up. Were we to lose our charitable status, we would lose big financial advantages. As it was, the WPA had been losing money year by year for some years. The director hoped that, if we could be shown to be in a better-organized state, people would feel more confident about making grants to us. Compliance with charity rules was thus linked at least in his mind to fund-raising. He and I set about upgrading the WPA's systems for management of its affairs. I ploughed in my experience of the RSPB and the way it ran itself, making allowance for the fact that the WPA was an infinitely smaller show. Step by step we put notes to the council for discussion. The council – in practice a loose-knit mix of formally elected trustees and the 'founding fathers' who played a dominant part in the trustees' discussions – took slight interest. But enough was done for the director to feel he had a better picture to paint in his applications for funds. There was only one problem: he was winning almost no grants. The only large grant he did secure was dissipated in a short time, spent on hiring a research assistant – and on the director's salary.

This tight financial position was as far as I could tell a new situation for the WPA to be in. In its early years the operations in developing countries had involved the injection of modest amounts of private money, with no ongoing commitment to running offices or paying salaries in or outside the UK. The commitment to a UK salary for the director on a par with a university lecturer was proving a heavy burden, and looked difficult to sustain. Our treasurer wrung his hands each year as he presented the accounts, Council members looked at each other, while the state of the budget grew worse and worse.

Around 2011, things were coming to a head. I had just been elected chairman, with support from the five scientist members of council, in the face of misgivings on the part of the ancien regime. I had stepped into a crisis situation. I was at least no stranger to crises, whilst clearly none of the other trustees had either the appetite or the experience to resolve the matter. It did not take long to detect that we really had two problems. There was the money, or lack of it. But there were also two competing visions for the future. The scientists on the council had formed around the director a view that the WPA could be turned into a niche scientific body, a specialist focus for scientific research into the conservation of the pheasant family of birds. Scratching the surface I soon found that this little group felt really quite intense hostility towards the amateur members of the association, and particularly towards those who had the breeding of birds in captivity as their main interest. So here we had a schism on our hands: two schools of opinion competing for the soul of the WPA.

I could understand that there could be two views on the value captive breeding could have for ensuring the survival of a species in the wild. There are indeed serious debates to this day on that issue, some arguing that if a species is in danger of dying out the only way of saving it is to help those birds that remain in the wild, by protection from predators and improvement of their habitat; that breeding up a stock of the birds in captivity is never going to produce birds in sufficient numbers to create a new population capable of surviving on its own in the wild. This is a strong case, but it is not cut and dried. Just occasionally captive breeding *has* saved a species that was about to die out in the wild. Peter Scott achieved it for the Né-Né goose of Hawaii. The Wildfowl Trust is trying it now with the Spoon-billed Sandpiper in Russia (as with Cranes in Britain). And the WPA may prove able to save the Edwards' Pheasant from extinction; none has been seen in the wild in its Vietnamese homeland for around twenty years, but a large number are kept in captivity. From these a stock could be bred to release into the wild. At the time of writing, this is work in progress.

I had little sympathy with our scientists on the question of amateur versus professional. Their disdain for amateurs' views seemed to me a narrow-minded attitude. I had many years of experience of scientists in government working patiently and respectfully in harness with people who might have little or no scientific training, but other objectives or preferences that needed to be steered by science. In the area of ornithology, the BTO was a shining example of scientists giving a steer to amateurs, and not being disdainful of the sometimes wayward contributions that the amateurs came up with.

In the end the problem with our scientists' vision for the WPA was that it was not shared by the founder members, the bankrollers; more than that, it clashed head-on with the interests of the majority of UK members, not to mention all the members on the continent. Additionally there was no sign that it would pay the director's salary.

Finding my way through this fraught situation caused me real stress and sleepless nights. We had two very tense meetings of the council over the summer of 2012. Discussions were acrimonious. Threats of resignation – from the scientists – became louder. The director's pleas to council members to pull their weight and work harder to raise funds met with a chill response.

In early autumn that year I called a summit meeting of just four of us: the two heavyweight founder members, the treasurer and me. We met on Holy Island in Northumberland, where the treasurer happened to have his day-job. The island is cut off by each high tide for three hours or so. This guaranteed us some clear time to think! It was agreed that we could not be dragged into bankruptcy, for which we and all the trustees might be legally obliged to pay. I had to present the director with an ultimatum: he was director of the whole WPA, he had very quickly to raise money by his chosen strategy, or time was up on that approach. The crisis then rolled rapidly to its conclusion. The director heard me through, as I explained what we needed of him. At the end of a glum discussion he signalled that he might be willing to leave, in exchange for compensation and a formal agreement. The deal was done. A six-month ordeal all round was cleanly ended.

Then came the question whether the WPA would survive. The scientist members of the council pulled out one by one, and as far as they were concerned the WPA then ceased to exist. What was left was a shell, of no scientific value, unscientific, disreputable. But was that to be the last word?

The story continued. I felt the WPA in the next phase needed a leader who had much deeper knowledge of and real keenness for the pheasants. Keith Chalmers Watson took over from me. Unduly diffident about his ability to chair meetings and speak in public, he soon proved excellent at both. He has presided over a regeneration, and expanded the family of branches into eastern Europe, with first the Czechs (amicably reunited for this purpose with the Slovaks) and more recently Poland and Hungary.

In 2015 the godfather of the founders, Keith Howman, hosted a 40th birthday party (1975-2015) to which key people from WPA operations worldwide were invited. The high point of the proceedings was when representatives from each country were invited to step forward and say a few words. Ten or eleven, including China, India, Pakistan, the US, Germany, France, the Czechs... Our best friend from Germany murmured to me that he had up till then thought the title 'World' Pheasant Association was a touch of British imperial arrogance, but now he could see it really was a worldwide brotherhood of operations. It is (my view now) an impressive thing for a handful of enthusiasts to have created on the back of some private wealth and a well-focussed idea distinctively developed.

My life with the WPA might have ended at that point, but for another chance. At our AGM in 2012 one of our speakers was from France: Edouard Jelen (the name is Polish). Bravely, because his English was then still very rocky, he made a presentation on common pheasants (black-necked pheasants, no white neck ring) in the near east, the Caucasus, and into Greece. This caught my interest. I followed up his appeal for the WPA to give some backing to conservation plans in Azerbaijan, Georgia and Greece. When I had looked into it more, the proposed actions in Azerbaijan and Georgia looked questionable.

But as for Greece, Poppy and I were planning to go to Thessaloniki the next spring and I found that we could meet two key people there: a leading light from the hunters' federation which was doing conservation work, and their chief scientist.

Over a meal on a pavement in a suburb of Thessaloniki we struck up a lively relationship with Apostolos and Christos. The organization they belonged to, Apostolos as a leading member and Christos as a paid official, was The Hunting Federation of Macedonia and Thrace. It is easiest to refer to it by its Greek initials: KOMATH. Hunting – in Britain it would be called shooting – is very popular in Greece. There are hunting clubs all over the country, and there are regional federations which draw these clubs together and provide some common services to them. KOMATH is one of the largest such federations, outdone by Athens/Attica in number of members, but the largest of all in its spread of territory, all across the top of the Greek mainland. KOMATH, if I have the figures right, has 40,000 members drawn from 60 local clubs. The small staff at its headquarters – a modern office on the outskirts of Thessaloniki – are a lively lot, and exercise quite considerable power and influence in the countryside. Most of the members are shooters, and conservation is a minority interest, but the minority who *are* interested are serious about it. Apostolos and Christos were our guides into this new world.

Two meetings with that pair and some emailing led to a first shot at an action programme that WPA might be able to support. I ran that past the WPA Council at a session in Dublin. It was judged to be a bit costly, but we agreed to send a leading expert from the Game & Wildlife Conservation Trust (remember Dick Potts from earlier in this story?), Roger Draycott, to the area, to assess what might be done. His report was encouraging and pointed to three or four worthwhile lines of action.

On that basis and after more emailing a concrete six-year programme of action was worked up. WPA's new scientific advisers (a panel of international authorities wisely set up by Keith Chalmers Watson to replace the scientists who had left us) gave it their stamp of approval. Roger and I met with the KOMATH president and top staff in Thessaloniki in December 2016 to seal a deal.

One year on, in November 2017, I returned to the scene. I made a two day visit with 3-4 hours of discussion in the smart KOMATH offices – largely conducted in Greek – and then a long day out in the Nestos Delta, mainly to be shown the work being done on the ground under our action programme to make better habitat for the pheasants. It rained, but the forest looked good with autumnal colour in the trees. We saw the ground work, we saw no pheasants (but I had glimpsed two the previous December). After three or four hours of driving around we adjourned for lunch. The local team of KOMATH game wardens in their smart uniforms, the team of KOMATH scientists – forestry and ecology experts who are overseeing the action programme, the president of the hunting club of Chrysoupoli, the main town in the delta, and the president of KOMATH – a big figure in this fraternity, we all sat down at a long table in the riverside restaurant and as this was a hunters' occasion we feasted on hunters' food. Woodpigeon and wild boar were the only meats on the table.

A local journalist was in attendance and in intervals in this feast he took me and the president of KOMATH outside for interviews.

As to what this joint Anglo-Greek – and French – operation is really about and its scientific value, I published an article in *The Field* in November 2017. This explained, in short, that the pheasants targeted for protection are of a particular type found in western Asia (Azerbaijan, Armenia, Iran and Georgia) that was also widespread in Greece 100 years ago, but through hunting and farming pressures has become so scarce there that the 150 or so in the Nestos Delta are the last to cling on. Pheasants of the common type range with variations of plumage from eastern China to western Asia but these in Greece are the only ones ever to have occurred naturally in Europe. They are interesting because of history (ancient Greek writers refer to them) and interesting to science (the birds at Nestos seem genetically purer than their cousins in the neighbouring countries to the east). One challenge for our project is to soften the general public hostility to hunters in Greece and to show that hunters in Greece as in Britain can sometimes do good conservation work. The evidence we bring of interest from outside Greece and our deployment of an internationally known game-bird scientist won early cooperation from some of the official agencies and won some sympathetic publicity.

In personal terms it has been great fun, a new window on Greece (see chapter 20) and a chance to make practical use of my slowly-growing ability in modern Greek. As I have got to know more about hunting in Greece my admiration for Greek hunters has grown. They have to be fit. Their form of hunting consists of one man and a dog, or a small group of friends and their dogs, walking up steep rocky hillsides tracking birds. They have to find their quarry species for themselves, and they rarely shoot many birds in a day. They are curious about the British form of shooting: shoots, guns in a line, birds driven towards them by beaters, and brought down in large numbers. It is clear to me, though they are too polite to say this, that my Greek friends regard the British style of shooting game birds with fair contempt.

Holkham NNR

The part of the north Norfolk coast which stretches from Burnham Norton in the west to Warham, just beyond the town of Wells, in the east is a National Nature Reserve (NNR). It is of interest to naturalists of many kinds, and to bird-watchers in particular. A great variety of creatures and plants can be seen there. But it is also much visited by tourists, horse riders and holiday-makers. The scene is well-known to many people: a long belt of pines stretching away to east and west from 'Holkham Gap', which is a break in the straight line of the coast where the sea cuts between two banks of sand dunes and forms a little bay. There is good sand for sandcastles, and a long beach where the Household Cavalry famously take their annual day at the seaside, soldiers in holiday kit riding through the surf on their smart horses released from London ceremonial duty. Other horse riders have fun on the beach here too. On the south side of the pine belt, facing inland, is a large area of wet grassland, grazing marsh, grazed by cattle but also, in autumn and winter, by thousands and thousands of Pink-footed Geese. In summer the same grazing marshes are home to nesting Redshank, Lapwing, Snipe – wader species that are becoming scarce across Britain as a whole. That is some of the nature interest, though there are other more specialised birds, and amphibians and insects in need of protection that flourish here too.

This area was declared a National Nature Reserve in the 1960s and was managed until around 2010 by the country's official organization for the protection of nature: once called the Nature Conservancy, then English Nature, now Natural England. Much of the land managed by Natural England was conceded to them by the Holkham Estate which owns it. In 2011 or 2012 the estate decided to 'take their land back in hand' and to manage it - for nature conservation – themselves. Holkham had no intention of changing the status of the land as a nature reserve; they embarked on the process of winning approval from Natural England to run this NNR fully in line with the requirements of the Wildlife and Countryside Act 1981, as the Act puts it 'preserving the flora, fauna, geological and physiographical features of special interest in the area and/ or providing opportunities for the study of, and research into, those features', along with (added by the Natural Environment and Rural Communities Act 2006) 'the provision of opportunities for public enjoyment of nature and/or open-air recreations'.

This would in any circumstances have been quite a tall order; strict requirements for a private landowner to meet. There was at the time only one precedent for a private individual meeting all the requirements and gaining approval from Natural England to run an NNR – known formally as Section 35 approval, after the section in the Wildlife and Countryside Act which empowers Natural England to hand over to an outside organization full authority to run an NNR. Our good friend Philip Merricks was for many years the one and only case of this, with his land at Elmley on the Isle of Sheppey.

This then was a bold decision by Viscount Coke, Tom, son of the Earl of Leicester, who was by 2011-12 in charge of running the Holkham Estate. To understand just how big the challenge was we need to take a detour through some earlier history.

Holkham Hall is a huge Palladian house, or palace, built 1734-64 with much internal decoration by William Kent (like Houghton Hall, Walpole's house not far from here, built at much the same time). It was made nationally famous by Thomas Coke, its second occupant, who farmed the estate according to the most modern methods of his time and attracted publicity from far and wide through his annual 'sheep shearings'. These were in effect an early form of agricultural show, to which everyone could come to learn about Coke's farming methods and see for themselves the quality of the end products. This 'Coke of Norfolk' was a key figure in the advancement of British agriculture. Not himself an innovator, he put into practice the latest ideas and took enormous pleasure in publicising them. He was part showman. His farming accomplishments put Holkham on the map, and – taken together with an active political career – eventually earned him a peerage with the title Earl of Leicester (1837). Then, from being a famous model farm in the first half of the nineteenth century, Holkham became famous later in the century as an innovative shooting estate. Driven shooting of pheasants and partridges was pioneered here. The shoots were, it is said, organized with military precision and it sounds as though they were carried through with military ruthlessness too. The quality of the shooting attracted many famous visitors including royalty.

Following the first world war large country estates ran into great difficulty. Many were sold up, their farmland dispersed, the great houses demolished. Holkham just survived; there was not the money to maintain let alone modernise the big house and it suffered from neglect, but the tradition of running the estate for game shooting lingered on. When Poppy and I first wandered in the park in the early 1970s we remember finding one or two gamekeepers' gibbets – corpses of stoats, weasels and crows strung out along barbed wire fences, evidence of predator control, the work record of a conscientious keeper. This was a grisly feature of rigorous gamekeeping which is rarely seen today.

Times changed again. A different branch of the Coke family inherited the title and the responsibility for Holkham. In 1973 a new Viscount Coke, Edward, took over the management from the sixth Earl. Edward had been brought up in Rhodesia and South Africa and brought new energy and a fresh outlook. Not burdened with too much respect for the Holkham traditions he set about turning the Hall from a crumbling ancestral home into a major tourist attraction. He inherited the title of Earl in 1994, continued vigorous modernisation of house and estate, then handed over day-to-day management to his son Tom in 2005. Edward continued to live on the estate but gave Tom free rein. Tom brought in an inspirational estate manager with rare talents, David Horton-Fawkes, and together they carried forward the campaign of forming a diverse and high-class business around the historic house, beautiful deer park and vast area of farmland that Holkham still owned. This was how things stood when the decision was taken to bring the NNR back under Holkham's direct management.

Against the background of past history it was not really surprising when it turned out that the path to Section 35 approval was going to be quite long. The estate had to live down its record as a mecca for the shooting fraternity and its game-keeping record of relentless killing of 'vermin' – every bird and mammal species that might compete with the shooters for their chosen prey, persecution that we suppose stayed mainly within the law... but there was always room for suspicion. Natural England in the politest possible way made clear that they wanted the estate to show on the ground over a period of several years just how it was going to match up to the standards expected of an NNR. Tom, Viscount Coke, Lord Leicester as he became when his father died in 2015, showed from the outset that he was entirely serious in wanting to turn a new page in Holkham's history. Shooting and management of the farmland for shooting was still very much alive as part of the business of the estate. But he wanted to show that this, and high quality intensive farming, could go hand-in-hand with management of the coastal strip, the NNR, in full compliance with the legal requirements for nature conservation; more than that, he aimed to show that the farmed area and the nature reserve could complement one another, and that the new Holkham could breathe a passion for excellence into both.

Tom saw at the outset that he would gain from some outside advice in getting this right and in convincing Natural England that he was getting it right. That is where I and three others came in. A little advisory board was assembled, four people from different backgrounds: Philip Merricks, clearly pre-eminently useful as the one private individual who had gained Section 35 approval up till then; a local farmer-naturalist, Keith MacDougall, who sadly died after a short time and was replaced by David Lyles, another local farmer, winner of a Norfolk conservation award; Dr (now Professor) Paul Dolman, senior lecturer at the University of East Anglia School of Environmental Sciences, appointed on my recommendation because his report on biodiversity in Breckland had impressed me by its rigour, range and depth; and then me, with my twin interests in birds and agricultural policy. We settled into a pattern of meeting twice a year with the Holkham staff involved on the NNR project (conservation manager Sarah Henderson in the lead here), generally with a member of NE's staff present too, to explain how we were doing in our progression towards the holy grail of Section 35 approval. Five years passed before, one fine day in July 2017, at a little ceremony attended by the Holkham trustees, local dignitaries and the press, a member of NE's Board handed over a certificate: Holkham

Estate thereby became the approved body to manage one of the UK's most important sites for nature.

It was satisfying to have helped in steering this project. Philip Merricks, the forerunner and role model, and Paul Dolman the high-grade environmental scientist, contributed more than I did. The nature of our task started to change once the essential approval had been achieved. From now on the challenge becomes to deliver Lord Leicester's ideal of taking this nature reserve to a new and higher level of excellence. The potential is there. Natural England should not be accused of having neglected the reserve in any way, but putting it under new and private management, with freedom to innovate and bring new thinking to bear, ought to be able to expand the conservation work in new ways, to focus on new species (the plant and insect life and the archaeology have not been fully explored), and to give higher quality attention to the needs of visitors. A new visitor information centre, opened in summer 2018, will be part of that.

Taking over the NNR is just one part of a programme of moving Holkham from its state of neglect 50 years ago to a state-of-the-art twenty-first century large landed estate, a profitable business meeting a variety of 21st century demands. Holkham Hall opens its superb state rooms to the public in the summer months but in addition hosts classical music concerts in the imposing (but acoustically challenged) marble entrance hall, and pop concerts in the park. The former stables which once housed a cramped cafe and a moth-eaten display of the very significant history of farming on the estate have been superbly renovated and now include a light and attractive shop (shopping being an essential part of the day out for today's tourists), a spacious cafe serving distinctive Holkham delicacies in a child-friendly atmosphere; whilst the display of farming has been entirely re-done with modern interactive exhibits covering not just the past history, Coke of Norfolk, but a lucid account of the farming year as it is today, introduced on video by Lord Leicester himself. Out on the ground the farming is being led by the outstandingly able Poul Hovesen and is once again making its mark nationally for innovative methods – a return to rotation, Coke of Norfolk style, but this time with not four but six year rotation – and for excellence of quality – Holkham malting barley has become highly prized by Britain's top brewers. For holiday-makers the sandy beach with beach cafe at the Wells end is the focus but nearer to the Hall a tree-top adventure playground has been introduced; sturdy, safe and, to judge by the difficulty parents have in enticing their children back down to earth, completely absorbing.

What has been achieved in all these different directions so far is the result of Lord Leicester having worked in complete harmony with David as estates director. For those of us involved in the newest enterprise, the nature conservation area, the bar has been set high.

20

BACK TO GREEK

2005 – 2018

At the height of the BSE negotiations the *Financial Times* published a little
article about me as leading negotiator, with the heading 'Classics scholar
who lives out of a suitcase'. The label of classical scholar had stuck to me during
a long and varied career entirely unrelated to classics. The brute fact was that
the demands of Whitehall and the fascination of weaving British interests into
the European Union's systems, which in many ways were an uncomfortable fit
for Britain, left no time for continuing study of classics, certainly not at the level of complexity which I had reached. After 1974 when my work on the papyrus
fragments of Sophocles was published (by De Gruyter, Berlin), I barely opened
a book on classical studies for the next 30 years. By 2005 when I emerged from
my career in the service of governments, I was much less able to read classical
Greek than I had been 30 years earlier, and Latin had become a struggle.

My interest in the classical world and the classical languages had been sup-
pressed, but it was not dead. It reasserted itself by several different routes. Poppy
was a constant encouragement. Her interest, particularly in the Greeks of the
fifth and fourth centuries BCE, burned bright.

One way in which we refreshed our interest was through a conference held
every three years, alternately in Oxford and Cambridge: the Triennial Conference of Classical Studies, or 'the Triennial' for short. This event lasted for
a week, and you were able to enrol to stay in one of the colleges in Oxford or
Cambridge for that time. Staying in a college was much the best way of getting
full value out of the programme, because events continued into the evening,
and of meeting and mixing with the other people attending. There were lectures on all aspects of Greek and Latin language, history, ideas and archaeology, given by people actively involved in teaching or research. People came from
all around the world to attend; a majority from British schools and universities but a good number, young and old, from other countries. For me, it was
a chance to catch up with a few who had been my contemporaries at Oxford

and who had gone on into academic careers; to hear about what they had done (what I might have done) over the intervening 30 years. Time for people to have risen to the top of the profession. 'Mister hReeve' had progressed from being star pupil in Eduard Fraenkel's seminars of the 1960s to the post of Kennedy Professor of Latin in Cambridge.

It was interesting to hear what steps had been taken to keep the classics alive, in the face of a steep decline in the subject at school level. Oxford had developed crash courses in the Greek and Latin languages for students who wanted to study classics intensively but had had no chance to learn the languages at their schools. These new courses, which one or two of my contemporaries helped to devise, have turned out to be really effective in bringing people fast forward inside two years and getting them to the stage where they can cope with reading the major works in the original.

It was equally fascinating to listen to some much younger scholars, in mid-career, working on subjects that had simply not featured in the curriculum in my time. A subject which meant nothing to us in the 1960s, 'reception studies', the study of how Greek and Latin classics have been interpreted and re-interpreted at different periods of history, in different countries, or just by imaginative individuals, has grown into a major area of interest in universities now. I was particularly pleased to meet Emily Greenwood whose book *Afro-Greeks* had opened my eyes to the way in which the stories from the classical past, Homer's Odyssey above all, had been reinterpreted by writers in the Caribbean. Perhaps it was my parents' past involvement in the West Indies that gave Emily's work a special interest for me.

Poppy and I attended the Triennial in Cambridge in 2005 and again in 2011. What about Oxford in 2008? I ran my eye over the programme but it seemed to lack variety and we did not feel fired up to set aside a week for that. Cambridge, in my opinion, put more of itself into creating a varied programme and the top scholars in Cambridge put more of themselves into it than their opposite numbers at Oxford appeared to do when their turn came round. Alongside the purely scholarly parts of the programme (which were interesting to me but not so much to school teachers and their pupils) there were some items of more general interest – on one occasion a debate chaired by Mary Beard on what to do (or not do) about preserving the streets of Pompeii from being trampled to dust by mass tourism – and more entertaining items – a performance by a pair of impromptu story tellers rattling through Homer.

It was a bitter disappointment to find, in 2017, when the turn of Cambridge came round again, that nothing was going to happen. The system had gone bankrupt; so much money had been lost on the previous occasion. It is very disappointing that the colleges of Oxford and Cambridge cannot find ways between them of re-floating the 'Triennial'. But there is no sign of a revival. That avenue for renewing my old interests is seemingly now closed.

There is another and longer tradition which seems alive and well: the Cambridge Greek Play. Every three years since 1882 an ancient Greek play has been staged in the theatre at Cambridge, performed entirely in ancient Greek. The plays are performed by undergraduates, not professional actors (though a number of them over the years have gone on to become professionals), and they have only a very short run of performances, over just three or four days at the start of the academic year, in early October. From the very beginning it has been part of the tradition that music is composed specially to go with the play (parts of Greek tragedies took the form of dances by a chorus, accompanied by music). Nowadays we have next to no idea what ancient music sounded like. The composers for the Cambridge plays – Parry and Vaughan Williams were among the past contributors – have freedom to use their imagination.

I went to one or two of these Cambridge Greek plays from school in the 1950s. Poppy and I picked up on them again in 2010, 2013 and 2016. The tradition is not just being kept alive; it goes from strength to strength. The performance of Aeschylus' *Agamemnon* in 2010 was powerful theatre, from the watchman on his tower who opens the play to Clytemnestra in all her fury at the end. It is hugely impressive that such fine performances can be given by undergraduates, some of whom have known no Greek beforehand and have learned their parts intensively over the preceding summer holidays. In 2013 two plays were performed: Aeschylus' *Prometheus*, a tragedy, but a very short one, paired with Aristophanes' *Frogs*, a comedy. This pairing of a tragedy and a comedy – the ancient Greeks would not have found it odd at all – went well. The *Prometheus* is a harrowing story, and the performance was bleak. Then came light relief, and the producer and cast gave it all they had. They took plenty of liberties with Aristophanes, mixed in some pantomime and contemporary jokes; it was high class entertainment.

For 2016 they followed the same formula of pairing two plays: Sophocles' *Antigone* and Aristophanes' *Lysistrata*. The *Antigone* was played straight, and powerfully. With the *Lysistrata* the performance took off to new heights of entertainment. The play that Aristophanes wrote is entertaining enough on its own, but the Cambridge team – Professor Simon Goldhill playing a leading part as scriptwriter, I think – superimposed two additional levels of fun. The actors spoke their parts in ancient Greek. A little panel above the stage showed sub-titles in English. It was hard to take in all the fast and furious action on stage, and keep an eye on the sub-titles too – but if you didn't, you missed out on the naughty asides that were woven in there. As for the action on stage, Aristophanes would have pretty much recognised his story line, but he would have been thrown by the rich and varied allusions to life and politics in the western world of 2016. Boris Johnson descending from heaven on a zip-wire, and conversing with Donald Trump? It was, once again, hugely funny, not short on innuendo and obscenity. The flame of ancient Greek culture burns bright in Cambridge on these occasions.

Somewhere around 2009 or 2010 with the repair work and painting of our large house in Norfolk far enough advanced for me to be allowed some days off, I discovered the University of the Third Age in Cambridge: U3AC. The University of the Third Age (U3A) is an institution with branches all over the country. It is run entirely by volunteers: people with some knowledge or skill that they are happy and willing to share with others, by organizing and leading courses or classes. The U3A does not conduct exams or award any qualifications. It is not a university in that sense. Nor is there any entry qualification, nor any firm definition of 'the third age'. You have simply to be someone who can plausibly be regarded as having finished full-time work. It exists to give a focus for older people with time to spare, who want to return to interests they had in the past, or to develop new ones. It runs on a spirit of volunteering and self-starting. Classes are led, so far as they are led, by volunteers with some expertise in the subject. The groups that gather around them work in a spirit of helping each other to learn. It is about learning for the satisfaction of learning, and sharing this with others at a similar stage of life.

At least, what I am describing is what I experienced from taking part in five or six different classes in the U3A in Cambridge (U3AC) over nearly ten years. U3A takes different forms in different areas. There are several branches in the rural part of Norfolk where we now live. At the smallest of these, the range of activities may be quite basic and quite simple: local history and taking healthy exercise may be the core programme. The local branch nearest to where we live is a little larger than some. It holds monthly morning meetings, social gatherings with a guest lecturer, and has quite a varied programme of classes on history, current affairs, languages (French and German), through to bridge, croquet (in the season) and bird-watching. Rising head and shoulders above its country cousins, U3A in Cambridge offers a variety of subjects which is unparalleled. Its annual prospectus runs to nearly a hundred pages. In Cambridge there is a plentiful supply of people with deep knowledge of an exceptionally wide range of subjects from history, philosophy and politics, languages, the arts, films and theatre, through to fitness and outdoor pursuits (bird-watching among them), the architecture of the college buildings and the botany in the college gardens.

I turned to U3AC to feed my enjoyment of languages. The annual prospectus offers a choice of courses in 15 languages. This includes six courses in modern spoken Greek. Over time I have dipped in and out of courses in German and Italian (reading modern novels and tuning up on colloquialisms) but Greek was my main target. It had irritated me for many years that with all the classical Greek I had in my head I had not taken the relatively short step from this to learning the language spoken and written in Greece now. It was a low-hanging fruit.

I made use of two of the six courses on offer. One, which lay towards the more formal end of the spectrum in U3A terms, consisted of working slowly through a succession of course books designed for people who knew some of the language already and wanted to improve their grammar and expand their vocabulary. The second 'course' consisted of an hour of free conversation, moderated with a light touch by a native Greek speaker. The two types of activity made a productive combination: an hour and a half on a Monday of exercises in how to use the language grammatically, with some homework required week by week – and we took it in turns to present little prepared pieces to the rest of the class. Then an hour on a Friday afternoon where a smaller group of us tried our hand at making free conversation without being too meticulous about whether what we were saying was terribly correct; but with our native Greek speaker on hand to unravel us if we got in a total tangle or to set us off on a new theme if we dried up.

Monday's leader entered into the spirit of the U3A by injecting enough push to make us do decidedly more than we would if left to our own devices (this was miles more effective than sitting at home with books and CDs) whilst leaving ample room for people of varied ability to make progress each at their own pace. In the groups both on a Monday and a Friday there were people whose ability varied widely. Two of us were coming to modern Greek with a high level of ability in ancient, classical Greek. This is a help and a hindrance. Others wanted this language because they had family or friends living in Greece, or because they regularly took holidays there. Those people tended to be familiar with the vocabulary you need for daily life on the streets, in buses, on trains, in shops, and they could manage quite fluidly in conversation about everyday matters. Those of us with memories of ancient Greek found it easier to understand when the subject matter got more complicated – because technical terms and words for abstract concepts are either the same in modern as in ancient Greek or easily recognisable. We the classicists were also quite comfortable with longer, compound words and could get our tongues round them. This exasperated those who were happier floating on the everyday, practical level; the more difficult it became to them, the more easily we seemed to cope. All in all though, we pooled our knowledge from our respective backgrounds and helped one another along. The U3A process worked well, all learning from each other.

Was that learning process effective as well as being happy and harmonious? The proof is in what I can do with my Greek. The first real test came about five years ago, when Poppy and I were on a bird tour with David and Jan Tomlinson. Our week in the north, at Lake Kerkini, completed, we were on our way back to Thessaloniki to catch a plane with not much time to spare. We were dropping down from the Kerkini area and within sight of the main road from north to south which we needed to join, when we saw ahead of us an elaborate barrier made up of what looked like interlocking farm machinery. Indeed it was a road-block put up by farmers protesting against cheap imports from Bulgaria (that country had been recently admitted to the EU). The farmers had expertly barred the north-south road and our access to it from our side road. I was deputed to get out of our car and find out what we could do. I strolled uncertainly towards the barricade, and a large bearded farmer ambled towards me. He started by saying we were not going to get through but my attempt at discussion of this starting point in my faltering Greek changed the temperature. In a more friendly tone the farmer explained that if we were to drop back a few hundred metres and took a field track for a mile or two in the southward direction then we would find ourselves on the main road we wanted, and as far as he was concerned we could speed on our way to the airport. David and Jan gave my Greek high marks on that occasion.

A new need for me to speak Greek came about through a new line of connection with Greece that the World Pheasant Association opened up for me. In my short time as chairman of the WPA I learned from one of our members in France, himself French but of Polish descent and adventurous in all the languages of the people he worked with, that a variety of pheasant lingered on in the north-east of mainland Greece which might be of conservation interest. Curious to learn more, I made contact with the local expert on this endangered population of pheasants, a scientist employed by a hunters' organization. The full story of these birds and the work that is being done to conserve them, a unique partnership between British and French pheasant enthusiasts and Greek hunters, is in the previous chapter. The interest here is that this project and the working partnership with Greeks that it has grown into gave me a real -life incentive to get my Greek into better working order. Of the people I find myself needing to talk to in Thessaloniki and on site in the Nestos Delta, one or two speak English quite well (but not very well), some have about as much English as I have Greek, and some speak no English at all. The president of the hunters has not a word; nor do some of the local field staff and game wardens in the Delta who have key influence over whether or not the project makes the progress we want. I really do need to speak Greek now to communicate for a purpose, not just for the sake of learning. At a riverside restaurant on the banks of the Nestos on a winter's afternoon with a steady supply of fish dishes appearing from the kitchen, and an air of expectancy around the table to hear from the English visitor, a little Greek goes quite a long way.

U3AC then has given me good value for the modest annual fee and for the many days I have spent to-ing and fro-ing from West Norfolk to Cambridge.

A link of a quite different kind, with Greece and its history and civilisation rather than with the Greek language, came about through another accidental encounter. Sometime in 2010 I ran into an old friend from school and St John's, David Dain. David, now Sir David, had retired from a Foreign Office career which had included time in the British Embassy in Athens and a posting as British high commissioner in Cyprus. He suggested I might like to join the Anglo-Hellenic League, of which he had become chairman in 2007.

In making this suggestion David had an ulterior motive, as he admitted. The Anglo-Hellenic League is a recognised charity and by 2010 it was at high risk of failing, of dying on its feet. David knew, because we had talked about it, that I had been involved as a trustee in one big charity (the RSPB) and then a smaller one, the WPA, which like the Anglo-Hellenic League was in a feeble state. So he wondered whether I could apply any of my experience in charity management to help the League. He asked me not just to join the League as a member but to come on to their council as a trustee. I was being invited to join a sinking ship.

Well, whether it was going to sink or not was something I thought I was unlikely to be able to influence very much, as a complete newcomer. But the organization itself sounded interesting. So I went along with the proposition.

The Anglo-Hellenic League celebrated its centenary in 2013. It was founded in the aftermath of the 1912-13 Balkan Wars in order to counter Bulgarian anti-Greek propaganda in the UK. Those were very different times. The UK with France and Russia had been the Great Powers who were given formal Treaty responsibility for protecting the independence of the fledgling Greek state when it was founded in 1833. In 1913 that era of the protecting powers was still quite a recent memory. There were people in Britain who felt a guardian's responsibility for Greece as well as interest in Greek culture and friendship for people in Greece.

The Anglo-Hellenic League reaches back into that period of history. Only a year or so after the League was founded in 1913, Greece acquired the province of Macedonia. The expanse of northern Greece that is an integral part of the country on today's maps was taken over amid fierce hostility from Bulgaria. The League is not itself a diplomatic organization but diplomats have often been leading members. It is one of a group of 'friendship organizations' that Britain has with several European countries – Germany, Fránce and Italy among them – and with some other more distant countries where our historic ties are strong. Of all of those the Anglo-Hellenic League has a particular quality, due partly to nineteenth century politics, partly to the long-running philhellenism of the British.

There have been several different strands to its activities over the years. One is charitable action. This goes back to the troubled period when it was founded, Greeks suffering at the hands of the Bulgarians. Relief of poverty is written into its objectives as a charity in English law, and it is far from being a dead letter. During the Second World War and just after, the League raised funds for the relief of poverty, for assistance to children's homes and for villages in deep distress; again after earthquakes in 1953. Then much more recently the League raised funds in 2013 for relief of hunger on the streets when the economic crisis at its height was driving more and more people in Greek cities to food banks, and again in 2018 to help people made homeless by terrible wildfires in Attica.

There have been times when literary activity was a prominent strand in the League's activity, as it is today. That ran most strongly just after the Second World War when, in a golden age for the British Council in Athens a number of English literary figures were resident there for various reasons: Patrick Leigh Fermor staying on after distinguished military service in Crete, Lawrence Durrell because his family had lived out the war years in Corfu, Rex Warner, a young classicist posted from London whose translations of Greek literature ancient and modern became widely read – and Steven Runciman.

Sir Steven Runciman, historian of the Crusades and Byzantium, soared to prominence in the League's affairs in the 1950s and became its longest-serving chairman: 1951 to 1967. In his memory a book prize was founded by one of his successors in the chairmanship (1979-86), Lord Jellicoe. Instituted in 1986, this Runciman Award has been going ever since. It is awarded 'for an original work wholly or mainly about some aspect of Greece or the world of hellenism, published in English in any country of the world in its first edition' in the previous year. The aim is to stimulate interest in Greek history and culture from earliest times to the present, and to encourage good and accessible writing – of which Steven Runciman's books are held up as models. The winners of the award have included some famous academic and non-academic authors.

Now it is time to return to the sinking ship. David Dain was one of a line of retired diplomats with Athens experience who had held the chairmanship of the League. This was not, let me say, the cause of its running into difficulties. The causes lay deeper: some leading past supporters of Greek nationality moving away from London, and a generational drop in the number of younger people inclined to join membership organizations were two factors at work. Be that as it may, the League's expenditure had been exceeding its income for several years when I came on the scene, and financial resources were running out. Council decided that we had to cut out the main fixed expenditure, the paid administrator. (The parallel with the situation at the WPA and their decision to cut out their paid director was really very close.) The administrator gone, there was an irreducible minimum of organization and administration to be done to keep the League's activities ticking over even at a low level; there was the Runciman Award to be looked after. A year or so on, it became clear that our treasurer had been landed with much of the work that the paid administrator had previously been doing. He was soldiering on conscientiously but it was too much for him. He made excellent work of looking after the finances but could not on top of that manage everything else. Various members of council stepped forward and volunteered to take over various tasks.

I volunteered to administer the book prize. There was a modicum of simple administration to this: mailing out information to nearly 100 publishers, logging in the books submitted for assessment, arranging meetings of the 4-5 judges, and organizing the award ceremony and accompanying reception and dinner. Alongside all that, of which I tried to make fast work, I found plenty to interest me, and tried to breathe new interest into the operation in several ways. Unlike the treasurer who had struggled, I had time to review and update the range of publishers whom we invited to submit their books. I added one or two academic publishers (including my own, De Gruyter in Berlin) but we began to feel that the field of books submitted was becoming too heavily academic so I explored – with help from the excellent Monica Williams, proprietor of the Hellenic Bookservice in North London and long-term friend of the League – and started to draw in publishers, including some based in Greece, of books of more general interest, including books on food and books for children.

I was able with my classical background to have more conversation with the judges and in this way (I hope) to create more of a collegiate atmosphere at their twice-yearly meetings, and to refresh and enliven their judging operations. They in turn, a rotating panel of four each year, some English and some Greek, reconnected me with the world of literature. Prompted by comments from several people with whom I discussed how to give our prize a higher profile (in a somewhat crowded field of book prizes) we set up in 2016 a dedicated website. It did attract interest, although it was not helpful that it crashed twice in its first two years, thanks to hackers. Using this website we introduced a set of interactive discussions with the authors of the five or six books short-listed by the judges, and in the six weeks or so between the short list being announced and the final winner being decided we ran these interviews, one a week. That certainly aroused some new interest.

Then the books themselves – it was a tremendous treat for me personally that one copy of each book submitted for the competition (there could be forty or fifty each time) was delivered to me to check over. A copy went to each of the judges too, and they were obliged to read each one, or enough of it to form a view on its qualities. I had the greater luxury of being free to choose what to read, to select and dip into those books that appealed to me most, some chiming in with my academic interest from many years before, some opening new windows on to Greece of the Byzantine period and modern times.

At the end of the process, once the prize had been awarded, the League was left with its 40-50 volumes and in the past those were offered to council members or friends, with a residue lingering on in the League's London office. That office has now been closed to save costs. I certainly have no room for an additional 40-50 books a year – and a backlog of 80 from the past. Instead I have started to put out feelers to schools with classics departments; for preference schools in the London area, with the idea that they can be interested both in taking books that fit in with school-level studies and in bringing groups of their pupils to League events in London from time to time. My hope is that outreach of this kind, feeding off the Runciman left-overs, may bring a younger generation of students and their teachers into the League's field of influence, so over time winning a younger crop of supporters.

The future for this little friendship organization looks uncertain. The chairman who took over from David Dain, through his contacts as a professional archaeologist, created a lively programme of events and lifted the League off the floor of despair to which it had sunk. He has been succeeded by another diplomat, recently British ambassador to Greece but a younger man, nowhere near retirement age. We are living in very different times from those when the League was founded. Greece, however, is once again in difficulty, a larger and more stable country but not far from hardship. Britain is willing itself into a new and much more uncertain future which could quite possibly bring economic troubles with it, perhaps social troubles too. The value in having channels for friendship between the two countries is strong. Be that as it may, I am grateful to the Anglo-Hellenic League for having given me a new channel for my interest in Greece, and I hope to play an active part in its next phase of life.